# THE HISTORY AND ARCHAEOLOGY OF PHOENICIA

# ARCHAEOLOGY AND BIBLICAL STUDIES

Brian B. Schmidt, General Editor

*Editorial Board:*
Aaron Brody
Annie Caubet
Billie Jean Collins
Israel Finkelstein
André Lemaire
Amihai Mazar
Herbert Niehr
Christoph Uehlinger

Number 25

# THE HISTORY AND ARCHAEOLOGY OF PHOENICIA

Hélène Sader

Atlanta

Copyright © 2019 by Hélène Sader

All rights reserved. No part of this work may be reproduced or transmitted in any form or by any means, electronic or mechanical, including photocopying and recording, or by means of any information storage or retrieval system, except as may be expressly permitted by the 1976 Copyright Act or in writing from the publisher. Requests for permission should be addressed in writing to the Rights and Permissions Office, SBL Press, 825 Houston Mill Road, Atlanta, GA 30329 USA.

Library of Congress Cataloging-in-Publication Data

Names: Sader, Hélène S., 1952– author.
Title: The history and archaeology of Phoenicia / Hélène Sader.
Description: Atlanta : SBL Press, 2019. | Includes bibliographical references and index.
Identifiers: LCCN 2019032588 (print) | LCCN 2019032589 (ebook) | ISBN 9781628372557 (paperback) | ISBN 9780884144052 (hardcover) | ISBN 9780884144069 (ebook)
Subjects: LCSH: Excavations (Archaeology)—Phoenicia. | Iron age—Phoenicia. | Phoenicia—Antiquities. | Phoenicia—Civilization. | Phoenicia—Religion. | Phoenicia—Economic conditions.
Classification: LCC DS81 .S23 2019 (print) | LCC DS81 (ebook) | DDC 939.4/4 —dc23
LC record available at https://lccn.loc.gov/2019032588
LC ebook record available at https://lccn.loc.gov/2019032589

## Contents

Abbreviations .................................................................................................vii
Preface ............................................................................................................xi

1. Introduction ............................................................................................1
   1.1. Origin and Etymology of the Term Phoenicia         1
   1.2. The Origin of the Phoenicians                      3
   1.3. Chronological and Geographical Setting             4
   1.4. The Problem of the Sources                         23

2. Phoenicia in Iron Age I ......................................................................33
   2.1. The Textual Evidence                              34
   2.2. The Archaeological Record                         36

3. Phoenicia in Iron Age II and III ........................................................51
   3.1. The Phoenician Polities                           51
   3.2. Physical Characteristics, Settlement Pattern, and
        Distribution of the Phoenician Sites              138
   3.3. The Political Organization of the Phoenician Kingdoms   143

4. Phoenician Culture ...........................................................................147
   4.1. The Language                                      147
   4.2. The Material Culture                              155

5. Phoenician Religion .........................................................................181
   5.1. General Characteristics of Phoenician Religion    181
   5.2. Phoenician Religious Architecture                 188
   5.3. Cultic Artifacts                                  205
   5.4. Foreign Influence on Phoenician Religion          210
   5.5. Phoenician Mortuary Practices                     216

6. Phoenicia's Economy .................................................................249
   6.1. Phoenician Trade                                    249
   6.2. Phoenician Agriculture                              276
   6.3. Phoenician Industries                               296

Conclusion ........................................................................................313

Bibliography.....................................................................................317
Ancient Sources Index.....................................................................363
Personal Names Index ....................................................................365
Place Names Index ..........................................................................369
Modern Authors Index....................................................................377

# Abbreviations

| | |
|---|---|
| *AA* | *Archäologischer Anzeiger* |
| *AAAS* | *Annales archéologiques arabes syriennes* |
| *ABSA* | *Annual of the British School at Athens* |
| *ActAr* | *Acta Archaeologica* |
| ADPV | Abhandlungen des Deutschen Palästina-Vereins |
| *AeL* | *Ägypten und Levante* |
| *AfO* | *Archiv für Orientforschung* |
| *AHA* | *Annales d'Histoire et d'Archéologie* |
| *AHL* | *Archaeology and History in the Lebanon* |
| *AION* | *Annali del Instituto Orientale di Napoli* |
| *AJA* | *American Journal of Archaeology* |
| *Anab.* | Arrian, *Anabasis* |
| ANESSup | Ancient Near Eastern Studies Supplement Series |
| *AnOr* | *Analecta Orientalia* |
| *AnSt* | *Anatolian Studies* |
| *Ant.* | Josephus, *Jewish Antiquities* |
| *Ash-Sharq* | *Ash-Sharq: Bulletin of the Ancient Near East: Archaeological, Historical and Societal Studies* |
| *Atiqot* | *'Atiqot* |
| AUSS | Andrews University Seminary Studies |
| AW | Antike Welt |
| AWE | Ancient West and East |
| BA | Biblical Archaeologist |
| BAAL | Bulletin d'Archéologie et d'Architecture Libanaises |
| BAH | Bibliothèque Archéologique et Historique |
| *BaM* | *Baghdader Mitteilungen* |
| BAR | Biblical Archaeology Review |
| BARIS | Biblical Archaeology Review International Series |
| *BASOR* | *Bulletin of the American Schools of Oriental Research* |
| BeirTS | Beiruter Texte und Studien |

| | |
|---|---|
| *Berytus* | *Berytus: Archaeological Studies* |
| *Bibl. hist.* | Diodorus Siculus, *Bibliotheca historica* |
| *BMB* | *Bulletin du Musée de Beyrouth* |
| *BO* | *Bibliotheca Orientalis* |
| *BolA* | *Bolletino d'Arte* |
| *BSFE* | *Bulletin de la Société Française d'Égyptologie* |
| *C. Ap.* | Josephus, *Contra Apionem* |
| *CAM* | *Cuadernos de Arqueología Mediterránea* |
| *CAM* | *Cuadernos de Arqueología Mediterránea* |
| *CHANE* | *Culture and History of the Ancient Near East* |
| *CRAI* | *Comptes-rendus de l'Académie des Inscriptions et belles-Lettres* |
| *CSF* | *Collezione di Studi Fenici* |
| *DRBZ* | *Dynastensarkophage mit szenischen Reliefs aus Byblos und Zypern* |
| *DE* | *Discussions in Egyptology* |
| *DWO* | *Die Welt des Orients* |
| EA | El-Amarna tablets. According to the edition of Knudtzon, Jørgen A. *Die el-Amarna-Tafeln*. Leipzig: Hinrichs, 1908–1915. Repr., Aalen: Zeller, 1964. Continued in Rainey, Anson F. *El-Amarna Tablets, 359–379*. 2nd rev. ed. Kevelaer: Burzon & Bercker, 1978. |
| *EBR* | Klauck, H.-J., et al., eds. *Encyclopedia of the Bible and Its Reception*. Berlin: de Gruyter, 2009–. |
| *EpAn* | *Epigraphica Anatolica* |
| *ErIsr* | *Eretz-Israel* |
| *Geog.* | Strabo, *Geographica* |
| HACL | *History, Archaeology and Culture of the Levant* |
| *HBAI* | *Hebrew Bible and Ancient Israel* |
| *Hist.* | Herodotus, *Historiae* |
| *IA* | *Internet Archaeology* |
| *IEJ* | *Israel Exploration Journal* |
| *IJNA* | *International Journal of Nautical Archaeology* |
| *Il.* | Homer, *Iliad* |
| IN | Ivories from Nimrud |
| *JAEI* | *Journal of Ancient Egyptian Interconnections* |
| *JArSci* | *Journal of Archaeological Science* |
| *JASR* | *Journal of Archaeological Science: Reports* |
| JB | Jerusalem Bible |
| *JEA* | *Journal of Egyptian Archaeology* |

| | |
|---|---|
| *JNES* | Journal of Near Eastern Studies |
| *KAI* | Donner, Herbert, and Wolfgang Röllig. 1973. *Kanaanäische und aramäische Inschriften.* Wiesbaden: Harrassowitz. |
| *KTU* | Dietrich, M., O. Loretz, and J. Sanmartín. *Die keilalphabetischen Texte aus Ugarit, Ras Ibn Hani und anderen Orten.* Münster: Ugarit Verlag, 2013. |
| *KUSATU* | *Kleine Untersuchungen zur Sprache des Alten Testaments und seiner Umwelt* |
| *LT* | *L'Archéo Théma* |
| *MAA* | *Mediterranean Archaeology and Archaeometry* |
| MadBeit | *Madrider Beiträge* |
| *MadMit* | *Madrider Mitteilungen* |
| *Méd* | *Méditerranée* |
| *MDOG* | *Mitteilungen der Deutschen Orient-Gesellschaft* |
| *MUSJ* | *Mélanges de l'Université Saint Joseph* |
| *Nat.* | Pliny, *Naturalis historia* |
| *NEA* | *Near Eastern Archaeology* |
| *NEAEHL* | Stern, E. *New Encyclopedia of Archaeological Excavations in the Holy Land.* 4 vols. New York: Simon & Schuster, 1993. |
| NIV | New International Version |
| *NMN* | *National Museum News* |
| *NumC* | *Numismatic Chronicle* |
| OBO | Orbis Biblicus et Orientalis |
| OBO.SA | Orbis Biblicus et Orientalis, Series Archaeologica |
| *Od.* | Homer, *Odyssey* |
| *Op.* | Hesiod, *Opera et dies* |
| *Or* | *Orientalia* |
| *QDAP* | *Quarterly of the Department of Antiquities in Palestine* |
| *QR* | *Quaternary Research* |
| QSS | Qatna Studien Supplementa |
| P.Bologna | Papyrus Bologna |
| *PAM* | *Polish Archaeology in the Mediterranean* |
| *PBSR* | *Papers of the British School at Rome* |
| PCEP | Publications of the Carlsberg Expedition to Phoenicia |
| *PNAS* | *Proceedings of the National Academy of Sciences of the United States of America* |
| *PRU* | *Palais Royal d'Ougarit* II. Paris: Imprimerie nationale, 1965–1970. |
| *RB* | *Revue biblique* |

| | |
|---|---|
| *RDAC* | *Report of the Department of Antiquities Cyprus* |
| *RÉS* | *Répertoire d'épigraphie sémitique*. Académie des Inscriptions et Belles-Lettres. Paris: Commission du *Corpus Inscriptionum Semiticarum*, 1905. |
| RGTC | Répertoire géographique des textes cuneiforms |
| RIMA | The Royal Inscriptions of Mesopotamia, Assyrian Periods |
| RINAP | Royal Inscriptions of the Neo-Assyrian Period |
| *RLA* | *Reallexikon der Assyriologie* |
| RS | Ras Shamra |
| *RSF* | *Rivista di studi fenici* |
| SAA | State Archives of Assyria |
| *SAAB* | *State Archives of Assyria Bulletin* |
| ScrHier | Scripta Hierosolymitana |
| *Sem* | *Semitica* |
| SER | Salvage Excavation Reports |
| SMA | Studies in Mediterranean Archaeology |
| *SMEA* | *Studi Micenei ed Egeo-Anatolici* |
| *StEb* | *Studia Eblaitica* |
| StMosc | Studi in onore di S. Moscati |
| StPhoe | Studia Phoenicia |
| StPohl | Studia Pohl |
| SupTranseu | Supplément à Transeuphratène |
| *TAJA* | *Tel Aviv Journal of Archaeology* |
| *Transeu* | *Transeuphratène* |
| VBBK | Verlag Butzon & Bercker Kevelaer |
| *VHA* | *Vegetation History and Archaeobotany* |
| VTSup | Supplements to Vetus Testamentum |
| WF | Wege der Forschung |
| ZAW | Zeitschrift für die alttestamentliche Wissenschaft |
| ZDPV | Zeitschrift des Deutschen Palästina-Vereins |

# Preface

The last three decades have witnessed the publication of several monographs dealing with the history and material culture of the Phoenicians: Glenn Markoe (2000), Brian Peckham (2014), Mark Woolmer (2017), Josette Elayi (2018), and Josephine Quinn (2018) published in English; Michael Sommer (2008) and Morstadt (2015) in German; and Michel Gras, Pierre Rouillard, and Javier Teixidor (1989); Claude Baurain and Corinne Bonnet (1992); Véronique Krings (1995); and Elayi (2013a) in French, to name only some recent examples. An Oxford Handbook dealing with all aspects of Phoenician and Punic history and archaeology has just been published. Several exhibitions, such as *I Fenici* (Moscati 1988), *Les Phéniciens et le Monde Méditerranéen* (Gubel 1986), *Liban, L'Autre Rive* (Matoïan 1998), *La Méditerranée des Phéniciens* (Badre, Gubel, and Thalmann 2007), and *The Sea-Routes: From Sidon to Huelva; Interconnections in the Mediterranean Sixteenth–Sixth c. BC* (Stampolidis and Karageorgis 2003), to name only the most comprehensive ones, have also focused in recent years on Phoenician culture, expansion, and commerce. The Phoenicians are thus still calling for the attention of scholars and able to raise the interest of the public.

The novelty of the present study is that it approaches the subject from a divergent perspective: it focuses exclusively on contemporary written sources and on the archaeological evidence of the homeland. To date, in the reconstruction of Phoenician history and material culture, almost all publications relied heavily on the accounts of classical authors and on the results of excavations in the Phoenician settlements of the Mediterranean because of the lacunar evidence of the homeland. To focus exclusively on the archaeological results from the homeland in order to reconstruct Phoenician history and daily life is possible today because the available archaeological documentation from Phoenicia is substantial enough to allow new insights into its material culture, in spite of the unequal distribution of the evidence between its northern and southern parts. New, illuminating evidence has and still is emerging from the Iron Age settlements of Dor, Akko, Akhziv, Tyre, Tell el-Burak, Sidon, and Beirut in south Phoenicia. Important investigations are also taking place at Tell Kazel, 'Amrit, Tell Sianu, Tell Iris, and Tell Tweini in north Phoenicia, adding new substantial information to the older Tell Sukas excavation results. The study of the local remains of the Phoenician kingdoms will correct the rather skewed image of Phoenician culture and economy that has been proffered by examining so-called Phoenician materials found outside Phoenicia. Indeed, the issue of defining what is *Phoenician* based on objects from the colonies has been repeatedly criticized (Martin 2017; Quinn 2018).

Furthermore, while most publications have dealt with Phoenicia as one state and the Phoenicians as one people, recent studies (most recently Quinn 2018) have rightly questioned these assumptions and have argued that there was no unified country known as Phoenicia but four different kingdoms spread on the territory of the Levantine coast that the Greeks called Phoenicia, and that there was nowhere evidence that their inhabitants considered themselves as one people and identified themselves as such (also Woolmer 2017, 2). While it is obvious why the Phoenicians never referred to themselves as Phoenicians—since this term was coined and used by the Greeks—they also never used a generic term of their own to speak of the inhabitants of all four city-states and never referred to all these inhabitants as one people. In short, "the identity and history of the Phoenicians have long been defined by outsiders" (Woolmer 2017, 1), and scholars who used and still use the term *Phoenicians* seem to imply an ethnicity and a feeling of belonging to one nation that are nowhere attested in the written sources. When a citizen of one of these kingdoms identifies himself, he does it always in relation to his home city. The absence in the Phoenician language of a term equivalent to the Greek words *Phoenicians* and *Phoenicia* is indeed problematic, and Quinn (2018, xviii) is correct in pointing out that the Phoenicians never presented themselves as a people or ethnic group. She suggests that they were invented when nation-states came into existence: "In the case of the Phoenicians, I will suggest, modern nationalism invented and then sustained an ancient nation," and she concludes that one cannot speak of the Phoenicians as "a people" but simply as "people." However, nowhere in her book does Quinn define what she means by *nation* and *people* in order to test whether these definitions would accurately apply to the Phoenicians.

Even if we acknowledge with Quinn that the Phoenicians were not "a people" but "people" living in four different kingdoms, on a coastal stretch referred to as Phoenicia by the Greeks, it is precisely these people that this book intends to investigate without a priori ideas about their ethnic belonging or identity. Whether the inhabitants of this coastal strip shared common cultural features that can justify identifying them as "a people" partaking in the same Levantine koine, or whether they turn out to have radically different cultural characteristics that would not support labeling them by the same generic term, is what the evidence collected exclusively from the homeland will assess.

Despite the fact that the term *culture-history* has been criticized (see Quinn 2018, 68–69, for a review), it seems useful to apply it here in order to understand why ancient Greeks perceived the Levantine coast as a geographic unit and its inhabitants as one undifferentiated group. Their assumption raises the following question: did all the inhabitants of the four Phoenician-speaking kingdoms share one common way of life dictated by similar environments and/or by their proximity to one another, as suggested by the Greek designation, or can one detect a clear distinction in lifeways in various parts of the Phoenician coast?

Another novelty this book claims is that it does not present a global history of Phoenicia but rather the history and archaeology of the geographical area occupied by the four kingdoms of Arwad, Byblos, Sidon, and Tyre. It will attempt to reconstruct and understand the way of life of these people in their home environment without filling in gaps with information from the western Mediterranean, as has been done previously. The latter approach has been largely misleading, as would be, for example, a history of Lebanon based on the achievements of the Lebanese diaspora. In this process, many of the clichés and stereotypes attached to the Phoenicians will prove to have no or little historical value.

In other words, the book focuses exclusively on the Levantine coast whose inhabitants spoke the same West Semitic dialect known as Phoenician during the Iron Age. Using the term *Phoenicians* to refer to the inhabitants of these four coastal kingdoms is comparable to the use of the term *Aramaeans* to speak of the population of the Syrian polities in the Iron Age: in spite of the fact that there were several kingdoms, sometimes with substantial differences in their material culture, all publications speak about *the Aramaeans*, implying that they formed one people with the same origin and culture (see Younger 2016), although there is no evidence that the Aramaeans themselves expressed this kind of awareness (Sader 2010, 261). What led scholars to consider them as such is first and foremost that they shared the same language and the same social structure based on kinship. The same applies to the Phoenician polities, whose inhabitants spoke the same language. This may justify continuing to call them Phoenicians despite the ambiguous and often misleading use of the term. In his critical approach to the Phoenician question, Erik van Dongen (2010, 471–74) agrees that "Phoenicia may be defined linguistically."

Notwithstanding the abovementioned reservations regarding the use and misuse of the terms *Phoenicia* and *Phoenicians*, the name coined by the Greeks to refer to the Levantine coast and to its inhabitants has survived for three millennia and has come to mean to any reader or Near East historian the geographical area that includes the territory occupied by the four kingdoms of Arwad, Byblos, Sidon, and Tyre. It therefore remains expedient to continue using it to refer to this area and to its inhabitants. So, for lack of a better term, we will keep calling the geographical area including the four Phoenician-speaking kingdoms *Phoenicia* and their inhabitants *Phoenicians*. Since this designation has been used for many centuries, there is no harm in continuing to use it, provided one is aware of the political subdivision of that area and the absence of evidence for a common Phoenician identity.

The approach employed here finds an additional justification in the description of Phoenicia as presented in the *Periplus* of Pseudo-Scylax, a Greek author who lived in the fourth century BCE. This author defined the area called Phoenicia and enumerated all the cities included within this geographical concept, acknowledging that some of them were royal seats that incorporated other cities (see 1.3.1.1).

This investigation will also provide the opportunity to set the record straight regarding the understanding and the historical implications of the terms *Phoenicia* and *Phoenicians* for modern Lebanese. Since the most famous cities of Phoenicia were located on the coast of modern Lebanon, the Lebanese found it justified to appropriate the Phoenicians for themselves. By the same token and in the absence of hard data from Lebanon itself, they adopted uncritically all the clichés, myths, and false information relating to some issues such as the invention of the alphabet as well as other discoveries ascribed to the Phoenicians, and these became part of the more recent historical memory of a large part of the Lebanese population. Scholars have discovered and discussed recently the impact of Phoenician history on the search of the Lebanese for their identity after the formation of the Grand Liban, which was created by the mandatory authorities with amputated segments of former Ottoman provinces: while some of them saw themselves as heirs of the Phoenicians, others have denied this ascendance and acknowledged an Arab origin (Sader 2001, 221; Quinn 2018, 14–16; Kaufmann 2014). All this highly speculative discussion had, of course, political motivations, which led to some groups using part of the past to serve present political interests. A few researchers have gone as far as to study the DNA of modern Lebanese to try to prove their genetic connection to the ancient Phoenicians (National Geographic 2004; University of Cambridge, Research News 2017). Elayi mentions these analyses without approving or rejecting them and cautiously says that "the latest fashionable research on the identification of Phoenicians by means of their DNA is extremely fragile."[1] With all sorts of questionable information now on the internet and in the media (such as https://phoenicia.org), it has become extremely difficult to correct the wrong assumptions relating to the Phoenicians. In addition, most of these stereotypes continue to be taught in schools and constantly repeated by officials on public occasions. There can be an immediate negative and even a hostile reaction if one expresses doubts about some of the achievements ascribed to the Phoenicians because people feel that someone is stealing something away from them. This book hopes to contribute to a more sober view of Phoenician history based on reliable historical and archaeological evidence rather than on myths and legends.

---

1. Elayi 2013a, 19: "les dernières recherches à la mode sur l'identification des Phéniciens par leur ADN sont extrêmement délicates."

# 1
# Introduction

## 1.1. Origin and Etymology of the Term *Phoenicia*

The etymology and origin of the terms *Phoenicia* and *Phoenicians* have been widely discussed. There is a large consensus among scholars today that *Phoenicia* derives from the Greek term Phoenix, from the root *phoinos*, meaning "red." This word can refer to different things (Bonnet and Lipínski 1992, 353): to the purple color, to the red-winged bird, to the palm tree, to a sort of cithara, and to red-faced people; also it "was regularly used by the Greeks to describe people from the Levant" (Quinn 2018, 26). Homer "does not use Phoenician as an ethnic demonstrative (ethnonym) as might be expected but rather as a term to denote people from one of the coastal cities of the Levant who were on or over the sea" (Woolmer 2017, 1).

The etymological root *phoinos*, "red," encouraged scholars to speculate about the reasons behind this designation. For example, it was suggested that the Levantines received this appellation from the Greeks because of the purple dye for which the Phoenicians were famous, an opinion still defended by Elayi (2013a, 15). However, others (Lipínski and Röllig 1992, 348) believe that it was because of the tanned color of their skin that they were called *phoinikē*. Elayi considers the latter two meanings as possibilities but categorically dismisses all the others: "In any case, the term Phoenician should not be related to the Greek name of the lyre, the palm tree, or the phoenix."[1] So there is still no final agreement on this issue, and the debate about the origin of the name is still open. The term *Phoenicians* appears for the first time in Homer's *Iliad*, which is generally dated to the eighth century BCE. It is one of the reasons why modern scholarship restricts the

---

1. "Le mot 'Phénicien' n'a rien à faire en tout cas avec le nom grec de la lyre, ni avec celui du palmier, ni avec le phénix."

use of the terms *Phoenicia* and *Phoenicians* to the Iron Age period, which extends from the twelfth century BCE, when the Late Bronze Age culture came to an end, until the coming of Alexander the Great in 332 BCE, an event that put an end to the existence of the Phoenician kingdoms.

One has to mention another suggestion to explain the origin and etymology of the term *Phoenicians*. Some scholars were of the opinion that the origin of the word was Egyptian. They linked it to the Egyptian term *fnḫ-w*, "woodcutters," which referred in some cases to those felling cedar trees in the Lebanon Mountains, hence its association with the Phoenicians (Nibbi 1986; Helck 1962, 22; Dils 1992). However, this explanation did not find many defenders because it rests primarily on a phonetic similarity.

In short, Phoenicia is a foreign, Greek designation of the Levantine coast. The Semitic-speaking inhabitants of the coastal cities did not call themselves Phoenicians and did not call the region Phoenicia for the obvious reason that these were foreign terms.

So what did the local inhabitants call their land? This question is difficult to answer in the absence of relevant textual sources, as no Phoenician or any other ancient Near Eastern text of the first millennium BCE mentions the geographical name of the Levantine coast. This omission can be ascribed mainly to the fact that the coastal strip called Phoenicia by the Greeks was divided in the first millennium BCE into four independent kingdoms, Arwad, Byblos, Sidon, and Tyre, which never formed a united political entity, except for a temporary union of the kingdoms of Sidon and Tyre, if we accept H. Jacob Katzenstein's proposition (1973, 247–48; see also 4.4 below). The available texts refer only to these city-states and to their inhabitants—Tyrians, Sidonians, Byblians, and Arwadians—and never use a generic name to speak of the whole geographical area they formed.

Despite the dearth of evidence from the first millennium BCE, there is a widely accepted assumption that the area was still called Canaan, a name attested in second-millennium BCE sources (Moran 1987). *Canaan* occurs already in the Mari texts, where it indicates the Lebanese Biqāʻ (Durand 1999, 156), and is preserved in the Bible (mainly Num 34:1–5). Quinn (2018, 30–31) has deconstructed all the arguments presented in favor of this assumption, mainly Saint Augustine's reference to the name Chanani, used by the inhabitants of North Africa to refer to themselves, which is considered to be a clear reference to their Phoenician origin. Quinn (35; Quinn, McLynn, Kerr, and Hadas 2014) argues that the use of this term is explained rather by a biblical passage relating to the emigration of biblical Canaanites to Africa. Quinn (2018, 36) compares the meaning of the two toponyms Phoenicia and Canaan and concludes that "these terms were used about different places and people. While the Greeks' Phoenicia was always a coastal strip, the Canaan of the Near Eastern sources, including the Hebrew Bible, was considerably larger, including the coastal cities but often extending as far inland as the River Jordan if not beyond." The only instances where Canaan is equated with Phoenicia are in the Septuagint, where the "land of Canaan" is rendered only five times in Greek as "Phoenicia" or "land of the Phoenicians" but 150 times as Chanaan. Much later, in the first century CE, Philo of Byblos mentions that the original name of Phoinix was Chna, and in the third century "Herodian says straightforwardly that Phoenicia's original name was Chna" (Quinn 2018, 37).

To conclude, there is no equivalent to the terms *Phoenicia* and *Phoenicians* that were used by the inhabitants of the Levantine coast to refer to that geographical area and to its inhabitants. The above terms were coined and used by foreigners and not by the local people, who identified themselves as citizens of their hometown or city-state. It seems that Phoenicia was not a well-defined and familiar area to the Greeks, who knew vaguely about its geographical location but probably ignored its political division into various kingdoms and made no difference between their inhabitants. The only city Homer and his contemporaries had heard of was Sidon, and this is why they often referred to Sidonians, probably because they were the only people with whom they came in direct contact with through trade as early as the eighth century, or maybe because the term *Sidonians* encompassed also the Tyrians, as suggested by the Phoenician inscription from Cyprus, which speaks of a governor of Qrtḥdšt who calls himself "servant of Hiram, king of the Sidonians" (Katzenstein 1997, 207). On the other hand, the Neo-Assyrian and Neo-Babylonian empires were more familiar with the area; in spite of the fact that they often refer to the "kings of the seacoast" in general, their records acknowledge the existence of the various kingdoms and mention them as well as several of their cities by name. The expression "kings of the seacoast" is purely geographic and does not carry any cultural or ethnic connotation. It includes not only the Phoenician but also the Philistine kingdoms.

## 1.2. The Origin of the Phoenicians

It is a longstanding tradition in Near Eastern archaeology to explain any change in the material culture of a given area by the coming of new populations. The cultural change that occurred on the Levantine coast at the end of the second millennium BCE was also explained in the same way. This is how many authors have traditionally seen the Phoenicians as newcomers to the area. The first to ascribe a foreign origin to them were the classical authors, such as Strabo and Pliny the Elder, who claim that they came from the Persian Gulf. Herodotus, on the other hand, speaks of the Red Sea as their country of origin (for a review of the various propositions and relevant references see Elayi 2013a, 18).

The idea that the Phoenicians were partly foreigners was also defended by Dimitri Baramki (1961, 10), who believed that the Phoenicians were a mix of the local Bronze Age population and settling Aegean or Sea Peoples groups: "by about 1100 B.C. the fusion of the two races, the Proto-Phoenician Semitic Canaanites and the Indo-European Aegeans, gave birth to a new and virile nation of seamen." However, recent archaeological evidence has established that the material culture of Iron Age I is clearly in continuity with that of the Late Bronze Age, and no evidence for Sea People materials was found in Phoenicia in the excavations that took place at Sarepta, Sidon, Tyre, Akko, and Dor (see ch. 2). In Dor, the excavators observed a clear continuity of the material culture with that of the Late Bronze Age, but they also found evidence for the presence of other population groups, mainly from Cyprus and northern Syria (Gilboa and Sharon 2008, 161).

In short, there is no evidence for invasion or migration of new populations to the Phoenician coast to justify a radical change in the Late Bronze Age population composition and ethnic affiliation. All that can be said is that the evidence from the southern Phoenician coast indicates an active commercial activity and suggests the presence of what appears to be trading communities in these cities in Iron Age I. Evidence for the presence of new groups of people settling on the coast in Iron Age I is more evident in northern Phoenicia and is attested by the presence of new ceramic types as well as by the introduction of the cylindrical loom weights in the textile industry (see ch. 2).

### 1.3. Chronological and Geographical Setting

#### 1.3.1. Issues of Geography

##### 1.3.1.1. The Geographical Boundaries of Phoenicia

What is the stretch of the Levantine coast that the Greeks included under the geographical term *Phoenicia*? There is absolutely no written evidence

# 1. INTRODUCTION

to fix the boundaries of this geographical unit, which remained a vague designation until the fourth century BCE, when Pseudo-Scylax defined it with considerable precision. In his *Periplus* this author describes Phoenicia in detail and mentions its main cities. This contemporary source is important to define what the Greeks and later classical authors understood under this concept.

> There is after Kilikia the community of the Syroi (Syrians). And in Syria there live, in the seaward part, the Phoinikes (Phoenicians), a community, upon a narrow front less than up to 40 stades from the sea, and in some places not even up to 10 stades in width.
> 
> And past the Thapsakos river is Tripolis Phoinikōn (of the Phoenicians). Arados island with a harbor, a royal seat (*basilea*) of Tyros (Tyre) with a harbor roughly 8 stades from the land. And in the peninsula is a second city of Tripolis: This belongs to Arados and Tyros and Sidon; in the same place are three cities, and each has its own circuit of the enclosure wall. And a mountain, Theou Prosopon, Trieres, <a city> with a harbor. Berytos (Beirut), a city with a harbor. <The river> Bostrenos, Porphyreōn, a city. <Leontōn Polis>, Sidon, a city with an enclosed harbor. Ornithōn Polis. Belonging to the Sidonioi is (the area) from Leonthōn Polis as far as Ornithōn Polis.
> 
> Belonging to the Tyroi is the city of Sarapta. The city of Tyros, having a harbor within a fort; and this island is the royal seat of the Tyrioi, and is distant 3 stades from the sea. Palaetyros, a city; and a river flows through the middle. And a city of the Tyrioi, <Ekdippa>, with a river. And Ake (Akko), a city. Exope, a city of the Ty<rioi. Karmelos, (Carmel)>, a mountain sacred to Zeus. Arados, a city of the Sidonioi. <Magdolos, a city> and river of the Tyrioi. Doros (Dor), a city of the Sidonioi. <Ioppe (Jaffa), a city;> they say it was here that Androm<eda> was <ex>posed <to the monster. Aska>lon, a city of the Tyrioi and a royal seat. (Shipley 2011, 77–78)

According to the *Periplus*, it appears that toward the end of the Persian period, the territory occupied by the Phoenician kingdoms extended from the territory of Arados in northern Syria to Jaffa on the southern Palestinian coast. The *Periplus* also ascribes two cities to the kingdom of Tyre located beyond these borders: Myriandros on the Gulf of Iskenderun and Ashkelon, a former Philistine city, on the southern coast of Palestine (see fig. 1.1). However, this wide territory had not always formed part of the Phoenician kingdoms and fluctuated, shrinking at times and expanding at others depending on favorable or hostile political circumstances. As we will see in chapter 3, both the northern extension of the kingdom of Arwad and the southern extension of the kingdom of Sidon seem to have happened during the Persian period, when the Achaemenid kings awarded new territories to the Phoenician cities as a reward for their naval support. While the awarding of Dor and Jaffa to the Sidonian king is attested in Eshmunazar II's inscription (*KAI* 14), the territorial extension of Arwad is only evinced by the archaeological record.

Regarding the Tyrian occupation of Myriandros and Ashkelon, there is no other contemporary source to corroborate the account of the *Periplus*. Although highly probable, this territorial extension of Tyre still needs additional evidence to be confirmed. In any case, these extensions happened later in the Iron Age, and the core territory of Phoenicia extended originally probably from 'Amrit in the north to the Carmel coast in the south to include Dor and Jaffa. This is suggested by the recent Dor excavations, which have clearly shown that Iron Age I Dor belonged to the Phoenician cultural sphere in the eleventh–tenth century BCE: "If by 'Phoenician' we mean a society that originated in the indigenous Late Bronze Age population of the Levantine coast mixed with new ethnic elements originating overseas; that was leading the way in establishing market-oriented maritime commercial entrepreneurship in the early Iron Age; and whose self-identity these activities gradually shaped, then Dor is a Phoenician site par excellence" (Gilboa and Sharon 2008, 161). According to Ayelet Gilboa and Ilan Sharon, this city was conquered in the ninth century BCE by the neighboring kingdom of Israel, while 1 Kgs 4–11 mentions Dor among Solomon's districts, suggesting a date in the tenth century BCE. The biblical passage has led Ephraim Stern to assume an Israelite conquest of the city circa 925 BCE, but he had to admit that the material culture of this occupation was still Phoenician (Gilboa, Sharon, and Bloch-Smith 2015, 56). Israelite presence at Dor is archaeologically attested first during the ninth century BCE: "In the mid-to-late-9th-century BC, most probably under the Omrides, the town of Dor underwent a thorough programme of urban renovation. After a protracted period of essentially the same layout … it was transformed into an administrative centre, with none of the previous buildings left standing. This constitutes the only such profound change throughout Dor's Iron Age history" (70). Regarding the chronological debate about the date of this second Israelite city, Gilboa, Sharon, and Bloch-Smith "propose that the relative date for the construction of the new administrative centre falls late within 'Late Iron Age IIA,' rather than Iron Age IIB, as was hitherto proposed. … according to all the

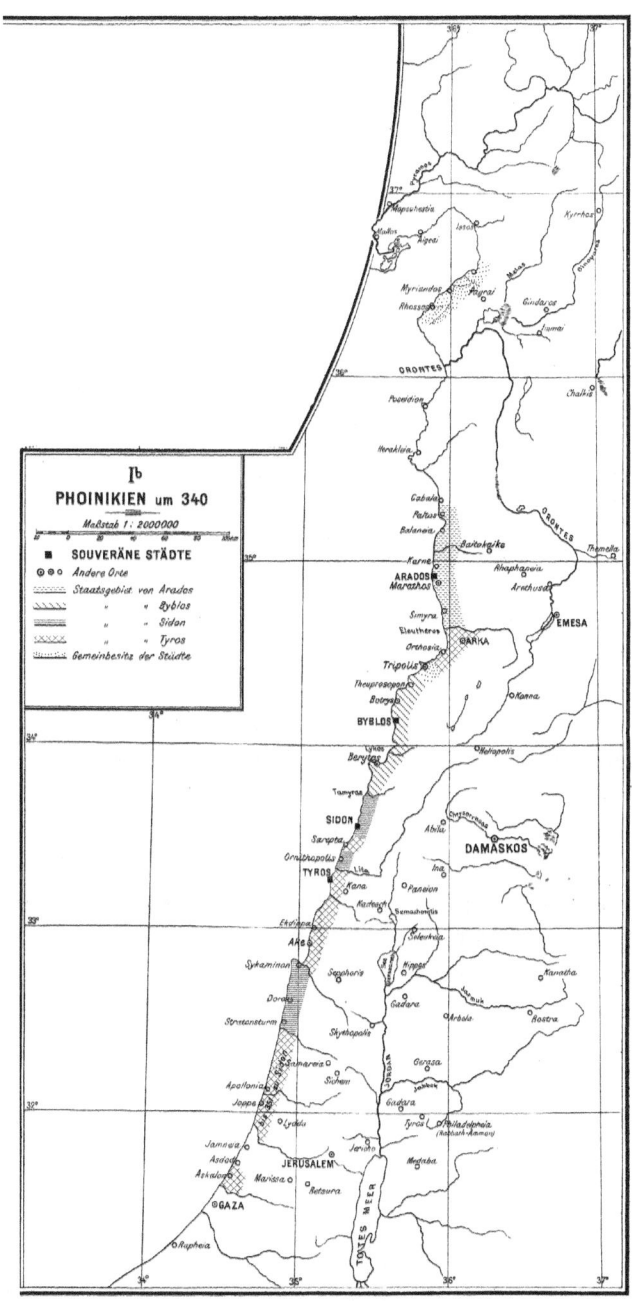

Fig. 1.1. Map of Phoenicia based on the *Periplus* of Pseudo-Scylax. After Kahrstedt 1926. Drawing Rami Yassine.

aforementioned interpretations of the radiocarbon data from Israel, the absolute date of the end of Iron Age IIA has moved about 100 years lower than was hitherto supposed. Therefore, Stern's attribution of the establishment of the 'four-chamber-gate-town' to the Omride Dynasty is definitely plausible" (70).

In the sixth century BCE, Dor was given by the Persian monarch to the king of Sidon as a reward for his services. Since then Dor was always counted as a Phoenician city, as it appears in the *Periplus* as well as later in Ptolemy's *Geography* (5.14.3). It is maybe not far-fetched to suggest that when the political circumstances changed, the kingdom of Sidon regained cities that once belonged to it. This is, of course, a mere hypothesis since Dor and Jaffa are never mentioned as part of the Tyrian or Sidonian territory but are also nowhere mentioned as forming an independent city-state. According to its excavators, Dor's culture is clearly related to that of Tyre and Sidon and not to that of the southern Philistine cities.

To sum up, the geographical extension of Phoenicia oscillated with the fluctuation of the territory of the kingdoms that formed it. It expanded when these kingdoms were able to enlarge their territories and shrank when these kingdoms, under specific historical circumstances, were amputated from some of their provinces. *Grosso modo*, the geographical boundaries of the area that the Greeks called Phoenicia were, for most of the Iron Age, the Carmel coast in the south and the Plain of 'Amrit in the north.

1.3.1.2. The Physical Characteristics of Phoenicia

**The Coastal Plain and the Harbors.** The coastal plain that characterizes the Phoenician homeland stretches along the Mediterranean coast and is interrupted at several points by promontories jutting out into the sea, blocking the coastal plain, and making land communication difficult. Twenty such promontories or capes are aligned on the coast of modern Lebanon only. The ones that form the main obstacles to land traffic are found also on the Lebanese coast, where from north to south one comes across Rās esh-Shaqʿa near Shekka, the Theouprosopon (God's Face) of the Greeks; Rās Nahr el-Kalb, the Lycus River of the classical authors, north of Beirut; Rās el-Abiad or Biyyāda, the *promontorium album* of Pliny (*Nat.* 5.19), south of Tyre; and Rās en-Nāqūra, north of Akko, to name the most important ones. The southernmost promontory is that of the Carmel. These promontories were difficult to cross, and sometimes steps were cut in the cliffs to make the passage easier. This is mainly the case of the Rās el-

Abiad, where stairs were sketched by Édouard Boudier from a photograph in 1897.[2] This is maybe what the ancients referred to as Scala Tyriorum, the "ladders of Tyre," although other authors (e.g., Renan 1864, 693 and n. 6) prefer to identify these "ladders" with Rās en-Nāqūra.

Some promontories were easier to circumvent by using roads going around the cape, as is the case of Rās esh-Shaqʻa (Davie and Salamé-Sarkis 1986). The promontory that formed a real, impassable barrier on the coast was Rās Nahr el-Kalb, first because it was almost impossible to circumvent it, and second because of the presence of the river at the foot of its northern and southern slope. It is perhaps because of its impregnable position that foreign invaders since Ramesses II carved their stelae on its southern cliffs (Weissbach 1922; Mouterde 1932, Maïla-Afeiche 2009). The presence of these promontories was maybe the reason why the inhabitants preferred to exchange their commodities by sea using small boats, a faster and easier means of transportation.

The coastal plain in Syria is wide in the ʻAmrit and Ǧabla areas but narrower in between. In Lebanon, it is not continuous because of the presence of the abovementioned promontories, which have created a series of small, narrow coastal plains. The largest plain is the valley of the Eleutherus River, the modern ʻAkkār, which stretches north of Tripoli on both sides of the modern Syro-Lebanese borders. It is circa 25 km wide on the Lebanese side and is thus the second largest plain after the Biqāʻ Valley. South of Tripoli, the coastal plain disappears or becomes extremely narrow circa 1 km in width. South of Beirut, the coastal plain widens only in Shwayfat and farther south in the area of ʻAdlūn to become 7 km wide between Sidon and Tyre (Buccianti-Barakat and Chamussy 2012, 76). The plain widens again substantially in the area of Akko, south of Rās en-Nāqūra.

The coastal plain is crossed by several small rivers that cannot be navigated but that irrigate the area abundantly. Water supply was provided also by numerous natural springs along the coast, such as those of ʻAyn el-Ḥayyāt in ʻAmrit, of Tell el-Burak south of Sidon, and Rās el-ʻayn near Tyre. This abundance of water made the plain extremely fertile and well suited for agriculture. However, given the density of the settlements, mainly in the southern part of Phoenicia, and given also that this plain is often very narrow, the available agricultural land may not have produced sufficient staples to feed its population. Agricultural land was gained prob-

---

2. View the photograph at https://tinyurl.com/SBL1724a.

ably by terracing the lower slopes of the nearby mountains, but no investigations about this activity have been undertaken yet.

The northern coast of Palestine between Rās en-Nāqūra and Mount Carmel is wide in the north and narrows toward the south. It is interrupted by the Carmel promontory. It separates the Jezreel Valley and the western Galilee from the Mediterranean Sea. South of Mount Carmel extends the Carmel coast and the Sharon Plain. It is a fertile area crossed by the Yarkon River.

Several harbors were active in the Iron Age along this coast: those of Gabala, Arwad, Ṭarṭūs, Tabbat el-Hammam, Tripoli, Byblos, Beirut, Sidon, Tyre, ʿAthlit, Akko, and Dor were among the best havens (see ch. 3). The presence of islands offshore, as in the case of Arwad, Tyre, and ʿAthlit, favored the installation of external harbors. Harbors were located generally north of a reef, of a line of islets, or of a promontory, which protected them naturally from the dominant southwestern winds and currents. Today most of these harbors are silted up and hidden under modern constructions far from the present shoreline, which makes the investigation of their installations difficult. With a few exceptions, little information is available about harbor installations in the Iron Age in spite of the fact that it was the period of great commercial expansion and active trade interaction in the eastern Mediterranean. The recent investigation of the harbor of ʿAthlit, which was used in the Iron Age only, with no later occupation in the Hellenistic and Roman periods, provided information about Phoenician harbor constructions (Haggi 2006; Haggi and Artzy 2007). Arad Haggi and Michal Artzy (2007) summed up the main characteristics of Phoenician harbors based on their study of the ʿAthlit harbor on the one hand and their review of other harbors on the Phoenician coast on the other. They concluded that the main harbor of a Phoenician settlement was located on the northern side of the promontory or island on which the city was built because it was better protected from the prevailing winds. Furthermore, Phoenician harbors presented the same building technique for the construction of quays, which were built with headers with their narrow sides facing the sea. Moles, when attested, were placed on a layer of pebbles and were built from two parallel header walls. The gap between the latter was filled with field stones. Finally, "the Phoenicians invested great effort in planning and building circulation and flushing systems. At ʿAthlit they used the natural settings of the northern bay to create a constant flow of water into the harbor. In other harbors, flushing channels were quarried at natural reefs and gaps were left in the moles to prevent silting" (83). A major conclusion of Haggi and Artzy's study is that the Phoenician harbor-building technique developed locally from ashlar construction techniques used on land and was not brought to the Levant by the Sea Peoples.

**The Western Mountain Ranges.** The coastal plain was separated from the hinterland by mountain ridges that border it from the east. In the north the Anṣariyah—also called Nuṣayriyye Mountains, with a maximum elevation of 1575 m—separated the land of Arwad from that of Hamath. The ʿAkkār Valley, known as the Homs Gap, separated the Anṣariyah Mountains from the Lebanon range and allowed easy access to the Orontes Valley. The Lebanon mountain range runs from north to south along the Lebanese coast over a length of 240 km, from east of Tripoli to east of Sidon. It is known in the cuneiform texts as $^{kur}Labnana$, the Lebanon Mountain (*RLA* 6:641–50), to which the modern state of Lebanon owes its name. It culminates in its northern part at 3,088 m at Qurnet es-sawdā. Except for the existence of a few passes, it forms an almost impassable barrier separating the coast from the Biqāʿ Valley. The Lebanon mountain range is a calcareous, mainly Cretaceous and Jurassic formation with volcanic basalt intrusions in the north (Buccianti-Barakat and Chamussy 2012, 79). Underground water flowing from the mountains emerges in marine springs mainly in the area between Beirut and Byblos. Deep valleys cut through it, and dense forests of evergreen trees covered it in antiquity.

South of the Litani a low mountain ridge, Ǧabal ʿĀmel, east of Tyre, culminates at 611 m. It does not hinder communication with the east and south. Two direct communication routes from Tyre to Palestine and Damascus were available for communication (Dussaud 1927, 22). Farther south, the upper and lower Galilee heights, culminating at Ǧabal Ǧarmak at an altitude of 1,200 m, are bordered to the south by the Jezreel Valley. A series of valleys on their western slopes allow access to the coastal plain and the Akko harbor (Suriano 2013, 17). The Carmel range stretches in a southeast direction southwest of the Jezreel Valley and separates it from the Plain of Sharon. It is 26 km long and circa 8 km wide, and culminates at 546 m. Its western slope comes very close to the sea and leaves a narrow coastal plain 180 m wide ("Mount Carmel" n.d.).

**The Communication Routes with the Hinterland.** The presence of this mountainous barrier has led to the assumption that the Phoenician coast was entirely cut off from its hinterland. "Were the Phoenicians driven to the sea because of their geographical situation, because they had little living space on the coast, squeezed by the mountains?"³ Many scholars have ascribed the maritime vocation of the Phoenicians to this geographical reality, assuming that contact with the hinterland was very difficult if not impossible. The reality is rather different, as communication routes are attested from the second millennium BCE linking the Phoenician coast to the Syrian hinterland and to Palestine. It can be even argued that had it not been for the possibility to trade with the hinterland, the Phoenician commercial enterprises would have been much more modest. As will be argued in chapter 6, the countries mentioned in the famous chapter 27 of Ezekiel's book suggest that the Tyrian trade network seems to have been geared mainly toward the hinterland. This would not have been possible without the existence of good communication routes. The overland trade of the Phoenicians has been investigated also by Peter van Alfen (2002).

Three well-attested routes linking the coast to the hinterland were used as early as the second millennium BCE: one, the Homs Gap, is located in north Lebanon and goes across the valley of the Nahr el-Kabīr al-Ǧanūbī to the Orontes Valley (Klengel 2000, 240, with relevant bibliography), and the other is in south Lebanon and linked Sidon to the Biqāʿ Valley across the mountains through the pass of Ǧizzin (Dussaud 1927, 409–10; Kuschke 1977; Hachmann 1983, 25; Kitchen 2000, 48 and fig. 6). René Dussaud (1927, 22) identified also routes linking Tyre to Palestine and Damascus.

One has to mention in this context also the so-called *via maris*, which linked Egypt to the Levant and passed by the Jezreel Valley that bordered the Phoenician territory to the south. This route branched off in northern Palestine into two segments: one continued across the Biqāʿ Valley and led to Syria, Anatolia, and Mesopotamia, and the second went west to reach all the Lebanese coastal cities (Aharoni 1967, 42; for a study of the *via maris* and related literature, see Sader 2000c, 67–85).

This ideal situation whereby maritime trade found its natural extension in inland trade placed the Phoenician cities at the heart of the ancient commercial network of the Levant and allowed them to interact with the cultures with which they came into contact. They played a major role in the transmission of Levantine culture to countries around the Mediterranean and in propagating some western traditions in the East.

---

3. Elayi 2013a, 26: "Les Phéniciens sont-ils poussés vers la mer par déterminisme géographique, parce qu'ils sont à l'étroit sur la côte, coincés par la montagne?"

**Natural Resources.** The Phoenician kingdoms were poor in raw materials. The only natural wealth they had was the timber and resins of their forested mountains, mainly those of the Lebanon range. Egypt, Assyria, Babylonia, and the Israelites coveted the highly prized cedarwood for the building of their palaces and temples. The Wenamun Report and the biblical account, as well as the Neo-Assyrian and Neo-Babylonian texts, refer abundantly to the cedar logs they took from the Phoenician cities: Wenamun (Sass 2002) was sent to get cedarwood for the Amun barge and reminded the Giblite king that this had been a long-lived tradition, and Hiram of Tyre provided cedarwood for the building of the Jerusalem palace and temple, according to the biblical account (1 Kgs 5:2). Sargon II depicted on the walls of his palace the transport of cedar logs to Assyria for the building of his new residence (see fig. 1.2), and Nebuchadnezzar II described in the inscriptions he left at Nahr el-Kalb and Wadi Brisa (see fig. 1.3) how he opened roads in the mountains to transport cedar logs for the building of his palaces in Babylon (for the bibliography relating to the above texts see chs. 2–3). It was mainly in exchange for cedar wood that the Phoenicians obtained the raw materials and goods they needed.

Fig. 1.2. Relief from the palace of Sargon II at Khorsabad depicting transport of cedar logs in boats.

Fig. 1.3. Inscription (see enlarged detail) of Nebuchadnezzar II from Wadi Brisa, northern Biqāʿ, Lebanon. Source: Rocio da Riva.

The nearby mountains provided them also with abundant limestone that could be easily quarried and hewn. They used it in their buildings, and this allowed them to develop building techniques of their own. In the mountains they hunted wild animals that were part of their diet, such as game and wild boars.

The Mediterranean Sea was another source of food and offered a variety of fish as well as the murex shells used in the purple-dye industry. The availability of timber and the proximity of the sea were prerequisites for the development of ship building, which became one of the main industries in the Phoenician kingdoms.

The limited natural resources may explain the scarce evidence for industries based on imported materials and the development of those based on agriculture.

**The Climate.** Like all Mediterranean countries, the Levantine coast is deeply influenced by the sea. It is characterized by rainy winters and by hot, dry summers. Rainfall averages between 800 and 900 mm in the Beirut area and decreases in the south and in the north of Lebanon (Buccianti-Barakat and Chamussy 2012, 85). Major precipitations come after December. The proximity to the sea provides a moderating influence on the climate, making the range of temperatures relatively narrow between day and night, although temperatures may reach above 38°C during the day and below 16°C at night. The average temperature for Beirut is 13.6°C in January and 28.7°C in August. The Cedars Mountain, at 1700 m altitude, has an average temperature of 0.3°C in January and 18.0°C in August (Buccianti-Barakat and Chamussy 2012, 84, tableau 3). The mountains enjoy a cooler climate in summer; they have a wider daily range of temperatures and less humidity than the coast. Winters are much colder there, with heavy snowfall and frequent frost.

Recent investigations suggest that a period of drought hit the Levant between 1200 and 850 BCE, which may have been caused by substantial changes in the climate (Kaniewski et al. 2008; 2010).

## 1.3.2. Issues of Chronology and Periodization

The chronology and periodization of the Iron Age is difficult to establish for all the Phoenician kingdoms: first, because of the discrepancy of the evidence between north and south, the latter being better documented, and second, because not all sites have yielded a complete sequence from the Late Bronze–Iron Age I transition to the end of the Persian period. In addition, very few sites have provided carbon-14 determinations to establish absolute dates for the chronological and stratigraphic sequence.

In northern Phoenicia the chronology of the events starts with a traumatic transition from the Late Bronze Age into the Iron Age: destruction of the Late Bronze Age occupation is attested at Tell Sukas, Tell Tweini, and Tell Kazel. At Tell Tweini it is dated to the first quarter of the twelfth century BCE based on the presence of Helladic III C pottery as well as on carbon-14 determinations. It is contemporary with the events at the other sites: "New 14C results and the fact that level 7A holds Late Helladic III C Early ceramics allows dating the destruction to the first quarter of the 12th century B.C.E. This date is comparable to the fall of Ugarit, Ras Ibn Hani, Tell Kazel, and many other sites probably destroyed by the Sea Peoples" (Bretschneider, Van Vye, and Jans 2011, 85; see also Al-Maqdissi et al. 2010, 139). These sites were not abandoned after the destruction but were reoccupied after a very short hiatus in Iron Age I (see also Badre et al. 1994, 345). They all present evidence for settling newcomers attested by the presence of new ceramic wares: céramique à la steatite, "barbarian," and Trojan ceramics, which disappear at the end of Iron Age I. This is in addition to local ceramics in the Late Bronze Age tradition as well as local imitation of Cypriot and Mycenaean vessels, which indicate continuity with Late Bronze Age traditions after the short period of abandonment. This Iron Age I period witnesses the beginning of a new era of urbanization with a new town plan and the emergence of public buildings.

A new wave of destruction occurred toward the end of that period, dated by carbon-14 determinations to 1050–1000 BCE at Tell Tweini (Bretschneider, Van Vyve, and Jans 2011, 82), and it is also attested at Tell Kazel, but no carbon-14 dates are available (Capet 2003, 117). The presence of cylindrical loom weights in the destruction levels seems to indicate the settlement of foreign groups related to the so-called Sea Peoples (Bretschneider, Van Vye, and Jans 2011, 83). The recent discovery of Luwian inscriptions attesting the creation of the Neo-Hittite state of Palastin (Hawkins 2009) may explain the displacement or migration of people from north to south.

Urbanization resumed in Iron Age II and was characterized by the erection of public buildings at Tell Tweini. Tell Kazel has a poorer residential area in Iron Age II, but the Late Bronze Age temple is rebuilt (Level V). There are no exact dates for this period, but a rough estimate is given by the excavators of Tell Tweini as circa 900–700 BCE. The marker that ushers in this period is the red-slipped burnished pottery as well as imports from Cyprus and the Aegean. This is the period of Assyrian expansion and the annexation of large parts of northern Syria. Written sources may help date some of the events identified in the archaeological record.

Toward the end of this period the cities in the northern territory of Arwad witnessed a major shift in their economy, which became based on wine and olive oil production. The problematic identification of the Neo-Babylonian period assemblages in northern Phoenicia makes their assignment to Iron Age II or III debatable. The excavators of Tell Tweini (Al-Maqdissi et al. 2010, table 1), which is the only site to have the whole chronological sequence of occupation, suggest the following periodization: Iron Age I (ca. 1190–900 BCE; but this period can be clearly divided into two subphases, one before and one after the destruction: Iron Age IA [ca. 1190–ca. 1050] and Iron Age IB [ca. 1050–ca. 900 BCE]), Iron Age II (ca. 900–ca. 700 BCE), and Iron Age III (ca. 700–333 BCE), which includes the late Assyrian and Neo-Babylonian as well as the Achaemenid

Persian periods. What appears clearly in the archaeological record is the change that took place in the seventh century BCE and continued through the Persian period.

To sum up, more evidence is needed to establish a solid chronology and periodization of the Iron Age in northern Phoenicia, more precisely in the kingdom of Arwad. From the available information, a preliminary periodization includes a transitional Late Bronze Age–Iron Age I; Iron Age IA and IB; Iron Age II, corresponding mainly to the Assyrian and possibly including the Neo-Babylonian periods; and Iron Age III, covering the Persian period (see table 1.1 on pages 18–19).

This periodization seems to be preferred by the excavators of Tell Tweini, Tell Kazel, Tell Sianu (Al-Maqdissi 2016b, 182), and 'Amrit (Al-Maqdissi and Ishaq 2016, 294).

The chronology and periodization of the southern Phoenician kingdoms are better established because of the existence of good stratigraphic sequences extending from the Late Bronze–Iron Age I transition until the end of the Persian period. The main sites that have provided long sequences of occupation of Iron Age strata are Sarepta, Tyre, Tell Keisan, and Dor. As opposed to the north, in southern Phoenicia the end of the Late Bronze Age was not violent, since sites such as Sarepta, Tyre, and Dor did not witness any severe destruction or abandonment at the end of the Late Bronze Age. No carbon-14 dates are available from either Sarepta or Tyre. The dates proposed by the excavators are based mainly on imported ceramics from Cyprus: the beginning of the period in both sites is set arbitrarily around 1200 BCE, and its end in the last quarter of the eleventh century BCE (see ch. 2).

Francisco Nuñez (2004, 354, 357), who studied the ceramic assemblages of the Tyre al-Baṣṣ cemetery, opted for the low chronology and proposed to set the end of Iron Age I at Tyre around 850 BCE because "we consider a good chronological anchor the $^{14}C$ date of ca. 850 B.C. obtained at Tell Dor." Nuñez also argues that his Period I, which includes both the Late Bronze Age–Iron Age I transition and the Iron Age I phase, coincides with the Cypro-Geometric I and II periods, dated 1050–900 BCE (Counts and Iacovou 2013, table 1). He does not offer any chronological subdivisions for this long period that he dates between the twelfth and the mid-ninth century BCE, setting the end of Iron Age I at al-Baṣṣ some two centuries later than Bikai's dating of Iron Age I in the Tyre sounding.

William Anderson (1988) and Issam Khalifeh (1988) identified two subphases in Iron Age I, Strata E and F and Periods V and VI respectively,

Table 1.1. Iron Age Periodization of the Northern Phoenician Sites

| Site | Periodization | Strata | Dates | Reference |
|---|---|---|---|---|
| Tell Tweini | LB IA transition | VII A / Niveau 6 G–H | 1200–1175 BCE | Bretschneider, Jans, and Van Vyve 2010, tableau 2 |
| Tell Tweini | IA IA | VII A / Niveau 6 G–H | 1175–1050/1000 BCE | Bretschneider, Jans, and Van Vyve 2010 |
| Tell Tweini | IA IB | VII B / Niveau 6 E–F | 1000–900 BCE | Bretschneider, Jans, and Van Vyve 2010, tableau 2 |
| Tell Tweini | IA IIA | VI A–B / Niveau 6 A–B | 900–700 BCE | Bretschneider, Jans, and Van Vyve 2010, tableau 2 |
| Tell Tweini | IA IIA | VI A–B / Niveau 6 C–D | | |
| Tell Tweini | IA IIIA | V A–B / Niveau 5 A–B | 700–500 BCE | Bretschneider, Jans, and Van Vyve 2010, tableau 2 |
| Tell Tweini | IA IIIB | V A–B / Niveau 4 A–B | 500–332 BCE | Bretschneider, Jans, and Van Vyve 2010, tableau 2 |

# 1. INTRODUCTION

| Site | Periodization | Strata | Dates | Reference |
|---|---|---|---|---|
| Tell Kazel | LB–IA transition | 6 upper in Chantier II<br>5 upper in Chantier IV | No dates | Capet 2003, 117 |
| Tell Kazel | IA I | 5 in Chantier II<br>4–3 in Chantier IV | No dates | Capet 2003, 117 |
| Tell Kazel | IA II | 4 in Chantier II<br>Absent in Chantier IV | No dates | Capet 2003, 117 |
| Tell Kazel | IA II | 3 in Chantier II<br>Absent in Chantier IV | No dates | Capet 2003, 117 |
| Tell Arqa | IA I | Phase J (no settlement) | 1200–? | Thalmann 2006, 15, fig. 3 |
| Tell Arqa | IA II | Level 10<br>Level 9 C, D, and E {Phase H, Niveau 10} | No date | Thalmann 2006, 15, fig. 3 |
| Tell Arqa | IA III | Niveau 9 | No date | Thalmann 2006, 15, fig. 3 |

with proposed dates, which are often hypothetical or controversial, according to Anderson (1988, 396). Both the Sarepta and Tyre excavators relied on the presence of Late Cypriot III pottery to date their Iron Age I sequence. They do not mention the presence of Cypro-Geometric I and II sherds in it. They ascribe the latter to the early phase of Iron Age II. This pottery first appears at Tyre in Stratum XIII, while in Sarepta it is attested already in Stratum E. Anderson (1988, 395) concluded, "It appears, therefore, that Stratum E is, in part, contemporary with both strata XIV and XIII at Tyre. The transitions were not simultaneous, possibly suggesting that no occupational gap occurred at either site." The latest dates for Late Cypriot III (1225/1200–1050 BCE) did not significantly change and still correspond to the Iron Age I dates proposed by the Tyre and Sarepta excavators. The discrepancy between their dating of the end of Iron Age I and that of Nuñez is due to the fact that the latter considers the occurrence of Cypro-Geometric I and II sherds as part of Iron Age I, as is commonly agreed today (Sharon 2013, 61), hence his adoption of 850 BCE for the end of the period.

The new evidence from Dor has provided a good chronology and a detailed periodization of Iron Age I: Late Bronze Age/Iron Age I Transition, Early Iron Age IA, Late Iron Age IA, Transitional Iron Age IA/Iron Age IB, Iron Age IB, and Transitional Iron Age IB/Iron Age IIA (Gilboa 2005, 52–53; see also the comparative table of the main sites of southern Phoenicia in Gilboa and Sharon 2003, fig. 21, with both traditional and carbon-14 dates). Iron Age IA is characterized by local pottery in the tradition of the Late Bronze Age vessels and a substantial number of Twenty-First Dynasty Egyptian imports, as well as local imitation of Cypriot pithoi (Gilboa and Sharon 2008, 155–56). Iron Age IA ended in a violent deflagration, which was interpreted by Stern as the result of a Phoenician invasion, an interpretation convincingly rejected by Gilboa and Sharon (2008, 161). Based on the pottery, this destruction is dated circa 1050 BCE, but carbon-14 dates are fifty to seventy-five years lower, that is, circa 910 BCE (Gilboa and Sharon 2003, table 19; 2008, 156). A transitional Iron Age IA/Iron Age IB phase was identified, during which there was evidence for rebuilding of previous structures according to the same lines, while other parts of the site remained unoccupied and were dedicated to animal penning. Monumental building activities, as well as the first appearance of Phoenician bichrome pottery and increasing evidence for contacts with Cyprus, illustrated mainly by the presence of Cypro-Geometric I tableware, characterize Iron Age IB. Iron Age IB ended peacefully toward 845 BCE, according to carbon-14 dates (Gilboa and Sharon 2003, fig. 20), contrary to Tell Keisan, where the Iron Age I levels were violently destroyed (Humbert 1993, 866).

To sum up, the chronology and periodization of Iron Age I in southern Phoenicia has been revised based on the evidence from Tel Dor. The traditional ceramic-based dating used for the sites of Sarepta and Tyre tends to be progressively abandoned in favor of the new carbon-14 dates retrieved at Dor, which suggest that Iron Age I ended in the mid-ninth century BCE, the period of the Assyrian expansion to the west. It is to be noted, however, that the datings by Gilboa and Sharon are according to the "low chronology" that has been corrected by Israel Finkelstein, who dates the end of Iron Age I and the beginning of Iron Age IIA to the mid-tenth century BCE (Finkelstein and Sass 2013, 180).

An attempt at a periodization of the Iron Age II in southern Phoenicia was made by Nuñez (2004; 2014) based on a chrono-typological sequence of the Iron Age material excavated at Tyre al-Baṣṣ. Nuñez's aim was to reach an internal Phoenician sequence based on stratified material from Lebanese coastal sites and thus "liberate" the chronological sequence or periodization of "Phoenician" pottery from Cypriot and Palestinian sequences.

Based on the development of the neck-ridged jug, which appears in Iron Age I contexts and continued to develop all through Iron Age II, Nuñez identified four chrono-sequential phases, Periods II–V, as the four different subphases of Iron Age II. Period II represents the transition between Iron Age I and II and is considered to be rather "obscure" (Nuñez 2004, 357–58; 2014, 335) and contemporary with the Cypro-Geometric III period attested at Dor after 850 BCE (ca. 850–775 BCE) and assigned to Iron Age IIA (Sharon 2013, 61). Period III represents the first stage of a new era, ushered in by the emergence of new pottery types, and is contemporary with Cypro-Geometric III and Cypro-Archaic I periods (Iron Age IIB; ca. 775–750; Nuñez 2004, 363). Period IV represents the full development of the Iron Age II ceramics or "standard Iron Age" (ca. 750–700; Nuñez 2004, 352–73 and fig. 241; 2014, 334). Both Periods IV and V (Iron Age IIC) are contemporary with the Cypro-Archaic I period, dated 750–600 BCE (Counts and Iacovou 2013, table 1). The end of Period V, and hence that of Iron Age II at al-Baṣṣ, is confirmed by a carbon-14 date from Period V Tomb 54. The date obtained is the end of the seventh to the beginning of the sixth century BCE (Nuñez 2004, 366). So the full Iron Age II period is subdivided into three subphases, represented by Periods III–V, which correspond to Stratum V–I of the Tyre sequence.

Nuñez (2004, fig. 241) established also a concordance between his own and Patricia Bikai's Tyrian and Cypriot periodization of Iron Age I and II. His periodization differs from that of Bikai, who assigns her Strata XIII–X to Iron Age II, while Nuñez ascribes them to Iron Age I. He also differs in dating the beginning of Iron Age II to 850 BCE and not to 1025 BCE, while he and Bikai agree on dating its end to 600 BCE.

Anderson identified two phases in Iron Age II, represented by Strata D and C, which are again subdivided into subphases D1 and D2 and C1 and C2, respectively. He ends Iron Age II in 650 BCE, slightly earlier than in the Tyre sequence.

There is no agreed upon periodization of the Persian period. In Sarepta, Anderson identified a transition phase between C1 and B2, which represents, he believes, an occupational gap, and two occupation phases, B2 and B1, characterized by a "marked change in decoration and area finishing techniques" (Anderson 1988, 420). He suggests a date in the sixth/fifth century BCE for Stratum B (Anderson 1988, 421). The presence of imported Attic pottery serves as a marker of the Persian period and contributes to its dating. According to Sharon (2013, 63): "Good assemblages of the end of the 6th century and the beginning of the 5th are as elusive as those of the Babylonian period.... 480 BCE forms a good heuristic cleavage point, inasmuch as Attic (and consequently Cypriot) pottery can easily be classified to Archaic versus Classical, and imports, especially of the former, become prevalent on mainland sites after the mid-5th century."

No Persian-period levels are mentioned in the Tyre sounding and Tyre al-Baṣṣ sequence. In Beirut important remains dating to Iron Age III were excavated in several areas mainly in Bey 010 (Elayi and Sayegh 1998; 2000). In the latter site Iron Age III is represented by Niveau IX (Fer III/Perse; Elayi and Sayegh 2000, 116). In Bey 003 Leila Badre identifies a transitional Late Bronze Age/Iron Age phase, and after an abandonment, a reoccupation in Iron Age II followed by a Persian-period occupation. No stratigraphic subdivisions and no chronological frame are proposed for any of the three Iron Age phases (Badre 1997, 60, 72, 90).

To sum up, if we combine the results of the most recent investigations that took place in southern Phoenician sites, we can conclude that the Iron Age is divided into three phases: Iron Age I (1190–850 BCE), II (850–600 BCE), and III (600–332 BCE), separated by transitional phases and subdivided into subphases. As previously mentioned, Finkelstein and Benjamin Sass (2013) place the end of Iron Age I circa 950 BCE. Iron Age I is subdivided into two main subphases: Iron Age IA and Iron Age IB;

1. INTRODUCTION 23

Iron Age II into three: IIA, IIB, and IIC; and for Iron Age III there is no known periodization yet. The only site where a subdivision into two periods is proposed is BEY 010 (see table 1.2 on pages 24–26). The chronology of the Iron Age can be related to the main historical events of the first millennium BCE attested in the written records. Iron Age I started after the Egyptian withdrawal, witnessed the migration of groups from Cyprus and northern Syria, and ended with the beginning of the Neo-Assyrian expansion to the west. Iron Age II covers the period of Neo-Assyrian and Neo-Babylonian occupation, and Iron Age III that of the Achaemenid Persian empire. The Iron Age ended with the conquest of Phoenicia by Alexander the Great in 332 BCE.

## 1.4. The Problem of the Sources

### 1.4.1. Scarcity of Contemporary Written Records

In almost all the publications there is a recurring statement that characterizes the Phoenicians as an "elusive" people. In other words, although seemingly well-known and familiar, the history and culture of the Phoenicians are difficult to grasp and to define. This elusive character is due to the scarcity of contemporary textual and archaeological records from their homeland.

Regarding the written record, only a dearth of inscriptions were left by the inhabitants of the four Phoenician kingdoms, and with a few exceptions they do not contain any historical information. The rare royal inscriptions from Byblos and Sidon (*KAI* 1–12, 13–16), as well as the variety of short graffiti found mainly on funerary stelae (Sader 2005; Lemaire 2001; Abou Samra and Lemaire 2014; Abou Samra 2018), seals (Sass and Uehlinger 1993; Bordreuil 1986; Avigad and Sass 1997; Deutsch and Lemaire 2000; Elayi 2013b; Schmitz 2014), and ceramics (Bordreuil 1982; 2003; Teixidor 1986: 209–10; Abou Samra 2009; 2014), retrieved either from the market and more rarely from regular archaeological excavations, do not enlighten us much about Phoenician history. Not one monumental inscription is known from Tyre and Arwad, and their history is almost totally dependent on foreign sources. Recently André Lemaire published two Tyrian inscriptions purchased on the antiquities market that mention the names of Tyrian kings (Lemaire 2013a). The first attests the name of Ittobaal son of Hiram and the second a certain ʿAbdalonim, whose great-grandfather was a king named Hirom. The scarcity of contemporary writ-

Table 1.2. Iron Age Periodization of the South Phoenician sites of Beirut, Sarepta, Tyre, al-Baṣṣ, Keisan, and Dor

| Beirut 003 | LB IA I transition | Not available | No date | Badre 1997, 60 |
|---|---|---|---|---|
| Beirut 003 | IA II | Not available | No date | Badre 1997, 72 |
| Beirut 003 | IA III | Not available | No date | Badre 1997 |
| Beirut 010 | IA I | hiatus | No date | Elayi and Sayegh 2000, 125 |
| Beirut 010 | IA II | hiatus | No date | Elayi and Sayegh 2000, 125 |
| Beirut 010 | IA III/Persian | Niveau IXa | End of the sixth century to mid-fourth century BCE | Elayi and Sayegh 2000, 127 |
|  |  | Niveau IXb | Mid-fourth to early third century BCE |  |
| Sarepta sounding Y | IA I | F | ca. 1200/1190–1150/1125 BCE | Anderson 1988, 386–96 |
|  | Area II, Y | E | 1150/1125–1050/1025 BCE |  |
| Sarepta sounding X | IA I | Period V | ca. 1275–1150 BCE | Khalifeh 1988, 102–24 |
|  | Area II, X | Period VI | ca. 1150–1025 BCE |  |
| Sarepta | IA II | Stratum D2 | ca. 1025/1000–950 BCE | Anderson 1988, 407 |
|  |  | Stratum D1 | 950–850/825 BCE |  |
| Sarepta | Iron Age II | Stratum C2 | 850/825–750/725 BCE | Anderson 1988, 419 |
|  |  | Stratum C1 | ca. 750/725–650 BCE? |  |

| Site | Period | Stratum | Date | Reference |
|---|---|---|---|---|
| Sarepta | Iron Age III transition C to B | Stratum C1/B2 | 650–600 BCE? | Anderson 1988, 419 |
| | | Occupational gap | | |
| Sarepta | Iron Age III | Stratum B2 and B1 | sixth/fifth century BCE | Anderson 1988, 423 |
| Tyre al-Baṣṣ | LB IA I transition and IA I | Period I | ca. 1200–850 BCE without chronological subdivisions of IA I | Nuñez 2004, 281–373 and fig. 241; 2008 |
| Tyre al-Baṣṣ | IA I–II transition | Period II | ca. 850–775 BCE | Nuñez 2004, 281–373; 2008 |
| Tyre al-Baṣṣ | IA IIA | Period III | ca. 775–750 BCE | Nuñez 2004, 281–373 and fig. 241; 2008 |
| Tyre al-Baṣṣ | IA IIB | Period IV | ca. 750–700 BCE | Nuñez 2004, 281–373 and fig. 241; 2008 |
| Tyre al-Baṣṣ | Iron Age IIC | Period V | ca. 700–600 BCE | Nuñez 2004, 281–373 and fig. 241; 2008 |
| Tyre sounding | Iron Age I | Level XIV | 1200 BCE to ca. 1070/1050 BCE | Bikai 1978a, 65–66 |
| Tyre sounding | Iron Age II | Strata XIII–I | ca. 1070/1050–1000 BCE–ca. 600 BCE | Bikai 1978a |
| Tyre sounding | IA II | Stratum XII | ca. 1000–925 BCE | Bikai 1978a |
| Tyre sounding | IA II | Strata XI–X | ca. 925–825 BCE | Bikai 1978a |
| Tyre sounding | IA II | Strata IX–VIII | ca. 825–800 BCE | Bikai 1978a |
| Tyre sounding | IA II | Strata VII–IV | ca. 800–750 BCE | Bikai 1978a |

| Site | Phase | Stratum | Date | Reference |
|---|---|---|---|---|
| Tyre sounding | IA II | Strata III–II | ca. 850–700 BCE | Bikai 1978a |
| Tyre sounding | IA II | Stratum I | ca. 700–600 BCE | Bikai 1978a |
| Tell Keisan | IA IA | Strata 12–9C | ca. 1160–1050 BCE | Briend and Humbert 1980, 27 |
| Tell Keisan | IA IB | Stratum 9A–b | ca. 1050–980 BCE | Briend and Humbert 1980, 27 |
| Tell Keisan | IA I/II | Stratum 8C | ca. 980–960 BCE | Briend and Humbert 1980, 27 |
| Tell Keisan | IA IIA | Stratum 8A–B | ca. 960–900 BCE | Briend and Humbert 1980, 27 |
| Keisan | IA IIB | Strata 7–6 | ca. 900–800 BCE | Briend and Humbert 1980, 27 |
| Keisan | IA IIC | Strata 5 and 4A–B | ca. 720–580 BCE | Briend and Humbert 1980, 27 |
| Keisan | IA IIIA | Stratum 3A | ca. 450–380 BCE | Briend and Humbert 1980, 27 |
| Keisan | IA IIIB | Stratum 3A | ca. 580–480/460 BCE | Briend and Humbert 1980, 27 |
| Dor | LB IA | B/14? G/11? | ca. 1190–1160 BCE | Gilboa and Sharon 2003 |
| Dor | IA IA early | B/13?–G/10 | ca. 1160–1120 BCE | Gilboa and Sharon 2003 |
| Dor | IA IA late | B12/G/9 | ca. 1120–1090 BCE | Gilboa and Sharon 2003 |
| Dor | IA IA/IB | B11/10, D2/12, G/8 | ca. 1090–1050 BCE | Gilboa and Sharon 2003 |
| Dor | IA IB | B10, 9b?, D2/11–9, G/7 | ca. 1050–980 BCE | Gilboa and Sharon 2003 |
| Dor | IA I/II | B1/9a, D2/8c, G/6b | ca. 980–960 BCE | Gilboa and Sharon 2003 |
| Dor | IA IIA | B/8, D2/8b, G/6a | ca. 960–900 BCE | Gilboa and Sharon 2003 |

ten records has led scholars to fill the gap by seeking information in the writings of later classical authors who did not have firsthand information and who filled in the blanks with myths and legends that were and still are often taken at face value. They became so deeply anchored in both the scholarly and the popular tradition that it is very difficult to deconstruct them at present.

It is unfortunate that no ancient Phoenician settlement of the homeland has yielded so far the equivalent of a state archive. This situation is all the more puzzling since such archives are known to have existed. The Phoenicians kept archives in which they stored legal, diplomatic, and administrative documents, as was the tradition in all the other kingdoms of the ancient Near East. These archives are mentioned in the Report of Wenamun. The Egyptian envoy says that Zakarbaal, king of Byblos, "had brought records from the time of his ancestors and had them read before me" (Goedicke 1975, 76). Josephus in his *Jewish Antiquities* (8.5.3) mentions also the existence of Tyrian annals that were translated into Greek by Menander of Ephesus. One plausible reason why such archives were never discovered, in spite of long-term and extensive excavations in the main Phoenician cities, may be that the inhabitants of the Levantine coast used scrolls of Egyptian papyrus to write their records. Papyrus is a perishable material that did not survive the humid climate of the Levantine coast (Lemaire 1981, 67); what survived are short inscriptions written on stone, pottery, and metal. Furthermore, no public building that can be identified as a city palace from the Iron Age period and not one likely to have stored state archives has thus far been unearthed in the homeland.

In the absence of historical records from the Phoenician polities, one has to look for other contemporary sources mentioning them and their inhabitants. The main sources of information are the Neo-Assyrian texts, and to a lesser degree the Neo-Babylonian texts and the Homeric epics, and to some extent the biblical record. The Egyptian texts that form the main written corpus for the second millennium BCE contribute hardly any information on the Levantine coast in the Iron Age. Instrumental for the history of the Phoenician kingdoms during the Persian period are Herodotus's *Histories*, since the Persian kings did not leave annals similar to those of the Mesopotamian monarchs.

Had it not been for the annals of the Neo-Assyrian kings who regularly undertook military campaigns to the west from the ninth until the early seventh century BCE, it would be hard to even sketch a political history of the Phoenician kingdoms. The annals of the Assyrian kings form the main corpus of contemporary texts relating to the Phoenicians. However, one has to keep in mind that the Assyrian scribes were interested mainly in glorifying the victorious king, in detailing the exemplary punishments he inflicted on the rebellious people, and in listing the tribute imposed on the subdued countries, and much less in the social and economic conditions of the lands they conquered.

The biblical account detailing the relations between Hiram of Tyre and David and Solomon, which were recounted partly by Josephus, a first-century CE historian, were also taken as facts and presented as evidence. However, the historicity of these tales as well as that of their heroes is doubted today by many scholars. At least, one cannot assign them securely to the tenth century, as has been traditionally suggested (Sharon 2013, 59–60).

In short, we owe most historical facts relating to the Phoenicians to foreign sources. This is why the archaeological record is of utmost importance not only to fill in the gaps left by the scanty written sources but also to get solid facts that are not distorted by political or economic foreign interests and that, if retrieved and interpreted properly, would give us an unbiased view of the historical reality.

1.4.2. Issues Relating to Phoenician Archaeology in the Homeland

Unfortunately, for many years the absence of substantial archaeological information mainly from the Lebanese coast, the heartland of Phoenicia, meant that the region's material culture was poorly documented, thereby contributing to the elusive character of the Phoenicians.

Despite investigations of the Phoenician cities starting in the nineteenth century, with the launch of Ernest Renan's *Mission de Phénicie* (1864), little was retrieved that could shed light on the history of Phoenicia. Arwad, Byblos, Sidon, and Tyre, the famed cities of the Phoenicians, were visited, and for more than a century large-scale excavations have taken place. However, puzzlingly, in none of these sites was the Phoenician settlement identified. Maurice Chéhab, the first director general of the Lebanese Antiquities, who remained in that position for some fifty years, made the investigation of Phoenician culture his priority. Working in tandem with Maurice Dunand, he monopolized the archaeological investigations in the three Phoenician capitals: Byblos, Sidon, and Tyre. Unfortunately, they both failed to establish solid stratigraphic sequences for their excavations, and their results remain unpublished. But while sensational discoveries were made in the Phoenician settlements in the west, and while scholars were eagerly expecting information from the homeland, the latter kept on disappointing them by failing to produce relevant archaeological evidence. For Wolfgang Röllig (1983a, 83), "The explanation for this is quite simple: over the millennia the important settlements were constantly being rebuilt due to their favorable location. Thus, 1) the sequence of levels was often disturbed by the clearance of earlier buildings. Nevertheless, 2) deposition of cultural remains often reaches a considerable height, so that the levels of the 2nd millennium lie quite deep. Finally, 3) recent settlements there permit excavation only in a quite confined area" (see also Pritchard 1975, 3). This explanation seems to have been corroborated by the Beirut evidence, on the one hand, and contradicted by the large-scale excavations on the site of ancient Tyre and Byblos on the other. In Beirut the Phoenician city was indeed buried under the remains of the old town district, but in Tyre and Byblos the ancient settlement was extensively excavated without yielding information about the Phoenician era.

Whatever the reason may be, the relentless focus on the main capital cities of the Phoenicians did not yield any important result. The investigation of these cities proved to be sterile, and after many years of excavations the authorities should have designed a new strategy to develop Phoenician archaeology. If one is allowed a comparison, a similar situation prevailed in Palestine when biblical archaeologists were trying to find evidence for the settlement of the Israelites and concentrated their efforts on the large Canaanite cities mentioned in the Bible. However, while precious information relating to the Late Bronze Age was retrieved, they found no evidence regarding the issue they were trying to solve (Finkelstein and Silberman 2001, 105) until they opted for a totally new strategy and started looking elsewhere.

The turning point for Phoenician archaeology in Lebanon was the Sarepta archaeological project, which opted for a smaller but intact settlement. James Pritchard's (1975, 3) "principal objective of the Sarafand expedition from its beginning had been the discovery of well-stratified remains of an urban settlement for the period of the Phoenician commerce and settlement in the Mediterranean (ca 1200–600 B.C.)." His choice proved a sensible one, as the Sarepta excavations were such a success that they paved the way for a new phase of Phoenician archaeology in Lebanon. For the first time extensive and stratified evidence could be retrieved from a Phoenician settlement, and Sarepta became a reference for those working on the Phoenician archaeology of the motherland. This success should have encouraged the Lebanese authorities to survey and protect all the small coastal sites of Lebanon; unfortunately, this did not happen, and many of them fell victim to the anarchic urbanization that developed during and after the civil war.

When archaeologists turned to other less famous coastal settlements, the long-sought evidence started to emerge. New hope for the Lebanese Iron Age has dawned with the beginning of new, post–civil war archaeological projects. Work concentrated, first, on the city center of Beirut, where Iron Age II and III remains were exposed. At the end of the 1990s, excavations began at Tyre al-Baṣṣ to investigate the Phoenician cremation cemetery that was accidentally discovered there (Seeden 1991). At the same time, a new archaeological project was started at Tell el-Burak, where a Phoenician settlement dating to Iron Age II and III was exposed. More recently, the island of Tyre started unveiling its Phoenician remains: a Persian-period temple was exposed, and new investigations in the area contiguous to Bikai's sounding have identified and partly exposed a segment of the Tyrian acropolis city wall as well as other Iron Age remains. The exposure of these layers is still work in progress. The remains in that area have clearly shown the scale of the destructions inflicted to the Iron Age remains by the later classical and medieval buildings.

New excavations were started also in Jiyye (Waliszewski et al. 2015), Chhim (Waliszewski et al. 2002), Sidon College Site (see Doumet-Serhal 2013 for a summary), and Yanūḥ (Monchambert et al. 2010; Monchambert 2011) in the mountains of Byblos, and Iron Age remains were identified in all these settlements. In Batrun, rescue excavations undertaken by the Department of Antiquities have exposed a promising sequence of Late Bronze Age and Iron Age remains in a small area opposite the famous sea wall. The recent investigation in north Lebanon at the site of Anfe, ancient Ampa, and the new excavation project of Tell Mirhan, ancient Šigata/Shekka—a site that Pritchard considered as a good candidate for his Phoenician project before he opted for Sarepta—promise new information about the Phoenician period.[4] The recent excavations have provided new and reliable stratigraphic and chronological sequences for the Phoenician Iron Age. One has to note in this context that in addition to these regular and long-term excavations, countless accidental discover-

---

4. The investigation at Anfe is an excavation project of the University of Balamand in cooperation with the Honor Frost Foundation. The excavation at Tell Mirhan is a joint University of Vienna\Austrian Academy of Science archaeological project.

ies and rescue excavations have taken place in the larger Beirut, Sidon, and Tyre areas, but it is very unfortunate that nothing has transpired from their results. Furthermore, several surveys are taking place in the coastal area of Lebanon: in the ʿAkkār Plain, in the area around the sites of Enfe, Shekka, and Tell Koubba in northern Lebanon, a region that is still almost completely unknown archaeologically. As for southern Lebanon, surveys of the area of Chhim as well as that of Tell el-Burak and Kharayeb will substantially contribute to the understanding of the Sidonian kingdom. Finally, a survey of the area around the city of Tyre and around the site of Oum el Amed was started a couple of years ago. So there is hope that in the near future and upon the publication of these survey results a picture of the Iron Age settlement of the Lebanese coast and its immediate hinterland will emerge. The only portion of the coast that remains unexplored is the area stretching from Byblos to Jiyye.

So Lebanon is progressively operating a comeback on the archaeological scene of the Phoenician homeland and is yielding new and important evidence for the understanding of its culture. It is adding to the substantial and generally well-documented information provided by the northern Palestinian sites, a territory that historically belonged to the Phoenician kingdoms of Tyre and Sidon. The excavations of ʿAthlit, Akhziv, Akko, Tell Keisan, Tell Abu Hawam, and Dor, to name only the most prominent Phoenician settlements, were instrumental for the understanding of the material culture and daily life of southern Phoenicia, as well as for the chronology and periodization of the Phoenician Iron Age.

In northern Syria new investigations are taking place in ʿAmrit, Tell Kazel, and the Plain of Ǧabla, shedding new light on the daily life in the territory of Arwad. However, with the exception of the Tell Sukas publications, only very short preliminary reports describe briefly the results of the new excavations.

2

PHOENICIA IN IRON AGE I

The beginning of the Iron Age or Phoenician period has been set traditionally in the twelfth century, starting around 1200 BCE, when the Late Bronze Age culture was either waning or had come to a violent end. After a short transitional period, the Iron Age proper started. Its earliest phase, Iron Age I, was and still is largely considered to be one of the most puzzling dark ages in the history of Phoenicia for two main reasons: the extreme rarity of the textual record on the one hand, and the absence of sufficient and reliable archaeological data on the other.

By contrast to the relatively abundant written record regarding the situation prevailing in Phoenicia during the Late Bronze Age, hardly any historical information is available for the last two centuries of the second millennium BCE, a crucial transition period that followed the collapse of Late Bronze Age culture in the Levant. The assumption has always been that Phoenicia, like its southern Palestinian and northern Syrian neighbors, suffered from the Sea Peoples invasion. This invasion theory was based on the accounts of the Egyptian pharaohs Merenptah and Ramesses III. The latter says in the inscription on his funerary temple at Medinet Habu that people coming from the midst of the sea invaded and destroyed the land: "From Ḫatti, Qode (Cilicia), Carchemish (on the Euphrates), Arzawa (Lycia, in southwestern Turkey), Alashia (on Cyprus) they were cut off" (Halpern 2008, 17). Today we know that these accounts have been exaggerated and sometimes invented: "Royal inscriptions walk a line between truth and risibility," says Baruch Halpern (18) in his discussion of Ramesses III's inscriptions. Indeed, neither Carchemish nor Ḫatti were destroyed by the Sea Peoples (Hawkins 2000; 2009 with relevant bibliography; Genz 2013). Furthermore, the material culture of northern Syria did not display any radical change in Iron Age I as compared to the Late Bronze Age culture (Venturi 2000; 2005). The only area that seems to have witnessed the arrival of new populations is the southern Palestinian coast with the emergence of Philistine culture. The archaeological evidence relating to Iron Age I south of Dor supports the view that Sea People groups coming from the Aegean, Asia Minor, and Cyprus settled on the southern coast of Palestine, at Gath, Ekron, Ashdod, Ashkelon, and Gaza. The presence of Shardana at Tell Abu Hawam and Sikils at Dor has been questioned (see below). The Philistine or Iron Age I culture of the southern Palestinian settlements has been abundantly discussed in the scientific literature (for a synthesis see Killebrew 2005, 197–245 with relevant bibliography; and more recently Harrison 2008; Killebrew and Lehmann 2013). Phoenicia, however, shows no tangible evidence for such an immigration, but there may be some evidence in north Syrian sites.

## 2.1. The Textual Evidence

Regarding the written sources, apart from short alphabetic inscriptions on arrowheads consisting of personal names (Bordreuil 1992b; Sader 2000b; Abou Samra 2014) and dated between the twelfth and the tenth century BCE, as well as the possible mention of a king of Byblos named 'Ozbaal on a small stone and on two arrowheads (Lemaire 2013b), only two texts with some historical bearing make a direct reference to Phoenician coastal cities: the annals of the Middle Assyrian king Tiglath-pileser I (1114–1076 BCE) and the Egyptian text known as the Report of Wenamun (Sass 2002).

### 2.1.1. The Annals of Tiglath-pileser I (1114–1076 BCE)

Tiglath-pileser I's account speaks of an expedition to Mount Lebanon to cut cedarwood for the building of the temple of the gods Anu and Adad, during which he conquered the land of Amurru and collected tribute from the lands of Byblos, Sidon, and Arwad:[1] "I received tribute from the lands Byblos, Sidon, (and) Arvad. I rode in boats of people of Arvad (and) traveled successfully a distance of 3 double hours from the city Arvad, an island, to the city Ṣamuru which is in the land Amurru. I killed at sea a nāḫiru, which is called a sea-horse" (Grayson 1991, A.0.87.3:20–21).

---

1. A cylinder seal found in Tyre was generally ascribed by Porada (1978, 77–79). to the Middle Assyrian period. There is, however, no clear evidence that it belongs to the later years of this period, more specifically to the reign of Tiglath-pileser I.

From this passage of the annals we learn that in the first quarter of the eleventh century BCE, the Phoenician cities existed and were even rich enough to arouse the greed of the Assyrian king, who imposed and received their tribute. The only important city that is omitted from the list of tribute payers is Tyre. The reasons for this omission will be discussed in chapter 3.

## 2.1.2. The Report of Wenamun

The Report of Wenamun describes the journey of an Egyptian official who was sent to Byblos to buy cedarwood for the Amun barge. It was first dated to the eleventh century BCE by Hans Goedicke (1975). This date was challenged by Wolfgang Helck (1994, 110), who argued that the text is not an actual report of a journey but was written some 150 years later to prove the power of the god Amun outside Egyptian borders. More recently Sass (2002, 247) discussed the various opinions relating to the nature of the text: they range from an authentic report of a journey to "the literary reworking of an administrative report, if not a piece of fiction pure and simple," and he opted for a date around 925 BCE. This text, whether dated to the beginning or to the end of the Early Iron Age, remains a useful source because "although likely to be fictitious, the account is nevertheless thought to present an accurate picture of prevailing political and social conditions at the time of its composition" (Woolmer 2017, 33). The text brings precious information about Sidon and Byblos and their political and economic situation. As for Byblos, the report mentions Zakarbaal, the ruling king of that city, who is otherwise unknown[2] and who is presented as the descendant of a well-established and uninterrupted royal lineage, since Wenamun refers to his father and grandfather. If this king is a historical figure at all, he is more likely to have ruled before Ahiram, that is, at the end of the eleventh century BCE, since five rulers of Byblos are attested in the tenth century BCE: Ahiram, Ittobaal, Yeḥimilk, Abibaal, and Elibaal. On the other hand, it seems that Byblos had renewed its friendly relations with Egypt in the tenth century BCE, as attested by the royal inscriptions of Abibaal and Elibaal, which were written on statues of Sheshonq I and

---

2. The name Zakarbaal on an arrowhead published by Jean Starcky (1982) cannot refer to the king of Byblos mentioned in the Wenamun report since his title reads clearly *mlk ʿmr*: king of Amurru? This identification was, however, proposed by Lemaire (2012).

Osorkon I respectively. Zakarbaal's unfriendly attitude toward the Egyptian envoy clearly indicates a period of drastic change in the relations of Phoenicia with Egypt. Egypt was not the almighty suzerain it used to be in the Late Bronze Age but seems to have lost power and prestige in its former provinces. Despite repeated attempts during the first millennium BCE, Egypt was not able to restore its previous hegemony and long-lasting rule over the Phoenician cities because of Assyrian presence in the area. Hence, it appears from the available sources that in the period covering the eleventh and tenth century BCE, the Phoenician cities were independent and not vassals of a foreign power. Furthermore, the overall picture is one of economic prosperity, as indicated by the situation of the cities of Byblos and Sidon. Twenty ships in active trade relations with Egypt in the harbor of Byblos and fifty in that of Sidon are mentioned by Wenamun and clearly illustrate the flourishing economy of these Phoenician cities. It is noteworthy that Sidon appears to be the prominent trading center of the Phoenician coast. It signals the power that this Phoenician city would enjoy in the first millennium BCE.

The above records suggest that the Phoenician cities were well-established urban centers with local royal dynasties in the eleventh–tenth century BCE. They were witnessing an important economic expansion, indicated by a large merchant fleet and a well-organized trading network run by both public officials and private merchants.

The biblical account is considered to be an important source for the situation of the Phoenician cities in the tenth century BCE, as attested mainly in the narratives relating to Hiram I of Tyre and his relations with David and Solomon (for a discussion of the historicity of these accounts see ch. 3).

## 2.2. The Archaeological Record

Now we have to turn to the archaeological record to see whether it corroborates the peaceful situation and economic prosperity suggested by the written sources. The Iron Age I period is unequally attested on the Phoenician coast. While it is poorly documented in the archaeological record of northern Phoenicia, it is better known in the southern part of the area.

### 2.2.1. Iron Age I in the Northern Kingdoms of Byblos and Arwad

With the exception of Tell Kazel, Tell Sukas, and Tell Tweini on the north Syrian coast, nothing is known about the Iron Age I in the territory of the Phoenician kingdoms of Arwad and Byblos. In Tell Sukas Iron Age I levels were excavated in Stratum H and in a cremation cemetery dated to the twelfth–tenth century BCE near the southern harbor, thus indicating a continuous occupation (Riis 1961–1962, 140; 1979, 51). At Tell Tweini a complete sequence ranging from the transition between the Late Bronze Age and Iron Age I until Iron Age II was excavated in Areas A and B. It is represented in the former by Stratum VIIA and VIIB, Levels 6G–H and 6E–F, and in the latter by Stratum VIIA and VIIB, Levels 7A–C, dated between 1200 and 900 BCE (Al-Maqdissi et al. 2010, table 1). A partial destruction marked the end of the Late Bronze Age, but settlement resumed after a short hiatus. The pottery of these levels, mainly the storage jars, are in the tradition of the Late Bronze Age pottery. Tell Tweini has no "barbarian" pottery like Tell Kazel, but its Iron Age I is characterized by the so-called *céramique à la steatite*, common at Ras Ibn Hani (Bounni, Lagarce, and Lagarce 1979, 254), and by craters with hatched triangular motifs painted black and red.

At Tell Kazel the last occupational phase of Level 6 upper floor in Area II and Level 5 upper floor in Area IV represent the transitional Late Bronze Age/Iron Age occupation: these levels were destroyed by fire. Level 5 in Area II and Levels 4–3 in Area IV represent Iron Age I, and they were also violently destroyed (Badre 2006, 69). In the transitional Late Bronze/Iron Age levels, the pottery is characterized by the emergence of the so-called barbarian or handmade burnished ware and by the presence of Trojan vessels (Capet 2008; Badre 2006, 92) together with the local pottery, which is in the tradition of the Late Bronze Age vessels. The "barbarian" pottery was locally made probably by potters who had migrated from their homeland (Capet 2008, 198). The Trojan pottery, on the other hand, was imported (198). Imports from Cyprus and mainland Greece are not attested, and local imitations of Mycenaean pottery (Mycenaean IIIC 1B) are produced and continue to be present in the later phases of the Iron Age I. They are closer to the Cypriot and north Syrian wares (196). No bichrome ware is attested yet in this transitional phase. These levels are dated by relative chronology to the twelfth century or the very beginning of the eleventh century BCE (204–5). No carbon-14 determinations are available. The architecture of this phase presents the same characteristics as those of the Late Bronze Age, mainly fieldstones with ashlars at the corners and doorjambs used also at Ugarit. The end of this phase is characterized by the disappearance of the "barbarian" pottery and the progressive disappearance of the Trojan imports. The publications (Badre 2006; Capet

2008) focus on the ceramics of this particular period to study the transition between Late Bronze Age and Iron Age I, and they do not detail that of the Iron Age I levels.

At Tell Arqa Phase J represents the Iron Age I period (Thalmann 2000, fig. 15; Thalmann 2006, 15 and fig. 3), but the site showed no traces of occupation during that phase, indicating a hiatus in the occupation. At Byblos, the remains of the Iron Age I and II could not be detected. According to Dunand (1939, 64, 79), "A Byblos les couches hellénistiques et romaines sont souvent superposées directement aux couches du Moyen Empire," a situation that partly explains the absence of Late Bronze and Iron Age remains at the site. With the exception of necropole K, hardly any Iron Age remains were found (Salles 1980).

2.2.2. Iron Age I in the Southern Kingdoms of Sidon and Tyre

The archaeological evidence for the southern kingdoms is more abundant and suggests a peaceful transition from the Late Bronze into the Iron Age.

2.2.2.1. Beirut

The evidence for Iron Age I in Beirut is highly controversial: in Area BEY 003, Badre (1997, 54, 64) identified a Late Bronze Age/Iron Age transitional phase characterized by the erection of a new fortification wall and glacis, which she calls Glacis II and which she dates to the end of Late Bronze Age II. The excavators of neighboring areas where the same structure (Glacis II) was attested suggest a much lower date for its building: Uwe Finkbeiner (2001–2002, 27–28) dates it to Iron Age II, and Hans Curvers (2001–2002, 57) to Iron II–III. On the other hand, in his reconstruction of the Beirut stratigraphy, Curvers (59) does not recognize any Iron Age I levels. This conclusion seems to fit the ceramic evidence retrieved on site, since no Iron Age I pottery is described or illustrated in any of the excavation reports.[3]

Further south, the Iron Age I is rather well represented: Sidon, Sarepta, Tyre, Tell Abu Hawam, Tell Keisan, Akko, and Dor have all yielded complete Iron Age I sequences.

---

3. All preliminary reports on the excavations of the upper city of Beirut have appeared in the second volume of *Bulletin d'Archéologie et d'Architecture Libanaises* (1997).

## 2.2.2.2. Sarepta

The best-preserved evidence for Iron Age I on the Lebanese coast comes from Sarepta Area II, sounding X, Periods V–VI (Khalifeh 1988, 102–24), and sounding Y, strata F and E (Anderson 1988, 386–96), and from Tyre strata XIV and XIII (Bikai 1978a, 65–66). The exposure of the Iron Age I remains is limited in Sarepta to these sounding areas (sounding X 800 m$^2$ and sounding Y 100 m$^2$). Stratum F in sounding Y at Sarepta was tentatively ascribed to the period between circa 1200/1190 and 1150/1125 BCE based on the presence of Late Cypriot III and Mycenaean IIIC pottery (Anderson 1988, 390), and Stratum E in the same sounding is dated to the period ranging between 1150/1125 and 1050/1025 BCE. Period V in sounding X is dated circa 1275–1150 BCE (Khalifeh 1988, 113), and Period VI circa 1150–1025 BCE (124). According to the Sarepta excavators (Anderson 1988, 386; Khalifeh 1988, 102, 113–14) there are no distinctive breaks in the occupational sequence and in the pottery traditions from G to F and from IV to V. Between Strata F and E and Periods V and VI, there is also a gradual transition, with no distinct break in either the stratigraphy or the characteristic pottery types. Based on this evidence, Anderson (1988, 424) concluded, "Sarepta—and possibly most of the Phoenician coast—was not directly affected by the massive disturbances, attributed to the 'Sea-Peoples,' which occurred at the end of the LBA in Syria, Palestine and elsewhere." This conclusion is confirmed by the evidence from Period V and VI of sounding X.

The evidence indicates that the industrial production of pottery attested by the presence of pottery kilns continued from the Late Bronze Age into Iron Age I. This large-scale production of pottery vessels as well as a clear increase in pithoi and storage jars (Khalifeh 1988, 106) may hint at trade activity. The Sarepta and the close-by Sidonian harbors were the places where these products were shipped to both local and Mediterranean destinations. This industrial production of amphorae suggests also that the country was producing wine and oil, as well as other commodities (see ch. 6). The evidence from Sarepta is thus in line with the intensive trade activity of the Sidonian harbor suggested by the Wenamun Report.

## 2.2.2.3. Sidon

More recently, the excavations at the College Site in Sidon have produced a sequence of occupation starting in the thirteenth and ending in the ninth century BCE, substantiated by carbon-14 determinations. In Sidon, the Iron Age I remains were exposed over a large area and brought more solid evidence for the situation prevailing in southern Phoenicia at this time. A temple dating to that period was excavated and had ten occupation Levels A–J. The building presented clear evidence for continuity, since it was rebuilt as is by the successive occupants. The ceramics of this long sequence will be detailed in a forthcoming publication (Doumet-Serhal forthcoming) and will allow a better understanding of the nature of the settlement during this period.[4] Further evidence for continuity in occupation was the discovery of a vase bearing the name of Queen Tawosret (Doumet-Serhal 2013, fig. 45) and dated around 1190 BCE. According to the excavator, it "constitutes a document of fundamental significance for relations between Egypt and Sidon for the period of great upheaval in connection with the Peoples of the Sea. At this time relations between Sidon and Egypt continue, and Sidon remains untouched by the instability of the period" (Doumet-Serhal 2013, 45). Trade activity with the eastern Mediterranean in the eleventh century BCE is indicated also by the finds in the Iron Age I temple, which consisted mainly of Egyptian alabaster vessels and faience necklaces, as well as Cypriot imports. The new Sidonian evidence will shed additional light on the heartland of Phoenicia in Iron Age I.

2.2.2.4 Tyre

The Tyre sounding was even smaller (150 m²) than those at Sarepta, and the remains were too fragmentary to allow any conclusions. However, the pottery sequence allowed an insight into the period. At Tyre Stratum XIV "extends from about 1200 BC to about 1070/50 BC and covers a period roughly equivalent to Palestinian Iron Age I and Late Cypriot III" (Bikai 1978a, 66). The date of the end of the stratum was determined by the absence of Cypriot white-painted sherds, which indicates that it must have ended before 1070/1050 BCE. Bikai ascribes only this stratum to Iron Age I and considers Stratum XIII in its two subphases to represent the beginning of Iron Age II, while other scholars in light of new evidence ascribe

---

4. This information was presented by Claude Doumet-Serhal at an international symposium held in Beirut in October 25–29, 2017. The proceedings of this symposium are planned to be published in a special volume of the journal *Bulletin d'Archéologie et d'Architecture Libanaises*.

this latter stratum also to a later phase of Iron Age I: Iron Age IB (Gilboa and Sharon 2003, table 21; Lehmann 2013, table 3a). Stratum XIV has yielded fragments of domestic architecture with a *tannur* and storage bins cut into the floors as well as evidence for a bead industry (Bikai 1978a, 8). A fire pit probably used for the firing of the beads was also found: "About 1886 red faience beads ... were found in this stratum.... It is likely therefore that the manufacture of beads, apparently begun in this area at the time of Stratum XVI, continued through Stratum XIV" (8). This evidence clearly indicates that the production of faience beads had a long tradition in Tyre and continued without interruption from the Late Bronze Age into the Iron Age I. Little is known about other activities in the Iron Age I city.

The recent excavations at the site of Tyre al-Baṣṣ (Aubet 2004; Aubet, Nuñez, and Tresilló 2014), where a cremation cemetery was found, have indicated that the latter was in use already in the eleventh century BCE. Period I, circa 1100–950 BCE (Aubet 2004, 465), represents this Iron Age I occupation (Nuñez 2004, 352 and fig. 241). According to the excavators, it corresponds to Tyre Strata XIV–X. No radiocarbon dating is available for this period because the Iron Age I ceramics were found scattered out of their original context. Since this cemetery was the burial ground of the island population (Aubet 2004, 466), it provides additional evidence for the continuous occupation of the insular city.

2.2.2.5. Akko

Tell el-Fukkhar, ancient Akko, has yielded evidence for Late Bronze–Iron Age I transition and Iron Age I levels in Areas A, B, AB, H, and F (Dothan 1993, 21). The transition period was dated circa 1200 BCE based on finds from the reign of Seti I. The occupation sequence in Iron Age I was not dealt with in detail. Evidence for several types of industry, such as purple dye, metal, and pottery, was found. Based mainly on the account of the *Onomasticon* as well as on the presence of Mycenaean IIIC 1B pottery, the excavators concluded that the site was settled by the ŠRDN, one group of the Sea Peoples, a conclusion challenged by Sharon and Gilboa (2013).

2.2.2.6. Tell Keisan

Tell Keisan has yielded a complete sequence for the Iron Age I in Area B, where Levels 13–9c (Briend and Humbert 1980) represent the period from the Late Bronze/Iron Age I transition until the end of Iron Age I. It is dated by the excavators between 1200 and 1000 BCE. The last phase of Iron Age I, Phase 9A–C, showed signs of revival. Level 9A was violently destroyed, probably as a result of local events (Humbert 1993, 866). In 9B Phoenician bichrome vessels appeared and Philistine ware disappeared. The pottery showed clear Cypriot influence as well as Aegean imports. This pottery attests to active trade during the Iron Age I, mainly with Cyprus and the Aegean. This trade was made possible by the proximity of the Akko harbor, which appears to have been extremely active during that period.

2.2.2.7. Tell Abu Hawam

At Tell Abu Hawam, according to the new evaluation of the Iron Age strata (Balensi, Herrera, and Artzy 1993, 10), the transition from the Late Bronze Age to the Iron Age I is represented by Stratum VC (thirteenth–twelfth century BCE), the Iron Age IB by Stratum IVA (eleventh), and Iron Age IA/IIA by Stratum IVB (eleventh–tenth century). The pottery showed clear evidence for active trade in Iron Age I based on the presence of large numbers of imports from Cyprus as well as other eastern Mediterranean sites.

2.2.2.8. Tel Dor

The recent evidence from Tel Dor is instrumental for the periodization and chronology of the Phoenician Iron Age I in southern Phoenicia. The Iron Age I at Dor was first interpreted by Stern as being divided into two phases. The earliest phase, which represents a Sikil or Sea People settlement, was violently destroyed. Stern (1990, 30; 2000, 201) ascribed the destruction to a Phoenician military conquest of the city. In his view, Dor became a Phoenician city only after this conquest. Gilboa (2005, 67; also Gilboa and Sharon 2008; 2013) challenged this view and saw in the Iron Age I city of Dor a Phoenician settlement since the very beginning of the Iron Age, arguing that the material culture of Dor is closest to the culture of the Phoenician cities of the heartland and different from that of the Philistine sites of southern Palestine: "The *Sitz im Leben* of the ceramic culture of Dor (like that of Tell Keisan) and its commercial vista is the coast north of it, including the very 'heartland' of Phoenicia—the Lebanese coast (and part of Israel's northern valleys), and that, on the other hand, these differ significantly from those in Philistia" (Gilboa 2005, 52; also Gilboa, Sharon, and Boaretto 2008, 117). She interprets the term *Sikil*, used by the Egyptians, as "referring to the mixed, but largely autochthonous population of the Phoenician coast" (see also Gilboa 2013, 634: "It is probably some of this new blend of Canaanite, Cypriot, and Syrian populations that is referred to by the Egyptians as *tj-k-r/SKL*"). She suggests elsewhere that the term may refer to a geographical concept (Gilboa and Sharon 2008, 159). On the other hand, the assumption that Dor is never mentioned as part of a Phoenician kingdom before the Persian period, when it was annexed to Sidon (*KAI* 14), does not necessarily mean that Dor did not previously belong to the Phoenician, and more particularly to the Tyrian and Sidonian, cultural sphere.

The Tel Dor excavations have produced a detailed sequence for Iron Age I, for which twenty-two carbon-14 determinations were obtained. The results of the latter seem to support the newly proposed low chronology (Gilboa and Sharon 2001). This new evidence has substantially contributed to a better periodization and chronology of Iron Age I in Phoenicia since "one can match the developments at Dor point-for-point with sites to its north (Tell Keisan, Sarepta, and Tyre), the most evident of which is the gradual change from Late Bronze Age 'Canaanite' to Iron Age 'Phoenician' culture" (Gilboa and Sharon 2008, 160).

The periodization of the Iron Age I at Dor includes the following phases: transitional Late Bronze Age/Iron Age I, Early Iron Age IA, Late Iron Age IA, transitional Iron Age IA/Iron Age IB, Iron Age IB, and transitional Iron Age IB/Iron Age IIA (Gilboa 2005, 52–53). Taking the Tel Dor periodization as a starting point, Gilboa and Sharon (2003) attempted to correlate the ceramic sequences of all the southern Phoenician as well as those of Israelite, Philistine, and Cypriot sites with the Iron Age sequence at Dor in order to establish a chronology of the Levantine Iron Age I period. The results of these correlations are presented in a table (Gilboa and Sharon 2003, table 21) with both the conventional and the new carbon-14 dates from Tel Dor. The latter lower the conventional chronology by circa one hundred years, giving a date range between 1160 and 880 BCE for the period extending from the Late Bronze Age/Iron Age I transition to the beginning of Iron Age II. Gilboa and Sharon (2003, 72; see also Gilboa 2005, 52) are reluctant to opt for one or the other debated chronologies: "The radiocarbon results, both from Dor and Tel Rehov, indicate that the low chronology can no longer be brushed off. However, we are in no position yet to proclaim this one correct or any other chronology obsolete. Thus with the current chronological maelstrom in Israel, we are unable yet to proclaim ex oriente lux, and the relative sequence proposed here is presented in the light of both chronologies." According to these authors, Iron Age IA starts after 1160 BCE and Iron Age IB "begins ca. 980/970 B.C.E. at the very earliest" (Gilboa and Sharon 2003, 62), and it is characterized by the emergence of Phoenician bichrome ware.

The Iron Age I ceramic repertoire at Dor presents no radical changes from the Late Bronze Age one. The pottery displays a progressive development of some forms that were identified and studied using a computerized, mathematics-based method (Gilboa and Sharon 2008, 156). However, some new features can be observed in all southern Phoenician sites during Iron Age I: First, painting tends to disappear on local pottery, and only small containers destined for export are painted. Second, the typical Phoenician bichrome ware appears in Iron Age IB levels. Third, there is a conspicuous absence or rare occurrence of Philistine monochrome and bichrome vessels in the Phoenician Iron Age I sites north of the Yarkon River. Finally, all display an increase of Cypriot imports and of locally made ceramics denoting Cypriot influence, suggesting active trade with the island and maybe the presence of a Cypriot community on the mainland.

2.2.3. Iron Age I Architecture

Little evidence is available for the domestic architecture of Phoenicia in Iron Age I. In northern Phoenicia only Tell Kazel, Tell Sukas, and Tell Tweini, ancient Ğabla, have yielded some limited evidence. In southern Phoenicia at Tell Keisan, Tell Abu Hawam, and Dor examples of domestic architecture were exposed. In Sarepta only parts of domestic dwellings have been exposed, but no complete plan could be reconstructed.

At Tell Tweini the architecture of the Iron Age I is well preserved in Area A. South of building A, Iron Age I structures were exposed: they are built with fieldstones, and they all display features typical of domestic dwellings (Bretschneider, Jans, and Van Vyve 2010, fig. 3.10). A number of domestic installations were found: one of the exposed rooms contained storage jars (Bretschneider, Jans, and Van Vyve 2010, fig. 3.1–3). A sounding under building A exposed Iron Age I structures consisting of a series of small rooms where a number of *tannurs* were found but no coherent plan could be reconstructed. Fragmentary remains of the Iron Age I were found also under building C.

At Tell Sukas domestic installations are represented by two poorly preserved successive buildings: complex V and VI were both only partly excavated, and their plan cannot therefore be fully understood (Lund 1986, 24 and pls. 9–12). North of complex VI a storage area was found, characterized by circular, stone-lined pits (Lund 1986, fig. 17) similar to the ones found at Tell Kazel (Capet 2008, fig. 15). Each one of these buildings had two occupation phases. Complex V was dated between 1170 and 1050 BCE and complex VI to 1050–850 BCE (Lund 1986, 40).

At Tell Kazel three houses, labeled southern, northern, and southwestern complex, were exposed clustered around a temple in Area IV and dated to the transitional Late Bronze/Iron Age I Level 5 (Badre and Gubel 1999–2000, fig. 30; Badre 2006, 77). These structures are large buildings with multiple rooms that had not been totally exposed at the time of the publication. They present the same building technique: fieldstone walls with ashlars at the corners and at the doorjambs, and hard-beaten floors. Some rooms, considered to be courtyards, were partly paved with stone flags. No definite house plan can be identified. This level was destroyed by fire and the "ruins of this area (level 4) are abandoned and disintegrated" (Badre and Gubel 1999–2000, 185 and fig. 42). In Level 3 hardly any architectural remains were found around the cella. In Area II, a short hiatus separates the destroyed Level 6 from the Iron Age I Level 5. No complete or coherent plan can be identified, but the orientation of the buildings changed. The building technique consists of stone foundations with a mudbrick superstructure and a heavy use of wood (Capet 2003, 101 and fig. 33).

In Sarepta no complete house plans were uncovered in strata F and E. Part of a pottery kiln and refuse pits were discovered in F, suggesting that "the architecture of this stratum was associated with the manufacture of pottery" (Anderson 1988, 88–89). The kiln continued to be in use in Stratum E2 and E1 (90, 93), and the presence of a large number of bread ovens, mainly in E1, attest the domestic character of the buildings. In sounding X, both Period V and VI are also characterized by a pottery-workshop area and the presence of kilns (Khalifeh 1988, 102, 113). In Period VI a new building technique known as "headers and stretchers" appears for the first time.

Tyre Stratum XIV has yielded fragments of domestic architecture, with a *tannur* and storage bins cut into the floors as well as evidence for bead industry (Bikai 1978a, 8).

At Tell Keisan the better preserved buildings were excavated in Area B. Four buildings were exposed. Their outer walls were made of stone, while the inner partition walls were made of bricks. The first consists of a courtyard and three rooms (Briend and Humbert 1980, figs. 51 and

52, rooms 501, 502, 503, and 512). Two rooms have stone-paved floors, and one of them had four column bases. In the northeast corner of this area there is another building characterized by the presence of silos in its courtyard. Two rooms border the courtyard to the north, and one of them was filled with storage jars (Briend and Humbert 1980, fig. 52). The walls are plastered, and they have stone foundations consisting of a base of smaller fieldstones, on top of which were larger, flat stones. The mudbrick superstructure rested on the latter. The Tell Keisan Iron Age I houses belong to types IB and IIA1 of Frank Braemer's typology (Braemer 1982, 102 and figs. 13b, 13c, 15d). In Area A fragments of walls were exposed, and no coherent plan can be reconstructed (Briend and Humbert 1980, fig. 53). The collected evidence indicates that the site was not fortified but was very well planned and had an important agricultural activity.

At Tell Abu Hawam, the Iron Age I settlement was fortified, and domestic houses of various types were excavated. Houses 41, 44, and 45 have a T-shaped separation walls, creating two identical back rooms and one front room (Braemer 1982, fig. 15a–c). The tripartite-type houses using occasionally monolithic pillars were built on the tell in Stratum IVA (Braemer 1982, fig. 16a). They were first scattered but were clustered later in parallel rows. They are built with fieldstones and ashlars at the corners. According to the excavators, this type of house may have a Hittite origin and could have been brought by emigrants from northern Syria (Balensi, Herrera, and Artzy 1993, 11). The use of pillars was ascribed to Israelite influence, although their use is attested in Late Bronze Age northern Syria at Tell Afis, for example (Venturi 2005, fig. 52.1). The Tell Abu Hawam Iron Age I houses belong to Braemer's (1982, 102) types IB and IIAI. In Stratum IVB, a large building, labeled 32, with storage galleries abutting it had a clear public character. An Iron Age I temple (Temple 30) was also exposed at the site on top of the Late Bronze Age Temple 50, indicating thus a continuity in the settlement population.

At Tel Dor the Iron Age I site was fortified, and houses were excavated in Areas G and D1 and D2. They consist of a courtyard surrounded on three sides by rooms, a plan in the tradition of Late Bronze Age "Canaanite" houses. In Area G a building was exposed in the early phase of Iron Age IA, Phase G/10, and was interpreted as a bronze-recycling workshop based on the finds. The same structure acquired a domestic character in the Late Iron Age IA, G/9, as attested by the food-processing tools and installations as well as by the presence of storage vessels (Gilboa and Sharon 2008, 154–55; Sharon and Gilboa 2013, 404). This house was destroyed violently but was rebuilt reusing the same walls. Two buildings of a public character were exposed in Area D1 and D2 dating to Iron Age IB: The first is an 18 m wide and 40 m long stone building built with large boulders and ashlars in its northwestern corner (Sharon and Gilboa 2013, 420), "one of the earliest attestations of this type of construction in the Iron Age" (Gilboa 2013, 632), but its function is not clear. The second is a mudbrick building (Sharon and Gilboa 2013, 426) that was destroyed and rebuilt in the same phase and abandoned at the end of Iron Age IB. It was apparently a storage and redistribution facility (Gilboa and Sharon 2008, 158). It was replaced by a domestic building built of fieldstones with ashlars at the corners.

2.2.4. Iron Age I Funerary Practices

A few tombs dated to Iron Age I have been found in all of Phoenicia. One is the doubtful Ruwayse example, where an inscribed arrowhead dated to the twelfth century was found (Guigues 1926), and the other is a twelfth-century BCE tomb from Beirut. The latter is a shaft burial consisting of a very narrow pit cut in the rock that contained a skeleton (Stuart 2001–2002, 88). A bone amulet bearing the cartouche of Ramesses IV (1153–1147) dates the tomb to the twelfth century BCE. There is an indication for the existence of an Early Iron Age cemetery on the northwest slope of the tell of Khaldeh, under Persian-period walls. Roger Saidah describes them as "inhumations from Iron Age I, earlier than those that have been exposed elsewhere," but they were not published.[5]

The Iron Age I period in Phoenicia is characterized by the introduction of cremation. Two cremation cemeteries were found and excavated on the Phoenician coast: one at Tell Sukas near the southern harbor, dated to the twelfth–tenth century BCE (Riis 1979, 51), and one in Tyre al-Baṣṣ (Aubet 2004; 2014). The recent excavations on the latter site have not yielded tombs from Iron Age I. Al-Baṣṣ Period I, which is dated by the excavators between the eleventh and the mid-tenth century BCE (Aubet 2004, 458, 465), has provided only isolated finds that were found out of context. The latest geomorphological investigations on site have clearly

---

5. Saidah 1967, 167: "des inhumations du premier âge du Fer, antérieures à celles mises au jour par ailleurs."

demonstrated, however, that Iron Age I tombs were embedded in a beach-rock layer. According to the excavator, the geomorphological study has established that the dunes in which the urns were buried can solidify at a very rapid pace. This phenomenon has led to the confinement of the Iron Age I tombs to a beach-rock layer. Their existence can be proven, but their excavation is impossible.[6]

To sum up, from the available archaeological evidence, a new picture of the so-called dark age is emerging, and it does not seem to be so dark after all. With a few exceptions, the archaeology indicates that the Phoenician sites, even those that witnessed a destruction at the end of the Late Bronze Age, continued to exist and were immediately resettled. Most of them even flourished during Iron Age I, and some, such as Dor, witnessed a substantial growth (7 ha) and can be qualified as urban (Sharon and Gilboa 2013, 460). Others, such as Tell Abu Hawam, were even fortified. Urban planning is difficult to reconstruct since most Iron Age materials came from limited soundings.

To conclude, in spite of clear evidence for domestic buildings, it is impossible to identify a clear Iron Age I Phoenician house plan because of the incomplete nature of most structures that have been excavated. Furthermore, in the same site different house plans are attested, as is the case at Tell Keisan and Tell Abu Hawam. The domestic character of these structures is clearly attested by the presence of silos, *tannurs*, food-processing tools, and storage vessels. Some, such as Keisan, had a clear agrarian economy, while others, such as Dor and Sidon, had active harbors and Mediterranean trade. The architecture was not restricted to domestic buildings, but there is also evidence for public monumental architecture, whether sacred, as in the temples in Tell Kazel, Sidon, and Tell Abu Hawam, or administrative, as at Tel Dor, where two such buildings were found: the so-called monumental building, used probably for administrative purposes, and a mudbrick storage one filled with jars and where evidence for fish industry was found (Gilboa and Sharon 2008, 158). Many sites displayed evidence for local industries: pottery production at Sarepta, bead industry at Tyre, purple-dye industry at Tell Keisan, fish industry at Tel Dor. At all these Iron Age I sites, there is evidence for continued trade activity, mainly with Cyprus and Egypt. So the international relations of the Phoenician cities did not stop, and some of their harbors were actively engaged in maritime

---

6. This information was communicated to me by Maria Eugenia Aubet.

trade. The evidence also suggests that possibly settlers from Cyprus and maybe also from northern Syria were physically present at some of these settlements and actively interacted with the local population, exchanging goods and influencing each other's productions, mainly ceramics. So far the evidence from southern Phoenicia has provided more substantial and homogeneous features than that of the northern cities, most probably due to a better documentation.

One may identify also regional differences in the material culture between northern and southern Phoenicia in Iron Age I, illustrated by the presence of ceramic wares such as the "barbarian" or handmade burnished ware, Trojan, and *céramique à la steatite* vessels, which are absent in the south. Another difference is that the northern sites all display a destruction level at the end of the Late Bronze Age, while in the south Sarepta, Tyre, and Sidon show no evidence of destruction. The textual and archaeological evidence strongly suggests that the Phoenician coast did not suffer from foreign invasions, for no evidence for a drastic change in the material culture can be observed between the Late Bronze Age and the Iron Age I culture. However, it displays strong evidence for Cypriot "presence in the region, especially along the Carmel coast.... Some of this population probably arrived in northern Canaan following the LCIIIA/IIIB disruptions on the island. Some newcomers from Syria are attested by designs on ceramics" (Gilboa 2013, 635) but a conspicuous absence of "Philistine" pottery. Phoenician bichrome ware is characteristic of Iron Age IB. Finally, we witness in Iron Age I the introduction of cremation, a new funerary practice that was not in use in the Late Bronze Age, at two Phoenician sites: Tell Sukas in the north and Tyre in the south.

# 3
# PHOENICIA IN IRON AGE II AND III

## 3.1. The Phoenician Polities

The available written sources inform us that in Iron Age II and III the land called Phoenicia by the Greeks was divided between four polities, which are from north to south Arwad, Byblos, Sidon, and Tyre (Sader 2000a). These Phoenician city-states and their main harbor city had the same name, preceded sometimes by the determinative URU, to indicate the city, or KUR, to indicate their territory. The territory of a polity can be approximately reconstructed from the mention in the texts of the cities and towns that belonged to it. The identification of these ancient toponyms with modern archaeological sites is not always easy and depends heavily on extensive land surveys and archaeological excavations. The territory of these kingdoms fluctuated with the political and military developments and was at times extended and at others deprived of some areas. In this chapter we will attempt to delineate the territory of each one of these polities as well as the changes that they underwent during the various periods of their existence. This will be followed by a brief survey of each polity's political history as revealed by the available written and archaeological sources.

### 3.1.1. The Kingdom of Arwad

#### 3.1.1.1. The Territory of Arwad

Arwad, modern Ruād, is an island located circa 2.5 km away from the shore, opposite the modern city of Ṭarṭūs.

Classical authors provide different estimations for the distance between the island and the mainland (see Belmonte-Marín 2003, 54). The toponym is mentioned in the Late Bronze Age texts from Tell el-Amarna

52   THE HISTORY AND ARCHAEOLOGY OF PHOENICIA

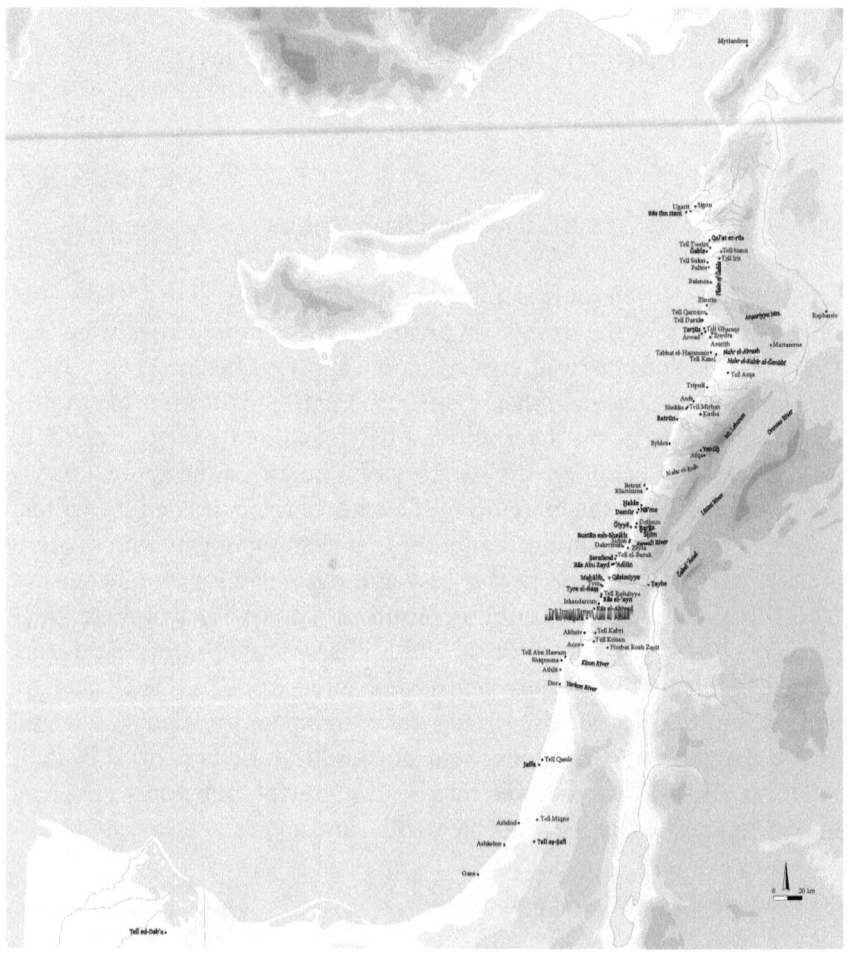

Fig. 3.1. (above) Map of Phoenicia within the Near Eastern world. (right) Detail of Phoenicia with ancient and modern toponyms. Source: Rami Yassine.

# 3. PHOENICIA IN IRON AGE II AND III

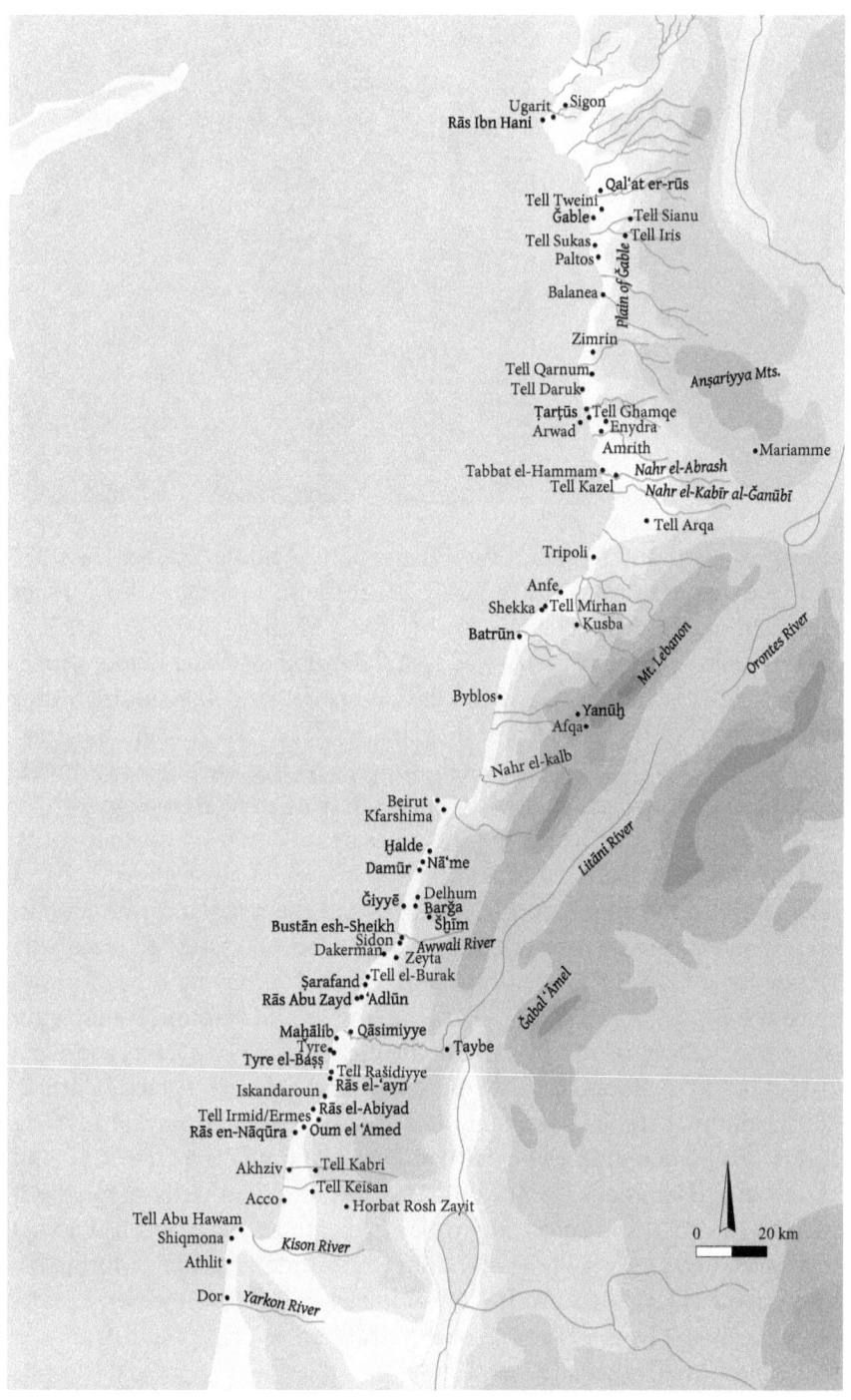

Fig. 3.2. Aerial photograph of the island of Arwad. Source: A. Poidebard.

and Syria (Belmonte-Marín 2001, 39) and in the Middle (Nashef 1982, 37) and Neo-Assyrian texts (Bagg 2007, 27–28) with varying orthographies (see Belmonte-Marin 2001, 54; Nashef 1982, 37; Bagg 2007, 27–28). The meaning of the place name Arwad is still debated. Michael Astour (1975, 262) suggested an etymology from the root *rwd*, "to wish, to desire," "thus probably expressing the idea of a desirable place," while Jean-Paul Rey-Coquais (1974, 92), following Renan, simply says that the name in Phoenician means "refuge" or "shelter" without referring to its etymology.

The island has an oval shape and measures 800 m from north to south and 500 m from east to west, and it has an area of circa 40 ha. It has a double, well-protected harbor looking toward the mainland with a natural reef separating the two coves. This harbor was investigated mainly by Honor Frost (1964; 1973a), who suggested that it may have been in use since the Bronze Age (1973a, 113). The little islands around it may have had small harbors related to those of the main insular city (Elayi and Elayi 2015, 17). On the shore opposite the island, harbors were located at ʿAmrit, 600 m southwest of the main temple or *maʿbed* (Elayi and Haykal 1996, 22 and n. 46; Al-Maqdissi 1993, 448), at Tell Qarnum (Elayi 2015, 23), and at Tabbat el-Hammam (Braidwood 1940). Arwad had wells supplying it with sweet water, and according to classical authors the island had access to a sweet-water spring in the sea, from which water was drawn through a leather pipe (Elayi 2015, 18–19; Rey-Coquais 1974, 60). However, in spite of its local supply, the island probably still had to bring water from the mainland (Rey-Coquais 1974, 60).

Arwad was famous for its fleet and must have had access to the forests of the al-Anṣariyye Mountains to get the wood necessary for the building of its ships. It also needed to secure food products and must have had control over a territory on the continent. However, the borders of its territory are extremely difficult to define during the pre-Hellenistic period because, except for the island city itself, no settlement belonging to it is explicitly mentioned in the texts. It may be revealing that in the Late Bronze and Iron Age texts the toponym Arwad is consistently preceded by the determinative URU = city and refers explicitly to the island, thus indicating perhaps that it did not have fortified or royal cities like the other Iron Age northern Syrian and Phoenician kingdoms. It is only in the annals of Aššurbanipal that Arwad is preceded by the determinative KUR = land. This may lead to the assumption that Arwad was able to extend its dominion over a larger portion of the continent after the annexation of its neighbors by the Assyrian Empire and their resulting weakness. This assumption is supported by the attitude of Iakinlû, a contemporary of Aššurbanipal, who felt strong enough to resist Assyrian power: "(As for) Yakīn-Lû, the king of the land Arwad, Mugallu, the king of the land Tabal, Sanda-šarme of the land Ḫilakku (Cilicia), who had not bowed down to the kings, my ancestors, they bowed down to my yoke" (Novotny 2016, prism B 003, II 63–74).

Since no city belonging to the territory of Arwad is mentioned in the Late Bronze and Iron Age texts, one has to look at the territorial extension of the neighboring kingdoms in order to determine what portion of land may have been left under the control of the island (for a detailed study of Arwad's territory see Belmonte-Marín 2003, 47–59).

The absence of reference to an Arwadian territory and to Arwadian cities in the texts has led Juan Antonio Belmonte-Marín (2003, 50) to conclude that Late Bronze Age Arwad was not a territorial state and was restricted to the island. According to him, the "island city" had no continental possessions but in exchange for its maritime support may have enjoyed a small territorial enclave tolerated by the kingdom of Amurru for agricultural and funerary purposes (also Briquel-Chatonnet 2000, 131).

Indeed, the territory of Arwad in the Late Bronze Age seems to have been reduced to the stretch of land facing the island and extending to the neighboring slopes of Ǧabal al-Anṣariyye. Ṣimirra, generally identified with Tell Kazel (Belmonte-Marín 2001, 252; Badre 2013; this identification was questioned by Sader 1990), and the whole Eleutherus Valley were part of the kingdom of Amurru, which controlled the Homs Gap, one of the main west-east routes linking the Mediterranean to the Orontes Valley.

This suggests that the southern limit of Arwad's territory coincided with the northern borders of the kingdom of Amurru. However, these borders cannot be defined with precision: the only certain fact is that they must have been located north of Ṣimirra, probably on the right bank of Nahr el-Abrach. The northern borders of Arwad's territory were delimited by Sianu, Ugarit's southernmost city (Yon 2006, 9). So it may be suggested that the Late Bronze Age territory of Arwad was very limited and may have extended from the area south of Nahr es-Sinn in the north to the area of Ṭarṭūs in the south. The western slopes of the al-Anṣariyye Mountains formed its eastern borders.

In the Iron Age, the territory of Arwad may have witnessed changes, but we are unable to define its limits. One thing, however, is certain: Arwad did not control the area previously occupied by the Late Bronze Age kingdom of Amurru or the territory that previously belonged to the kingdom of Ugarit, which seem to have disintegrated into smaller polities, as attested by the annals of Aššurnaṣirpal II and Šalmaneser III. "At that time I received tribute from the kings of the sea-coast, from the lands of the people of Tyre, Sidon, Amurru, Byblos, Maḫallatu, Kaizu, Maizu, and the city Arvad which is (on an island) in the sea" (Grayson 1991, A.0.101.1, iii, 86 and 101.2, 26–28). This passage from the annals of Aššurnaṣirpal II seems to imply that Arwad did not control the territory of the former kingdom of Amurru. Indeed, while Amurru in this text is a vague indication of the geographical area including the Lebanese and Syrian 'Akkār, the remaining cities of Maḫallatu, Kaizu, and Maizu (Bagg 2007, 163, 164, 131), which were also part of that kingdom, have to be looked for somewhere in northern Lebanon, at the southern edge of the 'Akkār Valley.

The following passage of Šalmaneser III's annals relating to the battle of Qarqar indicates that Irqanata—modern Tell Arqa in the 'Akkār Valley (Bagg 2007, 25–26), another city that belonged to the former kingdom of Amurru—as well as Usanata/Usnu, maybe Tell Daruk? (271), and Sianu, modern Tell Sianu (217), were not part of Arwad's territory but appear rather as small independent cities.

> Moving on from the city Arganâ I approached the city Qarqar. I razed, destroyed, (and) burned the city Qarqar, his royal city. An alliance had been formed of these twelve kings: 1,200 chariots, 1,200 cavalry, (and) 20,000 troops of Hadad-Ezer (Adad-idri), the Damascene; 700 chariots, 700 cavalry, (and) 10,000 troops of Irḫulēnu, the Hamatite; 2,000 chariots

(and) 10,000 troops of Ahab (Aḫabbu) the Israelite (Sir'alāia); 500 troops of Byblos; 1,000 troops of Egypt; 10 chariots (and) 110,000 troops of the land Irqanatu; 200 troops of Matinu-baʿal of the city Arvad; 200 troops of the city Usanātu; 30 chariots (and) [N],000 troops of Adunu-baʿal of the land Šianu; 1,000 camels of Gindibu of the Arabs; [N] hundred troops of Baʾasa, the man of Bīt Ruḫubi, the Ammonite. (Grayson 1996, A.0.102.2, ii, 89b–102)

From the above evidence it can be concluded that in the ninth century BCE the kingdom of Arwad kept the same limited extension it had during the Late Bronze Age and did not extend its dominion over cities previously belonging to the Late Bronze Age kingdoms of Amurru and Ugarit.

Information about Arwad's territory in the eighth century BCE is provided by the annals of Tiglath-pileser III, who enumerates the cities of the newly founded province of Ṣimirra in 738 BCE (Tadmor 1994, 148). These cities, as convincingly argued by Karlheinz Kessler (1975–1976) and followed by Jean Sapin (1989, 28), were part of the kingdom of Hamath. They are Gubla, the city of Ǧabla north of Tell Sukas (and not Byblos: see Tadmor 1994, 148 and n. 16), Usnu, Irqata, Zimarra (Zimrin? 13 km north of Ṭarṭūs; Bagg 2007, 275), Ṣimirra, Riʾiṣurri (Qalʿat ar-rūs? Bagg 2007, 203), and Kašpuna (identified with Kusba, south of Tripoli, or with a city north of Arwad; Bagg 2007, 138–39). In a recent article Éric Gubel (2018) argued for its identification with Et-Talle-Kastina at the mouth of Nahr el-Bared in northern Lebanon. This proposal implies that the territory of the kingdom of Hamath included part of Ugarit's and Amurru's former territory. The portion of the mainland that may have remained under the authority of Arwad could have extended roughly from ʿAmrit in the south to some 20 km north of Ṭarṭūs—if we accept the identification of Zimarra with Zimrin. So, if Arwad had a continental territory at all—which it most probably had since without it the island was not viable—it seems to have been a tiny enclave bordered north and south by the province of Ṣimirra. It can be concluded that during Iron Age I and II Arwad's territory did not witness substantial changes and kept the same extension it had in the Late Bronze Age.

As already mentioned, Arwad seems to have increased its political and military power toward the end of Esarhaddon's rule, under the reign of Iakinlû, who was subdued later by Aššurbanipal. Whether this empowerment was accompanied by an extension of the territory of his kingdom remains an open question and cannot be verified. Regarding the

Neo-Babylonian period, no information is available about the extension of Arwad's territory.

Although there is no direct evidence for the extension of the territory of Arwad in the Persian period, some information can be collected from the writings of later classical authors (Elayi 1982; Belmonte-Marín 2003, 52). However, one has to use this information with caution (Sartre 2001, 33), and one should not transpose it automatically to earlier periods. Herodotus (*Hist.* 7.98) informs us that the fleet of Arwad led by *mhrb'l*, probably the island's king, helped the Persians against the Greeks in the battle of Salamis. It would not be far-fetched to assume that this support was probably rewarded with a territorial gift granted by the Persian king. There is indeed another instance of such territorial gifts by the Persian king, namely, the gift of Dor, Jaffa, and the Plain of Sharon to the king of Sidon, Eshmunazar II, to reward him for his support (*KAI* 14). It is difficult, however, to know exactly what territories were given to Arwad. Pseudo-Scylax, who lived toward the end of the Persian period (fourth century BCE), is a reliable source, since he witnessed the state of the Phoenician cities before the coming of Alexander. He mentions a city of "Tripolis of the Phoenicians" before Arados, and Graham Shipley (2011, 179) is of the opinion that this toponym refers to "three mainland towns opposite Arados, … of which they were dependencies Karnos, Enydra, and Marathos." Information about Arwad's territory during the Persian period is generally inferred from Arrian's *Anabasis*, in which this second-century BCE author enumerates the cities that the last king of Arwad, Ger'aštart, controlled at the eve of Alexander's conquest of Syria. According to Arrian's account, the cities of Marathus, Sigon, and Mariamme as well as other territories were part of the Arwadian territory.

> Alexander appointed Menon son of Cerdimmas as satrap of "hollow" Syria, giving him the allied cavalry to protect the country, while he himself proceeded towards Phoenicia. On his way he was met by Straton son of Gerostratus, king of the Aradians and people near Aradus; Gerostratus himself was sailing with Autophradates, like the rest of the Phoenician and Cypriot kings. On meeting Alexander, Straton crowned him with a golden crown and surrendered to him the island Aradus and Marathus which lay opposite it on the mainland, a large and prosperous city, with Sigon and the city of Mariamme and all the other places under his control. (*Anab.* 2.13.7–8 [Brunt])

It seems that the territory of Arwad reached its maximal extension under Persian rule encompassing the area of the Plain of Ǧabla in the north to Nahr el-Abrach in the south. The cities mentioned in Arrian's account give the southern and northern borders of Arwad's territory. To the east, it reached the eastern slopes of the al-Anṣariyye Mountains. Strabo (first century BCE) enumerates the main cities included within this territory: Paltos, Balanea, Carne, Enydra, and Marathus. Tell Sukas, a harbor city south of Ǧabla, may have been included within Arwad's territory during that period.

> But the remainder of the coast from Laodiceia is as follows: near Laodiceia are three towns, Poseidium and Heracleium and Gabala; and then forthwith one comes to the seaboard of the Aradians, where are Paltus and Balanaea and Carnus, this last being the naval station of Aradus and having a harbour; and then to Enydra and Marathus, the latter an ancient city of the Phoenicians, now in ruins. Aradians divided up this country among themselves, as also Simyra, the place that comes next thereafter. (*Geog.* 16.2.12 [Jones 1932])

The available archaeological evidence does not help fill the gap left by the written sources regarding the extension of Arwad's territory in Iron Age I and II. The coastal area of northern Syria was neglected for a very long time, but a few decades ago interest in Phoenician Syria increased. Several sites in the area of Ṭarṭūs and the Plain of Ǧabla were investigated, and new results emerged regarding Phoenician presence on the north Syrian coast. Unfortunately very little has been published on these recent excavations.[1] As a result, little is known about the occupation of the territory mainly in the Early and Middle Iron Age, while most of the available evidence sheds light on the Late Iron Age or Persian-period occupation (Elayi 2000 lists the archaeological sites that have yielded evidence for Late Iron Age occupation; see also her fig. 1). This evidence seems to match the textual records, which do not mention any settlement in the area of Arwad for the Early and Middle Iron Age, while there are indications that the kingdom prospered in the Persian period and was able to extend its territory substantially. This is attested by the archaeological remains found on the main sites of the coast facing the island: at Ṭarṭūs, Tell Qarnum, Tell Ghamqe,

---

1. I am grateful to Dr. Michel Al-Maqdissi for providing me the latest information and publications on excavated sites in this area.

and 'Amrit, cities that have formed the heart of the Arwadian territory since the Late Bronze Age, as well as on sites located further north in the Ġabla Plain such as Tell Sukas, Tell Tweini, Tell Sianu, and Tell Iris.

Renan was the first to investigate Arwad, Ṭarṭūs, and 'Amrit. In Ṭarṭūs, classical Antarados, he observed a large necropolis with modest tombs and rich personal belongings (Renan 1864, 44), probably the cemetery of the island population. In 'Amrit, 5 km south of Ṭarṭūs, he described the Persian-period necropolis with its funerary monuments and the temple or so-called *ma'bed*. This important Persian-period religious complex was unearthed and published by Dunand and Nessib Saliby (1985), and several of the observed cemeteries were investigated later (Saliby 1989). Other French scholars visited the area and brought back with them finds that they offered to the Louvre Museum (Elayi and Haykal 1996, 19). The finds from Arwad and Ṭarṭūs, which are in the Louvre, range from the eighth to the first century BCE, and they were presented by Marguerite Yon and Annie Caubet (1993). Elayi and Mohamed Raïf Haykal (1996, 24–47) collected and presented the available evidence relating to the recent archaeological discoveries in the area of Ṭarṭūs and 'Amrit as well as a summary of all the recent excavations on the sites that are believed to have belonged to Arwad's territory (Elayi and Haykal 1996, 22–29). Most of the excavated sites have yielded cemeteries, and very few have yielded a stratigraphic sequence from the settlement. Rumat az-Zahab, 6 km south of Ṭarṭūs and 1 km northeast of 'Amrit, has yielded a Persian-period necropolis with anthropoid sarcophagi (Elayi and Haykal 1996, 49–78). In Bano, 7 km south of Ṭarṭūs and 3 km east of 'Amrit, a Persian-period necropolis and one marble anthropoid sarcophagus were found. A Phoenician inscription (*RÉS* 56) as well as a Persian period tomb in the area known as Ḥay al-Ḥamarat, and a third-century BCE marble anthropoid sarcophagus (Saliby 1970–1971; Elayi and Haykal 1996, 81), were unearthed in Tell Ghamqe. Another anthropoid sarcophagus was found near Tell Qarnum at the site of al-Kaisouneh. A tomb was found in Ṭarṭūs in the area known as the *zone des chalets* and contained five clay anthropoid sarcophagi (Elayi and Haykal 1996, 89).

Recent excavations on the tell of 'Amrit have demonstrated that the site was occupied since the third millennium BCE and witnessed an uninterrupted settlement until the twelfth century, when signs of a violent destruction appeared. Little evidence for Iron Age I and II was found, whereas the Late Iron Age showed the prosperity and the expansion of the settlement. The recent excavations exposed important cemeteries as well as religious monuments consisting of three temples and two cultic installations with niches for the deposition of *ex-votos* (Al-Maqdissi and Ishaq 2016; further discussion of these installations can be found in chs. 5 and 6). No evidence for a city wall or residential quarters—with the exception of a few houses for those in charge of the *maʿbed*—were found in ʿAmrit, which led Michel Al-Maqdissi to confirm Renan's opinion that ʿAmrit was not a city but simply a suburb of Arwad (Al-Maqdissi and Ishaq 2016, 295; 2017, 3) where the people of the island buried their dead and where they built their religious complexes. A small harbor that served to connect the site with the island was also identified.

In the Ǧabla Plain recent investigations at Tell Iris, 5 km east of Ǧabla (ancient Gabala) and 2 km southwest of Tell Sianu (Al-Maqdissi 2016a; Suleiman and Al-Maqdissi 2016) have revealed that the site was occupied without interruption from the late fourth millennium BCE and was destroyed at the end of the Late Bronze Age. Settlement resumed in the eighth century BCE, and a residential quarter was exposed. A large building dated to the Persian period was also excavated. Its public character is indicated by the presence of a Persian column base.

Tell Sianu in the Ǧabla Plain, 35 km south of Ugarit, is a circular tell that had an uninterrupted occupation from the fourth millennium BCE to the end of the Late Bronze Age, when it was heavily destroyed. Settlement resumed in the Late Iron Age, and "all the related monuments constitute the elements of a typical Phoenician city, with a fortress on the western part of the summit of the site, controlling the lowland areas associated with residential houses and, in particular, one religious monument of small dimensions" (Al-Maqdissi 2016b, 183).

Tell Tweini, located also in the Ǧabla Plain, was excavated by a joint Syrian and Belgian team (Bretschneider and van Lerberghe 2008; Al-Maqdissi et al. 2010; Al-Maqdissi, Badawi, and Ishaq 2016). The site is located 28 km south of Lattakia, not far from the site of Gabala. It had an active harbor and was occupied from the mid-third millennium BCE until the Byzantine period without interruption. It was destroyed at the end of the Late Bronze Age, and its occupation resumed immediately in Iron Age I on the ruins of the Late Bronze Age city (Al-Maqdissi, Badawi, and Ishaq 2016, 176). A small sanctuary dating to the same period was exposed. In Iron Age II a new urban plan with public buildings was designed. This Early Iron Age II city was destroyed by a violent fire, and toward the end of the eighth century an industrial quarter for olive production located in a residential area was built. According to the excavators, this industrial center disappeared with the Assyrian conquest. In the Persian period the city witnessed a new revival with the building of a new residential quarter with a large temple in its western part. All the finds are characteristic of the Persian-period Phoenician settlements, such as female terra-cottas and Persian riders.

The last site in the Ǧabla Plain is Tell Sukas, which was excavated by a Danish mission. These excavations have revealed a Persian-period Phoenician settlement, harbor, and sanctuary.

This review of the sites of the Ǧabla Plain seems to confirm that in the Persian period the territory of Phoenician Arwad extended as far north as Gabala. This period appears to be the most prosperous period in the Iron Age settlement of that region and seems to share the same characteristics, such as a simple architecture associated sometimes with more important buildings (Al-Maqdissi, Badawi, and Ishaq 2016).

Information about Arwad's territory is more abundant for the Hellenistic period, and Rey-Coquais (1974, 110) was able to define its borders. The island's territory extended from the city of Ǧabla, in the north, where coins dated from the era of Arwad were found (116), to Raphanée and Mariamme in the east, and Nahr el-Abrach in the south. So the territory of Arwad in the Hellenistic period covered a long coastal stretch, three agricultural plains, and the slopes of a nearby mountain, the largest extension this small kingdom ever reached. Whether this extension corresponds to the situation that was already prevailing in the Persian period remains an open question.

To sum up, for most of its history Arwad consisted mainly of the island city and had maybe some control over the area facing the island. It seems that the territory controlled by Arwad was, for most of its recorded history, very small, covering probably the area between Nahr es-Sinn and Nahr el-Abrach. The main cities that formed the core of the continental possessions of Arwad were Ṭarṭūs, Tell Qarnum, Tell Ghamqe, and ʿAmrit. Next to the main harbor on the island, small harbors located on the islets south of Arwad and on the coast facing the island at Ṭarṭūs, ʿAmrit, Tabbat el-Hammam, and Tell Qarnum, classical Carne, were also used and secured communication with the island. In the Persian period Arwad's territory seems to have extended to include some northern cities that previously belonged to the territory of the province of Ṣimirra, including Ǧabla, the northernmost of these cities.

## 3.1.1.2. A Political History of Phoenician Arwad

The first scholars to pay close attention to the history of the kingdom of Arwad were French historians Françoise Briquel-Chatonnet, who wrote a series of short articles (1996; 1997; 2000; 2005) dealing with various aspects of Arwad's pre-Hellenistic history, and Josette Elayi, who dedicated two exhaustive studies to this Phoenician kingdom: The first (Elayi 1996) discussed recent discoveries relating to funerary practices during the Persian period, and the second (Elayi 2015) compiled and discussed all the available written and archaeological sources relating to Arwad's history. In the latter, Elayi (2015, 11–12; see also 2000, 327–28) rightly pointed out that, contrary to the other Phoenician kingdoms, Arwad's history has been relatively neglected mainly because of the rarity of contemporary ancient sources. One obvious difficulty is that only the island city is mentioned in the pre-Hellenistic records, with no reference to its continental territory. Furthermore, the archaeological investigation of the north Syrian coast was lagging behind and witnessed only recently an increase in archaeological activity (Elayi 2000). Most of the recent excavations undertaken in the area still await publication. The rarity of written sources coupled with fragmentary archaeological evidence are the main reasons why important aspects of the history of this northern Phoenician kingdom remain in the dark. On the other hand, the history of Hellenistic Arwad is better known because of the abundance of the textual and material sources. Two major contributions by Rey-Coquais (1974) and Frédérique Duyrat (2005) explored the history of Hellenistic Arwad and its territory. Notwithstanding these difficulties, the broad lines of the history of Phoenician Arwad will be attempted.

It is noteworthy that Arwad is not mentioned in the Egyptian texts. Except for the mention of an "Arwadite" (P.Bologna 1086), the island does not appear in the Egyptian records. According to Briquel-Chatonnet (2005, 24) this omission may be ascribed to the fact that the Egyptians had no direct economic and strategic interests in the island: the city that was of key importance to Egypt was Ṣimirra because it controlled the route to inner Syria, the so-called Homs Gap.

Arwad is mentioned for the first time in the Amarna letters of the fourteenth century BCE. The occurrence of the toponym in earlier texts is still debated. While Giovanni Pettinato (1981; 1983) identified the place name '$a$-$ra$-$wa$-$ad$'$^{ki}$ and '$à$-$ur_4$-$ad$'$^{ki}$ of the third-millennium lexical texts of Ebla with Arwad, his identification was rejected by Marco Bonechi (1993,

46–47). The toponyms *A-ra-ʾà-du*ki, *A-ra-ʾa-ad*ki, and *ʾÀ-ra-ma-d*ki listed by Alfonso Archi (1993, 108, 133) are still discussed, and no final consensus about their identification with Arwad has been reached. Archi seems to equate *ʾÀ-ra-ma-du*ki with URU*ar-ma-at-ta* of the Alalakh texts. Furthermore, Belmonte-Marín (2001, 39) implicitly rejects the identification of URU*ar-ma-at-ta* of the Alalakh texts (Wiseman 1953, 71) with Arwad, since he does not list it among his second-millennium toponyms relating to Arwad, while Edward Lipiński (2004, 280–81) clearly adopts it. It was also suggested that the place name *ʾrtt* mentioned in the lists of Thutmosis III refers to Arwad, but this suggestion was also rejected in favor of the identification of the toponym with Ardata, a city located at Tell Arde in northern Lebanon (Elayi 2015, 46).

In short, the first undisputed reference to Arwad before the Iron Age is its mention in the Amarna letters, which are the only source for its history in the Late Bronze Age. The city appears in five of these letters as URU*Ar-wa-da* or *Er4-wa-da* (Belmonte-Marín 2001, 39). The political status of Arwad in the second millennium BCE is discussed by Briquel-Chatonnet (2000), who has convincingly argued that Arwad was not a hereditary monarchy during the Late Bronze Age, unlike the other Levantine cities. She bases her argument on the fact that no king of Arwad is ever mentioned. Furthermore, whenever a political agreement or action is taken, the protagonists are the "men (or the people) of Arwad" and not a monarch. These "men of Arwad" are clearly associated with the "boats of Arwad," which has led Briquel-Chatonnet (132) to assume that the political power was held by the owners of the boats, which formed the powerful fleet of the island. Jordi Vidal (2008, 13) understands the expression "men of Arwad" as referring to seafaring warriors, mercenaries, who were hired by neighboring kingdoms because of their skills as navigators. He compares them to the Shardana, who were hired as mercenaries by the Egyptians. According to the El-Amarna Tablets (104–5), Arwad was an ally of the kingdom of Amurru who hired Arwadian boats to block the way to Ṣimirra. The kingdom of Amurru needed a naval power to help it in its struggle against other coastal cities (Vidal 2008, 11). Vidal argues that after the fall of Ṣimirra into the hands of the Egyptians and the increased importance of its harbor, Arwad's commercial power declined, and the people of the island started hiring their boats to the continental kingdoms who needed a naval force and acted thus as mercenaries. This is how Amurru and Sidon hired the fleet of Arwad in their conflict with the city of Tyre (*EA* 149).

Additional support for Briquel-Chatonnet's theory that Arwad was not a monarchy in the second millennium BCE comes from the Middle Assyrian sources. Upon his visit to Arwad, Tiglath-pileser I does not mention a king of that city but only the "people of Arwad": "I received tribute from the lands Byblos, Sidon, (and) Arwad. I rode in boats of people of Arwad (and) travelled successfully a distance of 3 double hours from the city Arwad, an island, to the city Ṣamuru which is in the land Amurru. I killed at sea a nāḫiru, which is called a sea-horse" (Grayson 1991, A.0.87.3:20–21). Arwad was the first Phoenician city with which the Assyrians came into contact. This encounter seems to have been peaceful, and Tiglath-pileser I was impressed by the exotic animals—crocodiles, monkeys, *nāḫirus*—that he saw there as well as by his boat ride (Briquel-Chatonnet 1997, 58). Aššur-bēl-kala also mentions in his annals that he rode "in boats of the land of Arwad (and) killed a nāḫiru" (Grayson 1991, A.0.89.7, iv 1–3), but he does not name a ruler for that city. Briquel-Chatonnet (1997, 59) doubts the authenticity of Aššur-bēl-kala's account and suggests that he simply copied the event from his predecessor's annals.

The annals of the Neo-Assyrian kings are our main if not only contemporary source for Arwad's political history in the Iron Age. The Phoenician inscriptions that were discovered on the island are brief and do not contain substantial historical information. For the Persian period, besides coins, one has to rely almost exclusively on the accounts of later reliable classical authors, mainly Herodotus, Pseudo-Scylax, Arrian, and Strabo.

In the first half of the ninth century BCE, Arwad submitted to Aššurnaṣirpal II (Grayson 1991, A.0.101.1, iii, 85–87). The city paid the tribute, but no ruler is mentioned by the Assyrian king. Briquel-Chatonnet questions whether Aššurnaṣirpal II reached Arwad or not and finally opts for the probability of the visit. The island city seemed insignificant politically to the Assyrian king, probably because of the absence of a king, since Arwad was not invited to the banquet celebrating the building of his royal palace, whereas Sidon and Tyre were present (Grayson 1991, A.0.101.30, 145).

It seems that hereditary kingship was adopted as a government system in Arwad in the mid-ninth century BCE. The first time an Arwadian king is mentioned by name is in the annals of Šalmaneser III. In the anti-Assyrian coalition at the battle of Qarqar, Arwad participated under the leadership of its king, Mattan-Baal (I) (*mma-ti-nu-ba-'a-li* $^{uru}$*ar-ma-da-a-a*) and contributed two hundred troops (Grayson 1996, A.0.102.2, ii, 93). The small number of Arwadian troops participating in the battle is surprising and compares very poorly with those of the other coalesced forces. Elayi (2015, 86) argues that the small number may be explained by the fact that Arwad was a naval power and that its participation in the battle was merely symbolic. The same explanation is given by Briquel-Chatonnet (1997, 61). The circumstances under which hereditary kingship was established in Arwad remain unexplained in the absence of written sources. Did the Arwadians want to emulate other kingdoms? Was the need to have a leader born because of the Assyrian threat? Was kingship imposed peacefully or by popular consensus? All these questions cannot be answered given the current state of the evidence.

After the death of Šalmaneser III and during the period of internal troubles that followed, Elayi (2015, 90) argues that Arwad and the other Phoenician kingdoms came under the hegemony of Hazael, king of Aram-Damascus, not as vassals but rather as allies (Lemaire 1991c). However, this opinion is not based on strong and decisive evidence. In his recent and exhaustive study of the Aramaean polities, K. Lawson Younger Jr. (2016, 620–27 and fig. 9.7) discusses the extension of Hazael's empire, which included the Israelite and Philistine cities, but he does not mention that the Phoenician cities were included in his territorial expansion. He does, however, mention a "campaign of Hazael against Unqi (Patina)" and possibly Hamath (630).

The period of Assyrian weakness came to an end with the accession of Adad-nērārī III to the throne. The latter resumed Assyrian campaigns to the east and claimed in his 803 campaign to have erected his statue in the island of Arwad: "I marched to the great sea in the west. I erected my lordly statue in the city Arvad, which is on an island in the sea" (Grayson 1996, A.0.104.7, 10). Elayi (2015, 90) finds this statement "surprising" and doubts its authenticity since it is difficult for her to accept the idea that Arwad willingly allowed the Assyrian king to come to the island. She also notes that Adad-nērārī III says nowhere in his annals that he received the tribute of Arwad (Elayi 2015, 91) and tries to explain this fact by assuming that maybe special ties developed between Assyria and Arwad that led to the exemption of the latter from paying the tribute. If this assumption is correct, then it would not be surprising that the king visited the island as a friendly overlord and erected his statue there. Briquel-Chatonnet (1997, 62) explains the omission of the tribute by assuming that the tribute of Arwad must have been too insignificant to be mentioned and that it was the location and the marine environment of Arwad that impressed the king and were deemed worth mentioning.

Arwad appears again as a tributary of Assyria under the rule of Tiglath-pileser III, who received the tribute of several kingdoms of northern Syria and the sea coast, including the city of Arwad, whose king, Mattan-Baal (II; [mMa]-ta-an-bi-'i-il $^{uru}$Ar-ma-da-a-a; Tadmor 1994, 171), bore the same name as that of his ancestor, the contemporary of Šalmaneser III. This probably indicates that the same dynasty was still ruling in the kingdom. Briquel-Chatonnet (1997, 62), following Hayim Tadmor (1994, 268), argues that Arwad's tribute was paid during the campaign against Damascus (734–732 BCE) since Arwad is not mentioned in earlier tributaries lists.

After a period of silence, Sennacherib mentions a king of Arwad, Abdi-Li'ti, in the list of rulers who paid him a heavy tribute upon his campaign against Sidon in 701 BCE: "As for Minuḫimmu of the city Samsumuruna, Tu-Ba'lu of the city Sidon, Abdi-Li'ti of the city Arwad … all of the kings of the land Amurru, they brought extensive gifts, four times (the normal amount), as their substantial audience gift before me and kissed my feet" (Grayson and Novotny 2012, 4, 36).

Another Mattan-Baal (III), king of Arwad ($^m$ma-ta-an-ba-'a-al LUGAL URU a-ru-ad-da), is mentioned in the annals of Esarhaddon (Leichty 2011, 1.5.60; 5.6.11). He is the third king bearing that name, and this probably indicates that paponymy was a tradition observed by the royal family of Arwad. He is mentioned together with twenty-one other kings of the sea coast and Cyprus who were ordered to provide raw materials for the building of Esarhaddon's palace. It is difficult to determine which item in the list of stones and trees taken as booty came from Arwad.

This submissive attitude of Arwad toward Assyria changed under Iakinlû, who ruled toward the end of Esarhaddon's and during Aššurbanipal's reign. Aššurbanipal says that Iakinlû had rebelled against Assyria and had stopped paying the tribute: "(As for) Iakīn-Lû, the king of the land Arwad, who lives in the wide sea, (whose) location is situated like a fish in an unfathomable amount of water (and) the surge of powerful waves, who put his trust in the roiling sea and (therefore) did not bow down to the yoke, became frightened of my lordly majesty and (then) bowed down to do obeisance to me and (now) he pulls my yoke. Yearly, I imposed upon him (a payment of) gold, red-purple wool, blue-purple wool, fish, (and) birds" (Novotny 2016, tablet 003, r.33–37). In another passage Aššurbanipal says, "Yakīn-Lû, the king of the land Arwad, Mugallu, the king of the land Tabal, Sanda-šarme of the land Ḫilakku (Cilicia), who had not bowed down to the kings, my ancestors, they bowed down to my yoke. They brought (their) daughters, their own offspring, to Nineveh to serve as housekeepers, together with a [sub]stantial dowry and a large marriage gift, and they kissed my feet" (Novotny 2016, prism B, ii 63ff.).

When he was still a crown prince, Aššurbanipal was concerned with the rebellion of the Arwadian king and was wondering in a prayer to the god Šamaš how to deal with him and whether he would react positively to his message:

> [Ša]maš, great lord, give me a f[irm positive answer] to what I am as[king you] Should Assurbanipal, son of Esar[haddon, king of Assyria,] send Nabû-šarru-uṣur, the *rab mūgi*, to Ikkalû, who dwells in the city Arwad? If he sends him, will Ikkalû listen to and comply with the message which [Assurbani]pal is sen[ding] to Ikkalû by the hand of Nabû-šarru-uṣur, the *rab mūgi*? Does your great divinity know it? Is it decreed and confirmed in a favorable case, by the command of your great divinity, Šamaš, great lord? Will he who can see, see it? Will he who can hear, hear it? (Starr 1990, 104)

From the above texts it appears that breaking down the rebellion of Iakinlû was not easy even for powerful Assyria. The reason for this Assyrian concern can be found in the letter sent by Itti-Šamaš-Balaṭu to Aššurbanipal; in it the sender says that Iakinlû was threatening the economic interests of Assyria by forcing merchant boats to come to his harbors and not to those under the control of Assyria: "Ikkilu does not release the ships, (so that) they can not dock at the wharf belonging to the king my lord. He appropriates the wharf's receipts for himself. If a man comes to him (first), he speeds him on his way; but if a man docks at the Assyrian wharf, he kills him and confiscates his ship, saying, They have written from the court saying, Lo, (such a one) has stolen, he has done (so and so)" (Pfeiffer 1935, 104–5, no. 137). Arwad was using its maritime superiority to challenge Assyria's power, and this explains Assyria's concern: in spite of its military strength, Assyria was aware that it could not defeat Arwad at sea, and this is why Aššurbanipal was looking for a compromise. Two questions should be raised here: What made Iakinlû rebel against Assyria? How did Aššurbanipal force him to surrender? As for the reasons for Iakinlû's hostility toward Assyria, they remain unexplained. For many centuries Arwad had avoided an open conflict with Assyria and paid the tribute. The explanation can be sought in the politics of Assyria under Esarhaddon. Assyria had tightened its control over Phoenician harbors and had limited the cities' income from maritime trade, as attested by the treaty with Hiram of Tyre (Borger 1982–1985). Esarhaddon may have deprived Arwad also of one of its main sources of income, which led its king to rebel. Iakinlû felt himself invulnerable on his island and knew perfectly well that Assyria was unable to fight him at sea. This is the reason why Aššurbanipal chose to compromise, because he knew that military strength would be ineffective. It seems that Aššurbanipal's offer to the Arwadian king—the content of which did not come down to us—was successful and that the Assyrian king probably did not have to use coercion to stop Iakinlû's rebellion. This is suggested by the fact that Aššurbanipal does not say how he broke down Iakinlû's resistance. There is no mention of a siege, or a battle, or any other aggressive or armed encounter. Furthermore, the fact that the Assyrian king took Iakinlû's daughters "with a [sub]stantial dowry and a large marriage gift," most probably as wives for royal princes, suggests that the terms of the compromise were not humiliating for Arwad. This is also indicated by the respectful way Aššurbanipal treated the sons of Iakinlû after the latter's death: "After Yakīn-Lû, the king of the land Arwad, had gone to (his) fate, Azi-Baʿal, Abī-Baʿal, (and) Adūnī-Baʿal, the sons of Yakīn-Lû who reside in the middle of the sea, came up from the middle of the sea, came with their substantial audience gift(s), and kissed my feet. I looked upon Azi-Baʿal with pleasure and installed (him) as king of the land Arwad. I clothed Abī-Baʿal (and) Adūnī-Baʿal in garment(s) with multi-colored trim (and) placed gold bracelets (on their wrists). I made them stand before me" (Novotny 2016, prism B 003, II 75). If the above interpretation is correct, we would have an example of Assyrian *Herrschaftspraxis*, which secured the economic interests of both Assyria and Arwad and resulted in a win-win situation for both parties (for Assyrian policy in the Levant see Bagg 2011, 305–8).

Aššurbanipal appointed his vassal ʿAzi-Baʿal as king of Arwad and gained the submission of the island city. ʿAzi-Baʿal is the last king known to us until the Persian period. Arwad is not mentioned in the Neo-Babylonian annals, but Arwadites are mentioned in some Babylonian texts (Weidner 1939). It is only in the Persian period that substantial information about the Phoenician kingdom resumes.

The main source for the history of the Phoenician cities in the Persian period is Herodotus, though there are also later Greek authors. Herodotus mentions Arwad's participation in the battles fought by the Persians against Cyprus and the Greeks. In 480 Arwad, together with Sidon and Tyre, participated in the battle of Salamis (*Hist.* 7.98). The Arwadian contingent was led by Merbalos, Phoenician Mhrbʻl (for the controversial meaning of *mhr* in Phoenician see Benz 1972, 340–41), the city's king, son of Agbalos, probably a corrupt form of ʻAzi-Baʻal, "My strength is Baal" (Benz 1972, 374), who was probably also king of Arwad. The Phoenician maritime contingent was formed by the fleets of Sidon, Tyre, and Arwad: "After the commanders, the most notable men in the fleet were Tetramnestus the son of Anysus, from Sidon; Matten the son of Siromus, from Tyre; Merbalus the son of Agbalus, from Aradus" (*Hist.* 7.98 [Waterfield]). There has been a controversy concerning whether the commanders of the Phoenician galleys were kings of their cities or simple naval commanders because they are mentioned only by their names without a title. Elayi (2005, 68–69; 2015, 135) has convincingly argued that the leaders of the Phoenician fleet were the kings of the Phoenician cities and not simple leaders.

No other king of Arwad is mentioned for the rest of the Persian period, but the Arwadian fleet probably continued to participate in the naval battles on the side of the Persians. The series of defeats suffered by the Phoenician fleets must have weakened Arwad and is considered by Elayi to be one of the main reasons behind the introduction of coinage. For this author, both financial and political reasons were behind the decision to start minting coins (Elayi 2015, 140–41) in the second half of the fifth century BCE. Arwadian coinage was excellent propaganda to restore the prestige of the city after the series of defeats.

Until the end of the Persian rule there is no information about the kingdom of Arwad. The last king who was ruling when Alexander defeated the Persians and marched into Syria was Gerostratos, Phoenician Gerʻaštart, "Client of the goddess ʻAshtart" (Benz 1972, 298), who was absent from Arwad when Alexander reached the area (Arrian, *Anab.* 2.13.7–8). As already mentioned, he was met by Straton, Phoenician ʻAbdʻaštart, "Servant of ʻAshtart" (Benz 1972, 369–72), the crown prince, who "crowned him with a golden crown and surrendered to him the island Aradus and Marathus which lay opposite it on the mainland, a large and prosperous city, with Sigon and the city of Mariamme and all the other places under his control" (Arrian, *Anab.* 2.13.7–8 [Brunt]). The attitude of Straton toward Alexander and his immediate allegiance to him in the absence of the king, as well as his surrender without any resistance, have been given different explanations such as fear, political calculations, economic interest, or philhellenism (Elayi 2007, 102 and n. 26). According to Elayi (2000, 339; 2007, 104), the crown prince at Arwad may have had royal prerogatives in the absence of the king. The thorough analysis of Gerʻaštart's coinage has led the same author (Elayi 2007, 104) to conclude that this king came to the throne seven years before the coming of Alexander, that is, in 339 BCE, and that he continued to rule after 333 for several years. There is no evidence whether his son, Straton/ʿAbdʿashtart, ruled after him or not. The Straton of Arados mentioned in an inscription from Delos does not necessarily refer to the son of Gerʿaštart, as suggested by Rey-Coquais (1974, 153–54), but could refer to any man from Arwad, since ʿAbdʿaštart was a common Phoenician name (Elayi 2007, 103). There is no evidence indicating how long the dynasty of Gerʿaštart continued to rule after the coming of Alexander.

Arwad prospered under Persian rule, as evidenced by the archaeological remains (Elayi 2000 and see above) mainly from Ṭarṭūs, where large numbers of anthropoid clay and stone sarcophagi were found (Elayi and Haykal 1996), and ʿAmrit, where a monumental funerary and religious complex was found (Dunand and Saliby 1985; Saliby 1989; Al-Maqdissi and Ishaq 2016). The latter city was occupied since the Early Bronze Age and Middle Bronze Age (Saliby 1989, 21), but the older strata were not excavated. So far the Persian period remains are by far the most substantial evidence from Phoenician Arwad. As previously suggested, the strong support that Arwad brought to the Persian naval force may have been rewarded by granting the island city new territories on the mainland.

Nine kings of Arados are mentioned in the texts (Elayi 2015, annex 1). In her chronology of the kings of Arwad, Elayi adds a tenth name since she assumes that Straton, Gerʿaštart's son, ruled after his father's death during the early period of Alexander's reign, an assumption that is difficult to prove. There are substantial gaps in the history of the city, and the best-documented succession of Arwadian kings comes from the Neo-Assyrian annals. Six kings bear names theophoric of Baʿal, and two have names theophoric of ʿAštart, which clearly indicate that the divine couple, Baʿal-ʿAštart, was the patron deities of the royal family. Abdi-Liʾti can be considered also to be a theophoric of Aštart, since the second element of the name is the feminine form of the participle and means "the mighty one" from a root *lʾy*, "to be strong, to prevail" (Benz 1972, 336–37).

Unfortunately, we have no Phoenician royal inscription from Arwad to fill the gaps in the succession of Arwadian kings and to know more about the internal situation of the island and its cities. The Phoenician inscriptions that were found on the territory of Arwad are very short and mention personal and divine names that can be used for the study of Arwadian onomastics and religion. Among the most important inscriptions are those of ʿAmrit: an inscription on a stela representing a divinity identified by the inscription as Shadrapa (*RÉS* 88, p. 95; Dunand and Saliby 1985, pl. XLI, 1-2; see fig. 5.2 below), and a votive inscription (Dunand and Saliby 1985, 47 and pl. LIII) mentioning two personal names—one incomplete name, of which only the theophoric element Eshmun survives, and the other, *bdmlqrt*, constructed with the divine name Melqart (Bordreuil 1985, 222–23). This inscription attests to the cult of Melqart in 'Amrit's *ma'bed* together with statues representing this god as Heracles (Dunand and Saliby 1985, 38 and pls. XXXVIII, XXXIX, XL). Another Phoenician inscription from 'Amrit (Bordreuil 1985, 225–27) mentions the god Eshmun and attests the cult of the latter in that city. A short Phoenician inscription found in nearby Tell Kazel (Bordreuil 1985, 229) and bearing the personal name Na'areshmun provides support for the existence of an Eshmun cult in the kingdom of Arwad. Another Phoenician inscription in the Louvre Museum has only a personal name '*bd*', interpreted as a hypochoristic of 'Abdisis, "Servant of (the goddess) Isis," attesting to the influence of Egyptian religion in Arwad (Texidor 1986, 425, 51). Short Phoenician inscriptions and letters are found on Arwadian coins (Elayi 2015, annex 6).

Arwad is rarely mentioned in the Old Testament. In Gen 10:15–18, the island is listed as one of Canaan's sons. In Ezekiel's lamentation over the fall of Tyre, Ezek 27 describes the wealth and the fate of the city. In verse 8 the prophet says that men from Sidon and Arwad were the oarsmen of Tyre, and verse 11 says, "The sons of Arvad and their army manned your walls all round and kept watch from your bastions. They hung their shields all round your walls and helped make your beauty perfect."[2] These short biblical passages stress the characteristics of Arwad as a naval power and its people as skilled navigators and seafaring warriors. It may also indicate the alliance between the fleets of the major Phoenician cities attested during the Persian period.

Table 3.1. The Kings of Arwad (after Elayi 2018, table 2)

| Name of King | Date |
|---|---|
| 'Ozbaal (II?) | (< 480 BCE) |
| Maharbaal | (480 BCE) |
| Ger'aštart | (339–333 BCE) |
| Ger'aštart | |
| 'Abd'aštart? | |

---

2. Unless otherwise stated, all biblical translations follow the JB.

## 3.1.2. The Kingdom of Byblos

### 3.1.2.1. The Territory of Byblos

Byblos, ancient Gubla, Phoenician *gbl*, modern Ğbayl, is circa 45 km north of the capital, Beirut. The ancient settlement is located on a promontory overlooking a narrow and fertile agricultural plain bordered to the east by the forested mountain range of the Lebanon. These forests were the main source of wealth of the city over the millennia, providing cedar and other coniferous wood and resins, the raw material that Byblos traded and exchanged for the goods it needed.

The promontory on which ancient Byblos was founded consists of two hills separated by a depression: the higher hill is 28.3 m, the lower one 24.3 m high, and the depression 18.4 m above sea level (Margueron 1994, 14). Water supply is provided by the aquifer that surges in various parts around the promontory and feeds also a spring, called *'ayn el-Malak*, "the king's

Fig. 3.3. Aerial view of the tell of Byblos. Courtesy MAPS Geosystems. S.A.R.L.Beirut-Lebanon.

spring," located in the center of the settlement. Dunand (1960) describes the works that were done around it over the centuries. The presence of a water supply as well as natural coves north and south of the promontory made the site an ideal place for settlement, with its high defensive position and its access to both the sea and a fertile plain. The size of the settlement is rather modest, covering 7 ha, with only 5 ha for the city *intra-muros* (Thalmann 1990, 101; Margueron 1994, 16).

Jean-Claude Margueron (1994, 17) has raised the issue of the absence of archaeological remains on the higher hill. Indeed, all the excavated structures were found either in the depression or on the lower hill, whereas the higher hill presented virtually bare bedrock. He suggests that the archaeological remains were either totally destroyed by later classical buildings (see also Salles 1994, 54), or heavily eroded, or overlooked during the excavations. This may have been also the fate of the Iron Age remains, which could not be located on the promontory: "How is the absence of traces of the Iron Age occupation on the whole site to be understood? Do we always have to make the great works of the Persian period followed by those of the classical era responsible and hence assume a generalized erosion that would have been as strong on the low hill as it was on the highest summit?"[3] Donald Harden (1962, 28) suggests that the Iron Age city may have moved to the north of the tell area. No final answer can be given to these issues in the present state of the evidence.

Despite the fact that Byblos is abundantly attested in the ancient sources since the end of the third millennium BCE (see Helck 1994 for the earliest attestations), there is hardly any information about its territory before the Late Bronze Age. Although the texts refer to a land or country of Byblos, hinting thus that the city had a civic territory, no town or village belonging to it is explicitly mentioned. However, Egyptian texts refer to the mountains and forests of Byblos. One inscription of Sen-nefer, a contemporary of Thutmosis III (Helck 1994, 109), speaks of the "mountains of the land of the gods," that is, the mountains of Byblos, which are "above the clouds." There, Sen-nefer says that he made offerings to the goddess

---

3. Margueron 1994, 17: "Comment comprendre aussi la quasi-absence des traces d'occupation de l'âge du Fer sur l'ensemble du site? Faut-il toujours en rendre responsables les grands travaux de l'époque perse suivis de ceux de l'époque classique et donc penser à une usure générale qui aurait été aussi vigoureuse cette fois sur la colline 'basse' que sur le point culminant?"

Astarte, who allowed him to take cedar logs to the god Horus. So clearly the mountains to the east of the city belonged to the territory of Byblos.

In the Late Bronze Age, more substantial information about the territory of Byblos is available from the Amarna correspondence and, more specifically, from the letters king Rib-Adda sent to Pharaoh or to his vizier Amanappa. According to these letters, the territory of Byblos included coastal and mountain villages: "All my villages that are in the mountains ḫa-*a-ri* or along the sea have been joined to the 'Apiru" (Moran 1987, EA 74). Another letter mentions also the cities of Rib-Adda: "Be informed that the war against me is severe. He has taken all my cities; Gubla alone remains to me. I was in Šigata and I wrote to you: 'Give thought to [your] city lest 'Abdi-'Aširta take it'" (EA 90). In El-Amarna Tablets 76 he acknowledges the loss of Šigata, modern Shekka, and Ampi, modern Anfe: "He has just gathered together all the 'Apiru against Šigata and Ampi, and he himself has taken these two cities." The text does not say explicitly that both towns were part of Byblos's territory, but since there is no indication that they were independent entities, it seems likely that they were under the control of Rib-Adda. After the loss of Šigata and Ampi, Rib-Adda had only two cities left, Gubla and Batruna: "They have as a result been striving to take over Gubla and Batruna, and thus all lands would be joined to the 'Apiru. There are two towns that remain to me, and they want to take th[em] from the king." Batruna was also lost, and Gubla was the only city that remained under the control of Rib-Adda: "Gubla alone remains to me" (EA 90); "Now he has taken Batruna, and he has moved up against me.... Moreover, look, he strives to seize Gubla" (EA 88). One has to note here that two other cities of Byblos are mentioned incidentally in Rib-Adda's letters: Bit-Arḫa (EA 76) and Ibirta. According to Belmonte-Marín (2003, 76), both cities should be looked for along Nahr el-Ǧawz (Belmonte-Marín 2001, 57, 139). A survey in progress of this area, conducted by Stephen McPhillips, may help locate these cities.

What can be inferred from these texts is that the territory of Byblos in the Late Bronze Age may have originally extended to the city of Shekka and, maybe, as far as Anfe. The above sources seem to imply that Byblos before the rise of Amurru controlled all the coastal area north of the city as far as Tripoli as well as the countryside and the mountains close to the city. Belmonte-Marín (2003, 76) believes that the northernmost city of Byblos's territory was Batrun, but the textual evidence of the Amarna letters seems rather to suggest that Šigata and Ampi were also under the protection of Rib-Adda and may have belonged to him. It is after the loss of these two cities that he claims to have only two cities left. The territory of Byblos did not extend north of Tripoli because the city of Ullaza was not part of it. This city is believed to be located on the site of Tell Kastina (Belmonte-Marín 2001, 321), which is the site of the Nahr el-Bared old Palestinian refugee camp. This site is generally equated with classical Orthosia. The site was rapidly investigated after the armed conflict between the Lebanese Army and the armed militias inside the camp. Although the results were not published, an internal report of the directorate general of antiquities said that the site was occupied from the Early Bronze Age I until the beginning of the twelfth century BCE and that no Hellenistic remains were detected, thus throwing doubt on its identification with Orthosia (see Sader, n.d.). Also Irqata, modern Tell Arqa, in the ʿAkkār Valley, had a king and thus did not belong to the territory of Byblos (Moran 1987, EA 75). In spite of the fact that the territory of Byblos did not include the Lebanese ʿAkkār Valley, the city had access to the Homs Gap because Ṣumur, which controlled this road, was the residence of the Egyptian governor, an ally of Rib-Adda. Under the pressure of ʿAbdi-Aširta and the ʿApiru, Byblos progressively lost all its cities to the kingdom of Amurru.

The southern borders of the territory of Byblos in the Late Bronze Age are more difficult to define, since no city located south of Gubla is mentioned in the texts. It is highly probable that the territory of Byblos extended to the promontory of Nahr el-Kalb, classical Lycus River, because it is a natural barrier separating its territory from that of Beirut (Elayi 1982, 92; Belmonte-Marín 2003, 78).

The Iron Age sources mention only the city of Gubla, which makes it difficult to identify the borders of the city's territory. As is the case with Arwad, one has to determine the borders of the neighboring kingdoms—if available—in order to define the territory of Phoenician Gubla. The Phoenician royal inscriptions do not give any information about the extension of the territory and do not mention any city other than Byblos. The inscriptions of Aššurnaṣirpal II indicate that the territory of Byblos in the Iron Age did not reach beyond the city of Tripoli (Grayson 1991, A.0.101.1, iii, 86 and 101.2, 26–28; see also above for these place names). Furthermore, the cities of Anfe, Chekka, and Batrun that were lost to the kingdom of Amurru were obviously not reconquered by Byblos, as evidenced by the annals of the Assyrian king Esarhaddon. Among the cities that became part of the province of Kar-Esarhaddon that was founded on the territory of the kingdom of Sidon in 677 BCE (Leichty 2011, 6, 26′–27′), the cities of Bitirume, modern Batrun (Bagg 2007, 51); Sagû, modern Shekka (206);

and Ampa, modern Anfe (9), are listed. These cities obviously belonged to the kingdom of Sidon in the Iron Age. It is not clear when Sidon conquered or annexed these cities to its territory. However, the account of Menander reported by Josephus in his *Jewish Antiquities* (8.324) ascribes the foundation of Batrun to Ittobaal I, king of Tyre, who ruled in the ninth century BCE. It is possible that after the end of the Late Bronze Age and the collapse of the kingdom of Amurru, Batrun remained in a state of quasi-abandonment until the Tyrians occupied it, probably to secure a naval station on their route to northern Syria and Cilicia. No other mention of Batrun is known to us in the Iron Age. The site was never properly excavated. Recently, salvage excavations took place on the western edge of the tell facing the sea wall, but no results have been published so far. No information is available for the sites of Anfe and Shekka, since their only mention is in the above-mentioned annals of Esarhaddon. It may not be far-fetched to assume that the occupation of these two northern cities happened at the same time as the occupation of Batrun, probably to stop the advance of the kingdom of Hamat to take possession of the former kingdom of Amurru. Current excavations at the site of Anfe and at Tell Mirhan, the site of ancient Šigata/Shekka, may provide new information about the territory of Byblos in the Iron Age.

However, Byblos kept its control over the mountains east of the city, as attested in the Wenamun journey: the Egyptian envoy requested cedar logs from Zakarbaal, king of Byblos (Goedicke 1975), which indicates that the mountains were still part of the territory of Byblos. In the treaty between Esarhaddon and Ba'lu of Tyre, mountain villages belonging to Byblos are mentioned: "These are the ports of trade and the trade routes which Esarhaddon, king of Assyria, [entrusted] to his servant Baal: to Akko, Dor, to the entire district of the Philistines, and to all the cities within Assyrian territory on the seacoast, and to Byblos, the Lebanon, all the cities in the mountains, all (these) being cities of Esarhaddon, king of Assyria" (Parpola and Watanabe 1988, SAA 2.5.iii.18–21). The eastern limits of the territory may be beyond the area of Afqa, where the famous Adonis grotto is located (Elayi 2009, 33), while the southern borders were probably still defined by the promontory of Nahr el-Kalb. Recent excavations at the site of Yanūḥ in the mountains of Byblos have exposed Iron Age remains (Monchambert et al. 2010; Monchambert 2011). Future excavations will, one hopes, shed more light on the eastern extension of the territory of Byblos.

In short, the territory of Byblos was very modest, and the city seems to have lost its importance in the Iron Age. According to scholars who have investigated the Byblos harbors, "the poor quality of Byblos's ancient ports may partially explain the historical decline of this city, which, unlike the other three ports studied (Beirut, Sidon, and Tyre), no longer plays an important maritime role today."[4]

The results of the investigations undertaken by several scholars (Frost 1998–1999; 2001; 2002; Frost and Morhange 2000; Morhange 1998–1999; Stefaniuk et al. 2005) have indicated that the sea level has been stable since antiquity. They have also demonstrated that the modern fishing harbor could not have been the site of the old Bronze Age harbor of Byblos—where cedar beams were stored and loaded on Egyptian ships—due to its diminutive size, which was the same in antiquity, as indicated by bio-sedimentological indicators and by the present morphology of the harbor basin. Researchers assumed that Byblos had several harbors in antiquity, and this is suggested by the natural coves and bays present north and south of the promontory where the settlement is located. However, recent research seems to suggest that the Bay of el-Skhiny south of the tell is the largest, best-protected, and most accessible of all and may have been the harbor where the cedar beams were stored and loaded onto ships. The geo-morphological study of this bay has shown the absence of sediments that are usually found in a closed protected harbor. This suggests that el-Skhiny Bay may have been an open harbor (Stefaniuk et al. 2005, 35). More investigations are needed before a clear picture of the Byblos harbor installations is obtained. A new project conducted by Martine Francis-Allouche is seeking to identify the exact location of the ancient harbor (Grimal and Allouche 2012).

3.1.2.2. A Political History of Phoenician Byblos

The oldest mention of Byblos goes back to the third millennium BCE, to the period of the Sixth Dynasty, where the city name appears as Kbn. The texts of this period speak also of Byblos ships, which are special ships dedicated to the transport of timber (Horn 1963, 53; Helck 1994, 106). In the Twelfth Dynasty period the name of the city was changed to Kpn. In the cuneiform literature Byblos appears for the first time in Ur III texts from Drehem as Ku-ub-la (Sollberger 1959–1960). Pettinato's identification of

---

4. Stefaniuk et al. 2005, 39: "la médiocre qualité des ports antiques de Byblos pourrait expliquer partiellement le déclin historique de cette cité qui, contrairement aux trois autres ports étudiés, (Beyrouth, Sidon et Tyr), ne joue plus de nos jours, un rôle maritime important."

the place name in the Ebla texts of the mid-third millennium BCE was challenged and rejected by Bonechi (1993). The ancient name of Byblos in the cuneiform sources of the second and first millennium BCE is Gubla/Gubal (for the various orthographies, see Belmonte-Marín 2001, 95–97; Bagg 2007, 79–80). In the cuneiform texts of the second millennium BCE, Gubla appears often in the Amarna correspondence (Moran 1987, 389–90). It is also mentioned in the Ugaritic texts (Belmonte-Marín 2001, 95–97).

The Phoenician name of Byblos, which appears in the inscriptions and title of its kings (*KAI* 1, lines 9–11) is *gbl*. It means in Semitic "territory" or "border" (Jean and Hoftijzer 1965, 47). The old toponym survives in the place name Ğbayl, the modern name of the city. The Greeks renamed it Byblos because in the Hellenistic period it was the center for papyrus trade. The Greek name of the city was used by all classical authors and has survived in the Western literature dealing with the site.

There has been hardly any study of the Iron Age city of Byblos for two main reasons: the rarity of the sources relating to the city; and the almost total absence of archaeological evidence for the Iron Age. Most publications have dealt with the general history of the city (Dunand 1963; Jidejian 1977; Acquaro et al. 1994; Wein and Opificius 1963) or with some specific aspects of its history. Elayi (2009) has recently published a book on the history of Byblos from the reign of Tiglath-pileser III until the end of the Persian period (eighth–fourth century BCE). She explains the limited chronological scope of her study (11), saying that the book expands the research she had previously published in two articles, one on Byblos in the Neo-Assyrian and Neo-Babylonian period (Elayi 1985) and one on Byblos and Sidon in the Persian period (Elayi 2008). The difficulty in writing a political history of Byblos can be clearly detected in the book Elayi (2009) dedicated to the history of that kingdom. Indeed, for every period the author says that the history of Byblos, although not explicitly documented, can be inferred from that of the other Phoenician cities and can be read "en creux": "The political history of Byblos under Babylonian rule (609–539), and perhaps also under short episodes of Egyptian domination, is very badly known because the sources are scarce, lacunar, laconic, or distorted. It can be reconstructed by comparison with that of the other Phoenician cities, mainly Tyre, which is not as poorly known."[5] As a result,

---

5. Elayi 2009, 105: "L'histoire politique de Byblos pendant la domination babylonienne (609–539), et, peut-être de brefs épisodes de domination égyptienne, est très mal connue car les sources sont peu nombreuses, lacunaires, laconiques ou déformées.

large parts of the book discuss the political history of Phoenicia in general, and the share of Byblos in the discussion is minimal. The most recent history of Byblos was published in 2018 by Marc Abou Abdallah, who collected and discussed all the written sources relating to the city.

The best-documented historical period is the second millennium BCE because Byblos is often mentioned in the Egyptian texts of the Middle Kingdom (Helck 1994; see also Allen 2008), in the fourteenth and thirteenth century BCE Tell el-Amarna archives, and in the Ugaritic texts. The Egyptian texts of the Middle Kingdom shed light on the relations with Egypt and on the importance of Byblos's harbor for Egyptian trade (Helck 1994, 107). The inscription of the tomb of Khnumhotep III in Dahshur, however, indicates that "Although Byblos had been Egypt's trading partner in the Old kingdom, this seems not to have been the case in the first half of the Middle kingdom.... Instead the expedition's destination was probably Ullaza, some 50 km to the north, which appears numerous times elsewhere in the text." Ezra Marcus (2007, 173, 176) concludes his study of the Mit Rahina inscription by stating, "Only later in the 12th dynasty is the traditional relationship with Byblos renewed." The Mari and the hieroglyphic inscriptions shed light on the ruling dynasty of the Middle Bronze Age and portray the names of several kings who carry the title of "mayors of the city," an indication that Byblos was under Egyptian dominion (Helck 1994, 108).

During the New Kingdom period, Byblos's political history is unveiled partly by the large number of letters sent by its king, Rib-Adda, to the pharaoh. The Amarna letters have been studied in depth by several scholars and have shed light on the political and social situation of the Levantine cities in general and Byblos in particular during the fourteenth and thirteenth centuries BCE. Rib-Adda's letters reflect a period of unrest, insecurity, famine, and rebellion that led to his exile and murder. However, these events do not seem to have changed dramatically the situation in Byblos, since in the late thirteenth century its king, whose name is, unfortunately, not mentioned, sent a letter to the king of Ugarit (*KTU* 2.44).

The first source available for Iron Age I is the eleventh-century BCE annals of Tiglath-pileser I (1114–1076 BCE). The land of Byblos appears as a functioning polity and pays tribute to the Assyrian king. The other

---

Elle peut se lire en creux comme pendant la domination assyrienne, par comparaison avec l'histoire des autres cités phéniciennes, un peu moins mal connue, surtout celle de Tyr."

literary source relating to the history of Byblos in Iron Age I is the controversial Egyptian text known as the Report of Wenamun (see ch. 2 for references). If Zakarbaal, the king of Byblos mentioned in this report, is not an invented ruler of the tenth century BCE (for his, in my opinion, doubtful identification with Zakarbaal king of Amurru, see Lemaire 2012) he must have ruled before Abibaal and Elibaal, who wrote their inscriptions on Sheshonq I's statue and Osorkon I's bust, respectively (*KAI* 5 and 6) According to Lemaire, both kings had commissioned these two statues, but this should not be interpreted as a sign of vassalage (Lemaire 2006, 1709). It is surprising, however, that Zakarbaal is nowhere mentioned in the five royal inscriptions dating to that century. Donner and Röllig (1973, 9) have listed six kings who ruled in Byblos from circa 1000 until 880 BCE: Ahirom, Ittobaal, Yeḥimilk, Abibaal, Elibaal, and Shipitbaal. It is difficult to insert in this century a seventh king, and it seems more likely that his reign was at the end of the eleventh century BCE. If the text is a fiction, it would not be far-fetched to assume that the account describes a historical situation that was prevailing in the eleventh or in the tenth century BCE. The above records clearly suggest that in Iron Age I Byblos was a well-established urban center with a local royal dynasty and enjoyed economic prosperity. It had a respectable merchant fleet and a well-organized trading network. It was rich enough to have awakened the greed of the Assyrian king who imposed and received its tribute. It is also clear that the main trading partner of Byblos in Iron Age I was Egypt and that the main raw material provided by Byblos was cedarwood in return for silver.

The only sources for a history of Byblos in the tenth century BCE are the Phoenician royal inscriptions (*KAI* 1, 4–7). During this century six kings followed each other on the throne of the city, but there is no evidence regarding the origin of this ruling dynasty: Was it the same dynasty that was ruling in the Late Bronze Age, or was there a drastic dynastic change at the beginning of the Iron Age? It is difficult to answer this question with the present state of the evidence. However, the personal names of the tenth-century rulers, which are almost all theophoric of Baal, may hint at a dynastic change, since no ruler with this type of name is known to us before the Iron Age. The author of the Wenamun text seems to have been familiar with the royal names given to the kings of Byblos, and the Zakarbaal of his account, even if fictitious, received a name conforming to those of the dynastic rulers. It is worth noting that in the course of the tenth century Byblos may have witnessed a dynastic change with the accession of Yeḥimilk to the throne. Indeed, in his inscription, this king does not mention his father and grandfather, and this omission of his genealogy has been usually understood as an indication that the king was not legitimate and may have usurped the throne. Abibaal and Elibaal followed each other on the throne: Abibaal's father's name is lost in a break, but his successor, Elibaal, says that he is the son of Yeḥimilk. It would not be far-fetched to suggest that both Abibaal and Elibaal were brothers, sons of Yeḥimilk.

Little can be gathered about the history of Byblos from these local inscriptions, for they are either funerary or votive in character and provide little information about the situation prevailing in the city in the tenth century BCE. They speak about the repair of buildings in ruin (*KAI* 4), the offering of votive statues to the Lady of Byblos (*KAI* 5–6), and they mention some deities worshiped in the city. No details are provided about the internal and external situation of the kingdom. That there were ruined buildings that needed restoration suggests that Byblos may have known certain difficulties in previous years. From a historical point of view, the only interesting information comes from the iconography of the Ahiram sarcophagus regarding the funerary practices of the Phoenicians. The overwhelming majority of scholars date the sarcophagus in the thirteenth century BCE, while others opt for a date in Iron Age I (for the various dates of the sarcophagus see Rehm 2004, 15–19). On the other hand, most epigraphists place the inscription in the tenth century BCE based on the evidence that the sarcophagus was reused by Ittobaal for his father, Ahiram (Lehmann 2005, 2 and n. 12).

During the ninth century BCE Byblos is mentioned in the annals of the Assyrian kings Aššurnaṣirpal II (Grayson 1991, A.0.101.1, iii 86) and Šalmaneser III (Grayson 1996, 102.2, ii 92). In the annals of the former, the city is a tributary of the Assyrian king. In those of the latter, Byblos is a participant with five hundred troops in the anti-Assyrian coalition at the battle of Qarqar. It is remarkable that Byblos and Arwad are the two cities that contribute the smallest number of troops to the coalition. This has been interpreted either as a symbolic participation of both cities in the coalition or as reflecting the weakness of the kingdoms (Elayi 2009, 55). In his twenty-first year and upon his campaign against Hazael of Damascus, Šalmaneser III received the tribute of Tyre, Sidon, and Byblos (Grayson 1996, A.0.102.16, 162'). Katzenstein (1973, 179) finds it "surprising" that Byblos is mentioned in the context of this campaign. Regarding the passage of Josephus (*Ant.* 8.324) in which he mentions the annexation of Batrun by Tyre, Katzenstein (1973, 131) thinks that "by means of Botrys, the Tyrian king was able to keep an eye on the nearby city of Byblos and thus draw it under Tyrian sway."

For more than a century Byblos is not mentioned in the Assyrian annals. In the mid-eighth century BCE the Assyrian texts reveal another king of Byblos called Shipitbaal, ᵐ*si-bi-it*[*ti*]-*bi-'i-li*, a contemporary and a tributary of Tiglath-pileser III (Tadmor 1994, 69, 87, 107, 171). Another king of Byblos, Urumilki, ᵐ*ú-ru-mil-ki*, is mentioned in the annals of Sennacherib (Grayson and Novotny 2012, 4.36; 16, iii 18; 17 ii 78; 22 ii 53; 23 ii 50.9′). He paid the tribute to Assyria together with other kings of the sea coast. The information provided by the Assyrian annals of the eighth century BCE is restricted to the mention of the king's name and the payment of his tribute. Since the tribute received from all the Levantine cities is listed together, it is difficult to know what each city contributed.

Byblos is not recorded in the annals of Esarhaddon, but it is listed among the cities belonging to the king of Assyria in the treaty between Esarhaddon and Baʻlu of Tyre mentioned above. Esarhaddon's annals reveal the name of yet another king of Byblos, Milki-ašapa, ᵐ*mil-ki-a-šá-pa*, who was one of the twenty-two kings of Syria-Palestine and Cyprus who were summoned to build his palace (Leichty 2011, V 54–VI 78). Among the requested goods were "large beams, tall columns, (and) very long planks of cedar (and) Cypress grown on Mount Sirāra and Mount Lebanon." Those from Mount Lebanon came most probably from Byblos. The same Milki-ašapa was still king under Aššurbanipal, who lists him as a tributary together with twenty-one kings of Syria-Palestine and Cyprus (Novotny 2016, prism C, ii 25′–50′): "In total, twenty-two kings of the seacoast, the midst of the sea, and dry land, [serva]nts who belonged to me, carried their substantial [audience] gift(s) [before me] and kissed my feet."

Elayi (2009, 95) sums up the situation of Byblos under the Assyrian kings as follows:

> This city (i.e., Byblos) is rarely mentioned in the Akkadian texts, probably because it caused no major problem to the Assyrian kings, which allowed it to preserve a certain autonomy. It seems that it was able to better endure the yoke of the last Sargonids, mainly that of Ashurbanipal: the city did not have to provide the Assyrians with a war fleet since it did not own one.... Finally, it never had to suffer from Assyrian retaliations because it did not rebel.[6]

---

6. Elayi 2009, 95: "Cette cité (i.e. Byblos) est rarement mentionnée dans les textes

After the fall of Nineveh, the Phoenician cities came under Egyptian rule following the expeditions of Psammetic I (656–609 BCE) and his son Neco II (609–594 BCE). However, little is known about the fate of the Phoenician cities under Egyptian rule, and Byblos is not mentioned in the Egyptian texts of that period. The situation remained obscure until the rise of Nebuchadnezzar II, who succeeded in chasing the Egyptians out of Syria-Palestine and in establishing his hegemony on the land, as attested by his inscriptions on the cliffs of Nahr el-Kalb and in Wadi Brisa (Da Riva 2008; 2009), but no information about Byblos is available in the Neo-Babylonian texts.

Regarding the Persian period, while some information about the political history of the other Phoenician kingdoms can be gained from the texts, nothing is known about Byblos's political history. The reason is probably that the city had no warships and played a minimal role in the wars of the Persian army. The local Phoenician inscriptions as well as the Byblos coinage betray the names of kings who ruled over the city, but no information about its internal situation is available. Two Phoenician inscriptions shed light on a few members of the royal dynasty of Byblos. The inscription of the son of Shipitbaal (*KAI* 9) is very fragmentary. It is a funerary inscription that reveals the name of a king of Byblos called Shipitbaal and referred to as Shipitbaal III. The name of his successor is lost in the break, and no information about the situation in the city can be gained from this text. The so-called Yeḥumilk inscription gives the name of two kings who preceded Yeḥumilk on the throne: his father, Yḥrbʻl, who probably did not rule since his name is not followed by the title king of Byblos; and his grandfather, ʼrmlk, who bears the same name as the king contemporary of Sennacherib, $^m$*ú-ru-mil-ki*, and he is referred to as Urimilk II.

Byblos is not mentioned among the Phoenician cities that placed their fleet at the service of the Persian king, and only Tyre, Sidon, and Arwad were members of the war council of Xerxes before the Battle of Salamis in 480 BCE. This may lead to the assumption that Byblos had no warships or that it had a very small fleet that played no important role in the royal

---

akkadiens, sans doute parce qu'elle a posé peu de problèmes aux rois assyriens, ce qui lui a permis de conserver une certaine autonomie. Il semblerait qu'elle ait mieux supporté que les autres villes phéniciennes le joug des derniers Sargonides et en particulier celui d'Assurbanipal: elle n'avait pas à fournir de flotte de guerre puisqu'elle n'en avait pas … enfin, elle n'a jamais eu à subir des représailles assyriennes, ne s'étant pas révoltée."

fleet of the Persian king. Byblos was the first Phoenician city to mint coins, shortly before 450 BCE (Elayi 2009, 140). While the oldest coins represent a winged sphinx, those minted after the middle of the fifth century BCE represent a Phoenician galley with soldiers. This has led Elayi (146–47) to suggest that Byblos had become a small naval power in the second half of the fifth century BCE. The early coinage of Byblos betrays the name of a king and his title:*' lpʻ l mlk gbl*. He is probably the last king of the legitimate ruling dynasty. ʻOzbaal, son of Batnoam and the high priest Palṭibaal (*KAI* 11), became king of Byblos probably around 400 BCE, having usurped the throne (Elayi 2009, 154). The last kings of Byblos have left their names on the coins they minted. According to Lemaire (2013a), these kings are "indicated by coins and legends on the coins" and identified as Elpaal, 'LPʻL; ʻOzbaal, ʻZBʻL, abbreviated ʻZ; Urimilk, ʼWRMLK, abbreviated ʼK; and ʻAynel, ʻYNʼL, abbreviated ʻ or ʻL. Lemaire adds that "the third king of this series has, up to now, generally been read as Addirmilk (ʼDRMLK), but during our publication with J. Elayi of an important hoard from Byblos, we noted that the head of the second letter was never closed and always open, so that it has to be read as W and not as D.... Hence, although the list might still be incomplete, we now know eight kings of Byblos: in chronological order, Shipitbaal III, Urimilk II, Yeḥarbaal, Yeḥawmilk, Elpaal, ʻOzbaal, Urimilk III, and ʻAynel."

To sum up, in spite of the scarcity of the sources, it seems that Byblos had a quiet history away from the turmoil caused by the invasions of the Assyrians, Babylonians, and Persians. Its modest importance prevented it

Fig. 3.4. Silver shekel of ʻOzbaal minted in Byblos, depicting on the obverse three hoplites in a war galley with a hippocamp swimming below; on the reverse a lion attacking a bull above which Phoenician inscriptions read ʻZBʼL MLK GBL. Source: Classical Numismatic Group, LLC. Triton XXII, Lot 729. 29 mm, 18.88 gr. www.cngcoins.com.

from rebelling (Elayi 1985, 397) and protected it from the greed of the invaders. It paid them a tribute but did not oppose them openly in any way. Except for the short episode of the coalition at Qarqar, we do not witness any hostile attitude of Byblos toward foreign invaders. The city kept its trading relations with Egypt and continued exporting the timber of its mountains. On the whole, the image of Iron Age Byblos is far from the wealthy and glowing picture of the Middle Bronze Age city. It is the Phoenician kingdom that ranked last in political and economic importance. It always preferred to submit peacefully rather than resist the mighty invading armies. This submissive attitude is clearly illustrated in the way Byblos submitted itself spontaneously to Alexander the Great: "Alexander marched from Marathus and received the surrender of Byblus and Sidon; the Sidonians who loathed Persia and Darius called him in themselves" (Arrian, *Anab.* 2.15.6). Even when it lost its economic and political importance, Byblos was still considered to be a holy city, a place of pilgrimage, as attested by the epithets *gbl qdšt* and ΒΥΒΛΟΥ ΗΙΕΡΑΣ, which appear on its coinage (Elayi 2008, 110).

Table 3.2. The Kings of Byblos (after Elayi 2018, table 2)

| Name of King | Date |
| --- | --- |
| Zakarbaal | ca. 1090 BCE |
| Ahiram | ca. 1000 BCE |
| Ittobaal | ca. 1000–970 BCE |
| Yeḥimilk | ca. 970–950 BCE |
| Abibaal | ca. 943 BCE |
| Elibaal | ca. 922 BCE |
| Shipitbaal I | ca. 900 BCE |
| Shipitbaal II | ca. 737–732 BCE |
| Urimilk I | ca. 701 BCE |
| Milki-ašapa | ca. 673 BCE |
| Shipitbaal III | ca. 500 BCE |
| Urimilk II Yeḥarbaal? | |
| Yeḥawmilk | ca. 450 BCE |
| Elpaal | |
| ʿOzbaal | ca. 400 BCE |
| Urimilk III | |
| ʿAynel | |
| ʿAynel? | |

### 3.1.3. The Kingdom of Sidon

#### 3.1.3.1. The Territory of Sidon

Sidon, modern Ṣaydā, is located 40 km south of the capital Beirut. The city is located on a peninsula or maybe on a former island(s), as can be inferred from the description of the city in the Neo-Assyrian royal annals of Esarhaddon. Sidon is said to be "in the midst of the sea," *ša qé-reb tam-tim*, *ša ina* MURUB4 *tam-tim* (Leichty 2011, 1, ii 68; 2, i 14), an expression used normally to describe an island. On the other hand, the Phoenician inscriptions of Eshmunazar II and Bod'aštart speak of *ṣdn ym* and *ṣdn 'rṣ ym*, Sidon-of-the-Sea and Sidon-land-by-the-Sea, expressions that may also lead to the same assumption. The Bronze and Iron Age Sidon, which developed around the northern harbor where the Ottoman city stands today, was 5–6 ha large (Volney 1787, 207), almost the same size as Byblos.

A wide, unprotected, round cove borders the city to the south. Investigation of the latter led to the conclusion that it could not have served as a southern harbor (Poidebard-Lauffray 1951, 54). This conclusion was confirmed by recent investigations: "The round cove, the south bay of Sidon, was never a favorable milieu for harbor installations.… this bay may have been used as an open harbor in the Copper Age, when the site of Dakerman was occupied."[7]

The ancient northern harbor of Sidon, which is located on the site of the modern one, is protected by a band of reef and a series of small islands, which provide a natural shelter for the ships. It was investigated for the first time by Antoine Poidebard and Jean Lauffray (1951) in the mid-1940s upon an official request to help solve the recurrent problem of the harbor's silting. Lauffray recognized a closed harbor, *port intérieur*, delimited by the line of reef and a northern man-made mole built on a rock platform linking the shore to the island where the Crusader sea-castle stands today. Another eastern mole perpendicular to the shoreline and built entirely with stone blocks inside the above defined harbor created two basins: a northern one called *avant-port*, which communicated directly with the open sea, and an inner one, which communicated with the sea only through the

---

7. Morhange et al. 2005, 136: "la Crique Ronde, baie sud de Sidon, n'a jamais été un milieu portuaire favorable.… Cette baie a pu être utilisée comme port ouvert à l'âge du cuivre, au moment où le site de Dakerman se developpait."

Fig. 3.5. Aerial photo of Sidon showing the coastline, reef, and islands. Source: Amenagements du port de Saida. Source: Poidebard and Lauffray 1951, plate I.

*avant-port* (Poidebard-Lauffray 1951, plan II). Man-made constructions, which reinforced the protective role of the natural reef and quays, were identified along its inner side.

The most interesting thing about this harbor is that it presents an example of how ancient Sidonians solved the silting problem by using the flushing method. They used two openings in the natural reef, opposite which they cut in the rock reservoirs or tanks to allow the sea to enter and fill them. These were controlled by a sluice, which was opened when the harbor basin was flushed. The flow of water kept the silt particles floating and counteracted the incoming silt from the eastern harbor entrance, thus preventing the deposition of the particles: "Two alternating streams created a turbulence across the harbor that prevented the deposition of suspended particles and therefore did not allow them to enter the harbor from the east gate."[8]

---

8. Poidebard-Lauffray 1951, 67: "Deux courants de chasse intermittents créaient

Christophe Morhange's (Morhange et al. 2005, 145, 135) and Nick Marriner's (Marriner, Morhange, and Doumet-Serhal 2006) new studies of the harbor area demonstrated that more than half of the old Sidonian harbor was located under the old city's souks: "Part of the medieval and modern souk as well as the recent corniche are located above the ancient basins of the Bronze and Iron Age,"[9] which means that the harbor was much larger in antiquity. The results of the fifteen boreholes made near the northern and southern coves have demonstrated that there was "a semi-sheltered environment that served as a proto-harbour during the Bronze Age" (Marriner, Morhange, and Doumet-Serhal 2006, 1520). From the Persian to the Roman period the harbor was a closed one. There is hardly any evidence for the Phoenician period, and this is mainly due to repeated dredging in Roman times (1526).

Poidebard and Lauffray (1951, 73ff.) established also the existence of an external harbor, *port extérieur*, on the little island off the shore of Sidon called "Zire" by the locals, which displayed evidence for intensive harbor activity as well as evidence for a quarry. This harbor was also later investigated by Honor Frost (1973b) and Nicolas Carayon (2003). They identified a mole built perpendicular to the southern tip of the island, which protected the quays on the island shore from the swell and from the accumulation of silt. Its outer face is built with stretchers and 5 m long headers. Its inner face, as well as the island shore, served as quays, as attested by thirty-one mooring holes (Carayon 2003, plan I). In terms of harbor installations, some construction remains may indicate the existence of docks and fish tanks. These installations are Roman or post-Roman in date but, according to Lauffray (Poidebard and Lauffray 1951, 76; see also 80–81), may have been in use much earlier: "Despite the fact that none of the installations can be ascribed with certainty to the pre-Roman periods, it is likely that this anchorage may have been used much earlier."[10] This assumption was recently verified: the earliest use of the

---

à travers le port une agitation qui empêchaient le dépôt des matières en suspension et s'opposait à leur entrée par la porte Est."

9. Morhange et al. 2005, 145, 135: "une partie du souk médiéval et moderne ainsi que la corniche routière récente se localisent au-dessus des bassins antiques de l'Âge du Bronze et du Fer."

10. Poidebard and Lauffray 1951, 76: "Bien qu'aucun des aménagements reconnus ne puisse être attribué avec certitude aux époques pré-romaines, il est probable que l'usage de ce mouillage doit remonter très haut."

closed harbor in Sidon was dated to the Middle Bronze Age (Morhange et al. 2005, 140); an earlier date around 3000 BCE (Morhange et al. 2000) was contradicted by the recent investigations. These investigations demonstrated, however, that the efficient protection works should be dated to the Roman period.

Regarding the territory of the kingdom of Sidon, no information is available before the Late Bronze Age (for a detailed study of Sidon's territory in the Late Bronze and Iron Age see Belmonte-Marín 2003, 81–97; for the territory of the city in the Persian period see Elayi 1982; 1989, 81–106; see also Sader 1997; 2000a). Indeed, Sidon is mentioned for the first time in texts of the Late Bronze Age as Ṣiduna/Ṣiduni (Belmonte-Marín 2001, 248–49). Until today there is no evidence for an earlier mention of Sidon in the cuneiform sources. The absence of Sidon's name in the hieroglyphic texts of the Early and Middle Bronze Age is surprising since during that period Sidon had strong ties with Egypt, as evidenced by the finds in the Sidon College Site excavations (Doumet-Serhal 2006b, 35–39; Bader 2003; Forstner-Müller, Kopetsky, and Doumet-Serhal 2006; Doumet-Serhal 2013, 31–45 and figs. 37–40), as well as by the wall paintings discovered at Tell el-Burak, a site 9 km south of Sidon (Kamlah and Sader 2010b; Bertsch 2019). These wall paintings display a strong Egyptian influence. The Egyptians who traded actively with this harbor city in the Middle Bronze Age must have mentioned it in their inscriptions and may have used a toponym that has not yet been identified as referring to Sidon. Furthermore, in spite of the fact that Thutmosis IV (Moran 1987, EA 85) visited the city of Sidon, no mention of the city is known from the Egyptian texts of Thutmosis III, his father, or his successors.

When it first appears in the texts, Sidon was already a powerful city and had preeminence over the other Phoenician cities: "The available sources relating to Acco, Beirut, Byblos, Sidon, and Tyre, whether published or not, clearly show the preeminence of Sidon over the rest of Phoenicia."[11] According to the Amarna letters (Moran 1987, EA 148, 149), Sidon in the fourteenth century BCE occupied Ušû, the territory of continental Tyre. This indicates that the territory of Sidon extended at that time to include the land of Ušû, which stretches from north to south opposite the Tyrian island reaching modern Tell el-Rašidiyye, 5 km south of the island (for the

---

11. Arnaud 1992, 182: "Le tableau des sources disponibles, publiées ou non, pour Acre, Beyrouth, Byblos, Sidon et Tyr montre, presque matériellement, la prééminence de Sidon sur le reste de la Phénicie."

extension of Sidon's territory in the Late Bronze Age see Belmonte-Marín 2003, fig. 8). In the letters mentioned above, Abimilku of Tyre complains to Pharaoh that he cannot go to the mainland anymore to get water and food and to bury the dead. There is no information about the extension of Sidon's own territory before the conquest of mainland Tyre. However, the border between the two kingdoms is traditionally believed to be the Litani River, which ends in the Mediterranean in the locality of Qasimiyye, north of Tyre. This natural border is, however, an assumption that cannot be verified by the texts of that period but that becomes more evident in the Iron Age. In any case, the occupation of Ušû was only temporary, but it is difficult to estimate how long it lasted.

The northern extension of Sidon's territory in the Late Bronze Age was probably limited by the territory of the kingdom of Beirut, for which there is no information at all. Whether this territory reached south as far as the River Damūr, another natural boundary (Elayi 1989, 86), or stopped further north in the area of Khaldeh remains an open question.

To the east, Sidon's territory extended to the nearby mountains, at least as far as Jezzine, whose pass controlled the route to the Biqāʿ Valley. The route coming from Sidon passed through Jezzine, Mašǧara, and Kāmid el-Lōz before reaching Damascus. This communication passage, described by Arnulf Kuschke (1977), was used by the Egyptian armies on their way back from the Battle of Qadesh. It must have been under the control of Sidon to secure its connection with the Biqāʿ Valley and Damascus. The existence of this route linking the Sidonian harbor to the hinterland may have existed already in the Middle Bronze Age. This is suggested by the evidence from Tell Sakka, near Damascus, where a palace with Egyptianizing wall paintings was found (Taraqji 1999). It seems that in the Middle Bronze Age, Egyptian-Levantine relations did not transit exclusively from the northern harbors of Byblos and Ullaza but used also the southern harbor of Sidon to link Egypt to the Biqāʿ Valley and Damascus (Sader 2015). This is also attested by the discovery in Sidon of a seal engraved with hieroglyphs belonging to a local Sidonian prince, "Sadok-Re, a native of Lay," a locality in the ʿAkkār Valley. Doumet-Serhal (2013, 35) concludes: "This confirms the existence in the Levant, aside from Byblos, of a scribal tradition using hieroglyphs."

In the Iron Age, there is no information about Sidon's territory before the end of the eighth century BCE. The annals of Sennacherib and Esarhaddon shed light on the extension of the Sidonian territory, while the Phoenician inscriptions of Eshmunazar II, Bodʿaštart, and Baalshillem II mention mainly the various districts of the city as well as neighboring sacred places. Two brief biblical mentions of the toponym Sidon Rabbah (Josh 11:8; 14:28), equivalent maybe to Great Sidon, the Ṣidunu rabû of the Assyrian inscriptions, can be also added to the evidence, although they provide little information on the territory's extension.

The Assyrian inscriptions of Sennacherib enumerate a series of cities between Sidon and Akko, which belonged to Lulî, king of Sidon, and which were probably part of the still-unified kingdom of Sidon and Tyre. His third-year campaign, dated 701 BCE, marked the separation of the two polities that formed the unified kingdom, according to Katzenstein (1973, 252).[12] "On my third campaign, I marched to the land Ḫatti. Fear of my lordly brilliance overwhelmed Lulî, the king of the city Sidon, and he fled afar into the midst of the sea. The awesome terror of the weapon of the god Aššur, my lord, overwhelmed the cities Great Sidon, Lesser Sidon, Bīt-Zitti, Sarepta, Maḫalliba, Ušû, Akzibu, (and) Akko, his fortified cities and fortresses, an area of pasture(s) and water-place(s), resources upon which he relied, and they bowed down at my feet" (Leichty 2011, 4, 32–34).

The territory described here is located south of Sidon, as indicated by the enumerated cities. Lesser Sidon ($^{uru}$ ṣi-*du-un-nu ṣe-eḫ-ru*) is still not clearly identified and is thought to refer either to a district of Sidon or to a city south of the capital (for the various propositions regarding its location see Bagg 2007, 229–31). It should be noted in this context that the toponym is preceded by the determinative URU = city and that all the mentioned place names are said to be "fortified cities" and "fortresses," which speaks against the opinion that Lesser Sidon is a district of Sidon. However, one has to mention in this context a passage qualified by Daniel Arnaud as ambiguous and in which the reference to the city of Sidon is not ascertained. It speaks of a fortress *birtu*: "If the term refers to the Sidonian palace, the latter would have been a fortress, a castle inside the city itself."[13] If the reference to Sidon is accepted, this would justify the use of the term *birtu* for a local district of the city and would weigh in favor of Lesser Sidon being one.

---

12. Belmonte-Marín (2003, 89) places the end of the unified kingdom of Tyre and Sidon under the reign of Šalmaneser V in the year 725 BCE, when Sidon and other Phoenician cities decided to free themselves from the yoke of Tyre, which caused Assyria to intervene and separate the antagonistic polities.

13. Arnaud 1992, 184: "si le mot désigne le palais sidonien, celui-ci aurait donc été une 'citadelle,' un 'château,' à l'intérieur de la ville même."

The second city is Bīt-Zitti, probably Zeita, 9 km southeast of Sidon (Bagg 2007, 54). Then comes Sarepta, modern Sarafand (225–26). These cities fall within the traditional territory of Sidon and are all located north of the Litani River. The remaining cities of Maḫalliba, modern Maḫālib; Ušû, modern Tell el-Rašidiyye; Akzibu, modern Akhziv; and Akko (for all these toponyms see Bagg 2007, 167, 272, 4, and 3, respectively), are all located south of the Litani and most probably belonged to the Tyrian territory. This may be inferred from the fact that the cities of the Sidonian territory that formed later the province of Kar-Esarhaddon were all located north of the Litani River. In the year 677 BCE, Esarhaddon campaigned against Sidon and transformed the kingdom into an Assyrian province to which he gave the name Kar-Esarhaddon, "Esarhaddon's harbor."

> (As for) Abdi-Milkūti, king of Sidon, … I leveled Sidon, his stronghold, which is situated in the midst of the sea, like a flood, tore out its wall(s) and dwelling(s)and threw (them) into the sea.… I gathered the kings of Ḫatti (Syria-Palestine) and the seacoast, all of them, and had (them) build a city in another place, and I named it Kār-Esarhaddon. (The inhabitants of) the cities Bīt-Ṣupūri, Sikkû, Gi', Inimme, Ḫildua, Qartimme, Bi'rû, Kilmê, Bitirume, Sagû, Ampa, Bīt-Gisimeya, Birgi', Gambūlu, Dalaimme, (and) Isiḫimme, cities of the environs of Sidon, places of pasturing and watering for his stronghold, which I captured with the help of the god Aššur, my lord. (Leichty 2011, 1, ii, 65–82, and iii, 1–19)

All the cities enumerated in this account are "cities in the environs of Sidon," "URU.MEŠ-ni ša li-me-et URU. Ṣi-du-un-ni," more specifically north and northeast of it. I have argued elsewhere (Sader 1997) that the enumeration of the first group of cities located along the coast follows a strict south-north order: Bīt-Ṣupūri, Sikkû, Gi', Inimme, Ḫildua, Qartimme, Bi'rû, to be identified with Bṣfaray (?), Rmayle (?), Jiyye, Nā'me, Khaldeh, Kfarshima (?), and Beirut (for a discussion of all these toponyms see Bagg 2007). After skipping the territory of Byblos, the enumeration resumes with Kilmê, Bitirume, Sagû, and Ampa, which may be identified with modern Kalmin (?), 4 km east of Batrun; Batrun; Shekka; and Anfe respectively (for the identification of these toponyms see Bagg 2007). Belmonte-Marín (2003, 94) rejects the above identification of Kilmê, Bitirume, and Sagû on the basis of linguistic arguments but accepts the obvious identification of Ampa with Anfe.

Three localities of the second group of five cities—Birgi', Dalaimme, and Isiḫimme—can be identified with certainty with the modern localities of Barġa, Delhum, and Šḥīm. Gambulu is listed between Birgi' and Dalaimme and must therefore be located in the same area, although its precise location cannot be determined. All of these cities are located northeast of Sidon in the area known today as Iqlīm al-Ḥarrūb. The site of Šḥīm has provided evidence for Iron Age occupation (see Waliszewski et al. 2002), but the excavations did not expose large areas dating to this period. Bīt-Gisimeya is more problematic and could belong either to the coastal cities north of Anfe or to the cities northeast of Sidon, the latter of which is, in my opinion, more plausible (for the various opinions, see Bagg 2007, 49).

So the territory of Sidon in the eighth and seventh century BCE extended to the north to the city of Anfe, interrupted only by the small enclave of the kingdom of Byblos. The extension of Sidon's territory to the south is known to us from the above-mentioned inscription of Sennacherib. It included Lesser Sidon, Bīt-Zitti, and Sarepta. Upon the creation of the province of Kar-Esarhaddon, the Assyrian king cut off two localities north of the Litani, Sarepta and Ma'rubbu, that belonged to the territory of Sidon and gave them to the king of Tyre: "From among those cities of his [i.e., Abdi-Milkūti's] I handed over the cities Ma'rubbu (and) Sarepta to Ba'alu, king of Tyre" (Leichty 2011, 1, iii 15–16).

The southernmost city of Sidon was Ma'rubbu, which is to be sought at the site of Tell Ras Abu Zayd, the ancient settlement of modern 'Adlūn (Sader 1997, 369; see also Bagg 2007, 171), north of Qasimiyye. This very plausible identification of Ma'rubbu with 'Adlūn is in line with the assumption that the natural borders of Sidon to the south was the River Litani at Qasimiyye.

So in the early seventh century Sidon's territory had reached its maximum extension from the Litani River to Anfe with fortified settlements northeast of the capital, on the western slopes of the mountains. There is no information about its territory in the Neo-Babylonian period. When Sidon recovers its autonomy under Persian rule it seems to have kept the part of the territory which formed the province of Kar-Esarhaddon: the city of Sarepta was still in the hands of Tyre according to Pseudo-Scylax, who visited Phoenicia in the last years of Persian rule. It seems, however, that it had lost Beirut and the cities north of Byblos (Elayi 1989, 86–87) with the exception perhaps of the settlement area it controlled in Tripoli, since this city is said to have been founded by Arwad, Sidon, and Tyre

## 3. PHOENICIA IN IRON AGE II AND III

Fig. 3.6. Map showing the toponyms mentioned in the Neo-Assyrian texts belonging to the kingdoms of Tyre and Sidon.

according to Diodorus (*Bibl. hist.* 14.41.1), whose claim cannot be verified. On the other hand, the territory of Sidon was enlarged southward by the annexation of Dor and Joppa in the Sharon Plain that were given to Eshmunazar II by the Persian king as a gift in return for his help and assistance: "Furthermore, the lord of kings gave us Dor and Joppa, the rich lands of Dagon which are in the plain of Sharon, as a reward for the striking deeds which I performed; and we added them to the borders of the land that they might belong to the Sidonians for ever" (Gibson 1982, 109). These lands remained part of the Sidonian territory until the end of the Persian period and may have remained part of the Sidonian territory in the Hellenistic period (apud Lemaire 2013a, 33, who claims that Dor was lost to Tyre).

The Phoenician inscriptions of Eshmunazar II, Bodʻaštart, and Baal-shillem II mention some districts of the Sidonian territory that are not often easy to identify (Sader 1997). All three inscriptions refer to a place in the mountains called ʻn ydll where a temple of the god Eshmun stood. Eshmunazar II says *wʻnḥn ʼš bnn bt lʼšmn [š]r qdš ʻn ydll bhr*, "and we (it were) who built in the mountain a house for Eshmun, the prince, of the sanctuary of the ydll spring" (Gibson 1982, 109; see also Mathys 2005, 273). This temple is attested archaeologically 2 km northeast of Sidon in Bustan esh-Sheikh, on the left bank of the Awwali River, where its remains were excavated by Dunand (1966; 1967; 1969; 1973; see also Stucky 2005) in the 1960s and early 1970s. They also mention several expressions that were interpreted either as toponyms referring to administrative districts (Elayi 1989, 84) or as temple names. These are *ṣdn ym*, *ṣdn ʼrṣ ym*, *ṣdn šd/r*, *ṣdn mšl*, *šmm rmm*, *šmm ʻdrm*, *ʼrṣ ršpm*.

The expressions *ṣdn ym* and *ṣdn ʼrṣ ym* obviously correspond to the Assyrian designation of Sidon: *ša qé-reb tam-tim*, *ša ina* MURUB4 *tam-tim*. These refer most probably to one and the same district namely, the urban area built around the harbor, which roughly corresponds to the modern old city of Sidon. Elayi's (1989, 83) argument that each one of these three toponyms refers to a different district is not convincing.

The remaining expressions, *ṣdn šd/r*, "Sidon- the-Plain" or "Sidon-the- Prince"; *ṣdn mšl*, "Sidon rules" (Hoftijzer and Jongeling 1995, 702); *šmm rmm*, "High Heavens" (116); *šmm ʻdrm*, "Lofty Heavens"; and *ʼrṣ ršpm* (1087) were generally interpreted either as toponyms or as temple names. The latter meaning seems to have gained more consensus among scholars. *ʼrṣ ršpm* was interpreted as referring to a funerary temple located most probably in the royal necropolis of Sidon.

## 3.1.3.2. A Political History of Phoenician Sidon

As previously mentioned, the name of Sidon appears for the first time in the Late Bronze Age texts. There is so far no earlier mention of the city attested in either the cuneiform or the hieroglyphic texts. However, the archaeological excavations that took place in the city of Sidon proved its antiquity and filled the gap on the ancient history of the city.

The earliest evidence for a human permanent settlement in Sidon was found on the site of Dakerman, a Chalcolithic or EBA I village dated to the fourth millennium BCE (Saidah 1969, 122; 1979). This settlement is located at the southern edge of the modern city near the south cove, which may have been used by these early settlers. An extensive settlement with oval houses and an enclosure wall was discovered there. Under and between the houses the excavations exposed large pithoi used as jar burials, which contained adult individuals. No offerings or personal belongings were found in these tombs. This settlement is very similar to the "énéolithique" settlement excavated by Dunand in Byblos. For reasons that are still to be determined, this site was abandoned at the beginning of the third millennium BCE. One reason may have been that the southern cove was not appropriate for sheltering larger vessels and for more intensive trade activity. This may have led them to move to the area around the northern harbor. Unfortunately, no excavations were conducted there because of the presence of the still densely inhabited Ottoman old town. However, we know that part of the population moved to the top of the hill where the Crusader land castle stands today. This area, known as College Site because of the presence of a former American Protestant Mission College and a Marist college, has yielded evidence for an Early Bronze Age settlement, which lasted until the end of EBA III (Doumet-Serhal 2006a, 3 and table 1). The finds from the site indicate that Sidon was an urban settlement with a complex administration already in close contact with Egypt: "A large number of jars from Sidon were found in the Egyptian tombs at Saqqara and Abydos. The transport of these jars was justified by their content: oil or wine" (Doumet-Serhal 2013, 31). Whether the College Site was the only Early Bronze Age settlement of Sidon is still an open question since there has been no evidence thus far for an Early Bronze Age settlement on the coast, around the northern harbor. As previously stated, it is highly probable that an early settlement existed in this area for the shipment of goods to Egypt but the presence of the modern old town has prevented archaeological research.

At the end of the third millennium BCE, the Early Bronze Age settlement on College Site was covered with an up to 2 m high sterile sand layer and was turned into a large Middle Bronze Age cemetery. The inhabitants of the urban settlement that was on the hill must have moved to another location, most probably to the shore around the northern harbor but their new habitat has not been identified yet. The finds from the Middle Bronze Age tombs indicate that the Sidonian harbor was already very active and that Sidon traded with Crete, as attested by the presence of a Kamares Ware and by a locally made jar painted with leaping dolphins, a typical Cretan motif (Doumet-Serhal 2013, 31 and figs. 34, 35, 35a). That it also traded with Anatolia is attested by the silver finds, the metal of which originated in the Ala Dagh mountains. Egypt (selected bibliography: Doumet-Serhal 2006b, 35–39; Bader 2003; Forstner-Müller, Kopetsky, and Doumet-Serhal 2006; Doumet-Serhal 2013, 31–45 and figs. 37–40), and Cyprus (Doumet-Serhal 2006b; 2013, 31, 35, and fig. 36) were also trading partners of Sidon. It is therefore not surprising that Sidon appears in the Late Bronze Age texts as the most important harbor city of the Phoenician coast (Arnaud 1992). The status of Sidon as an important coastal city of the same rank as Ugarit is attested in the fact that the king of Sidon addresses the king of Ugarit as his brother, thus considering him as his equal (184). The Ugaritic texts also mention an incident between the Sidonians and some citizens from Ugarit who are said to have offended the weather god of Sidon. The Sidonians wanted a severe punishment while their king wanted to reach a compromise in order not to jeopardize the diplomatic relations with Ugarit (185, 187). The epidemic that hit the city of Sidon after this incident was considered to be the retribution of the gods for the nonimplementation of the punishment.

The importance of the weather god in Late Bronze Age Sidon is reflected in the fact that, with the exception of Imtu (R.S. 11.723) and Anni-Wa, son of Addūmu (AO 22361), all the other attested Sidonian royal names are theophoric of Adad, the weather god (Arnaud 1992, 193): Yapaʿ-Adad (R.S. 25.430 A), Adad Yašmaʿ (R.S. 86.2221 and 86.2234), Addūmu (known from a seal inscription 22362), and Zimridda, mentioned in the Amarna letters. The latter attacked the city of Tyre and occupied its continental territory. This ruler called himself "mayor [ḫazanu] of Sidon" (Moran 1987, EA 144), while Abimilku of Tyre speaks of him as the "ruler of Sidon" (Moran 1987, EA 146, 154). The question arises here whether Zimridda was an official or governor appointed by the Egyptian pharaoh or whether he was a legitimate king belonging to the ruling dynasty of Sidon. In any case, he seems to have experienced trouble in his own kingdom since he complains that the cities placed under his control by the pharaoh joined the 'Apiru (144). The archaeological excavations on the College site demonstrated that Sidon continued to be a prosperous and an economic power in the Late Bronze Age and traded with the whole Eastern Mediterranean, namely, the Aegean (Doumet-Serhal 2013, 42 and figs. 43, 43a–e, 44), Cyprus, and Egypt.

The transition from the Late Bronze to the Iron Age was smooth, with no evidence for destruction and abandonment on the College Site. On the contrary, the discovery of the above-mentioned vase bearing the name of Queen Tawosret (Doumet-Serhal 2013, fig. 45) and dated around 1190 BCE "constitutes a document of fundamental significance for relations between Egypt and Sidon for the period of great upheaval in connection with the Peoples of the Sea. At this time relations between Sidon and Egypt continue, and Sidon remains untouched by the instability of the period" (Doumet-Serhal 2013, 45). That Sidon did not witness any upheaval during that period is also attested by the fact that Tiglath-pileser I mentions the tribute he collected from the city toward 1100 BCE, thus indicating that it was still a prosperous metropolis rich enough to awaken the greed of the Assyrian king. The Report of Wenamun confirms this picture and mentions the presence of fifty ships trading with Egypt in the harbor of Sidon. Recent archaeological evidence from the College Site has exposed a massive Iron Age I temple dedicated to funerary rites and thus has confirmed the fact that Sidon remained unharmed in the twelfth–eleventh centuries BCE (Doumet-Serhal forthcoming).

Little is known about Sidon in the period between the tenth and the eighth century BCE from both the written and the archaeological record. The Neo-Assyrian royal annals of Aššurnaṣirpal II mention the tribute of the kings of the seacoast among whom was the king of the land (KUR) of Sidon (Grayson 1991, A.0.101.1, iii, 84–85). No other information about the city is provided. Šalmaneser III received in his eighteenth regnal year the tribute of the lands of Tyre and Sidon after his Damascus campaign and the erection of his statue on cape Baalira'si (Grayson 1996, A.0.102, 25). Šamši-Adad V also mentions that he received the tribute of Sidon. No other information is available about that kingdom during the ninth century BCE.

Adad-nērārī III received also the tribute of the people of the land of Tyre and Sidon (Grayson 1996, A.0.104, 7, 8) but his annals do not add any further detail. Sidon is not mentioned in the annals of Tiglath-pileser III; only Tyre is. This has been noted by Katzenstein (1973, 210), who assumed that Sidon and Tyre had united before the reign of Tiglath-pileser III: "This silence about Sidon, together with the fact that the governor of Carthage in Cyprus calls his lord 'Hiram king of the Sidonians,' leads us to state that Hiram (like his predecessors) ruled over the strip between Sidon and Tyre." For Katzenstein (224), "there is no question that from the days of Ethbaal I, the father-in-law of Ahab, until 701 B.C.E., Sidon was an integral part of the kingdom of Tyre."

Sidon reappears in the Assyrian texts in the annals of Sennacherib who described his victory over Lulî, king of Sidon. According to Katzenstein (1973, 222) Lulî must have ascended the throne between 729—the year when Tiglath-pileser III became king of Babylon—and 727 BCE, and "continued to rule throughout the reigns of Shalmaneser V (726–722 BCE), Sargon (721–705 BCE) and into the reign of Sennacherib (704–681 BCE)." If this opinion is correct, then Lulî was still the king of the unified territory of Tyre and Sidon when Sennacherib attacked him. Scholars who are of this opinion were led to assume that the city depicted on the famous relief of Lulî's flight was the city of Tyre and not Sidon. They based this assumption on the depiction in the relief of a temple façade with two free-standing columns, which they believed to represent the Tyrian temple of Melqart as described by Herodotus (*Hist.* 2.44). This is not necessarily true since a similar temple could have existed also in Sidon. The proposition of Belmonte-Marín (2003) to date the separation of the two kingdoms in 725 BCE finds some support in the fact that Sennacherib's annals consistently grant Lulî the title "king of the city Sidon" and not king of the Sidonians or of the land of Sidon: "On my third campaign, I marched to the land Ḫatti. Fear of my lordly brilliance over[whelmed] Lulî, the king of the city Sidon, and he fled afar into [the midst of] the sea and disappeared" (Grayson and Novotny 2012, 15, iii, 1–5). This observation could lead to the suggestion that the two kingdoms split before the coming of Sennacherib. However, this is contradicted by the fact that the cities of Lulî enumerated in Sennacherib's annals belong to the territory of both Tyre and Sidon (Leichty 2011, 4, 32–34) and this would favor Katzenstein's opinion that the split between the two kingdoms occurred in 701 BCE. There is, however, no mention of that split in the Assyrian annals. On the contrary, Sennacherib says that he appointed 'Tu-ba'lu as king over all the enumerated cities of Lulî:" I placed Tu-Ba'lu on the royal throne over them (i.e. the cities enumerated in the previous lines) and imposed upon him tribute (and) payment (in recognition) of my overlordship to be delivered yearly (and) without interruption" (Grayson and Novotny 2012, 16, iii, 13–14). Elayi (2013a, 177) correctly noted that the territory of Sidon after the defeat of Lulî continued to include the cities between Sidon and Akko leaving only the island of Ṣurru in the hands of a local king of Tyre. Sennacherib kept the territory of the unified kingdom after 701, but he placed it under the rule of a king loyal to Assyria, thus weakening the power and influence of Tyre. It is difficult to identify at which point in time the splitting of the two kingdoms took place. It is highly probable that after the departure of Sennacherib, Tyre took advantage of the fact that Tu-Baʻlu was left without Assyrian support, and regained its lost cities south of the Litani River sometime between 701 and 677 BCE. When Esarhaddon created the province of Kar-Esarhaddon, the only two cities that he cut off from Sidon's territory were Sarepta and Maʻrubbu, thus implicitly inferring that Tyre owned already the cities south of the Litani River.

From 701 until 677 there is no mention of Sidon in the annals. Information resumes with the revolt of Abdi-Milkūti of Sidon. There is no clue to ascertain whether Abdi-Milkūti was a legitimate descendant of Tu-Baʻlu, or of Lulî, or whether he was an usurper. In any case he took advantage of the dynastic problems Esarhaddon had to face after the murder of his father to rebel against his Assyrian overlord. He allied himself with a Cilician king called Sanda-uarri, king of Kundi and Sissû, and both of them received a spectacular punishment: Sidon was razed to the ground, its king beheaded, the royal family and the retinue deported and all the riches of the city taken as booty:

> As for Abdi-Milkūti, king of Sidon, (who) did not fear my lordship (and did not listen to the words of my lips, who trusted in the rolling sea and threw off the yoke of the god Aššur-I leveled Sidon, his stronghold, which is situated in the midst of the sea, like a flood, tore out its wall(s) and its dwelling(s), and threw them into the sea; and I (even) made the site where it stood disappear. Abdi-milkūti, its king, in the face of my weapons, fled into the midst of the sea. By the command of the god Aššur, my lord, I caught him like a fish from the midst of the sea and cut off his head. I carried off his wife, his sons, his daughters, his palace retainers, gold silver, goods, property, precious stones, garments with trimming and linen(s), elephant hide(s), ivory, ebony, boxwood, everything of value from his palace in huge quantities (and) took away his far-flung people who were beyond counting, oxen, sheep and goats, and donkeys in huge numbers to Assyria. (Leichty 2011, 1, ii 65–80 and iii 20–38)

Two stelae commemorate the defeat of Abdi-Milkūti of Sidon: the stela of Sendjirli (Wartke 2005, fig. 60) and that of Til Barsip (Thureau-Dangin and Dunand 1936, pls. XII and XIII). On both of them the Egyptian king Taharqa and the Sidonian Abdi-Milkūti are represented chained and kneeling in front of the Assyrian king. It is surprising to find that the Phoenician king represented with Taharqa is the king of Sidon although it is nowhere mentioned that Sidon and Egypt were allies and were defeated during the same battle. On the other hand, the Phoenician king who is said to be the ally of Taharqa, the king of Kush, is Ba'lu, the king of Tyre (Leichty 2011: 60, 6′–9a′), not Abdi-Milkūti of Sidon. Furthermore, the campaign against Sidon took place in 677 during Esarhaddon's third campaign, whereas the campaign against Egypt happened during the tenth campaign of Esarhaddon. If Abdi-Milkūti was executed very quickly as the annals say, he could not have survived to be captured together with Taharqa. There are two possible explanations for this situation: the stelae symbolically represent either the capture of the two main opponents of Assyria and the latter's two main victories in the west, or the scribe has confused Ba'lu of Tyre with Abdi-Milkūti of Sidon.

The ally of Sidon against Assyria is clearly Sanduarri, a Cilician king, and not Egypt. Both kings were defeated and beheaded during the same year (see also Marti 2014):

> Moreover, Sanda-uarri, king of the cities of Kundi and Sissû, a dangerous enemy, who did not fear my lordship (and) abandoned the gods, trusted in the impregnable mountains. He (and) Abdi-Milkūti, king of Sidon, agreed to help one another, swore an oath by their gods with one another, and trusted in their own strength. I trusted in the gods...., my lords, besieged him, caught him like a bird from the midst of the mountains, and cut off his head. "In Tašrītu (VII)—the head of Abdi-Milkūti! In Addaru (XII)—the head of Sanda-uarri!" I beheaded both in the same year: With the former I did not delay, with the latter I was quick. To show the people the might of the god Aššur, my lord, I hung their heads around the heads of their nobles, and I paraded in the squares of Nineveh with singer(s) and lyre(s). (Leichty 2011, 1, iii 20–38)

The capture of Abdi-Milkūti and the destruction of his city were followed by the creation of the province Kar-Esarhaddon which put an end to the kingdom of Sidon. It is only in the Persian period that Sidon will be reborn as an independent kingdom and will resume its role as the leading Phoenician polity.

After the fall of Nineveh and before the rise of Nebuchadnezzar II, Egypt tried to recover its hegemony over the Phoenician cities under the reigns of Psammetic I and his son Neco II. In 608 Neco II led his army along the Phoenician coast on his way to the Euphrates and reestablished Egyptian hegemony from the coast to the Euphrates. Neco II built for himself a royal residence at Riblah, in the Eleutherus Valley. The same pharaoh commissioned Phoenician sailors to circumnavigate Africa according to the account of Herodotus (*Hist.* 4.42). His relation with Phoenicia is attested in the stela fragment bearing his name that was found in the Eshmun temple (Mathys 2005, 272 and n. 9). Egyptian finds from the Eshmun temple indicate that Egyptian involvement in Phoenicia was significant during the Twenty-Sixth Dynasty and Egyptian presence continued through the Twenty-Ninth Dynasty, as attested by the discovery of an inscription of Hakoris, who led a campaign to Phoenicia between 385 and 383 BCE (Lopriano 2005, 271). According to Hans-Peter Mathys, the relations between Egypt and the Eshmun temple were intensive under Hakoris's rule. This is not surprising, since the latter wanted to stop the Persian advance to Egypt and looked for allies in Phoenicia, Cyprus, and Asia Minor. Nebuchadnezzar II was able to chase the Egyptians out of Phoenicia and Palestine. Elayi (2013a, 210) adopts the explanation provided by Diodorus Siculus that Pharaoh Apries, the Hophra of the Bible, son of Psammetic II, took advantage of the fact that Nebuchadnezzar II was occupied with the siege of Jerusalem to control Tyre and Sidon. It is under the rule of this pharaoh that the Tyrians established their camp in Memphis. During this Egyptian interlude and the Babylonian rule, the history of Sidon remained almost completely in the dark for more than a century.

Unfortunately, the archaeological excavations at College Site have not yet filled the gap left by the sources for the period extending from the ninth to the sixth century BCE, at least no finds from that period have been published so far. By contrast, information about the kingdom of Sidon are quite substantial for the period of Persian domination. For this period, Phoenician inscriptions are available (Elayi 1989; Mathys 2005; Zamora 2008) as well as contemporary accounts by Herodotus about the relations of Sidon with the Persians. The historians of Alexander and the Sidonian coinage provide also some additional information about the last kings of that city.

The oldest royal inscriptions from Sidon during the Persian period are dated to the end of the sixth century BCE (for a discussion of the date of the Sidonian dynasty see Martin 2017, 104). When they resume with the inscription of King Tabnit (*KAI* 13), Sidon is an independent kingdom with a ruling dynasty which must have been established after the departure of the Egyptians and the Babylonians. We do not know who the founder of this dynasty was. The first king mentioned in this lineage is Eshmunazar I, the father of Tabnit (*KAI* 13), and he may have been the founder of that dynasty, since Tabnit does not mention his grandfather, whereas all the other kings of Sidon go back at least two generations in their genealogies. The Tabnit inscription was written on an Egyptian stone mummy sarcophagus that was brought back from Egypt probably as part of the booty given to the Sidonian king by the Persian overlord after the campaign against Egypt (Lembke 2001, 117). In this inscription, Tabnit calls himself and his father "king of the Sidonians" and not king of Sidon. All his successors bear the same title while other Phoenician kings call themselves king of their city or their kingdom: *mlk* followed by their city name, as is the case with the kings of Byblos, who called themselves *mlk gbl*, king of Byblos. The reason for choosing this title is not clear: In the absence of older Phoenician royal inscriptions from Sidon, it is difficult to decide whether this title was held by the kings before the Persian period or whether it originated when kingship resumed in Sidon at the end of the Babylonian empire. The fact that the eighth-century Phoenician inscription from Cyprus calls Hiram II of Tyre "king of the Sidonians" may suggest that this was the title borne by the king of the unified territory of Sidon and Tyre and that Sidonians was a generic term to indicate the people of southern Phoenicia. One would then spontaneously ask: Why Sidonians and not Tyrians? Maybe because Sidon was indeed the "mother of Tyre" and that since the foundation of Tyre by Sidonian refugees all the inhabitants of this joined territory were called Sidonians (Katzenstein 1973, 62). This may explain also the fact that Homer uses it to refer to Phoenicians in general, as is generally assumed.

If the title originated later, in the Persian period, it may have to do with the way the founder of the dynasty came to the throne. Was he acclaimed king by the assembly of the people, *'m ṣdn*, and thus took the title of king of the Sidonians? If this assumption is correct, did popular acclamation become a tradition and were all the kings of this dynasty acclaimed by the people to become legitimate rulers? Elayi (1989, 116l) correctly notes that *mlk ṣdnm*, king of the Sidonians (*roi des Sidoniens*), has no equivalent in the other states of the region, but she interprets *ṣdnm* as representing a political entity. The title *mlk ṣdnm* expresses, according to her, "The Sidonian political entity is based on the duality of the people and their king:

Ṣdnm (Sidonians) referred certainly to the 'people' of Sidon as a political entity."[14] This explanation is not very convincing because it does not give the historical justification for such an interpretation and does not explain what is understood by the people of Sidon: the inhabitants of the city or those of the whole territory?

This enigmatic appellation, which has been linked often to the political event of the unification of Tyre and Sidon, was recently discussed by Philip Boyes (2012). After systematically reviewing all the occurrences of this title used by Sidonian and Tyrian kings, Boyes concludes that in the Persian period the title that appears in the Sidonian inscriptions refers very simply to the royal title of the Sidonian kings. For him the ambiguity is the use of this title in earlier periods by Tyrian kings. This, however, he believes does not reflect an actual hegemony of Tyre over Sidon but indicates perhaps that the Tyrian king used the title king of the Sidonians to assert his identity vis a vis his foreign environment since foreigners whether Greeks or Israelites called the southern Phoenicians "Sidonians": "When it is used by, or of, the king of Tyre, 'Sidonian' more often seems to be intended in the sense that foreigners often used it, meaning any inhabitant of southern Phoenicia: what is being asserted is not, in fact, Tyre's rule over the specific city of Sidon but rather its more generalized status as part of the Phoenician world" (Boyes 2012, 42). The legend "Mother of the Sidonians" on the Tyrian coins should be understood also along these lines. While considering that a political union between Tyre and Sidon is plausible in the eighth century he questioned the narrative according to which Ittobaal may have conquered Sidon. The only clear evidence for such a joint territory is found in the Assyrian account of Lulli's defeat where his possessions that include the Tyrian cities are enumerated: "From the Assyrian sources, it seems clear that Luli was a king of Sidon who controlled Tyre, rather than vice-versa" (39).

Analyzing the title "King of the Sidonians," Maria Giulia Amadasi-Guzzo (2013) argued that the term ṣdnm is a plural of Sidon, ṣdn, referring to the "cities" of Sidon enumerated in the Eshmunazar II inscription, rather than the plural of ṣdny, Sidonian. The title would be "king of the Sidons," a proposition immediately adopted by Quinn (2018), who used it systematically in her book. Her argument is a grammatical one and is

---

14. Elayi 2005, 75: "l'entité politique sidonienne par la dualité du people et de son roi: ṢDNM ('Sidoniens') désignait certainement le 'peuple' de Sidon comme entité politique."

based on the fact that the plural of ṣdny, "Sidonian," should be ṣdnym, not ṣdnm. However, as Amadasi-Guzzo (2013, 263) herself pointed out, the fact that the Cos bilingual inscription mentions 'bd'lnm mlk ṣdnym suggests that the royal title of the kings of Sidon may have been indeed "King of the Sidonians."

Tabnit's inscription does not shed any further light on the political situation of the kingdom. The text is mainly a curse against looters. More information about Sidon can be found in the inscription of Eshmunazar II, Tabnit's son (KAI 14; see fig. 3.7 below). The inscription says that the king was an orphan, which means that Tabnit died when the crown prince was still a child. The queen mother, 'm'aštart, was regent during the childhood of Eshmunazar II, who also died at a very young age, probably without offspring and without a male sibling since his successor, Bod'aštart, is his cousin. Indeed, the latter's father did not rule since Bod'aštart does not name him in his genealogy, but he asserts the legitimation of his own rule by mentioning his grandfather, Eshmunazar I (KAI 15), king of the Sidonians. Further interesting information about the Sidonian royal house is that incestuous marriages existed among members of the royal family. Both 'm'aštart and Tabnit were children of Eshmunazar I. This tradition may have been the result of Egyptian influence since pharaohs often married their sisters. Elayi (1989, 110) believes that these consanguine marriages were meant to strengthen the royal lineage. Such marriages are attested in Ugarit as well as in Phoenician myths recounted by Philo of Byblos. The Eshmunazar inscription speaks of the building of several temples dedicated to the god Eshmun and the goddess Astarte, both in the mountains and in the harbor city as well as other places within the civic territory. No wonder that the kings of Sidon were mainly preoccupied with the building of temples, because one of their main roles or functions was to serve as high priests of the goddess Astarte, as attested in the Eshmunazar inscription. Both he and his father Tabnit are said to be khn 'štrt, high priest of Astarte.

Eshmunazar II is also the king who received the territories on the southern Palestinian coast as a gift from the Persian king and thus extended the territory of the kingdom and controlled two main harbors of the Palestinian coast: Dor and Jaffa (see above). He was too young and probably too sick to have participated personally in the Persian wars against Egypt, but his father and probably other members of the royal family did.

Eshmunazar's successor, Bod'aštart, left several inscriptions (Mathys 2005, 274 and n. 12; Chéhab 1983, 171; Xella and Zamora 2004), which

Fig. 3.7. Eshmunazar II's sarcophagus. Source: Wikimedia Commons.

were found in the podium of the Eshmun temple in Bustan esh-Sheikh. There is no reason to doubt that the lineage initiated by Bodʻaštart continued to rule in Sidon until the coming of Alexander the Great (for a list of Sidonian kings see Elayi 1989, 248). Mathys divides Bodʻaštart's inscriptions into three groups: one bears the name of the king, the month of his accession to the throne, and the name of the goddess Astarte; the second group mentions that he is the grandson of Eshmunazar I and that he built several temples in various places; a third group mentions the name of *ytnmlk*, the legitimate heir to the throne, as well as the building of a temple to Eshmun at the *Ydll* spring. The most recently discovered inscription of Bodʻaštart was found on the right bank of the Awwali River by Chéhab (1983, 171), who mentioned its discovery and gave a summary of its content. It has since disappeared, but Paolo Xella and José Zamora (2004) studied the text of the inscription based on the archives of the Directorate General of Antiquities. The search for the inscription provided the opportunity to explore the area of the Awwali River and to try to identify the remains of the works done by the Sidonian king to bring water from the river to the temple site (Xella et al. 2005). The inscription is not very clear and its reading is difficult, but some passages clearly indicate that it describes adduction works done by Bodʿaštart. Xella and Zamora (2004, 294) attempted a chronological sequence of the Bodʿaštart inscriptions and hence of the main achievements of his reign.

Bodʿaštart's inscriptions present him as a great builder who restored or built temples in the various districts of Sidon and who achieved the major task of adducting the waters of the Awwali River to the temple site. This intensive building activity indicates clearly that Sidon was in a very prosperous economic state since it was able to secure the means for major undertakings.

The sequence of Sidonian royal inscriptions stops after Bodʿaštart's rule. Between the inscriptions of Bodʿaštart (end of the sixth century BCE) and that of Baalshillem II (end of the fifth century BCE) there are no royal inscriptions from Sidon. Bodʿaštart says that he had a male heir, *ytnbʿl*, who was the crown prince, but we have no information about his rule.

After the rule of Bodʿaštart, the only sources that bring information about the political history of Sidon are the classical sources, since the Persian sources are almost mute. However, with the exception of Herodotus, Xenophon, and Thucydides, all classical sources are very late and will be used only selectively and cautiously to fill the gap left by the local inscriptions. These classical authors are mainly preoccupied with the role the Phoenicians played in the naval wars that the Persians undertook against the Greeks and against Egypt. The role of Sidon in particular is emphasized under the rule of Xerxes (486–465 BCE), who established privileged relations with Sidon and gave preeminence to its king in his protocol (*Hist.* 8.67–68). The commander of the Sidonian fleet is cited always before those of Tyre and Arwad (8.98). The preeminence of Sidon over the other Phoenician cities appears clearly from these passages. However, after the defeat of Salamis in 480 BCE, these relations deteriorated when Xerxes decided to execute the Phoenicians responsible for the Persian defeat.

Herodotus (*Hist.* 8.98) mentions a commander of the Sidonian fleet called Tetramnestus son of Anysus, contemporary of Xerxes. As we have seen previously, the fleet commanders are assumed to be the kings of the Phoenician cities. If this assumption is correct there would be two Sidonian kings who must have ruled in the second quarter of the fifth century BCE.

From the end of the fifth century BCE, we have the Phoenician inscription of Baalshillem II (Gibson 1982, 29) which was found in Bustan esh-Sheikh. It mentions four Sidonian kings: Baalshillem I, Baʻna, Abdamun, and Baalshillem II: "This (is the) statue that Baalshillem, son of King Baʻna, king of the Sidonians, son of King Abdamun, king of the Sidonians, son of King Baalshillem, king of the Sidonians, gave to his lord Eshmun at the Ydll Spring. May he bless him!" Nothing else is known about the rule of these four kings. Since the inscription is dated to the end of the fifth century, the first in this genealogy of four kings, Baalshillem I, must have ruled shortly after Tetramnestus since the rule of three kings, Baalshillem I, Baʻna, and Abdamun, should be fitted in the second half of the fifth century BCE. Baalshillem II, who was probably an adult when the inscription was written (Elayi 2005, 31), may have ruled in the last years of the fifth and first years of the fourth century BCE. Elayi (32–33) discusses in detail the various opinions relating to the dates of the reigns of these four kings, which generally fall within this chronological range mid-fifth to the first half of the fourth century BCE. She concludes that giving precise dates to their reign is difficult but that she is able to fix a *terminus post* and *ante quem* for their reign. The *terminus post quem* is the year 478, when Tetramnestus is mentioned as king of Sidon and the *terminus ante quem* is the year 365 when Straton I sat on the throne of Sidon according to Elayi's study and interpretation of the Sidonian coinage (Elayi 2005, 33).

The fourth century witnesses a series of defeats of the Phoenician fleets (Elayi 1989, 168–69; 2005, 58–61) in the Persian wars against Egypt and this situation may have led first to the Satraps' revolt and, second, to a conflict between the Phoenicians and the Persian kings (Elayi 1989, 173). Under the rule of Artaxerxes II (404–358 BCE) there is mention of a Sidonian fleet led by the king of the city at the battle of Cnidos in 394 BCE. Elayi (1989, 174) assumes that the king was Baalshillem II, the predecessor of Straton I. After the battle of Cnidos, we witness a shift in the foreign relations of Sidon. There is evidence for the deterioration of the relations with the Persian Empire and the birth of friendly relations with Egypt and Athens. The relations with Egypt are attested by the abovementioned inscriptions of Hakoris in the Eshmun temple and a new era of friendly relations with Athens was inaugurated by Straton I after the victory of Cnidos. They are attested by the Athenian decree in favor of the Sidonian king (Elayi 1989, 180) and the Phoenician merchant community established in Athens (Woolmer forthcoming). Straton I, Phoenician ʻAbdʻaštart, known also as "Straton Philhellene" (365–352), is known to us from a Greek inscription that was exhibited in the Athenian Acropolis (for a detailed study of the reign of this king, see Elayi 2005):

Fig. 3.8. Statue of Baalshillem II. Source: Directorate General of Antiquities.

> ... and to reply to the man who has come from the king of Sidon that, if in the future he is a good man to the People of Athens, he will not fail to obtain from the Athenians what he needs. Also Straton the king of Sidon shall be proxenos of the People of Athens, both himself and his descendants.... Let the Council also make tokens with the king of Sidon, so that the People of Athens may know if the king of Sidon sends anything when in need of the city, and the king of Sidon may know when the People of Athens sends anybody to him. Also invite the man who has come from the king of Sidon to hospitality in the city hall tomorrow." (Attic Inscriptions online IG II2, 141)

However, as underlined by Mark Woolmer (forthcoming), in this inscription the most significant honor was bestowed on the Phoenician merchant community established in Attica by exempting them from Athenian commercial taxes: "Effectively, this decree frees a number of Sidonian merchants from all financial obligations that were normally imposed by Athens on foreigners of metic or isotelēs status.... The hierarchical distinction that the decree bestows on the Sidonians may well be a reflection of their political system, in which wealthy merchant families exerted influence over the city's political life by their involvement in the king's council—hence the decree's insistence on characterizing the traders as, 'those who take part in the government,' in Sidon."

According to Elayi (2005, 105) this Athenian decree made the Sidonians privileged commercial partners of the Athenians and this is translated archaeologically by an increase of Attic vases in the fourth century in Sidon (for a recent study of Attic ceramics from Sidon see Haidar 2012). Straton I is known also from other sources to have brought from all parts of Greece young girls who served as singers and dancers (Elayi 2005, 94). The establishment of these new and friendly relations with Athens are attested by the influence Greek art had on Phoenician artifacts. The most striking examples are the Phoenician anthropoid sarcophagi which started representing Hellenizing features. Athenian craftsmen skilled in the working of marble may have been brought to the Sidonian workshops to teach the local stonecutters how to work marble stone (Lembke 2001, 117; Elayi 2005, 111; see fig. 3.9 below). This argument is rejected by Rebecca Martin (2017, 71), who thinks that these typical Phoenician objects were made by Phoenician artists:

> The two typical approaches to these objects, one emphasizing the important role of Greek sculptors in the invention of the type, the other stressing their gradual Hellenization away from the Egyptian type, are not supported by extant evidence. The peculiarity of the type and the experimentation evident in its many variations reinforce the idea that these attempts to assign ethnocultural identities to the objects' makers is unwise. The final artistic result only seems to us a pastiche, one that is surely indicative of specific, if unknown to us, Phoenician ideologies.

Another telling example of Greek influence during that century is the famous marble sarcophagus representing a Greek Ionian temple and weeping women, which may have belonged to Straton I, as suggested by many and adopted also by Elayi (for bibliography, see Elayi 2005, 106).

Finally, many have suggested that the Eshmun Tribune, which depicts mythological scenes involving Greek gods, was also completed under the reign of Straton I. The various opinions regarding the author (Straton I, Evagoras, or Straton II), date (Persian or Hellenistic) and meaning of this monument (whether Greek gods were adopted in the Sidonian pantheon) were discussed by Elayi (2005, 113–15), who finds it difficult to opt for one or the other opinion with the present state of the evidence. In her recent work, Martin (2017, 107) opts for an early Hellenistic date and suggests that the sculptor of the Alexander sarcophagus is also the creator of the tribune (see fig. 3.10).

Fig. 3.9. Anthropoid sarcophagi from Sidon: The Ford Collection. Source: Directorate General of Antiquities.

Scholars propose that the beginning of the Satraps' revolt against the king of Persia was the result of two successive defeats by Egypt. Sidon, together with other Phoenician cities, revolted against the Persians. At the time of the revolt, Straton I was still king of the city and may have revolted primarily because Persian demands and wars had pressured the Sidonians to the point that the situation had become unbearable. In 359 BCE, Straton I put an end to the alliance with the Persians for the first time in the history of Sidonian relations with Persia. Sidon's revolt was crushed by Artaxerxes III as attested by a Babylonian tablet mentioning the deportation of Sidonian prisoners to Babylon and Susa and dated to the fourth year of this king, in 355 BCE (Elayi 2005, 130). The punishment inflicted on Straton I was not terrible, since he was left on the throne but the control of the satrapy was now in the hands of the Persian satrap Mazday, who minted coins in Sidon (132, 138). Straton I is said to have died a violent death but the details of this event are unknown. The only remark is that his and his friend Nikokles's deaths were always mentioned together without further details (141).

Straton I's successor was Tennes, whose Phoenician name remains unknown (for the various proposals, see Elayi 2005, 144). He was favorable to the Persians and may have been appointed by them, as suggested by Elayi (145).

Fig. 3.10. Eshmun Tribune. Source: Directorate General of Antiquities.

Tennes inherited a bad economic situation and he had to submit to the will of a large part of the population who rebelled against the Persians. The latter's bad treatment and impositions had become intolerable. Frightened at the size of the Persian army he betrayed his city and his people. The only source that provides a detailed description of this event is Diodorus Siculus, but the historicity of his account is still questioned by some scholars:

> Tennes, ... with five hundred men, marched out of the city, pretending that he was going to a common meeting of the Phoenicians, and he took with him the most distinguished of the citizens, to the number of one hundred, in the role of advisers. When they had come near the King he suddenly seized the hundred and delivered them to Artaxerxes. The King, welcoming him as a friend, had the hundred shot as instigators of the revolt.... So Sidon by this base betrayal was delivered into the power of the Persians; and the King, believing that Tennes was of no further use to him, put him to death. (*Bibl. hist.* 14.45.1–6)

Those who stayed in the city burned their ships to prevent anyone from escaping, and as Artaxerxes entered the city they preferred to burn themselves with their families inside their houses instead of surrendering. The Sidonian houses contained so many riches that the looters were able to collect large quantities of melted silver and gold. As a result of this event it has been conjectured that the Persian king placed a foreigner on the throne of Sidon, a certain Evagoras who ruled from 346 to 343 BCE. His rule was bad and he was followed on the throne by ʿAbdʿaštart II, who ruled until the coming of Alexander the Great. The latter removed ʿAbdʿaštart II and replaced him on the throne of Sidon by a certain Abdalonymos, ʿbd ʾlnm. Scholars have suggested that the so-called Alexander Sarcophagus that was found in the royal necropolis of Ayaa may have belonged to this last king of Sidon (for a discussion of this suggestion and relevant bibliography see Martin 2017, 138). We do not know who followed him on the throne of Sidon, but kingship was abolished in this city definitely in 278 BCE (Sartre 2001, 149).

Table 3.3. The kings of Sidon (after Elayi 2018, table 2)

| Name of King | Date |
|---|---|
| Ittobaal | (ca. 701 BCE) |
| Abimilku | (ca. 677 BCE) |
| *Assyrian province* | (677–610 BCE) |
| Eshmunazar I | (ca. 575–550 BCE) |
| Tabnit | (ca. 550–540 BCE) |
| Amoashtart | (ca. 539 BCE) |
| Eshmunazar II | (ca. 539–525 BCE) |
| Bodʿaštart | (ca. 524–515 BCE) |
| Yatonmilk? | (after 515 BCE) |
| Anysus? | (before 480 BCE) |
| Tetramnestus | (480 BCE) |
| Abdamun | (401–366 BCE) |
| Baʿna | |
| Baalshillem II | |
| ʿAbdʿaštart I | (365–352 BCE) |
| Tennes | (351–347 BCE) |
| Evagoras II | (346–343 BCE) |
| ʿAbdʿaštart II | (342–333 BCE) |

3.1.4. The Kingdom of Tyre

3.1.4.1. The Territory of Tyre

Tyre, ancient Ṣurru, modern Ṣūr, "the rock" in Semitic, is located 40 km south of Sidon and circa 80 km south of the capital Beirut. The topography of Tyre drastically changed over the centuries. According to the

Fig. 3.11. Bronze coin of Tyre minted in the reign of Emperor Gallienus (253–268 CE) depicting an olive tree flanked by two ambrosial rocks and the hound of Hercules standing before a murex shell. Source: Classical Numismatic Group, LLC. Triton XXII, Lot 729. 29 mm, 18.88 gr. www.cngcoins.com.

ancient sources, Tyre was an island circa 750 m away from the shore (for the various estimates of this distance, see Katzenstein 1973, 10). More recently, geomorphologists working in Tyre estimated the distance to be 2 km (Carmona and Ruiz 2004, 207). The Neo-Assyrian sources describes it as being *ša qabal tâmtim*, "in the midst of the sea," and it is represented as an island on Shalmaneser III's famous gates of Balawat (Pritchard 1954, fig. 356). The city kept its insular character until its conquest by Alexander the Great, who built a mole to link it to the mainland in 332 BCE. According to Nicolas Carayon (forthcoming), who investigated the island as well as the opposite shore, there was a proto-tombolo on top of which Alexander's mole was built. This mole is to be looked for under the modern tombolo.

Josephus (*C. Ap.* 1.113) reports that Tyre was built on two islands that were joined together by King Hiram I to enlarge the area of the city. The legend about the two Ambrosian rocks says that they were floating in the sea with an olive tree; after a sacrifice was offered, they came to rest, and the city was built on them (Hill 1910, cxii). They are represented on Tyrian coins of the second and third century CE (Hill 1910, 281, no. 430, plate XXXIII, no. 15; see fig. 3.11 above). No modern geomorphological investigation was done to verify the legend. Jules De Bertou (1843, 89) speaks of a canal that linked the northern harbor to the southern one: "The military harbors separated by the island itself communicated through a canal that crossed the city, and their only entrance was directed toward Sidon."[15] His statement has not been evinced by recent investigations.

---

15. De Bertou 1843, 89: "Les ports militaires, séparés par l'île elle-même, avaient

There is no consensus among scholars about the area of Ṣurru after the joining of the two islands (Belmonte-Marín 2003, 110–11). Katzenstein (1997, 10) is of the opinion that the island was 57.6 ha in size, while Constantin-François Volney (1787, 10) speaks of 42 ha. Bikai (1987a, 76; 1992, 68) estimated the area of the island to be 16 ha. According to the recent marine surveys, part of the city is now underwater, and it is thus difficult to assess its exact ancient size.

Until the 1940s one could see on aerial photographs (Poidebard 1939, pl. I; see fig. 3.12) the boundaries of the former island, which is located on the tip of the peninsula created by the deposition of sand along the sides of the mole built by Alexander. The tombolo formation was investigated, and geomorphologists found a large depression in the al-Baṣṣ area where the Phoenician necropolis is located. It was a lagoon in antiquity that became a swampy area that still existed in the nineteenth century (Carmona and Ruiz 2004, fig. 121). Recent filling activities reclaimed large areas of the sea on the southern side of the mole and enlarged substantially its area. The anarchic urbanization that started at the end of the 1960s filled the latter as well as the former island area with buildings which have almost completely obliterated the island's ancient topography.

The island of Tyre had two harbors, according to Arrian (*Anab.* 2.20.9–10): one facing Sidon and one facing Egypt. The investigation of the harbors of Tyre was the pioneering work of Poidebard (1939), who, for the first time, made a combined use of aerial photography, maritime, and land investigation. His work focused on the southern or Egyptian harbor (23 and carte II), where he thought he recognized, opposite the island's shore, a 750 m long and 8 m thick mole with one entry in its center (25), called Bab el Mina by the locals (27), as well as several other moles, which formed the harbor basins. Poidebard investigated also a natural reef, *rade sud* (carte III), which stretches from the western corner of the island in a north-south direction over a length of 1,200 m and which, according to him, was enhanced by human made walls, to form a natural shelter (31–32). However, the mere existence of this southern harbor was proven wrong by Frost (1971, 105ff.; 2005, 45), whose investigation also showed that there were no stone blocks in the reef, that the fissuring was natural, and that Poidebard's divers mistook the layering of the rocks with masonry.[16] She accepted, however, his

---

été mis en communication par un canal qui traversait la ville, et leur unique entrée, tournée vers Sidon."

16. The same mistake was recently made by Sidonian divers who spread the news

Fig. 3.12. Aerial photograph of the island of Tyre. Source: Poidebard 1939, plate I.

interpretation of the structure as an offshore anchorage. Recent investigations have also confirmed that the *rade sud* is a natural reef (Morhange 2005, 130).

Recent investigations by interdisciplinary teams (El-Ammouri et al. 2005, 106; Frost 2005, 47–48) have clearly shown that there were no southern harbor installations at Tyre in the area investigated by Poidebard and that—as already suspected by Frost (1971, 108)—the whole "harbor" area is but an immersed industrial urban district: "The Egyptian harbor of Poidebard seems to correspond to an ancient urban district, a type of fill reclaimed from the sea, submerged, and eroded."[17] The southern harbor, if it existed, should be sought at another location on the southern shore of the former island. Boreholes were done at the southeast corner of the island next to the so-called Algerians tower but they have not identified any harbor installations. However, "The coastal stratigraphy clearly demonstrates that this leeward coastal fringe was a well-protected façade from the Bronze Age onwards. Although no diagnostic harbour facies have been found, we hypothesise that this area was the most conducive envi-

---

that they had found an immersed city opposite the shore of Tell el-Burak, confusing the layering of rocks with masonry. See Mainberger 2001, 191–93.

17. Morhange 2005, 129: "Le port égyptien de Poidebard semble correspondre à un quartier urbain antique, de type terre-plein gagné sur la mer, immergé et érodé."

ronment for the establishment of a second anchorage haven at Tyre" (Marriner, Morhange, and Carayon 2008, 1304).

Regarding the northern or Sidonian harbor of ancient Tyre, it was thoroughly investigated recently by a multidisciplinary team of specialists (Carayon 2005; Marriner et al. 2005b; Noureddine and El-Hélou 2005; Marriner, Morhange, and Carayon 2008). Its location is indicated by the modern harbor. However, the results of various boreholes (Marriner et al. 2005a, fig. 2; 2005b; 2008) and underwater reconnaissance "indicate that the harbour basin was much more extensive in its southern portion, and was most probably installed within the confines of a semi-protected natural cove" (Marriner et al. 2005a, 85; Marriner, Morhange, and Carayon 2008, 1282). According to Marriner, it was 40 percent larger than the actual one during the Middle Bronze Age (Marriner et al. 2005b, fig. 17) and is today under the Ottoman and medieval city. As was the case with Sidon's northern harbor, the Tyrian Bronze Age northern harbor was a semiopen marine cove until the first millennium BCE. This proto harbor is dated to the Middle Bronze Age (Marriner et al. 2005b, 1319). As was also the case in Sidon, the first-millennium strata were absent, and this is due to intensive dredging in the Roman period. The experts concluded that "the city's current coastal physiography differs significantly from the Phoenician, Hellenistic, and Roman periods" (Marriner et al. 2005a, 85).

Ibrahim Noureddine and Michel El-Hélou (2005, 156) say that they have retrieved evidence for the Persian period harbor. They dated a mole to Iron Age III based on its building technique. Carayon (forthcoming) is of the opinion that it was not substantial enough to shelter boats and that it might have served rather as a quay for the unloading of goods. Marriner (with Morhange and Carayon 2008, 1290–91), however, thinks that there is some evidence for "a well-protected harbor during the Persian period" but admits that "insights into Tyre's Phoenician and later Persian ports are marred by the relative absence of Iron Age sediments."

Next to the northern and southeastern harbors of Tyre, recent investigations (Marriner, Morhange, and Carayon 2008, 1307) have identified other harbor complexes: some are outer anchorages that have exploited the reefs and ridges north and south of the city, while others were on the mainland at Tall Mashuq, Chawakir, and Rašidiyye, respectively east and south of the city.

Sweet-water supply was one of Tyre's main problems because water was not available on the island. There is evidence that it was brought by boats from Ras el ʿayn, an abundant natural spring south of Tyre, near Tell el-Rašidiyye. The latter was identified as ancient Ušû, the Palaetyrus (Old Tyre) of the Greeks (Bagg 2007, 272–73). Evidence for Tyre's dependence on the mainland for water supply is clearly expressed in letters from the El-Amarna archives sent by its king Abimilku to Pharaoh: "May the king give attention to his servant, and may he charge his commissioner to give Usu to his servant for water, for fetching wood, for straw, for clay" (Moran 1987, EA 148). Papyrus Anastasi 1 brings also the same information about water being brought from Ušû: "Where is the stream of Netchen (i.e. Litani River)? What is Uzu like? They tell of another city in the sea, Tyre-the-port is its name. Water is taken over to it in boats, and it is richer in fishes than in sand" (see Fischer-Elfert 1986, §17). Cisterns were also built to collect and store water and wells were dug to get water in time of siege (Katzenstein 1997, 15).

That the island of Ṣurru controlled a large territory on the mainland is suggested by the fact that the Assyrian annals speak of the land of Tyre, $^{kur}$ṣurri as well as of the city of Tyre, (Bagg 2007, 235), which obviously refers to the island city and to the mainland area it controlled. Tyre's territory in the Late Bronze Age (see also Belmonte-Marín 2003, 104) extended on the mainland opposite the island city. The main source of information about it are the Tell el-Amarna letters. To the south it was limited probably by Rās en-Nāqūra, since Akko was at that time an independent city-state and included probably the plain extending between Rās en-Nāqūra and the bay of Akko. A Ugaritic text (Malbrant-Labat 1991, 57) mentions rāš ṣūri, the cape of Tyre, as belonging to the territory of the city. This cape was identified with Rās el Abiad, the White Cape south of Tyre (Bordreuil 1992a; Belmonte-Marín 2001, 231). To the north, it probably reached the Qasimiyye River, which formed a natural boundary, but there is no explicit reference to this fact except maybe the above-mentioned passage in Papyrus Anastasi I, which seems to describe the territory of Tyre as extending from the Litani River to Rās en-Nāqūra. Tyre lost the portion of its territory that extends from the Litani River to Ušû to Sidon, when Zimridda, mayor of Sidon, attacked Tyre (Moran 1987, EA 151), occupied its territory as far as Ušû, and deprived the island from its water, clay, and straw supply (Moran 1987, EA 149). We do not know how long the Sidonian occupation of the Tyrian territory lasted.

Information about Tyre's territory in the Iron Age comes from the Hebrew Bible and from the Assyrian royal annals. According to the biblical account, "King Solomon gave Hiram twenty towns in the land of Galilee"

(1 Kgs 9:11). Lemaire (1991b; see also Katzenstein 1997, 105) has identified these sites and has argued that until the creation of the province of Dor and Megiddo, the southern limit of Tyre's territory was Mount Carmel: "Since 945 until the annexation of Megiddo and Dor by the Assyrians, the southern border of the kingdom of Tyre … seems to have been located at the foot of Mount Carmel."[18] The archaeological evidence from the lower Galilee sites has demonstrated that all this area had a material culture very similar to that of Phoenicia and that the excavated sites—Horbat Rosh Zayit (Gal and Alexander 2000, 198), Keisan (Briend and Humbert 1980) and Abu Hawam (Balensi 1985; Balensi, Herrera, and Artzy 1993)—have yielded evidence for large scale cereal as well as olive oil production, commodities badly needed by the Tyrians and requested as payment for their contribution to the building of the Jerusalem palace and temple (1 Kgs 5:23).

The evidence from the Assyrian royal annals seems to confirm Lemaire's conclusion. The earliest mention of a Tyrian city is found in the annals of Shalmaneser III. After the Damascus campaign during his twenty-first regnal year, the Assyrian king went to the land of Tyre and erected a statue in the temple of the city Laruba: "Baʻal, the man of [Tyr]e, submitted to me (and) I received tribute from him. I erected my royal statue in the temple of the city Laruba, his fortified city. Now the tribute of the inhabitants of the lands Tyre, Sidon, (and) Byblos I received" (Grayson 1996, 102.16, 161'). The king of Tyre, Baʻal, mentioned in the inscription is probably the same person referred to as Baʻali-Manzēri, king of Tyre (Bagg (2007, 157), who was also a contemporary of Shalmaneser III (Grayson 1996, 102.10, iv, 10). Laruba is an enigmatic city and cannot be identified with certainty. According to the itinerary followed by Shalmaneser III after his campaign against Hazael, this city should be sought probably on the coast, south of Tyre. Between Rās en-Nāqūra and Rās el-Abiad there are two identifiable tells mentioned by travelers: Tell Irmid/Ermes and Tell ed-Dabaa, but they have not been investigated, and we do not know whether they were occupied in the Iron Age. A third candidate for Laruba is Ṭaybe, an archaeological site 89 km south of Beirut, from where the inscribed throne of Astarte (*KAI* 17), now in the Louvre Museum, is said to come. According to Denyse Le Lasseur (1922, 124), the throne was found "encastré et couvert de ciment" (embedded in and covered with cement), which says little about the nature

---

18. Lemaire 1991b, 152: "de 945 à l'annexion de Megiddo et de Dor par les Assyriens la limite méridionale du royaume de Tyr … semble avoir été située au pied du Mont Carmel."

of the building and the site. But since these Astarte thrones were usually *ex-votos* offered to the temple, it is possible that the building had a religious nature if the throne was still in situ when found. The identification of Laruba must await a thorough survey of the Tyre area. The difficulty in identifying this city has led Shigeo Yamada (2000, 209) to suggest amending it to *ma-ru-ba* and identified it with Maʾrubbu.

Cities belonging to Tyre are mentioned in the annals of Sennacherib, who enumerated the conquered cities of the unified kingdom of Tyre and Sidon. As we have already seen, this kingdom extended from Anfe in north Lebanon to Mount Carmel in the south. The cities located south of Sarepta, "Maḫalliba, Ušû, Akzibu, (and) Akko" (Leichty 2011, 4, 32–34), respectively, Maḫalib, north of Tyre; Tell el-Rašidiyye near Rās el-ʿayn, 5 km south of Tyre; Akhziv, modern ez-Zib, 15 km north of Akko; and Akko, modern ʿAkka (Bagg 2007, 164, 272, 4, 3, respectively), belonged to the territory of Tyre (see also Katzenstein 1997, 106). That Tyre's territory did not reach beyond the Litani River in the Iron Age may be inferred from a passage of Esarhaddon's annals where the Assyrian king says that he cut off the cities of Sarepta and Maʾrubbu from the territory of Sidon and gave them to the king of Tyre: "From among those cities of his [i.e., Abdi-Milkūti's] I handed over the cities Maʾrubbu (and) Sarepta to Baʿalu, king of Tyre" (Leichty 2011, 1, iii 15–16). These two cities were probably the natural northern extension of Tyre's territory beyond the Litani River. So since the tenth century BCE the territory of Tyre extended from the Qasimiyye River in the north to Akko in the south. In 677 it was enlarged to the north by the addition of Sarepta and Maʾrubbu. To the east it extended to the hills overlooking the coast leading across the mountains to Palestine (Dussaud 1927, 21–22), and included the twenty villages of the Galilee sold by Solomon to Hiram according to the Bible.

Tyre seems to have kept control of this large territory until the Persian period. This is attested on the one hand by the fiscal seals from the reign of ʿOzzimilk, who was ruling when Alexander conquered the city. These seals mention several localities belonging to the kingdom of Tyre (Lemaire 1994): Lbt, identified with Tell Abu Hawam; Sarepta; Bt-Zt, identified either with Bīt-Zitti or with Zayta; Akshaph, identified with Tell Keisan; and Bt-Bṭn, biblical Beten, 8 miles from Akko (see also Belmonte-Marín 2003, 117–18). It is attested also by the *Periplus* of Pseudo-Scylax (104): Tyre not only had kept its territory but seems to have enlarged it at the expense of Sidon, which was weakened by its conflict with Persia. Tyre had extended its dominion over the Plain of Sharon with the exception of Dor, and over the city of Ashkelon. Belmonte-Marín (2003, 118) is, however, of the opinion that Dor too became part of the Tyrian territory, as assumed also by Lemaire (2013a, 34).

### 3.1.4.2. A Political History of Phoenician Tyre

The history of the kingdom of Tyre has been dealt with by Wallace Fleming (1966) and Katzenstein (1973; 1997). The latter made an exhaustive study of the city's history from the Middle Bronze Age until the end of the Neo-Babylonian period, using Egyptian, Assyrian, Babylonian, classical, and biblical sources. His book remains a major reference on the history of the kingdom and has not been superseded by any other publication on that topic. Katzenstein's (1979) history was complemented by several publications on the city's history during the Persian period (Elayi and Elayi 2009; Elayi 2013a, part 4; Lemaire 1991a; 1994). The only updates to his history are the recent archaeological investigations in and around Tyre and in the Galilee and their implications.

The economic and political heart of the kingdom was the island of Tyre. The insular city settlement was founded around 2700 BCE, according to the account of Herodotus: "I talked to the priests of the god (Heracles) there and asked them how long ago the sanctuary was founded, and I discovered that they too disagreed with the Greek account, because according to them the sanctuary of the god was founded at the same time as Tyre, which was 2,300 years ago, they said" (*Hist.* 2.44 [Waterfield]). The results of Bikai's (1978a, 72) archaeological sounding on the island of Tyre concur with the date given by the priests for the city's foundation, since the earliest evidence from the sounding was dated to 2700 BCE. The area next to Bikai's sounding is being investigated by the University of Pompeu Fabra at Barcelona, and the results may throw new light on the island's settlement history.

There is no evidence for the foundation of Ušû, called Palaetyrus by the Greeks, and located on the modern Tell el-Rašidiyye. There may have been an older settlement there, near the abundant Rās el-ʿayn springs. However, the only excavations that took place on that site were those of Theodor Macridy Bey (1904, 564–70) and the salvage excavations that the Department of Antiquities undertook in a very hasty way in the early 1970s (Chéhab 1983; Doumet 1982). Both excavations reported Iron Age inhumation and cremation tombs, but no information was published about the occupation history of the site. The actual establishment of the Tyrian polity must have awaited the foundation of the settlement on the island, which developed soon into a maritime stronghold with an active harbor.

The earliest mention of Tyre is in the Egyptian execration texts dated to the early Thirteenth Dynasty (Helck 1962, 53). The city is mentioned as ṣu-u-r-u-ja and was ruled by a king whose name is lost partly in the break (58). This mention of a king of Tyre ruling in the eighteenth century BCE is somewhat puzzling since the island city was not inhabited in the Middle Bronze Age, as demonstrated by the results of Bikai's (1978a, 72) sounding, who raised this issue. Archaeological excavations revealed that the settlement was covered by a layer of sterile sand without any trace of occupation from circa 2000 to circa 1600 BCE, as was also the case of the College Site in Sidon. According to Bikai (72): "It is unlikely that that there was any city of Tyre during the period of the Execration texts." Was the king mentioned in the execration texts ruling before the abandonment of the city? Or was he ruling from another place on the mainland? There is no satisfactory answer to this question. In any case, this mention indicates that Tyre was already an independent polity with a monarchical system as early as the Middle Bronze Age.

Tyre is not mentioned in the inscriptions of the Eighteenth Dynasty kings, and its second occurrence in the Egyptian records is in the inscriptions of Seti I (see above), but it appears in the Late Bronze Age texts of Ugarit and in the Amarna letters (Belmonte-Marín 2001, 253–54).

Both Ṣurru and Ušû are mentioned in these texts, and the former is clearly the insular city, capital of the kingdom and residence of its king, whereas Ušû, modern Tell el-Rašidiyye, is the continental settlement near the natural springs of Rās el-ʿayn. The Tell el-Amarna letters are our main source for the political history of Tyre in the Late Bronze Age. In these texts Tyre appears as a very wealthy and prosperous city, and the palace of its ruler is said to be as beautiful as that of Ugarit: "Will the king not make an inquiry about the mayor of Tyre? For his property is as great as the sea. I know it. Look, there is no mayor's residence like that of the residence in Tyre. It is like the residence in Ugarit. Exceedingly [gr]eat is the wealth in it" (Moran 1987, EA 89). In spite of the close relationship of the Tyrian royal family with Egypt and its loyalty to Pharaoh, we hear from Rib-Adda of Byblos that during a rebellion the royal family of Tyre, to which he was related through the diplomatic marriage of his sister with the Tyrian king, was murdered by the people of the city. Pharaoh took no action to help his loyal mayor, and even after the murder of the latter Pharaoh did not punish the usurper: "I made connubium with Tyre; they were on good terms with me. But now they have, I assure you, killed their mayor together with my sister and her sons.... He wrote again and again to the king, but his words went unheeded. And so he died" (Moran 1987, EA 89). Both the ruler's and the usurper's name are not mentioned. Most probably, the wealth of the Tyrian ruler caused the greed of his opponent, who fomented a rebellion against him and seized the throne. The wealth of the city is emphasized by Rib-Adda in order to incite Pharaoh to avenge the dead king and reclaim his property. These events happened in the last years of Amenhotep III or in the tenth year of Akhenaten (Katzenstein 1997, 31–32 with bibliography).

Katzenstein (1997, 32) suggests that after Akhenaten's military intervention in Syria "the usurper disappeared and the former (?) royal dynasty was returned to power." Information about Tyre resumes with the letters of King Abimilku, who was an ally and an appointee of Egypt: "The king, my lord, charged me with guarding Tyre.... I am a commissioner of the king, my lord, and I am one that brings good news and also bad news to the king my lord" (Moran 1987, EA 149). While all other rulers are called ḫazanu, Abimilku bore the higher title of rabiṣu. He was a trustworthy commissioner and reported to Pharaoh about the situation in Canaan (Moran 1987, EA 151). His letters are dated to the second half of Akhenaten's reign (Katzenstein 1997, 33). His intended trip to Egypt was the reason for the attack of Zimridda of Sidon: "He heard that I was going to Egypt, and so he waged war against me" (Moran 1987, EA 151). The occupation of Ušû by Zimridda deprived Tyre of its water, wood, and clay supply as well as the burial ground of its people.

After the letter of Abimilku, information about the situation in Tyre stopped. It seems that the conflict between the Hittites and Egypt weakened the latter's control over its provinces, which tried to regain their autonomy. This is inferred by the inscriptions of Seti I, who led a campaign against the Levant to reimpose his dominion over its cities (Helck 1962, 200): Both Ṣurru and Ušû are mentioned in his lists of conquered cities (202), which implies that Tyre, too, had tried to free itself from the Egyptian yoke.

The Ugaritic texts do not contribute much information about Tyre's internal political situation in the Late Bronze Age. The thirteenth-century BCE legend of Keret mentions a temple of Asherah in Tyre (*KTU* I, 14, IV 32–39, 201). Three documents shed light on the trade and diplomatic relations between the two kingdoms (Belmonte-Marín 2003, 103–4). The kings of the kingdoms seem to have been of equal rank. Noteworthy is the mention of Tyre's dyed textiles as one of the main goods exported by the city. Close commercial and political relations between the kings of Ugarit and Tyre are also attested elsewhere (*KTU* 2.38). In this letter, the king of Tyre returns all the goods from a recently wrecked Ugaritic vessel to its owners.

In sum, Tyre in the Late Bronze Age was a monarchy, was a vassal of Egypt, was under the reign of Abimilku, and was in conflict with the neighboring kingdom of Sidon. In spite of the great wealth and economic prosperity of the kingdom, the internal situation was not always stable, and rebellions could break out and bring usurpers to the throne. Tyre tried to free itself from Egyptian dominion, but Seti I's campaign put an end to this attempt for autonomy.

The transition from the Bronze to the Iron Age went smoothly, and no disruption was evidenced in the archaeological record (Bikai 1978a, 73): "In this small excavation, there was no evidence of a massive destruction level between Strata XV and XIV but in so limited an area this is not decisive." Like Sidon and Sarepta, the island of Tyre witnessed no destruction, disruption, or radical cultural change that could be ascribed to the Sea Peoples or to any other major military event. There is a clear continuity in settlement and material culture, which are in the tradition of the previous Late Bronze Age culture. One has to mention in this context the tradition reported by Justin and Josephus that Tyre was refounded by Sidonian refugees after the destruction of the Phoenician cities by the king of the Ashkelonians, one year before the Trojan War or 240 years before the building of the temple of Jerusalem, circa 1200 BCE (Katzenstein 1997, 59–62, 84). This implies that Tyre was destroyed by the Sea Peoples and rebuilt by the Sidonians, a fact that is contradicted by the available archaeological record. However, this tradition seems to have been part of the Sidonian historical heritage and is illustrated on the Sidonian coins (Houghton, Lorber, and Hoover 2008, 83, no. 1454). But Tyrian coins claim exactly the opposite, namely, that Sidon was refounded by Tyre: *lṣr ʿm ṣdnm* = "of Tyre, mother [city] of the Sidonians" (Houghton, Lorber, and Hoover 2008, 85–86, nos. 1463–65)! Both these claims are very late and date to the Roman period. Their historicity can be doubted, and they may have been the result of the long-standing competition between these two cities for the economic and political supremacy over Phoenicia in classical times. Notwithstanding the above evidence, the destruction of Tyre is nowhere documented in contemporary sources, but some scholars have interpreted the absence of Tyre in the annals of Tiglath-pileser I (Grayson 1991, A.0.87.3:20–21) as evidence for its destruction. Tyre is mentioned in the Report of Wenamun only as a stopover of the Egyptian envoy on his way to Byblos, while he mentions the large commercial fleet of Sidon that impressed him. This has also been interpreted as evidence for the political irrelevance of Tyre versus the importance of Sidon in Iron Age I.

Whether the above-mentioned tradition of Tyre's refoundation by Sidon commemorates a historical event or not, the available evidence seems to suggest the preeminence of Sidon over Tyre at the end of the Late Bronze Age and beginning of the Iron Age. This might explain, as previously mentioned, the use of the generic term *Sidonians* to refer to the (southern?) Phoenicians in both the Homeric epics and the biblical text.

There are unfortunately no contemporary sources relating to Tyre before the reign of Šalmaneser III, except maybe some reliefs on the Balawat gates of Aššurnaṣirpal II (Barnett, Curtis, and Tallis 2008, 14, table 2.1, R3; probably also 52, table 4.1, L4, L5, and R4; see fig. 3.13), which may represent the city of Tyre. The Iron Age kings of Tyre, unlike those of Byblos and Sidon, left no inscriptions or official documents. The only contemporary historical sources are the Neo-Assyrian royal annals and a few economic and administrative documents from Assyria and Babylonia. The most famous are the so-called Nimrud letters, mainly those of Qurdi-Aššur-lamur (Saggs 2001), which show that the merchants of the Phoenician harbors of Tyre and Sidon were taxed and expected to boycott Assyria's political enemies, at that time the Philistine cities and Egypt. The recent archaeological evidence from the Tyre al-Baṣṣ cemetery has proven that the inhabitants of the island were using the burial ground since the eleventh century BCE (Aubet 2004). So the island was settled and prospered, but no written documents inform us about that period.

All the accounts of the books of Kings and the Chronicles as well as the account of Josephus dealing with the relations between Tyre and the Israelite kings during the tenth century BCE are later than the events themselves and should be used critically (for the relations of Tyre with the kings of Israel and Judah, see Briquel-Chatonnet 1992). The annals of Tyre translated into Greek by Menander of Ephesus and mentioned by Josephus are often quoted by ancient authors as their reliable source for the history of the city, mainly for the relations between Hiram I and Solomon. Unfortunately, the original Phoenician archives, as well as the work of Menander, has not survived, but the existence of the Tyrian archives cannot be doubted and has been universally accepted. They were still

Fig. 3.13. Tyrians transporting the tribute from the island to the mainland as depicted on the Bronze gates of Balawat. Source: British Museum.

available for consultation in the first century BCE according to Josephus (*C. Ap.* 1.111; 8.55). Another problem concerning the historicity of the narrated events relating to the relations between Hiram I and the Israelite kings is the recently raised issue about the historicity of David and Solomon. For instance, doubt has been cast on the accounts involving them, and it has been argued on the basis of the archaeological evidence that Jerusalem was not a major city in the tenth century BCE and could not have housed a large palace and temple complex:

> The David and Solomon narratives have recently been called into question. The actual extent of the Davidic "empire" is hotly debated. Digging in Jerusalem has failed to produce evidence that it was a great city in David or Solomon's time. And the monuments ascribed to Solomon are now more plausibly connected with other kings. Thus the reconsideration of the evidence has enormous implications. For if there were no patriarchs, no Exodus, no conquest of Canaan—and no prosperous united monarchy under David and Solomon—can we say that early biblical Israel … ever existed at all? (Finkelstein and Silberman 2001, 124)

In addition, both kings are absent from extrabiblical sources except for the Tyrian annals. The expression "house of David" mentioned in the Tel Dan inscription (Biran and Naveh 1995) is not a decisive argument to prove the historicity of the biblical king.

Notwithstanding these issues, it has been an accepted tradition to start the history of Iron Age Tyre with the reign of Hiram I, who is known to have provided raw materials and technical support for the building of the palace and the temple of Jerusalem. The main actions attributed to Hiram I are the joining of the two islands that formed the city of Ṣurru, the beginning of colonization in Cyprus with the foundation of Kition, modern Larnaca, and the rebuilding of the Tyrian temples (Katzenstein 1997, 85–86). He is also the king who received as payment for his services to Solomon agricultural products for his household (1 Kgs 5:24–25): "So Hiram provided Solomon with all the cedar wood and juniper he wanted, while Solomon gave Hiram twenty thousand kors of wheat to feed his household, and twenty thousand kors of pure oil," as well as twenty villages in the Galilee (Lemaire 1991b). The economic expansion of Tyre under his reign is also illustrated by the joint maritime expeditions of Tyre and Israel to Ophir, from where they brought back gold, ivory, and precious wood (for more details on the reign of Hiram and his achievements see Katzenstein 1997, 77–115; Briquel-Chatonnet 1992).

However, in a recent paper at a workshop in Mainz, Omer Sargi (2018) argued convincingly that all the deeds ascribed to Solomon should be ascribed to Jeroboam II and suggested that the latter's contemporary is "Hiram II," thus implicitly denying the existence of "Hiram I" and dating the incorporation of the Akko Plain within the Tyrian territory to the eighth century BCE.

The successors of Hiram on the throne of Tyre are listed by Josephus (*C. Ap.* 1.121–125): there are nine kings who ruled after his death and until the foundation of Carthage in 814 BCE (Katzenstein 1997, 116–17). Three of them were usurpers and accessed the throne after the murder of their predecessor. These are Methusastartus, Phelles, and Ittobaal. The latter established a stable dynasty that ruled without interruption until the foundation of Carthage in 814 BCE. Josephus's list, which is considered to be authentic, is the only information we have about the rule of these kings, although some have been identified with kings mentioned in the Neo-Assyrian annals, as will be seen below. Noteworthy is the fact that, with the exception of Phelles, they all have names built with either Baal's or Astarte's name.

With the reign of Ittobaal the kings of Tyre enter contemporary historical records. This Tyrian king was a contemporary of Ahab of Israel, with whom he contracted a diplomatic marriage by giving him his daughter Jezebel (1 Kgs 16:31). Ahab was a contemporary of Šalmaneser III and participated in the Battle of Qarqar as a member of the anti-Assyrian coalition. Although a contemporary and an ally of Ahab, the king of Tyre is not mentioned in contemporary extrabiblical sources and appears only in the classical texts. In the Bible he is referred to as "king of the Sidonians," which has led Katzenstein (1997, 133–34) to suggest that the unification of Sidon and Tyre may have taken place already under his reign. The Tyrian king Baʻali-Manzēri was the successor of Ittobaal, most probably his son. He was a contemporary of Jehu, son of Omri, king of Israel, and both of them are mentioned in the annals of Šalmaneser III (for the relations of Tyre with the Assyrian Empire see Kestemont 1983). Their tribute was collected after the campaigns against Hazael of Damascus that Šalmaneser III undertook in his eighteenth and twenty-first regnal years. It is interesting to note that the king of Tyre is mentioned there by name: "I received tribute from Baʻali Manzēri of Tyre (and) from Jehu (Iaua) of the house of Omri (Ḫumrî)" (Grayson 1996, A.0.102.10, iv 10–11), while elsewhere the tribute collected is said to be that of "the people of the land of Tyre" (Grayson 1996, A.0.102.12, 29–30). Baʻali-Manzēri has been identified with the Balezor of Josephus's text and is referred to by Katzenstein as Baalazor II. This author indeed suggests that the Balbazer of Josephus's list is Baalazor I, and Balezor is Baalazor II (Katzenstein 1997, 167; see also the discussion on 116 and n. 2).

In the list mentioned above, Baalazor II is followed by his son Mattan I, not to be confused with the Metenna of Tiglath-pileser III's inscriptions. His son Pygmalion, Phoenician Pumiyaton, ruled after him, and, according to Josephus (*Cg. Ap.* 1.125) it was in his seventh year of reign that his sister Elissa fled and went to build Carthage: "The reign of Pygmalion opened a new leaf in the illustrious history of Tyre with the foundation of Carthage; his reign also brings a chapter of Tyre's glorious history to an end" (Katzenstein 1997, 192).

After the reign of Pygmalion, no other king of Tyre is mentioned by name until the reign of Tiglath-pileser III. Tyre paid tribute to Adad-nērārī III at the end of his Damascus campaign against Mariʾ, but its king's name is not mentioned: "I (text he) received the tribute of Joash (Iuʾasu), the Samaritan, (and) of the people of Tyre and Sidon" (Grayson 1996, A.0.104.7, 7–8). This anonymous king of Tyre was a contemporary of Joash of Israel and was ruling at the beginning of the eighth century BCE.

In the annals of Tiglath-pileser III, three kings of Tyre are mentioned. The first one, a king named Tubaʾil, *tu-ba-il*, Ittobaal (II), is mentioned on the stela from Iran (Tadmor 1994, stela III A: 6), and he may have been the direct successor of Pygmalion (Katzenstein 1997, 194). He is a contemporary of Rezin of Damascus, Menahem of Samaria, and Shipitbaal of Byblos because he is listed with them paying the tribute to the Assyrian king. The second king mentioned, Hiram (II), *Ḫi-ru-um-mu*, appears in a list of tributaries, some of whom were also the contemporaries of Tuba'il. So he must have been the direct successor of the latter, probably his son. He allied himself with the king of Damascus against Assyria. He was defeated and had to pay a heavy tribute: "[Hi]ram of Tyre, who plotted together with Rezin [...] I captured Mahalab, his fortified city, together with (other) large cities. [Their] spoil [...]. He came before me and kissed my feet. 20 talents of [gold...] multi-coloured [garments], linen garments, eunuchs, male and fem[ale] singers ... [...horses] of Egypt [...I received] (Tadmor 1994, summary inscription 9, 5–8). Hiram II is mentioned also in a Phoenician inscription from Cyprus, which speaks of a governor of Qrtḥdšt, who calls himself "servant of Hiram, king of the Sidonians" (Katzenstein 1997, 207). This inscription is an additional confirmation of the existence of Tyrian colonies in Cyprus. The third king of Tyre mentioned by Tiglath-pileser III is Metenna, Mattan II, who succeeded Hiram II on the throne of Tyre. He paid a huge tribute to the Assyrian king, which testifies to the immense wealth of Tyre at that time: "I sent an eunuch of mine, the Chief-Eunuch, to Tyre. From Metenna of Tyre, 150 talents of gold (and) [2000 talents of silver his tribute I received]" (Tadmor 1994: summary inscription 7, rev. 16'). Katzenstein (1997, 218–19) suggests that Mattan II was maybe a usurper and bribed the Assyrian king with this enormous sum in order to keep the throne. Whether he belonged to the royal house remains an open question. Lemaire (1976) suggests adding another Tyrian king contemporary of Tiglath-pileser III and who would have preceded the above three kings. He bases his hypothesis on short Phoenician epigraphic inscriptions bearing the name of a certain Milkiram. However, in none of these inscriptions is Milkiram said to be king of Tyre. Further decisive evidence is needed to include him in the list of the eighth-century BCE kings of Tyre.

The next king of Tyre, Lulî, is mentioned in the inscriptions of Sennacherib as "the king of the city of Sidon" (for the rule of this king, see 3.3 below). According to Katzenstein, he was the king of the still-unified kingdom of Sidon and Tyre. After his escape to Cyprus, he was replaced by Tu-Ba'lu (Ittobaal III), who was appointed by the Assyrian king.

As previously argued, it is difficult to identify at which point in time the splitting of the two kingdoms took place. It is highly probable that after the departure of Sennacherib, and taking advantage of the fact that Tu-Baʾlu was left without Assyrian support, Tyre was able to regain its lost cities south of the Litani River sometime between 701 and 677 BCE. When Esarhaddon created the province of Kar-Esarhaddon, the only two cities that he cut off from Sidon's territory were Sarepta and Maʾrubbu, thus implicitly implying that Tyre owned already the cities south of the Litani River. It is not clear how and under which circumstances both polities split. All that we know is that Esarhaddon is the first king after Adad-nērārī III to mention Tyre and Sidon as two different polities. Indeed, his annals mention a king of Tyre called Baʿlu, Baal I, (Katzenstein 1997, 259), and a king of Sidon called Abdi-Milkūti. This clearly indicates that the two polities had separated and had now-distinct rulers.

The Assyrian king signed a treaty with Baal I of Tyre (Borger 1982–1985; Parpola and Watanabe 1988) that regulated the landing places of Tyrian ships and the trade routes for Tyrian traders, and established the rules concerning the shipwreck of a Tyrian vessel. According to Katzenstein (1997, 268), the treaty "clearly demonstrates the important status of the Tyrian king." The fact that Baal of Tyre is listed first in the famous list of the twenty-two kings of Ḫatti who were requested to provide all the raw materials for the building of the Assyrian king's palace in Nineveh (Leichty 2011, 1, v, 54–vi, 1) demonstrates the preeminence of the king of Tyre and indicates that he was the leader of this bloc (Katzenstein 1997, 263). The treaty mentions also the elders of Tyre, who probably were the merchant princes of the city. Their status and their relationship with the king is not clear. However, Baal I did not respect this treaty for long, and when the opportunity presented itself he allied himself with Egypt to free his country from the Assyrian yoke. The text says that he allied himself with Taharqa, the king of Kush, against Assyria (for a possible confusion between Baʿlu and Abdi-Milkūti, see 3.3 below). This alliance had disastrous consequences for Tyre: "I conquered Tyre, which is in the midst of the sea, (and) took away all of the cities (and) possessions of Baʿalu, its king, who had trusted in Taharqa, king of Kush" (Leicthy 2011, 607′–8′). We hear another, more detailed episode of Baal's rebellion, which led to the dispossession of his cities on the mainland: "[…Baʿalu, king of Ty]re, who dwells [in the midst of the sea…], who threw off [my] yo[ke,…] … heavy [tribu]te, his daughters with [their] dowr[ies, …] all of his [annu]al [giving] which he had stopped, […] (and) he kissed my feet.[…] I took away from him cities of his (that were on) dry land [… I] established and returned to Assyrian territory" (Leichty 2011, 31 rev 1′–11′). This passage has led some scholars to assume that Tyre was turned into an Assyrian province after this episode. Others, however, think that this transformation occurred later, after the campaign of Aššurbanipal (Katzenstein 1997, 282–83). In spite of this severe punishment Baal I was not executed and continued to rule in Tyre. He did not give up the hope to free his city from Assyrian rule.

After the death of Esarhaddon, Baal I took advantage of the internal troubles of Assyria, caused by the succession problems, and stopped paying tribute. During his first campaign against Egypt, Aššurbanipal, son and successor of Esarhaddon, received the tribute of twenty-two kings of the sea coast and dry land without a military confrontation. Heading the list of tributaries was Baal I, king of Tyre, who submitted without a fight:

> In the course of my campaign, Ba'alu, king of the land Tyre, Manasseh, king of the land Judah, Qa'uš-gabri, king of the land Edom, Muṣurī, king of the land Moab, Ṣil-Bēl, king of the land Gaza, Mitinti, king of the land Ashkelon, Ikausu, king of the land Ekron, Milki-ašapa, king of the land Byblos, Yakīn-Lû, king of the land Arwad,…—in total, twenty-two kings of the seacoast, the midst of the sea, and dry land, [serva]nts who belonged to me, carried their substantial [audience] gift(s) [before me] and kissed my feet. (Novotny 2016, prism B, 006, ii, 25)

But Baal I soon rebelled and probably refused to pay the tribute, which caused the immediate retaliation of the Assyrian army, which besieged the mainland and the island and starved the people until they surrendered. The text seems to imply that the Assyrian king had the support of the fleets of the other Phoenician cities to be able to successfully block the harbor of Tyre. After the surrender, Aššurbanipal showed mercy to Baal, gave him his son back, and dismantled the blockade he had imposed. Katzenstein (1997, 292) assumes that Baal continued to enjoy special rights and privileges on the mainland and that maybe a new treaty was signed between both kings.

> [On] my [third ca]mpaign, I marched against Ba'alu, the king of the land Tyre [who resides in the mid]dle of the sea. [Because] he did not honor my ro[y]al [com]mand(s) (and) [did not o]bey [the pron]ouncement(s) from my lip(s), I set up [blockad]es [again]st him. [To prevent his] people [from leav]ing, [I rei]nforced (its) garrison. [By sea and] dry la[nd, I] took control of (all of) his [rout]es (and thus) cut off (all) access to him. I made [water and foo]d for the preservation of their lives scarce

[for the]ir [mouths]. I confined them [in a harsh imprisonment from which] there was no escape. I constricted (and) cut short [thei]r [lives]. I made them (the people of Tyre) bow down [to] my [yoke]. [He brought] before me [(his) daughter], his [own off]spring, and the daughter(s) of [his] brother[s to serv]e as housekeep[ers. He brought his son, who had never] cross[ed the s]ea, to do obeisance to me. I received from him [his daughter and] the daughter(s) of his brothers, [together with a lar]ge [marriage gift. I ha]d [mercy] on him an[d] (then) I gave [(his) son, his offspring, back to him]. [I dismantled the blockades that I had constructed against Baʿalu, the king of the land Tyre. By sea and dry land, I] opened (all of) his [ro]utes, [as many as I had seized. I] received from him [his substantial payment. I turned around (lit. "I turned the front of my yoke") and returned safely to Nineveh], my [capit]al [city]. (Novotny 2016, prism B, 007, iii 16′–iii 38′)

It is surprising that Assyria showed on several occasions such magnanimity for Baal I in spite of his repeated rebellions. Assyria normally severely punished rebellious kings. It seems that the economic interests that it gained during the rule of Baal I were vital for the empire and the Assyrians could not jeopardize them by killing the Tyrian king. Punishing him and forcing him to obey was guarantee enough that Assyrian interests would be respected in the future. Therefore, in spite of this merciful attitude toward Baal I, Assyria kept a master card in its hand; it did not restore Tyre's total dominion over its mainland and placed Assyrian governors to rule it. Indeed, upon the second expedition of Aššurbanipal against Arabian tribes, the king is said to have collected tribute from Ušû and to have punished and deported its people who had not obeyed their governors and paid the tribute: "On my return march, I conquered the city Ušû (Palaetyrus), whose location is situated on the shore of the sea. I slew the people of the city Ušû who had not been obedient to their governors by not giving payment, their annual giving. I rendered judgement on (those) unsubmissive people: I carried off their gods (and) their people to Assyria" (Novotny 2016, prism A, 011, ix 115). This text suggests first that the mainland of Tyre known as Ušû had become incorporated into an Assyrian province under the rule of Assyrian governors and, second, that the island of Ṣurru was not part of it.

No information about Tyre is available after this episode until the reign of the Neo-Babylonian king Nebuchadnezzar II. During the rule of this king all of the land of Ḫatti, including the Phoenician city-states, came under Babylonian rule and replaced a short-lived Egyptian hegemony in the Levant. Historical records relating to Phoenicia are rare in the Neo-Babylonian texts in spite of the fact that Nebuchadnezzar II campaigned in his first four regnal years against the cities of the Levantine coast. Direct mention of the situation in Tyre during his reign is hardly available in his own inscriptions, even in those found in Lebanon, in Wadi Brisa and Nahr el-Kalb (Da Riva 2008; 2009; Weissbach 1922). Tyrian mariners and craftsmen are mentioned in two tablets from Babylon (Weidner 1939). We also know of a *bīt ṣuraa*, probably a Tyrian quarter in southern Mesopotamia.

The siege of Tyre by Nebuchadnezzar II is the major event relating to Tyre's history in the Neo-Babylonian period. It is reported by Josephus (*C. Ap.* 1.156–159) and not by the Babylonian king himself. The events narrated by Josephus were taken from the Tyrian archives:

> In the reign of king Ithobalos, Nabuchodrosoros besieged Tyre for thirteen years. After him Baal reigned for 10 years. Thereafter judges were appointed: Ednibalos, son of Baslechos, was judge for 2 months, Chelbes, the son of Abdaeos, for 10 months, Abbalos, the high priest, for 3 months, Myttynos and Gerastartos, son of Abdelimos, were judges for 6 years, after whom Balatoros was king for 1 year. When he died they sent for Merbalos and summoned him from Babylon, and he reigned for 4 years; when he died they summoned his brother Eiromos, who reigned for 20 years. It was during his reign that Cyrus became ruler of the Persians. So the whole period is 54 years, with 3 months in addition; for it was in the seventh year of the reign of Nabuchodrosoros that he began to besiege Tyre, and in the fourteenth year of the reign of Eiromos that Cyrus the Persian seized power. (Barclay 2007 and nn. 520–22, where he discusses the controversy about the dates for the reign of Nebuchadnezzar and Eiromos of Tyre)

The historicity of the siege of Tyre was confirmed by the text published by Eckhard Unger (1926, 316), which speaks about provisions being sent "for the king and the soldiers who went against the land of Tyre."

Two kings were ruling during the siege: Ittobaal III and Baal II, after whose reign the monarchy in Tyre seems to have witnessed an eclipse. Indeed, without any justification for the transition, Josephus names five judges who followed Baal II as rulers in Tyre. That judges existed in Tyre and that their function seems to have been transmitted within the same family is attested by a Tyrian inscription today in the Louvre (Teixidor 1979, pl. I). The inscription, dated to the third century BCE (Teixidor

1979, n. 2), enumerates the genealogy of the man who erected the stela, a certain Adonbaal, a suffete, whose ancestors held the same function. Javier Teixidor (13–14) rightly states that it is very difficult to understand the origin as well as the extent of the powers of the judge in the eastern Mediterranean before the Hellenistic period. He also underlines the difficulty of understanding the real function of a suffete in the Phoenician cities. He suggests that the suffete did not enjoy important powers and that he was a simple judge obeying the orders of a governor appointed by the Babylonian king (13), as was the case for Judah after its conquest by Nebuchadnezzar II (2 Kgs 25:22).

Katzenstein (1997, 327–28) assumes that monarchy resumed again in Tyre with Balatoros. He argues that, since the last two rulers were brothers who had to be fetched from Babylon, they must have belonged to the ruling family. Whether these were descendants of Baal II, the last named king of Tyre, remains an open question.

What remains also in the realm of speculation is the reason for the shift operated in the government system of Tyre: Was the royal family exiled in Babylon, as suggested by the mention of a king of Tyre in the "Court List" of Nebuchadnezzar II (Unger 1931, 35), and was the change in the type of government imposed by the Babylonian king? Or was this measure a solution foreseen by the Tyrian constitution, namely, to appoint a judge at the head of the state in the absence of a member of the royal family? Since this was the government system prevailing in Carthage, it may not be far-fetched to assume that the people of Tyre suggested the adoption of this type of governance. Another question comes to mind regarding the identity and status of the judges: Was the appointed judge one of the nobles of Tyre? A letter dated to the forty-second year of Nebuchadnezzar II written in Tyre and found in Babylon mentions a delivery of dates to "the chiefs of the town of Tyre" (Katzenstein 1997, 340). It would not be far-fetched to see in these chiefs and nobles a possible reference to the aristocracy of the kingdom (see below). In any case it seems that after the death of Nebuchadnezzar II, monarchy was restored in Tyre by Nergal-šar-uṣur, known as Neriglissar, to reward a Tyrian maritime support (Elayi 2013a, 226). This made it possible for the Tyrians to request the return of members of the royal family to restore kingship.

The Assyrian and Babylonian wars against Tyre weakened the kingdom, which lost its wealth and prosperity. The loss of its western colonies, mainly Carthage (Katzenstein 1979, 24), and the emigration of its inhabitants contributed to the economic and political downfall of Tyre (Elayi

2013a, 228; Katzenstein 1979, 29). It is thus a weakened polity that we encounter at the beginning of the Persian period.

When Cyrus came to power, Hiram III was in his fourteenth year of reign (*C. Ap.* 1.158–159). The Tyrian exiles in Babylon as well as all the members of the royal family were allowed to go back to their homeland. Tyre progressively regained its role as a maritime power, and the king of Tyre was second to the Sidonian king in the command of the Phoenician fleet.

The first important news relating to Tyre is that Hiram III was probably still ruling at the beginning of the reign of Cambyses. His son, Mattan III, must have succeeded him toward the end of Cambyses's rule, because he was king under Xerxes I. After his conquest of Egypt, Cambyses wanted to attack Carthage, but "the Phoenicians, however, refused to obey; they were bound by their solemn oaths, they said, and it would be wrong for them to attack their own sons.… Cambyses decided not to try to force the Phoenicians to go, because they had joined the Persian forces of their own accord and the whole navy depended on them" (*Hist.* 3.19).

In spite of the loss of their colonies, the Tyrians continued to have an important fleet, as well as settlements in the eastern Mediterranean, to support their trade. One of the better-known settlements during that period is the famous Tyrian Camp in Memphis, Egypt, which is described by Herodotus: "To this day there is in Memphis, south of the temple of Hephaestus, a particularly fine and well-appointed precinct which was his. The houses around this precinct are inhabited by Phoenicians from Tyre, and the whole district is called the Tyrian Camp" (*Hist.* 2.112 [Waterfield]). Katzenstein (1979, 30) rightly suggests that this camp existed probably before the Persian period and that it was not the only one in Egypt. He also believes that since the camp was built around a temple dedicated to Hephaistos, the Tyrian craftsmen established there may have produced some of the metal bowls with Egyptian motifs. That this settlement rivaled Tyre economically is illustrated by the fact that the city struck its first coins around 450 BCE, with a standard weight of 13.56 g, but they do not bear the name of the king who issued them (for Tyrian coinage see Elayi and Elayi 2009). They represent a leaping winged dolphin and the owl with Egyptian royal insignia.

Around 385 BCE, under the reign of Artaxerxes II, Evagoras I king of Salamis, attacked Tyre. According to Elayi (2013a, 274–75), he took advantage of the fact that the Persians were busy in Egypt. He was unable to conquer the island, but he occupied Ušû, the mainland territory. The rebellion of the Cypriot king was broken down by the Persians, who reimposed their rule over Tyre. When Sidon was destroyed by Artaxerxes III after its rebellion, part of its territory was given to Tyre. Taking advantage of Sidon's weakness, Tyre rose again to become the most prominent Phoenician city.

In the mid-fourth century BCE, the city witnessed an economic crisis attested by the devaluation of its coinage (Elayi 2013a, 284). Its participation in the Persian Wars caused huge expenses and impoverished the Tyrian state. This major economic crisis caused a rebellion of the city slaves. Elayi (2013a, 285) believes that, although reported by Justin, a very late source, the information can be trusted because it is corroborated by a Greek oracle, a Phoenician inscription, and monetary legends. The slaves are said to have killed their masters and to have taken their possessions as well as their wives and daughters. They appointed, as king, a certain ʿAbdʿaštart, the only Tyrian master who had escaped the massacre. In 349 or 348 BCE, his successor, ʿOzzimilk, accessed the throne, and he ruled for seventeen years, until the coming of Alexander in 332 BCE.

When Alexander reached the Phoenician shore, all the cities surrendered to him without resistance. The Tyrian king ʿOzzimilk was at sea fighting at the side of the Persian king. Nevertheless, a delegation of noble citizens including his son went to meet Alexander in Ušû with symbolic gifts expressing their allegiance. When the Macedonian king requested to go to the island to sacrifice to Melqart-Heracles in his temple, the Tyrians refused. After a six-month siege and the building of a mole using the ruins of the devastated city of Ušû, Alexander stormed the island city, destroyed it, massacred part of the population, and took the rest as captives (Arrian, *Anab.* 2.16–24): "The rage of the Macedonians was indiscriminate, as they were embittered by the protracted nature of the siege and because the Tyrians had captured some of their men sailing from Sidon. Some eight thousand Tyrians fell.... As for those who fled to the temple of Heracles, including among the Tyrians themselves the men of most authority and king Azemilcus, as well as some Carthaginian envoys.... Alexander granted them all complete pardon; he enslaved the rest; some 30,000 were sold" (*Anab.* 2.24.3–5 [Brunt]). Soon after Alexander's victory, Tyre ceased to be a kingdom with a local dynasty.

Table 3.4. The Kings of Tyre (after Elayi 2018, table 2)

| Name of King | Date |
|---|---|
| Weret or Mekmer | |
| Abibaal | < 970 |
| Hiram I | ca. 970–936 |
| Baleazoros | ca. 935–918 |
| Abdastratos | ca. 918–909 |
| Methusastartus | ca. 909–897 |
| Astharymos | ca. 897–889 |
| Phelles | ca. 889–888 |
| Ittobaal I | ca. 888–856 |
| Balezoros | ca. 848–830 |
| Mattan I | ca. 830–821 |
| Pumiyaton | ca. 821–774 |
| Milkiram? | ca. 750 |
| Ittobaal II | ca. 740 |
| Hiram II | ca. 739–730 |
| Mattan II | ca. 729 |
| Lulî | ca. 728–695 |
| Baal I | ca. 677–671 |
| Ittobaal III | ca. 591–573 |
| Baal II | ca. 572–563 |
| *Period of the judges* | 563–556 |
| Eknibal/Chelbes/Akbar | ca. 563–562 |
| Matta/Gerʻaštart | ca. 561–556 |
| *Return of the kings* | ca. 556 |
| Balazor | |
| Maharbaal | ca. 555–552 |
| Hiram III | ca. 551–533 |
| Ittobaal IV? | > 532 |
| Hiram IV? | < 480 |
| Mattan III | 480 |
| ʻAbdʻaštart | (after 354–350) |
| ʻOzimilk | (349–333) |
| ʻOzimilk | |

## 3.2. Physical Characteristics, Settlement Pattern, and Distribution of the Phoenician Sites

As previously said, the Lebanese coast and the neighboring mountains have not been systematically surveyed, and only a few sites have been or are being excavated. Notwithstanding the current state of the sources, we shall combine the evidence from both the written and the archaeological record to try to understand the physical as well as the organizational structure of the Phoenician polities.

Regarding the physical characteristics of the Phoenician sites, the large majority of them were located on the coast: on promontories, such as Sidon, Sarepta, Byblos, Anfe, and Beirut; or on islands, such as Tyre and Arwad. All the identified sites were very small because they could not extend beyond the edges of the island or the promontory where they were located. The largest, Arwad, had an area of 40 ha, while on the Lebanese coast their area could be as small as 2.5 to 3 ha, as is the case of Beirut and Tell el-Burak (Finkbeiner and Sader 1997). However, all these figures refer to the size of the ancient acropolis and not to the area of the Iron Age settlement, which most of the time has not been identified and entirely excavated. It may have been either smaller or larger than the tell itself if extending beyond the *intra muros* city. The example of Tell el-Burak and Beirut is telling: at Tell el-Burak, while the artificially created Middle Bronze Age tell was entirely occupied by a monumental palace building, the Iron Age settlement was much smaller and occupied only the southern and southwestern slope of the site (Kamlah, Sader, and Schmitt 2016a). On the other hand, the Beirut Iron Age settlement extended outside the stronghold located on the promontory to cover the plain surrounding it to the west and the south, thus extending beyond the 3 ha limits of the cliff (Curvers 2001–2002). Upper and lower cities are clearly attested at Tell Arqa, Beirut, Tell el-Burak, and Byblos. The Phoenician city was subdivided into areas or districts with different functions. Residential areas with domestic buildings were identified in the southwestern part of the city of Sarepta and in Beirut around the harbor northwest of the settlement (Curvers 2001–2002; Elayi and Sayegh 2000, 157–224 and figs. 36–37). Industrial quarters were also identified in Sarepta: pottery kilns, metal workshops, and crushed murex shells were excavated in sounding X northeast of the settlement (Anderson 1978). Beirut also produced evidence for industrial areas at the southern edge of the lower city (Curvers 2001–2002; Curvers and Stuart 2005), and more recently, at Tell el-Burak, an industrial installation was exposed at the foot of the mound, outside the enclosure wall (see fig. 6.3 below). However, hardly any evidence is available about the areas dedicated to administrative and religious buildings within the settlement.

Each Phoenician polity consisted of a fortified capital and the territory it controlled. In this territory were other fortified settlements, which are known to us from the written sources and which help define the boundaries of the polity's territory.

Regarding the settlement pattern within the Phoenician polity, the available evidence indicates that the main economic, political, and administrative center was the city where the main harbor was located. We know from the texts that the residence of the king and the temples of the main city gods and goddesses were also built there. However, this capital, which was located on an island or peninsula, did not stand isolated from the mainland, and it seems to have had a corresponding center there that played an important role in the kingdom's life. It was in a way the continental extension of the capital where the latter could expand to house larger numbers of people and develop all sorts of economic and religious activities. It is clear from the archaeological evidence that 'Amrit, for example, played such a role for Arwad, as attested by the harbor, the religious buildings, and the necropolis that were exposed there. This function is also apparent in the fact that, in the classical period, Ṭarṭūs and its surroundings were called Antarados. This term refers to the land opposite the island of Arados/Arwad. According to the written and archaeological record, Tyre had also a corresponding city on the mainland, called Ušû in the ancient texts and Palaetyrus in the classical ones. It is identified with Tell el-Rašidiyye. This settlement was of vital importance for the island since, as we have seen, it controlled the water source of Rās el-'ayn, housed a temple of the god Melqart, and used the territory opposite the island as a burial ground. Ušû was a vital extension of Ṣurru, where all the natural supplies necessary for the island's survival were found. The same applies to Byblos, which had also a corresponding city on the mainland, called Palaebyblos, but its location is still unidentified. Sidon was no exception since the Phoenician texts speak of ṣdn ym, Sidon-by-the-Sea, and the fortified city called Lesser Sidon, ṣidunu ṣeḫru. That the latter received the same name as the main capital seems to be an additional support to the suggestion that it may have played the role of a second capital for the kingdom. In short, there seems to have been a sort of organic relationship of proximity and dependence between the harbor capital and its mainland correspondent.

Next to this important city on the mainland, the texts and the archaeology bring evidence for the existence of other fortified settlements for the protection of the territory as well, for the safe storage of processed agricultural products. Some were coastal settlements, while others were located in the neighboring mountains. The number of fortified cities was proportional to the importance of the territory. Hence the unified kingdom of Tyre and Sidon, which is best documented, had in addition to the two capitals twenty-seven fortified cities, twenty of which were located on the coast, presenting the same physical characteristics: they are all located near small natural coves protected by islets and bands of reef forming a good chain of stopovers along the coast. Their small harbors, with a few exceptions, seem to have limited their activity to internal rather than international exchange. Some, such as the harbors of ʿAmrit, Beirut, and Akko, seem to have been very active in international trade during the Iron Age and continued to develop their maritime activities in later periods.

The cities belonging to the territory of Sidon and Tyre, for example, are mentioned in the Assyrian texts, where they are said to be "places of pasturing and watering for his stronghold," thus clearly indicating their role and function as providers for the capital and the king's household. The recent excavations at Tell el-Burak and Sarepta have yielded evidence for the role of these satellite cities. Sarepta was an industrial center for pottery production as well as purple and metal industry (Pritchard 1978, 71–76), and Tell el-Burak provided evidence for the production and storage of olive oil and wine in the Iron Age (Kamlah, Sader, and Schmitt 2016a; see also Schmitt et al. 2018). The coastal settlements were very close, within a distance not exceeding 5 km from each other. They occupied the whole shoreline north and south of the capital. Their identification with ancient tells demonstrates that the southern Phoenician coast was very densely occupied.

The texts also speak of settlements on the western slopes of the mountains overlooking the coast. There is unfortunately little evidence for these mountain settlements to allow a better understanding of their role. But it is not far-fetched to assume that they were rural settlements with an economy based on agricultural production and wood cutting. One of their main functions may have been to secure the communication routes with the hinterland. The control of these communication routes was essential for the development of Phoenician trade. Indeed, and contrary to the common assumption that the development of Phoenician maritime expansion was due to the fact that the coastal settlements were cut off from the hinterland by the mountain barrier, we know today that one of the main reasons for the Phoenician expansion was the quest for raw materials, mainly metals, which were sold to the inland polities that badly needed them. The study of their territory has clearly demonstrated that only those kingdoms that had good relations and easy communication with the Syrian hinterland prospered. It has also explained the decline of Byblos, which was cut off from its hinterland because it did not control anymore the Homs Gap, its main passage to inland Syria. The same applies also to Arwad, which started to prosper when the Assyrians neutralized the kingdom of Ḥamat, thus liberating the passages to the hinterland.

However, little is known about the internal administrative organization of the Phoenician polities: we do not know whether they were divided into provinces or districts, and how the latter were related to the central administration in the capital. The mention of the term *skn* in the inscription of Ahiram king of Byblos may hint at the existence of provinces or districts ruled by a governor. Lipiński (1991, 165) suggests that Tyre's territory was divided into six districts based on the evidence from the book of Joshua: "The text of the book of Joshua seems to reflect the existence of six districts, which cover the whole territory." No other information is available about this issue. But by analogy with the Aramaean polities of Syria or with the Israelite kingdoms, one can assume the existence of administrative units that helped in the management and control of the territory.

To sum up, there is enough evidence to assume that the Phoenician polities were very densely populated. This is mainly true for Tyre and Sidon, the southern Phoenician kingdoms. The exiguity of the arable coastal plain and mountain slopes may explain their need to import staple food from neighboring countries. This need is illustrated by the food requested by Hiram I in exchange for his help in building the temple and palace of Jerusalem, as well as in the transfer of twenty villages of the Galilee with good agricultural yields to the territory of Tyre.

On the other hand, from the evidence relating to the Sidonian and Tyrian kingdom, one may infer the existence of a site hierarchy within the polity. Four tiers of settlements can be identified in light of the above evidence: the capital city with the main harbor, the corresponding capital on the mainland with an active harbor, the fortified cities used to store agricultural products and control the communication passages, and, finally, the rural or village sites, some of which specialized in the exploitation of the forest resources. Their existence is attested in the treaty between Esarhaddon and Baal I of Tyre, which explicitly mentions "all the cities in the mountains" (Parpola and Watanabe 1988, iii 18). On the other hand, we know that Byblos continued to trade with Egypt, and the main commodity exported was wood. The recent discovery of substantial Iron Age remains in Yanūḥ, in the mountains east of Byblos (Monchambert et al. 2010; Monchambert 2011), brings archaeological confirmation for villages in the mountains whose main role was to cut and transport wood to the Byblian harbor.

A more refined understanding of the settlement pattern and territorial organization of the Phoenician polities will have to await more evidence from both surveys and excavations.

## 3.3. The Political Organization of the Phoenician Kingdoms

To discuss the political organization or government system of the Phoenician kingdoms is not easy in the absence of sufficient textual materials. One has to collect here and there shreds of evidence to be able to reconstruct a partial picture of the Phoenician government system (see Baurain-Bonnet 1992, 143–50).

One thing is certain and evidenced by the Phoenician royal inscriptions themselves: the Phoenician polities were hereditary monarchies. At the head of the state was a king, *mlk*. His function as head of the state is symbolized by the "scepter of his rule," as expressed in the Ahiram inscription. The Byblos and Sidon royal inscriptions give the king the titles *mlk gbl* and *mlk ṣdnm* respectively. The Assyrian texts, when they speak about the rulers of Syria and Phoenicia, speak of "kings of Ḫatti and the seacoast."

Kingship was hereditary, and the son, normally the eldest, succeeded his father on the throne. This appears clearly in the genealogy that a ruling king provided when presenting himself, on which at least his father and grandfather are listed. The absence of such a genealogy in the inscription of a ruling king suggests that the latter usurped the throne and was not the legitimate successor of the previous one. Sometimes, if the king died without leaving an heir, the throne went either to one of his brothers or to the closest member of the royal family. This is attested in the rule of Bodʿaštart of Sidon, who succeeded Eshmunazar II. He does not name his father because he did not rule but names his grandfather, Eshmunazar I, king of the Sidonians, who was also the grandfather of Eshmunazar II. This implies that Bodʿaštart was probably a cousin of the dead king. The royal lineage continued with the descendants of the ruling king, who was considered to be the founder of a new dynasty. If a ruling king died and his heir was still a child, the queen acted as regent, as was the case of *ʾmʿštrt*, the mother of Eshmunazar II. We have also instances where the royal lineage was forcefully interrupted by the Assyrian or Persian kings, who appointed kings loyal to them and caused thus dynastic change.

One instance of incestuous marriage of kings is attested in Sidon, where the royal couple, Tabnit and *ʾmʿštrt*, were both children of Eshmunazar I. Whether this was a one-time occurrence or a regular tradition cannot be decided on the basis of the available evidence.

Other information about the ruler that can be inferred from the Phoenician royal inscriptions is that the king was also the head of the clergy and acted as high priest of the goddess Astarte. This is clearly attested in the inscription of Eshmunazar (*KAI* 14) and implied by the relief on top of the stela of Yeḥumilk, in which the king is represented as a priest presenting an offering to the seated Lady of Byblos (Jidejian 1977, fig. 188). We learn also that the queen was the high priestess of Astarte, as attested by the title of *'mštrt*, Eshmunazar II's mother.

One of the king's duties and privileges was to build and repair the temples of the gods and goddesses. This is again attested in the inscriptions of Eshmunazar II, Bodʿaštart, and Yeḥumilk of Byblos. The first two say that they built the temples of Eshmun and Astarte and the latter repaired the temple of the Lady of Byblos.

The king was also the commander in chief of the army and led it during the battle. This is widely attested in the annals of the Neo-Assyrian kings, who always mention the king of the polity commanding his army and being taken captive or escaping during the battle. As we have already seen, the Phoenician kings were commanding their fleet in the naval battles they fought at the side of the Persian king. Eshmunazar II speaks of his own as well as his family high (military) deeds, which were rewarded by the granting of new territories.

Finally, the king represented the state in the international diplomatic relations of the kingdom. He was the person entitled to sign international treaties—such as the treaty between Esarhaddon and Baal of Tyre—and to conclude political alliances and economic agreements (as attested in the diplomatic marriages that the kings of Tyre made with the Israelite kings as well as the joint trade expeditions of Hiram I and Solomon).

There has been only one instance known to us where the monarchy was abolished or rather suspended to be replaced by suffetes: this is the case of Tyre after the siege of Nebuchadnezzar II. These judges were obviously appointed by the Babylonian king, but we have no clue regarding their status from the Phoenician texts. We also do not know from which social category they came and what exactly their prerogatives were. Whether they were members of an existing judicial institution or any other council involved in the affairs of the state remains an open question.

Indeed, there is no clear mention in the Phoenician inscriptions of another public institution involved in the administration of the state and sharing with the king the privilege of participating in the polity's government. There may have been such institutions or councils, but they are nowhere explicitly mentioned in the texts. It can be inferred from the written record that an important class of traders or merchants developed in the Phoenician cities, such as those mentioned in the Report of Wenamun.

These merchants are mentioned by Ezekiel (27:27), who refers to the "commercial agents" of the king of Tyre. The annals of Esarhaddon mention the "nobles" of Sidon, around whose necks he hung the head of their defeated king Abdi-Milkūti: "To show the people the might of the god Aššur, my lord, I hung their heads around the heads of their nobles, and I paraded in the squares of Nineveh with singer(s) and lyre(s)" (Leichty 2011, 1, iii 38). There is another reference to noblemen and advisers of the king in Diodorus's account of the Sidonian revolt, where it is said that the Sidonian king Tennes "took with him the most distinguished of the citizens, to the number of one hundred, in the role of advisers" to meet the Persian king (*Bibl. hist.* 14.45.2). This passage seems to suggest that Tyre had an assembly composed of a hundred advisers similar to the one attested in Carthage, where the title *rb m't* occurs. The same title was read on an ostracon from Shiqmona and interpreted either as a military rank or an assembly (Lemaire 1980, 18). However, this assumption remains conjecture: "However, in the present state of our knowledge of the ancient history of Tyre, it is only conjecture."[19] We also hear of "men of most authority" forming the delegation that met Alexander (Arrian, *Anab.* 2.24) and of "the chiefs of the town of Tyre" mentioned in the Babylonian text referenced above. That these "nobles," "advisers," "chiefs," and "men of most authority" influenced the action of the king or shared in the national decisions can be assumed, but it is nowhere clearly evidenced.

The only civic community was formed by the people of the city: this is attested by the title "king of the Sidonians," as well as by the fact that the coins of Tyre are dated after the era of the people of Tyre. As we have previously mentioned, Elayi (1989, 116l; 2005, 75) interprets *ṣdnm* as representing a political entity. Whether the people was represented in an assembly or council is difficult to decide. However, the people may have exercised a strong pressure on the king, who had to take into account their demands or inclinations. The only hint for the existence of such a representative assembly comes from the Report of Wenamun, where the king Zakarbaal appears surrounded by his assembly: "When morning came, he had his assembly summoned. He stood in their midst." Another hint for the existence of a council of elders can be inferred from a passage in the treaty of Esarhaddon with Baal of Tyre: "the elders of your country [convene to

---

19. Lemaire 1980, 18: "Cependant, dans l'état actuel de nos connaissances de l'histoire ancienne de Tyr, il ne s'agit là que d'une conjecture."

take] counsel." Ezekiel (27:8–9) also mentions the "sages" of Tyre and the "elders" of Byblos. If the existence of an assembly of the people and a council of elders seems attested, nothing is known about their composition and their prerogatives.

# 4
# Phoenician Culture

In the previous chapters we established that the area called Phoenicia by the Greeks is a geographical concept that covers the largest part of the Levantine coast from the area south of Ugarit to the Yarkon River, south of the Carmel. In spite of the fact that this geographical area was divided into four different polities, it has been generally assumed that it presents a cultural unity, which justifies considering it as one country and its inhabitants as one people. When modern scholars speak of Phoenicia and the Phoenicians, readers are always under the impression that they are speaking about one group that shared a common origin, religion, and material culture. In this chapter, we shall attempt to dissect the main aspects of the culture of this area in order to see whether we can isolate identifiers or specific features that can justify considering the culture of the Levantine coast as homogeneous and specific to its inhabitants, or whether we can detect substantial differences singling out individual cultures.

## 4.1. The Language

### 4.1.1. Evidence for the Use of the Same Language

Language is a major cultural identifier, and the question is whether the inhabitants of the Phoenician coast spoke and wrote the same language, a question that is not easy to answer because of the scanty and fragmentary written evidence. However, since the language of both the official and individual inscriptions found on the Phoenician coast is the same, it is assumed that it was used by the large majority of the population as a means for oral and written communication. While the archaeological record betrays the presence of foreign groups in Phoenicia, their presence cannot be detected in the available written sources, more particularly in the onomastics. Almost all foreign names appear in Punic texts, and hardly any are attested in the inscriptions found in Phoenicia (Benz 1972, 186–96). Three names that may be of Indo-European origin are attested on Tyrian stelae: ʾgrp, which may be identified as the Phoenician writing of Agrippa, as suggested by Philip Schmitz orally to the author (Sader 2014a, 376–78); and four other names of difficult interpretation: ʾpyn and tʾnpy, which can be of Indo-European origin, and ʾyprṣk and mg/pš/llš, of unknown origin and etymology (Abou Samra and Lemaire 2014, 203).

The bulk of the available evidence regarding the language comes from what is known as the heartland of Phoenicia, namely, the Lebanese coast (for a recent update on the epigraphic material from Lebanon, see Sader forthcoming) and the territory of Arwad. The most important corpus of Phoenician documents comes from Byblos and Sidon, which are the only cities to have yielded royal inscriptions of local kings (*KAI*; Gibson 1982; see also Elayi 1989, 41–45; Mathys 2005, 275; Xella and Zamora 2004; Zamora 2008). The rest of the epigraphic material consists of votive or funerary texts written by the common people, such as the funerary stelae from Tyre, Jiyye, Sidon, and Tell el-Burak (Sader 2005; Abou Samra and Lemaire 2013), northern Palestine (Delavault and Lemaire 1979; see also Xella 2017), Rašidiyye (Bordreuil 1982; 2003), Tell Arqa (Bordreuil 1977), Umm el-Amed (Dunand and Duru 1962), and the votive inscriptions from ʿAmrit (Dunand and Saliby 1985, 38, 47; pls. XLI, LIII), Sarepta (Pritchard 1988, figs. 1, 4; see also Teixidor 1975), Kharayeb (Kaoukabani 1973, fig. 2; Chéhab 1953–1954, pl. CI), Ṭaybe (*KAI* 17), and Maʿṣub (*KAI* 19). A Phoenician inscription was found also in Akko (Dothan 1985; Cross 2009; Lipiński 2009; Xella 2017). All these inscriptions witness the use of the same language, as do a large number of short graffiti (Sader 2017b), inscribed seals (Bordreuil 1986; Kaoukabani 2005), inscribed weights (Elayi and Elayi 1997; Sader 2014b; Kletter 1994; 2000), and ostraca (Sader 1990; 2017b; forthcoming; Vanel 1967; 1969; Bordreuil 2011, 236–37 and fig. 1; Doumet-Serhal 2013, 110, fig. 102). Except for the royal inscriptions, the available documents are very short and often restricted to personal names, single words, or short and often incomplete sentences. This evidence has led Röllig (1983b, 375) to say that Phoenician "remains the worst transmitted and least known of all Semitic languages" because of the scarcity of the attested words and the absence of long texts that can allow the study of the syntax and the grammar. After 130 years of research, "there are around ten thousand texts in the extant corpus and we know only about two thousand words total" (Martin 2017, 97).

## 4. PHOENICIAN CULTURE

Notwithstanding this limited evidence, the epigraphic material discovered so far in this area is written in the same Semitic language and the same alphabetic script that have been conventionally labeled Phoenician. This material presents linguistic characteristics that singled out the written language from the other contemporary languages of neighboring Syria and Palestine (Röllig 1992) and conferred to it a proper identity. With the development of Phoenician studies and the discovery of new inscriptions, scholars noted the existence of regional differences in the Phoenician material and identified Phoenician dialects, which are to be expected in such a wide geographical area as Phoenicia.

The Phoenician inscriptions found outside Phoenicia, namely, in Turkey and Cyprus, are considered by most scholars to reflect a southern Phoenician or Tyrian dialect. In spite of the absence of Phoenician inscriptions from Tyre, this similarity is based on the assumption that Tyre initiated the colonization movement in Cyprus and Asia Minor. Giovanni Garbini (1977), after reviewing previous attempts at identifying Phoenician dialects, concluded that there were three dialects of eastern or homeland Phoenician: the Byblos dialect, the Tyre-Sidon dialect, and the Arwadian dialect. The dialect that can be better studied given the relative abundance of texts and their distribution over several centuries is that of Byblos. In the third edition of the *Phönizisch-Punische Grammatk*, Friedrich, Röllig, and Amadasi-Guzzo indicate that dialectal differences can be better identified between the Byblos and other inscriptions of the homeland as well as between the earlier (*altbyblisch*) and later (*byblisch*) inscriptions of that city. They note, however, that "Within the Phoenician language *stricto sensu* the differences are not very strongly marked. Tyre and Sidon seem to have been the determining centers."[1] Garbini observes that the dialect of Byblos started to be influenced by that of Tyre and Sidon in the fifth century BCE, and this unification of the language was the result, in his opinion, of the growing importance of these two cities (Garbini 1977, 287). His study indicates that the dialects of Tyre and Sidon, which are known only from the later Persian and Hellenistic periods, are identical (288) and display clear differences with the Byblian dialect. He explains the similarity between the Sidonian and the Tyrian dialects by a common ethnic origin since, according to a later classical tradition, Tyre was destroyed

---

1. Friedrich, Röllig, and Amadasi-Guzzo 1999, 3: "innerhalb des phönizischen im engeren Sinn sind die Unterschiede weniger geprägt. Tyros und Sidon scheinen die bestimmenden zentren gewesen zu sein."

by the people of Ashkelon and rebuilt by Sidon (Katzenstein 1997, 59–62, 84). Garbini finally identified a dialect specific to the kingdom of Arwad, which he labeled northern Phoenician. This dialect is attested in the 'Amrit inscriptions and also in some Cypriot inscriptions, which may suggest that Arwad played a role in the Phoenician colonization of the island (Garbini 1977, 290).

In spite of these dialectal differences, it is clear that the inhabitants of Phoenicia shared the same language. This major identifier is the main—but not the only—argument in favor of the shared identity of the inhabitants of the Levantine coast in the Iron Age. Furthermore, they had the same scribal tradition, and the Phoenician script can be clearly distinguished from the neighboring Hebrew and Aramaic ones as early as the ninth and eighth centuries BCE respectively. Onomastics from all four kingdoms share the same characteristics, and no differences can be noted between the personal names in southern and northern Phoenicia. That the classical authors continued to call the area Phoenicia and did not change its name is also due to the fact that the area was considered to form a clear cultural unit, since Phoenician language continued to be spoken during the Hellenistic and early Roman periods before it was progressively replaced by Aramaic (Briquel-Chatonnet 1991).

4.1.2. The Place of Phoenician within the Semitic Languages

The Semitic languages were divided traditionally into East, West, and South Semitic groups based on cultural and geographical principles (Faber 1997, 5 with relevant bibliography). Phoenician was considered to be part of the West Semitic languages, and more specifically of the Northwest Semitic Canaanite group. This traditional subdivision of the Semitic languages was challenged by Robert Hetzron, who promoted "a genetic scheme of classification" (Huehnergard 1996, 258) of these languages and divided them into two main groups: East and West Semitic. To the former belongs only Akkadian, while the latter is divided into Central and South Semitic. Canaanite (Hebrew, Phoenician, Moabite, Ammonite, and El-Amarna) languages were placed in the Central Semitic group together with Arabic. Other linguists modified Hetzron's classification and added Eblaite to the East Semitic group and subdivided the West Semitic group into Central Semitic, Northwest Semitic, and South Semitic. They placed Arabic alone in the Central Semitic group and Canaanite, Ugaritic, and Aramaic in the Northwest Semitic group of the West Semitic languages (Faber 1997, 6).

In sum, Phoenician is a language that presents specific features that differentiate it from its closest kin, Hebrew and Ammonite. It is a language in its own right and has its place in the classification of the Semitic languages. Its affinities with the el-Amarna Semitic glosses (Faber 1997, 10) are an indication that the Iron Age population was in its majority a direct descendant of the Late Bronze Age inhabitants of the Levantine coast. Additional evidence for this population continuity comes from a tablet discovered at Sarepta written in the Phoenician language with the cuneiform alphabet of Ugarit, as identified by Pierre Bordreuil (2007, 77). So Phoenician was spoken already in the thirteenth century BCE, and in the Iron Age it was the language used in all four Phoenician kingdoms. The onomastics reflect the same name types in both northern and southern Phoenicia. In his discussion of the Phoenician personal names found in north Palestinian inscriptions, Garbini (1979, 327) concluded that in the first millennium BCE the southern Phoenician area present onomastics similar to those of northern Phoenicia, which justifies assigning northern Palestine to the Phoenician cultural sphere.

### 4.1.3. Did the Phoenicians Invent the Alphabet?

All the Phoenician inscriptions were written in a linear alphabetic script that is generally referred to as Phoenician. This designation was borrowed from the account of Herodotus about the transmission of the alphabet to the Greeks by the Phoenicians. Acknowledging this cultural transfer, Herodotus coined a name for the alphabetic signs and called them *Phoinikea grammata*, Phoenician letters or alphabet, because they were taught to the Greeks by the Phoenicians. This designation of the alphabet is still used by modern scholars.

> The Phoenicians who came to Greece with Cadmus, among whom were the Gephyraei, ended up living in this land and introducing the Greeks to a number of accomplishments, most notably the alphabet, which, as far as I can tell, the Greeks did not have before then.... At this time most of their Greek neighbours were Ionians. So it was the Ionians who learnt the alphabet from the Phoenicians; they changed the shape of a few of the letters, but they still called the alphabet they used the Phoenician alphabet, which was only right, since it was the Phoenicians who had introduced it into Greece. (*Hist.* 5.58)

Fig. 4.1. Bronze coin of Tyre minted in the reign of Philip I (244–249 CE) showing on the reverse Cadmus presenting the alphabet to the Hellenes. Source: Classical Numismatic Group, LLC. Triton XXII, Lot 729. 29 mm, 18.88 gr. www.cngcoins.com.

Although stating only that the Phoenicians transmitted the alphabet to the Greeks, Herodotus's account has led to the assumption that the Phoenicians also invented the alphabet. This opinion is abandoned today by the large majority of scholars, but it continues to be widespread in popular opinion all over the world and is still strongly defended by the Lebanese people, who count the invention of the alphabet as one of their major contribution to world history and take pride in it. That the Ahiram inscription is the oldest inscription written with the Phoenician alphabet currently known has strengthened this assumption. It is indeed very difficult to explain to the people that the alphabet was not invented overnight by a specific group of people from Byblos or Tyre but that it was developed in Egypt and that its formation process took several centuries to reach the standard form coined "Phoenician" by Herodotus.

Based on discoveries made during the twentieth century, the so-called Phoenician alphabet is considered today by the overwhelming majority of scholars to have been developed in Egypt by West Semitic–speaking people. The latter adapted the hieroglyphic and maybe hieratic scripts to create signs to render their own language (see mainly Tropper 2001; Darnell et al. 2005; Goldwasser 2010; 2012; 2015). The evidence for this theory came from the so-called Proto-Sinaitic inscriptions that were discovered by William Matthew Flinders Petrie (2009) at Serabit el-Khadim in the Sinai Peninsula, and in Wadi el-Ḥôl by John Darnell (Darnell et al. 2005). Alan Gardiner (1916) identified the script of the Serabit el-Khadim graffiti as an alphabet and their language as West Semitic and dated them to the fifteenth century BCE. The Wadi el-Ḥôl inscriptions (see fig. 4.2), which were written with the same signs, were dated earlier, to the late Twelfth or early Thirteenth Egyptian Dynasty, that is, to the first two centuries of the second millennium, between 2000 and 1800 BCE. The Proto-Sinaitic alphabetic script is still only partly deciphered and had probably a larger number of signs that were later reduced to twenty-seven in the Ugaritic and twenty-two in the Phoenician alphabet. So the available evidence strongly suggests that the alphabet was developed in Egypt in the early years of the Middle Kingdom by Canaanites working or trading there. Helmut Satzinger (2002, 26) even thinks that it was developed "in Egypt, by Egyptians in co-operation with speakers of a Semitic language, with the scope of facilitating communication with Canaanite personnel."

Fig. 4.2. Wadi el-Ḥôl inscription. Photographs by Bruce Zuckerman and Marilyn J. Lundberg, West Semitic Research, Courtesy Dept. of Antiquities, Egypt. Drawings by Marilyn J. Lundberg, West Semitic Research.

The identity of these Canaanites cannot be defined with more precision, but they came most probably from the Levantine coast of Palestine, Lebanon, and Syria, an area that was in close political and economic contact with Egypt, as attested by the Middle Kingdom Egyptian texts such as the Mit-Rahina inscription (Marcus 2007) and by the famous archaeological objects found in the Middle Bronze Age obelisk temple and royal tombs of Byblos. The alphabet was born using the acrophonic principle already familiar to the Egyptians and is characterized by the fact that it is written only with consonants.

It is noteworthy to mention in this context that, while Canaanite groups were experimenting with the alphabet in Egypt, the people of Byblos developed during the Middle Kingdom a local script inspired from the Egyptian hieroglyphs and known as the pseudo-hieroglyphic script of Byblos (Sznycer 1994) (see fig. 4.3). This script has not been deciphered yet but it clearly indicates that Egyptian hieroglyphs have deeply influenced the writing habits of the Levantine people. The pseudo-hieroglyphs of Byblos are another telling example of the influence Egyptian scripts had on the development of west Semitic writing systems. It is not surprising to see the influence Egypt had on the inhabitants of the Lebanese coast, since

Fig. 4.3. Bronze plaque with pseudo-hieroglyphic inscription from Byblos. Source: Directorate General of Antiquities.

it was one of their most important trade partners and enjoyed power and prestige in the Levantine kingdoms of the Bronze Age.

The development of the alphabetic signs invented in Egypt took several centuries to reach the standard or classical form the Phoenician alphabet had at the end of the second millennium BCE. The alphabetic script used at the beginning pictographs inspired from Egyptian signs and modified them with time to more stylized forms and reduced them to a minimal number of twenty-two. It is this standard Phoenician alphabet that was transmitted to and modified by the Greeks. It is also this same script that spread via Palestine and Phoenicia to Jordan, the Arabian Peninsula, and northern Syria in the first millennium BCE.

It is important to mention also the existence of another alphabet of thirty cuneiform signs that was developed in Ugarit in the thirteenth century BCE. The writing material used was clay, and the language written with this alphabet was a local West Semitic one. Whether the cuneiform signs of this alphabet derive from the proto-Sinaitic signs or whether they have a different origin remains a debated question. This cuneiform alphabet that was used also in Phoenicia disappeared at the end of the Late Bronze Age and was replaced by the linear alphabet.

To sum up, the alphabet "was not created by the Phoenicians, around 1000 BC, as tradition has it" (Satzinger 2002, 26) but was rather developed in the second millennium BCE in Egypt and not in Phoenicia by people speaking a West Semitic dialect. These people came from the West Semitic–speaking areas of the Levant, and according to Orly Goldwasser (2012), were not slaves or elites but common people with varied skills working for the Egyptians.

### 4.1.3. The Role of the Phoenicians in the Transmission of the Alphabet

Despite the fact that the Phoenicians cannot be credited with the invention of the alphabet, they played nevertheless an instrumental role in transmitting it to the people around the Mediterranean and along the Atlantic coast of Europe and Africa (Lemaire 2017). This transmission is attested by the presence of Phoenician inscriptions in all the regions where the Phoenicians chose to settle. It was also used as a second language and script in southern Anatolian kingdoms. This transmission is also attested in the Semitic name of the alphabetic signs. The name of this alphabet will be therefore always associated with that of the Phoenicians, as clearly acknowledged by Herodotus.

## 4.2. The Material Culture

The question that we shall attempt to answer in this chapter is whether one can identify elements of the material culture, namely, specific features of the architecture, the objects of daily use, and the pottery, that can be considered markers of their homeland culture.

### 4.2.1. Phoenician Architecture

Phoenician architecture is better understood today in the light of new discoveries and presents characteristic features that can be isolated from recently exposed buildings in the homeland, mainly in southern Phoenicia. One typical feature of Phoenician architecture is the particular use of stone ashlars in both domestic and public structures. Sharon (1987, 37) studied the use of stone ashlars at Dor in the Persian and Hellenistic periods and concluded that it was of Phoenician origin.

#### 4.2.1.1. Building Techniques

Building techniques are tributary of the natural environment and of the availability and accessibility of building materials such as stone, wood, and clay. On the Levantine coast the proximity of the mountains and the nature of the limestone that could be easily quarried determined one major characteristic of Phoenician building techniques, which is the use of ashlar blocks. Ashlar blocks could be also obtained by quarrying sandstone, which is easily accessible along the shore. The ashlars were hewn into rectangular blocks with smooth faces that could be fitted together with little, or even without, mud mortar. The way these ashlars were used in the Iron Age buildings is characteristic of Phoenician architecture, and their use can be best followed at Tell el-Burak, where some structures had a life span of three centuries (Kamlah and Sader 2003; Kamlah, Sader, and Schmitt 2016a). Other examples of this ashlar masonry are attested at Sarepta (Anderson 1988), Beirut (Elayi and Sayegh 2000), and Tel Dor (Sharon 1987). Examples are also known from Horbat Rosh Zayit (Gal and Alexandre 2000), in the hinterland of Akko. At Tell el-Burak, two of the exposed buildings, House 1 and House 3, were built entirely with stone in the early seventh century BCE and present no evidence for the use of mudbricks. In the seventh century BCE, the walls of these houses were built with fieldstones and had two smooth facings with rubble in the middle. However, the corners were built with neatly cut ashlars placed in three rows: A stretcher sandwiched between two rows of two headers each (see fig. 4.4). The ashlar corners remained a characteristic feature of the Tell el-Burak buildings all through the site's existence. In Sarepta the buildings present the same characteristic (Anderson 1988, 51). The openings are also characterized by the use of ashlars for the threshold and the doorjambs. In the latter the ashlars are placed in three rows consisting of alternating header and stretcher each (see fig. 4.5). Such ashlar-built corners and doorjambs are also attested at Dor, and Sharon (1987, 28) has pointed out their wide chronological and geographical distribution. At Horbat Rosh Zayit, "the ashlar masonry is a significant feature of the construction, the doorjambs and corners of the fort being built with ashlars laid in headers and stretchers technique, a style of Phoenician affinity" (Gal and Alexandre 2000, 198; see also figs. II.6 and II.17). This building technique is attested at Tell Kazel in northern Phoenicia since the thirteenth century BCE in the Level 5 temple and is good evidence for the cultural continuity of the area since the Late Bronze Age: "A characteristic of the masonry technique of the substructure is the use of two faces of sizable rubble stones with the interior filled with smaller rubble stones. This rubble masonry is enhanced by setting larger, regular blocks at the angles" (Badre and Gubel 1999–2000, 170, 198).

Some buildings, such as the Sarepta shrine (Pritchard 1978), were built entirely with ashlar blocks placed as headers and stretchers. This more sophisticated building technique was used for important public buildings such as shrines and temples, and it continued to be in use all through the

Fig. 4.4. House 2 at Tell el-Burak, the corner of the eastern room built with ashlars, west of House 1. View from the southwest. Source: Tell el-Burak Archaeological Project.

Fig. 4.5. Doorjambs built with ashlars in Tell el-Burak House 3. Source: Tell el-Burak Archaeological Project.

Iron Age in Phoenicia. The Persian-period temple of Tyre (Badre 2015) was built also with the same headers-and-stretchers technique.

A major development occurred in Phoenicia in the sixth century BCE when a new building technique was introduced, the so-called pier-and-rubble walls, which spread all over the homeland and became another characteristic feature of Phoenician architecture. This technique uses piers made of ashlars placed as headers and stretchers in the fieldstone wall. At Tell el-Burak the walls had only one central pier built with alternating rows of two juxtaposed stretchers to obtain the same width as that of the overlying row of two headers (see fig. 4.6). The same type of ashlar piers is found also in Beirut, where it is labeled by the excavators "Type A irrégulier." In that latter site five other types and two special structures of ashlar pillars are attested (Elayi and Sayegh 2000, 200–203 and figs. 43–46). While at Tell el-Burak only one central pier is attested in the fieldstone wall, two ashlar piers are placed in the walls of the Beirut houses. The pier-and-rubble building technique is characteristic also of other Persian-period settlements on the southern Phoenician coast, such as Sarepta (Pritchard 1975, 51), Jiyye (Waliszewski et al. 2015), Dor (Sharon 1987, fig. 7), Horbat Rosh Zayit (Gal and Alexandre 2000, 163), and Tell Abu Hawam (Hamilton 1934, 78). The northernmost evidence for this type of wall is found in Level F at Tell Sukas (Lund 1986, 142 and figs. 43, 103). This building technique survived well into the Hellenistic period and has been considered by archaeologists to be a characteristic feature of Phoenician architecture. The earliest evidence known so far for this technique is attested in the Tell el-Burak first enclosure wall in Area 3, which is dated to the end of the eighth century BCE (see fig. 4.7).

Mudbrick architecture is known in Phoenicia and is attested at Phoenician Tell Keisan, for example. The unavailability of stone in its immediate neighborhood led the Iron Age inhabitants to use sundried mudbricks with stone foundations (Briend-Humbert 1980, 27–28; Braemer 1982, 123). This cannot be considered, however, to be a characteristic feature of Phoenician architecture.

Regarding the roofs, we lack decisive evidence, but some observations indicate that they were flat and made of earth and wood. Stone rollers were found in Iron Age sites and were used to repair the flat roofs. At Tell el-Burak they were found on the site's area, and it is difficult to assign them to a specific period. The doors were obviously made out of a perishable material, most probably wood, and they have left no traces. The floors of the houses were either made of beaten earth, often white-plastered, or were paved with

Fig. 4.6. Pier-and-rubble wall of House 1 at Tell el-Burak seen from the south, to the lower right corner of a house built with ashlars. Source: Tell el-Burak Archaeological Project.

Fig. 4.7. Enclosure Wall 1 in Area 3 at Tell el-Burak seen from the south and showing the pier-and-rubble building technique. Source: Tell el-Burak Archaeological Project.

stone flags, as is the case in Houses 2 and 4 at Tell el-Burak (see fig. 4.8) and Level 4 and 5 structures at Tell Keisan (Briend and Humbert 1980, 133, 156, and fig. 38), for example.

Fig. 4.8. Flagstone pavement of House 2 at Tell el-Burak seen from the north. Source: Tell el-Burak Archaeological Project.

This review of the building techniques used in Phoenician sites demonstrates that the use of ashlars in the buildings is a common marker of the Iron Age architecture of the Phoenician coast. The disposition of the ashlars in headers and stretchers is also characteristic, but the patterns may vary from one site to the other or from building to building within the same site. These ashlars can be the exclusive building material in important buildings, where they were placed in the typical headers-and-stretchers pattern, but they were more commonly used only in the corners and doorjambs or as piers within the fieldstone walls. All scholars agree on considering the above-described building techniques as characteristic of Phoenician architecture.

4.2.1.2. Fortifications

Archaeological evidence for Phoenician fortifications is rare and unequally distributed over the Phoenician coast. Most of the evidence comes from southern Phoenicia, mainly Beirut, Tell el-Burak, Tell Abu Hawam, and

Iron Age I Dor. The lacuna in the archaeological evidence is unfortunately not compensated or complemented by the written record, because the latter is very parsimonious when it comes to the description of the Phoenician cities. What can be gathered from the contemporary Neo-Assyrian annals is that some Phoenician urban sites were fortified, and this feature is represented on Assyrian reliefs. Most famous is the representation of Tyre on the bronze gates of Balawat (Pritchard 1954, 356) and Sidon on the relief from Sennacherib's palace in Nineveh representing the flight of Luli, king of Sidon (Markoe 2000, fig. 6). Both depict the city's fortifications, walls, and gates. Needless to say, both cities have not yet yielded archaeological evidence for their fortifications to cross-check the iconographic evidence. The few excavated examples have exposed only segments of the fortification wall, and no complete plan of a complex fortification structure can be offered presently.

A well-preserved but incomplete example of a Phoenician fortification was exposed in Beirut. The city had a complex fortification system protecting its upper city, which was located on a rocky promontory. It consisted of a 30–35° sloping ramp or glacis and a vertical wall with one or more city gates. Large sections of the glacis were excavated, revealing at least two building phases and several repairs (Jablonka 1997, 126; Finkbeiner 2001–2002, 27). In the southeastern sector of the glacis a ramp and a staircase leading up to the city gate were also excavated (see fig. 4.9). Belonging to the earliest building phase is a guardroom and remains of an adjoining room that is still partly hidden under the later glacis. So the Phoenician city of Beirut had at least one city gate in the southeast, but it may have had another one in the west, as suggested by a paved road leading up from the harbor to the stronghold (Curvers 2001–2002, 55) (see fig. 4.10). In the Persian period, two retaining walls (Finkbeiner 2001–2002, 29–30) and one casemate wall (Badre 1997, 76–88, figs. 40a and b; Curvers 2001–2002, 58–59) were built behind the Iron Age II fortification. Unfortunately, the upper part of the glacis together with the vertical wall and gates were destroyed when modern buildings were erected in the 1960s. The Beirut fortification system was built most likely in the Late Iron Age I or in the Early Iron Age II period (Finkbeiner 2001–2002, 28; Curvers 2001–2002, 57; for an earlier date of the glacis in the Late Bronze Age, see Badre 1997, 60–64).

Stone glacis seem to have been part of Phoenician fortifications, mainly when the city was located on a promontory or on a tell summit. We know of the existence of a stone glacis as part of the fortification at Byblos and at

Fig. 4.9. (above) Iron Age glacis and staircase in Beirut seen from the west. (below) Detail of staircase and guardroom from the older phase of the glacis. Source: The Beirut 020 Archaeological Project.

Horbat Rosh Zayit (Gal and Alexandre 2000, 12–14). In the latter site, it was later replaced by stone walls built with fieldstone and preserved to a substantial height (Gal and Alexandre 2000, plan 5).

Two well-preserved enclosure walls that also served to protect the settlement in Area 3 were exposed at Tell el-Burak (Kamlah, Sader, and Schmitt 2016a). Both were built on the Middle Bronze Age glacis that covered the slopes of the mound. However, it seems that their purpose was not only defensive, that they were built mainly to protect the structures on the southern slope from sliding because of the steepness of the mound sides. The first wall was built at the end of the eighth century BCE, when the Iron Age settlement was founded, and the second at the end of the seventh or early sixth century BCE after the collapse of the former. The oldest wall is a massive enclosure circa 4 m thick, built with fieldstones that were stabilized by piers made of ashlars placed as headers and stretchers. The inner face of the wall was leaning directly against the Middle Bronze Age rampart. Noteworthy is, first, the use of ashlar piers in Iron Age II fortifications, a feature attested here for the first time, and second, the use of this technique as early as the late eighth century BCE.

Fig. 4.10. Beirut: Iron Age paved street leading from the harbor to the acropolis, thus indicating the probable existence of a western city gate. Courtesy of Hans Curvers.

This first wall was replaced by a second one a few meters north of it built partly with fieldstones and partly with two parallel rows of ashlars placed as headers. The same type of masonry is used in a Persian-period house adjacent to the city gate at Dor (Sharon 1987, 26, fig. 4). This second enclosure wall was reinforced by two buttresses built with ashlars placed as headers and stretchers (see fig. 4.11).

Two other wall segments were exposed in Areas 2 and 3. Their connection with the enclosure walls of Area 3 has not been cleared yet. However,

Fig. 4.11. Enclosure Wall II at Tell el-Burak in Area 3, seen from the east and showing two rows of ashlars placed as headers and two buttresses built with ashlars placed as headers and stretchers. Source: Tell el-Burak Archaeological Project.

the wall in Area 2 was not leaning on the glacis but had an inner face built also of fieldstones (Badreshany and Schmitt 2019). Its outer face was constructed with pillars of large ashlars placed vertically at 3 to 4 meter intervals and filled in with fieldstones. Its construction technique "is directly comparable to the so-called pillar and rubble technique, commonly found in Phoenician architecture during the Persian and Hellenistic periods" (280). Finally, a recent geo-physical survey has revealed the existence of two enclosure walls running from the foot of the tell in the southeast to its summit in the northwest. Future excavations will say more about their date and their function.

At Tell Arqa a very badly preserved casemate wall surrounded the Iron Age settlement (Thalmann 1998). In spite of its bad state of preservation, it is the only clear example of a casemate fortification wall. In Beirut the defensive nature of a casemate structure cannot be ascertained, since it has variously been described as a casemate wall, a casemate building, or a casemate wall-building (Curvers 2001–2002, 57–58; Badre 1997, 76, 80, fig. 40b). These different designations clearly indicate that the excavators were not certain about the nature of this structure. Some of its rooms were used as storage facilities, as attested by the discovery of large numbers of amphorae in them (Badre 1997, 80, fig. 40). This storage area was hence located at the edge of the urban settlement either inside of or directly next to its fortifications and may have been used to expand storage space within the stronghold (Curvers 2001–2002, 63). Badre (1997, 76–88 and figs. 40a, 40b) suggests a date earlier than the Persian period for its construction, while Curvers (2001–2002, 58, 59) and Finkbeiner (2001–2002, 29–30) opt for later.

Byblos has yielded some evidence for the Persian-period fortifications. The city witnessed an extension to the east, which led to the building of a retaining wall in front of the Iron Age II glacis toward the end of the seventh or beginning of the sixth century BCE. A monumental podium was built at the end of the sixth century BCE, the northern face of which was leaning on the Iron Age II glacis. It is made of neatly cut, large slabs with a bossed face of different lengths varying from 1 to 6.4 m and 1.05 m high (Dunand 1969, 94). They were placed as headers and stretchers in order to strengthen the building's structure. A lion protome was placed at one of its corners (Dunand 1966, pl. I). To the east of the podium, a glacis was built against its eastern façade in the fifth century BCE with neatly cut, flat slabs of stone. This podium served as a terrace for a rectangular building with two rows of four square pillars each. This structure, which was razed to the ground, was dated to the Persian period by the Attic pottery found in it (Dunand 1969, 96).

At the end of the fifth or beginning of the fourth century BCE, a massive building called a "fortress" by the excavator was added east of the podium. It consists of two rows of towers built with the same type of bossed slabs. It is 84 m long and 45 m wide, and it was preserved to a height of 9.5 m. The fortress could be accessed only from the podium area. The Iron Age II tower was rebuilt with the same bossed stones and regained its previous function as a watchtower. It had no connection with the fortress and was obviously rebuilt when the latter had fallen into disuse. The fortification system, which witnessed continuous rebuilding over three centuries, clearly indicates an ongoing planning process in Byblos in the Persian period.

There is hardly any evidence for fortifications in northern Phoenicia. Even in southern Phoenicia the available examples of fortifications do not indicate that they were built according to the same technique and plan. Their shape was determined by the location and morphology of the site. On the other hand, there is not one single example of a fortification system in which all the components are preserved. Fortifications cannot be used therefore as markers for Phoenician culture.

### 4.2.1.3. Domestic Architecture

Beirut, Tell el-Burak, Tell Abu Hawam, and Tell Keisan have provided ample evidence for domestic architecture for southern Phoenicia all through the Iron Age. In northern Phoenicia Tell Sukas and Tell Kazel have yielded examples of domestic architecture. At Tell Kazel domestic installations dating to Iron Age I were excavated, but their plans are rather difficult to reconstruct because of their bad state of preservation (Capet 2003, 99–100, fig. 33). At Tell Sukas several domestic structures with no coherent or complete plan were exposed and were dated to Iron Age I and III (Lund 1986). They are typically multiroom structures, and their domestic character is indicated by the presence of silos and food-processing installations (Lund 1986, 10, pl. 12, figs. 18, 19), but not a single house plan can be identified. Their building technique in Phase F is identical to that of the southern Phoenician houses, using fieldstones for the walls and ashlars for the corners and doorjambs.

In southern Phoenicia more examples of domestic houses are available. Nine different house plans were identified in Beirut: these Phoenician houses had fairly large sizes and consisted of three to ten variously organized rooms of different shape and sizes (Elayi and Sayegh 2000, 157–224 and figs. 36–37). The domestic character of the building was based on the presence of installations such as *tannur*s and silos. No decisive evidence for the existence of upper stories was found. All houses had well-preserved doors up to a height of 1.4 m, and they were generally located at a room angle that required the building of only one doorjamb. Doors giving access to the street were wider than internal communication doors and could reach a width of 2.1 m. The floors were either lime plastered, or covered with flag- or pebble stones mixed with sand and earth, or made of beaten earth.

At Tell el-Burak four houses were exposed (see fig. 4.12). House 1 was built in the early seventh century BCE. It is a multiple-room structure that includes a tripartite unit consisting in a front room extending over the entire width of the house and two back rooms separated by a wall and communicating with each other through doors. The southern room opened to the exterior through a door. Two other rooms north of this unit were probably part of that building, but more evidence is needed to verify this assumption.

House 3 consists also of a core unit including two backrooms communicating with each other and opening to a front room that may have

Fig. 4.12. Tell el-Burak Area 3: Houses 1 and 3 seen from the west. Source: Tell el-Burak Archaeological Project.

served as a courtyard. House 3 shares a wall with House 1, which indicates that they were built simultaneously. Whether it formed with House 1 one and the same building is a possibility that cannot be verified at that stage. However, while House 3 was suddenly destroyed at the end of the seventh century and its remains covered up, House 1 continued to exist until the mid-fourth century BCE and witnessed three repairs of its walls. The third structure, House 2, was built a century later and consists of two rooms with stone-paved floors, which do not communicate with each other but communicate with the open space outside that resulted from the covering up of the collapsed House 3. In fact, one could speak of two individual monocellular buildings sharing one common wall. The plan of House 2 is different from that of the previous two but like them does not display any domestic installation. In short, Houses 1 and 3 at Tell el-Burak share roughly the same tripartite core plan, while House 2 had a different one. None of them share a common plan with any of the Beirut houses.

West of House 2, House 4 was exposed. Its walls were too eroded to identify doors except for maybe one at the western side of the building. It has two aligned rooms with a drain in the wall separating them, which suggests an activity producing a liquid. West of them was a third large room with a floor characterized by the presence of broken pebbles, which suggests maybe an open courtyard. This plan is not basically different from that of Houses 1 and 3. However, more rooms seem to have belonged to House 4, and some wall corners have been identified along its northern side. Future excavations will hopefully complete its plan.

The same tripartite plan observed in Tell el-Burak is found in Houses 44 and 45 at Tell Abu Hawam (Braemer 1982, 162–63). At this latter site four different house plans from the Iron Age were exposed (160–64). They were all built with fieldstones, and the doors were placed at the wall corners, like the Beirut and Tell el-Burak examples. The same feature was observed at Horbat Rosh Zayit (Gal and Alexandre 2000, 154, plan 7), but one of the excavated structures, Building 49, was a two-room house with a division wall made of a row of five monolithic pillars and fieldstones filling the space between the pillars. The olive press and silo installation suggest that the building had an industrial rather than a domestic character or maybe served both purposes. A large four-room house with two rows of pillars dividing the space was exposed. In the courtyard olive-press installations were found (163, plan 9). The plan of these structures at Horbat Rosh Zayit is different from those of other Phoenician sites but presents the same building technique. However, in Area C one of the house plans finds a close parallel at Tell el-Burak: Buildings 330 and 302 (Area C plan 10) form a complex identical to Tell el-Burak House 2. Finally, at Tell Keisan (Braemer 1982, 244–49), several different house plans from the various Iron Age levels were exposed. Some of them, such as House 618, have a tripartite plan that can be compared to Tell el-Burak House 1 and Houses 44 and 45 at Tell Abu Hawam.

The available evidence suggests that the domestic architecture of Phoenicia did not follow one type of house plan. No characteristic Phoenician house plan such as the Israelite three- or four-room house can be identified. There are a variety of plans as attested in Beirut and Tell Keisan, and none of them is represented at all excavated sites. There are some similarities between Tell el-Burak and Tell Abu Hawam houses and between Tell el-Burak and Horbat Rosh Zayit houses, but there is no recognizable "Phoenician" house type. This wide variety in house plans is difficult to explain, but one of the reasons may be the nature of the site and the activities that were taking place inside the dwellings. Some combined commercial, storage, and residential functions, such as some of the Beirut houses, while others served industrial as well as residential purposes, such as the Horbat Rosh Zayit and Tell el-Burak dwellings.

### 4.2.1.4. Religious Architecture

See 5.1.2.

### 4.2.2. Phoenician Pottery: General Characteristics and Main Types

There is an assumption held by several scholars that artisans in a particular culture create commodity forms and decoration that become distinctive of that culture (for example, Hodder 1991). This certainly applies to Phoenician pottery.

"Pottery represents … the single, most significant class of artifacts recovered during the course of an archaeological excavation" (Anderson 1988, 42). With this statement Anderson has clearly highlighted the importance of pottery for the understanding of any period of human culture. The specific features presented by the whole body of retrieved ceramics, the study of the development of the main types, and the reasons behind the emergence of others can help define the culture to which a site belongs. Archaeologists rely today more and more on the material culture alone to try to reconstruct and to understand the situation prevailing in a certain place at a certain time. Pottery, the most significant element of this material culture, can be used as an objective criterion to classify a site within a certain chronological period but also within a specific cultural area. It also provides information about a site's economic situation and its participation in regional and interregional networks.

This is the reason why pottery can be used as an important and useful marker to identify Phoenician culture. For instance, when discussing the Iron Age I pottery of Dor, Gilboa and Sharon did not hesitate to classify the site as Phoenician based on the similarity of its pottery with that of sites located north of the Carmel and which belonged to the traditional territory of the Phoenician kingdoms. For them, pottery and its developments was *the* marker uniting these sites within one cultural sphere, since "one can match the developments at Dor point-for-point with sites to its north (Tell Keisan, Sarepta, Tyre), the most evident of which is the gradual change from Late Bronze Age 'Canaanite' to Iron Age 'Phoenician' culture" (Gilboa and Sharon 2008, 160).

The Iron Age pottery of southern Phoenicia has been unanimously considered to derive directly from Late Bronze Age types. This was observed at sites with uninterrupted sequences, such as Dor: "The pottery of this period [i.e., Iron Age I] is generally very ordinary and overwhelmingly of Canaanite ancestry, but with some idiosyncrasies" (Gilboa and Sharon 2008, 155; Anderson 1990, 36), and Sarepta, where the pottery of Stratum F is, according to Anderson, in the tradition of the Late Bronze Age pottery (Anderson 1988, pls. 29–30). In northern Phoenicia the same continuity in the ceramics between the Late Bronze Age into Iron Age I was observed (Venturi 2000; 2005).

Notwithstanding the fact that the pottery of the Phoenician coast continued to produce vessels similar to Late Bronze Age types, it nevertheless developed specific types of surface decoration that became landmarks of Phoenician culture and which characterize the pottery in almost all Phoenician settlements in southern Phoenicia (for a recent study of southern Phoenician Iron Age I–II pottery see Stern 2015). It is sometimes difficult to identify the presence of Phoenician ceramic types in the northern Phoenician sites for lack of detailed publications of the Iron Age pottery.

One of the oldest and most characteristic Phoenician pottery types that emerged in Iron Age IB is the so-called Phoenician bichrome ware. It appeared almost simultaneously at all south Phoenician sites and is clearly different from the Philistine bichrome ware typical of the southern coast of Palestine. It has a characteristic "enclosed band decoration" consisting of one wide band surrounded by two thin bands painted, in most instances, red and black, respectively: "This mode of decoration is usually considered one of the most conspicuous material attestations of the early Phoenicians, and of their commercial endeavors" (Gilboa and Sharon 2008, 158). According to the Dor excavators, this type of decoration was born under the influence of Cypriot vessels and was first used on small containers such as pilgrim flasks and strainer-spouted jugs, for trade purposes. It later spread to be used on all types of vessels. The decoration is applied in single bands or groups of red and black bands and also as vertical concentric circles, depending on the vessel type. At Dor, petrography has shown that this pottery was produced mainly locally, but some examples came from Lebanon (159). This type of pottery continued to be in use in the Early Iron Age II period but then progressively disappeared. Next to the bichrome decoration, geometrical motifs such as triangles were also popular and demonstrate Cypriot influence; they are found mainly on strainer jugs, are typical of Iron Age I Phoenician pottery (Anderson 1990, 37–38 and fig. 2).

Phoenician Iron Age II pottery was studied by Anderson (1988) based mainly on the Sarepta sequence. From the technological point of view, the Iron Age II pottery is overwhelmingly wheel-made. Some vessels were handmade, then turned on a slow wheel, and some were entirely handmade. In wheel-made vessels, some parts such as the handles could be handmade separately and then applied to the vessel.

The Phoenician Iron Age II pottery is characterized by typical surface finishing and decoration and by specific vessel shapes that start to emerge toward the end of Iron Age I. The most common, however, remained vessels with plain area finish, which have no slip or paint and which are not burnished or decorated in any fashion. Very often plain-surface Iron Age II pottery was wet-smoothed, meaning that it was wiped with wet hands or with a wet cloth to smooth the outer surface. This finish erases all the traces of a pot's manufacture technique by homogenizing the surface.

Burnishing is a characteristic of Iron Age II Phoenician pottery,[2] and its use clearly increased at the beginning of this period. It produces a lustrous finish, and it was applied in Iron Age II either by hand, or while the vessel was turned on the wheel, or by combining both. While combined burnishing was common at the beginning of the period, it was later replaced almost completely by wheel burnishing. The most characteristic feature of Iron II pottery is, however, the red-slipped[3] burnished ware, which is a distinctive feature of Phoenician vessels of the eighth and seventh centuries BCE. The pigment used to obtain the red color came either from red ochre or from an iron hydroxide. The vessels finished with burnished red slip are mainly bowls, plates, jugs, and flasks. The ware of the red-slipped burnished vessels was coarse in the early phase of the Iron Age II and became finer in the later phases (Anderson 1988, fig. 7). Phoenician shallow bowls made of a characteristic fine clay with burnished red slip are usually referred to as "Samaria ware" bowls, after the name of the site where they were first found.

Anderson (1988, 425) recognized two major periods in the development of Phoenician Iron Age II pottery. The first is represented by the pottery of Sarepta Stratum D and is characterized by bichrome decorated plates and jugs with concentric bands together with red-slipped bowls which were both hand- and wheel-burnished. The second major period is represented by the pottery of Sarepta Stratum C (Anderson 1988, pls. 35–38; see also Bikai 1978a, figs. 17–25), which combines bichrome deco-

---

2. Burnishing is "the deliberate compression of the surface clay of a leather-hard vessel with a smooth, hard, round-faced tool" (Anderson 1988, 337).

3. "A slip is an aqueous suspension of finely levigated clay applied as a separated coat to the surface of a vessel before firing" (Anderson 1988, 343).

rated jugs with horizontal bands and wheel-burnished red-slipped bowls and jugs. The latter develop two characteristic forms: the trefoil-mouthed and the mushroom-lipped jugs. The trefoil-mouthed jug is a ceramic imitation of metal prototypes, as indicated by the red color and highly lustrous finish as well as by the ridges at the juncture of the neck and body, which represent the soldered areas on the metal prototypes. Nuñez (2004) has studied the development of the ridged-neck jar from the Late Bronze until the Late Iron Age and argues that the typical Phoenician mushroom-lipped jug developed from this Late Bronze Age prototype. These two types of jugs have become hallmarks of Phoenician pottery in Iron Age II. They were found in all the Phoenician settlements both in the homeland and in the colonies, mainly in funerary contexts.

Storage jars developed from a bag shape and rounded bottom to a thinner body and an accentuated carination (Anderson 1988, fig. 24), which was due to the fact that the upper and lower part of the vessel were made separately and joined together. These Iron Age II jars became a typical Phoenician type of vessel and were recognized as such wherever found. Perfumed oil bottles and dipper juglets are also among the common Phoenician types attested in Iron Age II. The lamps are flat saucers with a wide rim and a pinched mouth for the wick. Double-spouted lamps are also attested in Sarepta and Sidon Dakerman (Pritchard 1975, fig. 60, no. 3; Saidah 1983, pls. LIII, no. 1, and LV, no. 1), and an inscribed bronze example is found in the Beirut National Museum (Dunand 1939, 124; Teixidor 1986, 372–73; Lipínski 1983, 143–44; 1995, 202 n. 69). Double-spouted lamps are common in the Phoenician colonies. These vessel types are attested in all Lebanese coastal sites where Iron Age II levels were excavated.

The pottery of Iron Age III in Lebanon and Syria was comprehensively dealt with by Gunnar Lehmann (Lehmann 1996; 1998 for an English summary), who correctly pointed out the absence of in-depth studies dealing with the local pottery of this period. The author noted that "the major changes in the pottery repertoire took place in fine drinking vessels, cooking pots, and transport amphorae" (Lehmann 1998, 32). All through the period there is a clear decrease in pottery forms and a standardization of the pottery repertoire, with amphorae, cooking pots, *mortaria*, and lamps being the main forms (Khalifeh 1988, 153). This decrease in shapes can be ascribed to an increase in regional centers of production (Lehmann 1996, 78, 86).

Red slip and geometrical motifs including concentric circles, which were very widespread in Iron Age II, progressively disappeared and were replaced by horizontal bands of either black or red paint as well as wavy and zigzag lines mainly on bowls. The large number of amphorae in all excavated sites—which in Sarepta (Anderson 1988, 420), Beirut (Jabak et al. 1998, 33; Lehmann 1996, 94–95) and Tell el-Burak (Schmitt et al. 2018) for instance, form more than half of the pottery repertoire—indicates the expansion of Phoenician trade in that period (Khalifeh 1988, 155; Anderson 1988, 419–20; Schmitt et al. 2018). Most typical is the hole-mouth or neckless amphora, with a flat, horizontal, and carinated shoulder. Various subtypes are attested in Beirut (Jabak et al. 1998, figs. 9–16), and this jar type is referred to as the "Lebanese Transport Jar" by W. J. Bennett and Jeffrey Blakely (1989, 207–8). These carinated shoulder amphorae are another marker of Phoenician pottery. Petrography indicated that the production centers of these Phoenician amphorae were mainly on the southern Phoenician coast, thus suggesting that they were a local product. The petrographic analysis of all the amphorae types across the four hundred years of the Tell el-Burak occupation (ca. 750–350 BCE) showed that the vast majority of the samples share a common fabric and likely originated from workshops located in relative proximity to each other, somewhere on the southern Lebanese coast (Schmitt et al. 2018). The fabrics are consistent with those known from Sarepta (Sarafand). Given the large number of kilns discovered at Sarepta and its proximity to Tell el-Burak, it likely represents the production center of at least part of the vessels from Tell el-Burak. On the other hand, Elizabeth Bettles (2003), who analyzed Persian-period amphorae from Sarepta and northern Palestinian sites, suggests also that one production center was in Sarepta, while others were probably along the north Palestinian coast. Some of the amphorae she analyzed may have been produced in the northern Levant, maybe in the Hatay area, at Myriandros or el-Mina (Bettles 2003, 190). This is an indication that the whole Phoenician coast was producing the same type of amphorae.

Next to the locally made pottery, a series of imported vessels were also identified. Most of the imports come from Cyprus, the most typical being the so-called black-on-red vessels (Schreiber 2003). This Cypro-Phoenician pottery originated in Cyprus and is characterized by a lustrous red slip and painted black circles. Its most typical forms are jugs and barrel-shaped juglets typical of the ninth century BCE. Other types of Cypriot imports are attested mainly in Sarepta (Koehl 1985, 210, fig. 9; 212–13, fig. 9; 220, fig. 10; 221–23), Tyre (Nuñez 2004, figs. 153–54, 245; Bikai 1978a, pls. XXI, XXIIa; for a detailed presentation of Cypriot imports in Tyre see also Aubet and Núñez 2008), Tell el-Burak (Kamlah, Sader, and Schmitt

2016a), and Khaldeh (Doumet-Serhal, Karageorghis, and Loffet 2008, figs. 78–80; Mura 2015). Greek imports dated to the ninth/eighth centuries BCE are also attested (Coldstream 2008, 168–88), and the most common imported type in Iron Age II was the Sub-Proto-Geometric skyphos, examples of which were found in Tyre (Núñez 2004, fig. 234), Sarepta (Koehl 1985, fig. 12, 248–49), Khaldeh (Saidah 1971, 197a and b; Doumet-Serhal et al. 2008, figs. 59–60), and Sidon (Doumet-Serhal, Karageorghis, and Loffet 2008, 16, fig. 19; 2008, 61–62). Ionian cups and pyxides are also attested (Saidah 1983, pl. LIII, 1; 1977, 141). Iron Age III pottery is characterized by the disappearance of Cypriot imports and red-slip platters and bowls and by the increase of Greek imports (Lehmann 1998, 21). The most typical groups of the latter are the Attic black- and red-figured and the black-glazed pottery, which made its first appearance at the very beginning of the sixth century BCE but rapidly became the largest imported ceramic category present at almost every single Levantine site with an Iron Age III occupation (Stewart and Martin 2005; Nunn 2014; Salskov Roberts 2015; Chirpanlieva 2010; 2015).

To sum up, there is a discrepancy in the available ceramic evidence between northern and southern Phoenicia except for Iron Age I. While the pottery of this period is well attested in both northern and southern Phoenicia, regional differences in the ceramics are obvious and were noted in chapter 2. Northern Phoenicia displays a different ceramic repertoire due to its geographical position and its proximity to northern and central Syria. On the other hand, southern Phoenicia witnessed more or less the same developments in Iron Age I: under the influence of Cyprus, the Late Bronze Age pottery repertoire progressively changed, and new characteristic wares were born.

In Iron Age II it is more difficult to study the characteristics of the pottery in northern Phoenicia because of the rarity of the publications. Common features with the south are exemplified by the red slip and the black-on-red pottery, which are found all over the Phoenician coast. However, the pottery of southern Phoenicia follows the same development pattern and produces the same new types. Its pottery repertoire is homogeneous, and the typological analyses of the Tell el-Burak sequence indicate a steady increase in the standardization of the carinated-shoulder amphora, a typical Phoenician vessel, from the eighth–fourth centuries BCE, and a great reduction in the number of types after about 650 BCE. Aaron Schmitt and his colleagues, who conducted a study on the Tell el-Burak amphorae, came to the following conclusions:

During the Persian period (Phases C/B/A), a greater scale of production is coupled with a perceptible decrease in the quality of the finish, though not a significant decrease in standardization.... The perceived reduction in vessel quality, however, is synchronous with the amphorae becoming smaller and seemingly sturdier. This gradual development likely led to a product that exhibited variable and often poor finishing but would experience less breakage and was more effective for transporting goods, which was of primary importance (Schmitt et al. 2019, 30–31)

To sum up, the pottery in the southern Phoenician sites shows common features, witnesses the same developments, and undergoes similar changes.

### 4.2.3. Artifacts Commonly Considered as Phoenician but Not Found in Phoenicia

In all the international exhibitions on the Phoenicians, such as *Les Phéniciens et le Monde Méditerranéen*, held in Brussels in 1986; *I Fenici*, held in Venice in 1987; and *La Méditerranée des Phéniciens*, held in Paris in 2008, to cite some of the most famous ones, one finds a wealth of objects said to represent Phoenician art and crafts, such as Phoenician metalwork, Phoenician ivories, Phoenician tridacna shells, and Phoenician ostrich eggs, to name the most famous items. When trying to trace the same objects in the Phoenician homeland, archaeologists are faced with the disappointing fact that almost none of them are attested in the sites of the Phoenician coast (for a discussion of this issue and relevant bibliography see Quinn 2018, 70; also van Dongen 2010, 474; Martin 2017). In this section, we shall briefly survey the evidence relating to each one of these items, and we shall raise the issue of their identity: What are the criteria used by scholars to ascribe them to the Phoenicians? Why were such objects not found in Phoenicia proper?

#### 4.2.3.1. Phoenician Metal Vessels

Among the most famous finds ascribed to the Phoenicians are metal vessels made of bronze, silver, or gold. They consist mainly of Phoenician metal bowls, which were studied by Markoe (1985), as well as other types of containers, mainly jugs and tripods, that were found around the Mediterranean.

Regarding the bowls, they were made of bronze and silver using the same production techniques. They combine elements from different Mediterranean cultures as well as influences from northern Syria and Assyria but display "uniformity in scheme and composition, which betrays a common artistic heritage and justifies the assignation Phoenician" (Markoe 2000, 148). They were found from Italy to Mesopotamia, but not one example was found in Phoenicia, although we know from Homer's *Iliad* that such bowls were made also in Phoenician cities. Homer (*Il.* 23.65) says that one such bowl made by Sidonians was given as a prize to the winner of the funeral games in honor of Patroclus. There is only one example of a bronze bowl attested so far in Phoenicia: it was found in Kefar Veradim and bears an early Phoenician inscription dated to the eleventh century BCE (Alexandre 2006, figs. 9, 10). It is much earlier and of a different type from the metal bowls published by Markoe (2000).

As for metal jugs, believed to be the prototypes after which the typical Phoenician burnished, red-slip, trefoil-mouthed and mushroom-lipped jugs were made, they were found mainly in Spain (*La Méditerranée des Phéniciens*, cat. nos. 189–93, 197), but also in Italy and Cyprus. Not one was found in the homeland. Their Phoenician identity is derived mainly from the fact that two of the most typical Phoenician pottery types with their lustrous red finish are believed to be the cheaper equivalent of these vessels. In addition, some of the motifs decorating the metal prototypes, such as the palmette, are usually considered to be a typical Phoenician motif.

With only a couple of exceptions, metal thymiateria or incense burners common in the Phoenician settlements of the Mediterranean, mainly Spain and Cyprus, were not found in the homeland. They must have existed, since they are represented in the local iconography: on scaraboid seals from Akko, Byblos, and Sidon (Morstadt 2008, 311–12, pl. 1, 1a1–1a4; see also Ghadban 1998, 148, not included in Morstadt's work), and on stone reliefs from the area of Tyre (Morstadt 2008, 374, pl. 21, 1–2). Most examples are dated to the Persian and later Hellenistic period. The only archaeological examples from Phoenicia are two complete bronze incense burners from the tomb of the Sidonian king Tabnit dated to the late sixth century BCE (Morstadt 2008, 435–36, pl. 50, OF 2b and 2c). They are, however, of a type different from those represented on seals and reliefs. We know also of two fragments of bronze thymiateria from Akko (Morstadt 2008, 447, pl. 53, 4b1 and 4b2).

The almost total absence of such luxury objects in the Phoenician homeland is enigmatic. Apart from the fact that these precious items were taken as booty or paid as tribute, as attested in the Neo-Assyrian annals and reliefs, they were most probably recycled locally since raw metal was not always available.

### 4.2.3.2. Phoenician Ivory Work

Another much-celebrated Phoenician craft is ivory work, but as is the case of metal vessels, ivory objects were not found in the homeland: "One of the paradoxes of the Phoenician ivories is that the large majority of finds come from a geographical area external to the Phoenician culture: they have reached these areas either as booty, tribute, gift, or merchandise."[4] Not one of the famous Phoenician ivories was found in Phoenicia, where only a few fragments, as well as some ivory cosmetic tools, were retrieved. The ivory comb found in Mgharet Tablun and displayed in the National Museum of Beirut and the ivory head found in the Sarepta shrine are two rare examples from the homeland. The latter (Pritchard 1975, fig. 43, 1; 1988, fig. 29, 26) is similar to the famous "woman at the window" motif common among the Nimrud ivories. The most famous Phoenician ivories are known mainly from Nimrud (Barnett 1975; Herrmann and Laidlaw 2015; Aruz and de Lapérouse 2014), Fort Shalmaneser (Herrmann 1992; Herrmann, Laidlaw, and Coffey 2008), Arslan-Tash (Thureau-Dangin, Barrois Dossin, and Dunand 1931; Fontan 2018), and Samaria (Crowfoot, Crowfoot, and Sukenik 1938). These ivory panels were used to decorate wooden furniture such as thrones, chairs, and beds (for Phoenician furniture, see Gubel 1987). The Phoenician character of the ivories was established based on several criteria, namely, the representation of Egyptian motifs and the use of polychrome inlays made of glass or semiprecious stones (Caubet et al. 2007, 213). Phoenician workmanship used also specific techniques such as ajouré, cloisonné, and champlevé.[5] An additional criterion is the occasional use of Phoenician letters on the various parts of an ivory panel to make their assem-

---

4. Caubet et al. 2007, 206: "L'un des paradoxes des ivoires phéniciens est que la majorité des trouvailles proviennent d'un domaine géographique extérieur à la culture phénicienne: ils sont parvenus comme butin, tribut, cadeau ou marchandise."

5. *Ajouré* is open work, *cloisonné* is to create closed spaces in the raw material which can be inlaid, and *champlevé* is deep carving "in which the background is whittled down in order to make the foreground decoration stand out" (Woolmer 2017, 142).

blage easier. The absence of ivory objects and the absence of evidence so far for ivory workshops in Phoenicia is therefore enigmatic, since it is well attested in the texts that ivory was one of the main items of the tribute imposed on the Phoenician cities. It is difficult to believe that all the Phoenician ivory-work production taken as booty was not replaced by the royal workshops of Phoenicia over the years. On the other hand, unlike metal, ivory cannot be recycled, so what happened? The absence of this luxurious item in the archaeological record of Phoenicia cannot be ascribed only to the haphazards of archaeological excavations. Is it possible that famous and skilled craftsmen left their homeland to serve other monarchs, either freely or under coercion? Because of the impoverishment of their local sponsors, who were ruined by repeated Assyrian incursions and tribute imposition, they established ivory workshops in more prosperous countries, and it would not be far-fetched to assume that the abundant ivory objects found in the capitals of Near Eastern kingdoms were produced, at least partly, by hired Phoenician craftsmen, as suggested, for example, by the fragments of elephant tusks found in Samaria. Their identity is betrayed by the occasional use of Phoenician letters on the ivories. These itinerant craftsmen who offered their services to other countries transmitted their know-how to locals who perpetuated the craft. Since most "Phoenician" ivory work found in East and West presents the same characteristics that single them out as "Phoenician," one could assume the existence of a well-established Phoenician "canon" in the homeland by which all craftsmen were abiding.

4.2.3.3. Phoenician Tridacna Shells

Tridacna shells are found in large quantities in the Red Sea. They were used as cosmetic containers and are decorated with incised motifs that are normally found on other well-known Phoenician objects. In spite of the fact that they continue to appear in all the catalogues of the Phoenician exhibitions, these items are not considered anymore to be of Phoenician manufacture. As argued by Rolf Stucky (2007, 223 with bibliography), the centers of production of these shells were in Palestine and Jordan, and they were exported most probably from the harbors of southern Palestine. Not one was found in a Phoenician site of the homeland or in Cyprus, although they are attested in a wide geographical area from Elam to Etruria. Stucky concludes his study saying that these items should not be considered Phoenician but rather Syro-Palestinian: "If this hypothesis is verified, the incised Tridacna shells would not be Phoenician but Iron Age II Syro-Palestinian luxury items."[6]

### 4.2.3.4. Phoenician Painted Ostrich Eggs

Ostrich eggs were widely used in the ancient world, mainly as containers and symbols of life regeneration. Ostriches lived in the steppes at the margin of the river valleys in Mesopotamia and Syria as well as the Nile Valley and the North African hinterland. This is why ostrich eggs were found in large numbers mainly in North Africa and the Balearic Islands (Caubet 2007, 227).

> The fragment of ostrich eggshell, placed in a child's grave, may have held symbolic protective or regenerating qualities as the egg is associated with the concepts of life and birth. This interpretation is based on studies of ostrich eggshells, eggshell containers, and decorated eggshells that come from later Phoenician tombs from the western Mediterranean. In the context of these seventh-to second- century BCE tombs, ostrich eggs are viewed as having apotropaic qualities, and are linked to magical ideas of regeneration as a symbol of life placed in a context related to death (Moscati 1988, 456; Gras, Rouillard, and Teixidor 1991, 138–40). (Levy 2010, 132)

The egg being a symbol of life regeneration, most of these items were found in funerary contexts. They were decorated with geometrical and figurative motifs, some of them with an apotropaic function. However, no such decorated ostrich eggs were found in the Phoenician homeland in spite of the fact that many burials have been excavated in various sites and in spite of the fact that ostrich eggs are attested as early as the Chalcolithic period in Byblos (Artin 2009, 93 A, B, C) and in Tell Hizzin, where fragments of an ostrich egg were found, but no information about their archaeological context is available.

The issue that the above items, mainly metal bowls and ivory carvings, have been used since the eighteenth century to study the characteristics of "Phoenician art," in spite of the fact that none of them was found in Phoenicia, was raised and discussed recently by Martin (2017, 94), who—rightly

---

6. Stucky 2007, 223: "Si cette hypothèse se révélait être juste, les coquilles de Tridacne à décor gravé ne seraient pas des objets de luxe de la Phénicie mais de la Syro-Palestine de l'âge du Fer II."

so—rejected categorically their use as a basis to study Phoenician art: "I maintain that the 'Phoenician Art' of the Iron Age is an invention of modern scholarship and insist that it does us little good to continue to study ivories and metal bowls as examples of it." This author thinks that "it is both historically tenable and intellectually responsible to talk about Phoenician art and identity in the Persian, Hellenistic, and Roman periods," because there is evidence for it from the homeland.

The remaining typical Phoenician items such as glass and glyptic are attested in Phoenician sites, but only in rare examples, which come most of the time from the antiquities market and hence are of unknown provenance. For a very long time the Phoenicians were credited with the discovery of glass, based on the account of Pliny the Elder, who reported in his *Natural History* (26) a legend according to which some merchants stopped on a beach in southern Phoenicia, near Akko, and lit a fire, which caused the formation of glass. The most typical Phoenician glass items are the colored amphoriskoi and the colored beads in the shape of a human mask or representing an eye. Both types are dated to the Persian and/or Hellenistic period. A number of amphoriskoi made of colored glass are displayed in the Beirut National Museum, but they are of unknown provenance. One such vessel said to come from Sidon is today in the Louvre Museum (*La Méditerranée des Phéniciens* 2007, cat. no. 255). The colored beads in the shape of human masks are very common in the Mediterranean, but only a few examples were found in Phoenicia, mainly in Sidon (Doumet-Serhal 2013, 106, 106a; *La Méditerranée des Phéniciens* 2007, cat. nos. 258, 261, 259). These two types of glass objects are the only glass items from the homeland that can be ascribed to the Phoenician period.

# 5
# Phoenician Religion

In recent years several books have dealt at length with Phoenician religion: Lipínski's (1995) *Dieux et déesses de l'univers phénicien et punique*, Herbert Niehr's (1998) *Religionen in Israels Umwelt*, Corinne Bonnet and Niehr's (2010) *Religionen in der Umwelt des Alten Testaments II: Phönizier, Punier, Aramäer*, and most recently, Bonnet and Niehr's (2014) *La religion des Phéniciens et des Araméens*. In addition, several books studied in depth some of the main Phoenician divine figures: Astarte (Bonnet 1996), Melqart (Bonnet 1988), and Baalšamen (Niehr 2003). In spite of this very abundant literature on Phoenician religion, Bonnet, in her own work on that same topic, questions the existence of one Phoenician religion, since there was, in her opinion, no Phoenician "nation" and no Phoenician "pantheon." However, she observes that, in spite of the existence of different polities, their religions shared common grounds: "Even if we are not allowed to speak of a 'nation,' and therefore of Phoenician or Punic 'religion,' with its own 'pan-Phoenician' pantheon, the multiplicity of local contexts does not preclude a certain convergence."[1]

## 5.1. General Characteristics of Phoenician Religion

The question raised by Bonnet is legitimate, and one is entitled to ask with her whether the inhabitants of the four Phoenician kingdoms shared the same religious beliefs, worshiped the same gods, and practiced the same rituals—in short, whether their religion was one and the same, with some local variations as expected in any large geographical area.

---

1. Bonnet and Niehr 2014, 55: "même si l'on n'est pas autorisé à parler de 'nation,' donc de 'religion' phénicienne ou punique, avec un panthéon 'panphénicien' qui lui serait propre, la multiplicité des contextes locaux n'empêche pas une certaine forme de convergence."

These questions are difficult to answer in the absence of written texts left by the inhabitants of Phoenicia. Indeed, the total absence of written records relating to religion is a major handicap that cannot be easily overcome. In order to compensate for it, scholars reverted either to earlier or to later sources. Starting with the assumption that the fundamentals of Canaanite religion in the Late Bronze Age did not drastically change in the Iron Age, scholars used the Ugaritic religious texts to fill the gaps left by the absence of Phoenician documents, and tried to identify the changes that were introduced to them in the Iron Age (see mainly Xella 1995): "Thereby, the rich mythological and ritual corpus of Ugarit forms a fundamental comparative standard to measure the ratio of continuity and innovation between the Late Bronze and Iron Age cults."[2]

Scholars sought information also in the wealth of later Greek and Latin sources mentioning Phoenician gods and cults and which sought to syncretize some of these gods with their own. However, in these later texts, it is always difficult to disentangle the original Phoenician from the later Greek or Roman borrowings. It is indeed impossible to follow the development of Phoenician religious beliefs and rituals, which have probably changed over the years under the influence of surrounding cultures and through the contact the Phoenicians had with a variety of populations.

One classical source, however, stands out and is considered to be important for Phoenician religion: this is Philo of Byblos's *Phoenician History* (Baumgarten 1981). Indeed, this work was written by a first-century CE scholar, a native of Byblos, and it is a document said to reflect the teachings of a Phoenician priest of Beirut called Sanchuniaton, whom Philo places before the Trojan War but who lived probably in the Hellenistic period. According to Quinn (2018, 146), "The basic text may in fact have been Philo's own, or he may have exploited an existing work, but the structure, themes, and rationalizing euhemerism of the work mean that any 'original' could not have been written earlier than the Hellenistic period." Only excerpts of Philo's work came down to us, quoted by a fourth-century CE bishop, Eusebius of Caesarea, in his *Evangelical Preparation*. The credibility of Philo's sources is acknowledged today, and the surviving passages of his *Phoenician History* remain our main source for the study of Phoenician cosmogony and theogony (Bonnet and Niehr

---

2. Bonnet and Niehr 2014, 46: "Ainsi, le riche corpus mythologique et rituel d'Ougarit constitue-t-il un terme de comparaison fondamental pour mesurer la part de continuité et d'innovation entre les cultes du bronze récent et ceux de l'âge du fer."

2014, 31). His text should be read, however, with caution, given the various layers of tradition that it used. It is indeed difficult to disentangle from this mixture of traditions what was actually Phoenician. It is to be noted, for example, that Phoenician cosmogony as related by Philo is very different from the other Semitic traditions that came down to us, such as the Babylonian and the Ugaritic ones. In the latter traditions cosmogony is built on the following pattern: victory of a new world order represented by a young god triumphing over watery chaos, represented by Tiamat in Babylon and Yam in Ugarit. This basic pattern of Semitic cosmogonies is absent from Philo's account. He ascribes the origin of the cosmos to wind and an undefined mixture coming together to form Desire: "When the wind lusted after its own sources and a mixture came into being, that combination was called Desire. This was the beginning of the creation of all things.... From the same interweaving of the wind Mot came into being.... From this substance came every seed of creation and the genesis of the universe.... There were some living creatures without sensation, from which came intelligent creatures.... They were formed roughly in the shape of an egg.... At the crash of the thunder the intelligent creatures previously mentioned awoke" (Attridge and Oden 1981, 37–39). The breaking of the cosmic egg corresponds to the separation of heaven and earth. Bonnet correctly observed that this account reveals borrowings from a variety of cultures: "No one escapes the feeling of déjà vu or *fritto misto*. The Ionian, Neo-Platonic, Egyptian, and biblical influences are obvious."[3]

Scholars have exploited also the rare information about religion that can be found in the Phoenician epigraphic documentation that came down to us. These texts have yielded a series of divine names, their epithets, and their cult places as well as personal names containing theophoric elements, which portray how the worshipers viewed their gods and what they expected from them. Some information about Phoenician gods can be found also in contemporary Neo-Assyrian and Neo-Babylonian sources. The most commonly cited is the treaty between Esarhaddon of Assyria and Baal I of Tyre, where Phoenician gods are listed as witnesses to the treaty (see also 3.1.4). Finally, the Old Testament contributes some information about Phoenician religion.

---

3. Bonnet and Niehr 2014, 118: "nul n'échappe à la sensation de déjà vu ou de fritto misto. Les réminiscences ioniennes, néoplatoniciennes, égyptiennes, bibliques sont évidentes."

The written record being what it is, one has to admit that without archaeology little would have been known about Phoenician religion. Indeed, the archaeological record often complements the written documentation and provides precious information about the cult places and the religious performances, sacrifices, and rituals that were taking place there. As seen previously, cultic installations, *ex-votos*, and cult objects can shed some light on various aspects of Phoenician religion. Another instrumental tool for the study of Phoenician religion is iconography: representation of divine figures and of cultic scenes contributes in visualizing the image of a deity as conceived by the Phoenician worshipers, and in understanding some religious performances. Many examples are known from the glyptic repertoire and from stone reliefs such as the stela of Yeḥumilk, king of Byblos.

Looking at the evidence from the various Phoenician kingdoms, one cannot help but observe the same basic pattern in their individual pantheons, variations on the same theme (Bonnet and Niehr 2014, 63: "des variations sur un même thème"). All kingdoms had at the head of their pantheon a divine couple in which the female goddess is always Astarte and the young male god is the young city god, usually the weather god. That the latter appears under different names and with varying functions in every kingdom does not speak against the fact that we are dealing with the same divine male figure: the Baal, or lord, of the city (63). All the Phoenician kingdoms had Astarte as their main female goddess (see Bonnet 1996 for a detailed study of this goddess). Little is known about her powers from the texts, but she is revered as the Lady or the Queen and symbolizes power, fecundity, and sexuality. She often had preeminence over the male god, as in the Byblos royal inscriptions, where only Baalat Gebal is repeatedly mentioned. Anna Zernecke (2013, 242) thinks that Baalat Gebal is not the title of Astarte but rather represents a distinct goddess whose true name is Baalat Gebal, a suggestion that goes against a tradition in Semitic religions of naming the main goddess after the city where she was worshiped in the same manner that the Virgin Mary is the Lady of the place where a main sanctuary is dedicated to her. Astarte's preeminence is also clear in the rituals honoring the god Adonis, the male god of Byblos: all the cultic performances in honor of this god were performed in the temple of the goddess and not in his own, if such a temple existed. In Sidon, she held the same prominent position, as inferred by the Sidonian royal inscriptions where temples for the two main gods of the city, Astarte and Eshmun (for this god, see Lipiński 1995, 154–68), are mentioned. In addition, the king and the queen were respectively high priest and high priestess of the goddess. In Tyre, we witness the preeminence of Melqart (see Bonnet 1988 for a detailed study of this god; see fig. 5.1 below) over Astarte, or at least this is what the enumeration of the Tyrian gods in the treaty of Esarhaddon and Baal I of Tyre seems to imply: there, Astarte is mentioned after Melqart. In Arwad no royal inscriptions came down to us, and no inscriptions mention the gods of the polity. However, ʿAmrit, which is considered to be a suburb of Arwad on the mainland, has yielded evidence for the worship of the two main Phoenician gods, Melqart and Eshmun, as well as a third god, Shadrapa, known, like Eshmun, for his healing powers, as attested by the etymology of his name, which is formed by the Egyptian divine name Shéd and the Semitic root rp', which means "to heal" (Lipiński 1995, 195; see fig. 5.2 below). This god is worshiped also in the kingdom of Sidon, as attested by an inscription from Sarepta (Lipiński 1995, 195). The cult of the female goddess is attested in the female figurines that were found in several excavated sites of Arwad's territory.

Bonnet (Bonnet and Niehr 2014, 63) sees in the royal couple the reflection in real life of the divine one. The main temples are dedicated to the divine couple, who were active in the official cult. This couple is present in the pantheon of all the Phoenician kingdoms, for in spite of the different names the male god was given, the divine couple represents the same religious concept and embodies the most important divine figures of the pantheon. The archaeological record attests to the popularity of the female goddess in all the Phoenician kingdoms, where she is represented with the same features expressing her fertility and her sexuality. This indicates that her essence was understood and her powers venerated in the same way by all the inhabitants of the four kingdoms.

Next to this divine couple, a divine being of a cosmic nature is mentioned in the Phoenician royal inscriptions: Baalšamen, the Lord of Heavens (for a detailed study of this god see Niehr 2003), who was worshiped also in all the Phoenician kingdoms. The oldest mention of this god is in the Byblos royal inscription of Yeḥimilk (*KAI* 4), which attests to his cult in that city. We know him also from the Karatepe inscription (*KAI* 26), where he is called in the Luvian version "Lord of the Heavenly Storm." This god was also worshiped in the kingdom of Arwad since the Persian period, and he had a temple dedicated to him in Ḥuṣn Suleiman, classical Baitokaike (Niehr 2003, 47 and n. 61). Baalšamen was also worshiped in Tyre: he is listed first before Baal Malagê and Baal Ṣaphon in the invocation of Tyrian gods in the treaty of Esarhaddon with the king of Tyre.

186	THE HISTORY AND ARCHAEOLOGY OF PHOENICIA

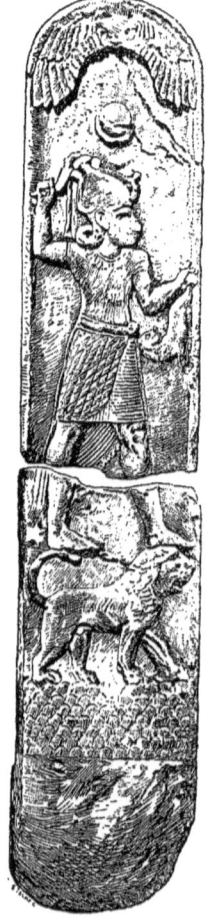

Fig. 5.1. Melqart stela from Breij, near Aleppo. Source: Museum of Aleppo.

Fig. 5.2. 'Amrit stela representing the god Shadrapa standing on a lion and holding a mace in his right hand and a small lion in his left. Source: Brent Strawn.

According to Niehr, all three were weather gods of the Levantine coast: "This is in relation to their association with sea journeys and the fact that we are dealing here with weather gods."[4] Herodotus mentions a temple of Baalšamen in Tyre, and he assimilates him to Zeus. His cult continues to be attested in that kingdom during the Hellenistic period, as suggested by an inscription from Umm el-Amed (*KAI* 18). Rey-Coquais identifies the god Zeus mentioned in a second-century CE Greek inscription from Sidon with Baalšamen: "Under his Greek name, Zeus in Sidon was the great Semitic god, Baalshamin, god of the storms and fertilizing rains,"[5] but Niehr (2003, 43) is more cautious in adopting this interpretation. In sum, this divine figure was also an important member of the pantheon of all the Phoenician kingdoms.

Other, more minor gods are attested, but they do not seem to have played an important role, or at least there is no evidence attesting it (for all these deities, see Lipiński 1995). Almost nothing is known about their nature and their cult, and it is therefore difficult to decide what role they played in the religious life of the Phoenicians. The mention of Tanit-Astarte in the Sarepta inscription, for example, is still enigmatic and does not shed light on the nature and cult of this goddess in Phoenicia (for a detailed study of Tanit, see Lipiński 1995, 199–215). The goddess Tanit or Tinnit was believed to be an African goddess, since her cult was not attested in the homeland (Hvidberg-Hansen 1979). The discovery of the Sarepta inscription betrayed the worship of this goddess in Phoenicia. Additional evidence came from the funerary inscriptions of Tyre (Sader 2005) and from the inscription on a double-spouted bronze lamp displayed today in the Beirut National Museum (Teixidor 1986, 372–73). The survival of toponyms such ʿAytanit and ʿAqtanit, respectively, in the Biqāʿ Valley and the Sidonian area indicate also that the goddess was worshiped in these areas.

This survey of the main deities of the Phoenician kingdoms has clearly shown that all these pantheons are very similar. Not only do they have at their head a divine couple, but all their main gods were worshiped in all the cities. None was exclusive to a city, and they were all equally venerated in all parts of Phoenicia. This evidence speaks in favor of a common religion

---

4. Niehr 2003, 44: "Dafür sprechen ihr Bezug zur Seefahrt und die Tatsache, dass es sich bei ihnen um Wettergötter handelt."

5. Rey-Coquais 1982, 398: "Sous son nom grec, Zeus était à Sidon le grand-dieu sémitique, Baalshamîn, dieu des orages et des pluies fécondantes."

in all four kingdoms. There is really no serious ground to assign individual pantheons to each polity. Nothing in the texts or in the archaeological record suggests differences in religious beliefs and practices. For instance, all the inhabitants of the Phoenician coast represented their gods anthropomorphically and with the same specific traits that made them easily identifiable by all worshipers. The evidence for the cult of the same gods, their identical anthropomorphic representation, the same cultic installations, the same type of ritual sacrifices and personal offerings, and the same language used for all the attested votive inscriptions and dedications all combine to suggest that the inhabitants of all the Phoenician kingdoms shared the same religion with only regional differences, indicated by the choice of a preeminent figure that was probably imposed by the physical context and the natural environment where the cult developed. Hence, for example, water played a very important role in 'Amrit given the abundance of its natural springs, and in Sidon because of the presence of the Awwali River, which led to emphasis on the powers of purification, cleansing, and healing of the main god. Other places dependent on maritime trade attributed to their main divine figure protective powers from storms and from the dangers of the sea. Some religious features can be explained by the proximity and hence easier and more frequent contacts with neighboring cultures: northern Syrian influence on northern Phoenicia and Egyptian influence on southern Phoenicia exemplify such regional differences.

I believe that in spite of the fragmentary evidence one can safely argue for one Phoenician religion: one common set of beliefs, one common set of divine figures, and common cultic traditions. Regional preferences for specific divine figures or aspects of a divine figure are common to all religions, even the monotheistic ones.

## 5.2. Phoenician Religious Architecture

The Phoenicians shared the same religious beliefs and worshiped the same gods in all their kingdoms. They also built places of worship to honor their divinities in almost all their settlements. The purpose of this section is to review the available evidence relating to temples to see whether a typical Phoenician temple plan can be identified in the archaeological record or whether there are typical features that may allow a religious building to be identified as Phoenician.

For decades scholars have assumed that the typical Phoenician temple plan was a rectangular tripartite building of the *in antis* type, with two freestanding columns at the entrance. This assumption was based on Herodotus's description of the Melqart temple at Tyre. "So I sailed to Tyre in Phoenicia, since I had heard there was a sanctuary sacred to Heracles there, and I found that the sanctuary there was lavishly appointed with a large number of dedicatory offerings. In it were two pillars, one of pure gold, the other of emerald which gleamed brightly at night" (*Hist.* 2.44). The biblical account regarding the building and description of the Solomonic temple strengthened this view. Indeed, the Jerusalem temple was built by the Phoenicians, mainly the Tyrians, and since its plan as described is of the *in antis* type, with two columns at the entrance, it was assumed that it was built according to a Phoenician prototype, such as the Melqart temple described by Herodotus. In addition, the representation of a building with two columns at its entrance overlooking the harbor on the relief from Sennacherib's palace at Nineveh depicting Luli's flight brought additional support to this view, because the building was interpreted as the Melqart temple and the flight scene as having taken place in Tyre and not in Sidon (see 3.1.4).

This type of temple *in antis*, with two freestanding columns at the entrance, has not been attested so far in Phoenicia in spite of the discovery of several religious buildings. It is in fact known today to be of Syrian origin and to represent the typical Syrian Iron Age temple, which developed from the Middle Bronze Age Syrian temples such as those of Ebla (Matthiae 2013, pl. 81). Iron Age examples were found at several Syrian sites, the most famous being the temples of Tell Tayinat (Haines 1971) and ʿAyn Dara (Abou-Assaf 1990). The only probable attestation of the existence of such a temple plan with wooden pillars at the entrance in Phoenicia is the Tell Sukas temple (Riis 1979, fig. 23), but as it is the northernmost Phoenician settlement it is not surprising to see north Syrian influence on its building plan.

Let us turn now to the archaeological evidence. Several temples and shrines were exposed on the Phoenician coast: from north to south we have temples at Tell Sukas, Tell Sianu, Tell Tweini, ʿAmrit, Tell Kazel, Tell Arqa, Beirut, Sidon, Bustan esh-Sheikh near Sidon, Sarepta, Tyre, and Tell Abu Hawam. The sacred buildings at Ǧabal al-Arbaʿin/Mișpē Yammīm and ʾElyākīn are believed to date to the Persian period. However, Jens Kamlah, who discussed their plan and finds, could not find conclusive evidence for their use before the Hellenistic period: "It is not certain that Mișpē Yammīm and ʾElyākīn were cultic centers during the Persian period. Regarding ʾElyākīn, it is only conjecture in the present state of the evidence.... A decisive evaluation of the sacred character of Mişpē Yammīm must await the publication of the final results."[6]

### 5.2.1. Tell Sukas

At Tell Sukas the Danish mission exposed a temple dated to the seventh century BCE, and they interpreted it as a Greek building based on its orientation and plan. The temple had a *temenos* wall and consisted of a rectangular, one-room building. An altar and a large stone with a hole, which probably served to fix a cult statue, stood at its western end. A column may have stood in the middle of its entrance (Riis 1979, fig. 18). P. J. Riis considered the reconstruction of the temple plan as hypothetical. East of this temple stood an altar and a structure that Riis labeled "Phoenician high place" (Riis 1979, fig. 19). This temple was destroyed and rebuilt in the sixth century BCE with a different plan consisting of a rectangular building with an inner tripartite division and two columns at the entrance (Riis 1979, 69, fig. 23). Inside was a stone altar and a base for a cult statue. The excavators considered this plan also to be hypothetical. The altar remained in use, and the Phoenician high place was reshaped (Riis 1979, 60, fig. 31). If the above reconstruction is verified, the Tell Sukas temple was built after

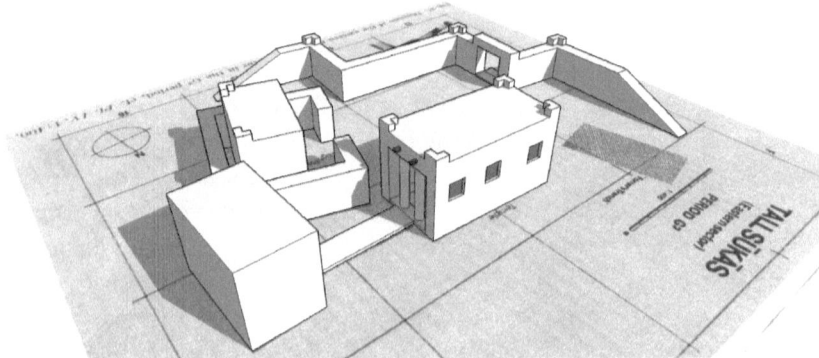

Fig. 5.3. 3-D reconstruction of the Persian period temples of Tell Sukas. Courtesy Michel Al-Maqdissi.

---

6. Kamlah 1999, 182: "Es ist nicht sicher ob Mişpē Yammīm und 'Elyākīn als Kultorte der persischen Zeitalters gelten können. Für 'Elyākīn ist dies beim jetzigen Stand der Dinge nur eine Vermutung.... Für eine abschliessende Bewertung des sakralen Charakter vom Mişpē Yammīm muss die vollständige Veröffentlichung der Grabungsresultate abgewartet werden."

the typical north Syrian temple plan, which is not surprising given that it is the northernmost Phoenician settlement. It was first believed to be dedicated to the Greek god Helios, as suggested by a Greek ostracon mentioning the name of this god, but the Near Eastern character of the building, as well as the large number of stag bones, the animal symbol of the god Reshef, led Tamar Hodos (2006, 58) to suggest that this Phoenician god was worshiped at Sukas, arguing that Helios was identified with Apollo and Apollo with Reshef. She concluded that the temple had a Phoenician character and was dedicated to the cult of Reshef.

5.2.2. Tell Tweini

Tell Sianu and Tell Tweini have yielded also Iron Age temples, which, unfortunately, are not published in detail. At Tell Tweini an Iron Age I temple was exposed. It has a rectangular cella with an altar which was found surrounded by offerings. The cella is separated by a wall from a narrow back room with two lateral entrances (Al-Maqdissi, Badawi, and Ishaq 2016, fig. 4). It is very similar to the Tell Kazel Late Bronze Age and Iron Age I temple (see below) as well as other Syrian temples of the Late Bronze Age. In Iron Age III a new sanctuary was built at Tell Tweini in the western part of the site. It consists of a courtyard, where a well and a lustration basin were found, and of an antecella and a cella with a stone-paved floor (Al-Maqdissi, Badawi, and Ishaq 2016, fig. 6).

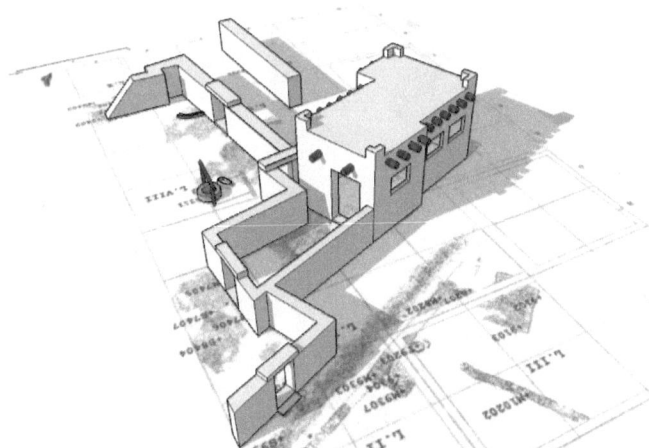

Fig. 5.4. 3-D reconstruction of the Persian period temple of Tell Tweini. Courtesy Michel Al-Maqdissi.

### 5.2.3. Tell Sianu

Tell Sianu was not occupied in the Early Iron Age but became an important settlement in Iron Age III (Al-Maqdissi 2016b). An Iron Age III religious complex was excavated there: it consists of a square building 18 m long opening onto a courtyard, where an altar stood (Al-Maqdissi 2016b, fig. 8). West of it and sharing the same courtyard is a tripartite sacred building: the first room had a stone base, probably for the cult image, and a large clay vessel for purification rituals; and the other two rooms had benches for offerings and a well. According to Al-Maqdissi (183): "This monument belongs to a tradition of the late Phoenician period, also attested at the sites of Tell Tweini and Tell Sukas."

Al-Maqdissi summed up the common characteristics of these three temples of the Ǧabla Plain (Al-Maqdissi 2007, 62–63): the Tell Sukas, Tell Tweini, and Tell Sianu temples all have a *temenos* wall, a main entrance leading to an inner open courtyard paved with pebbles where cultic installations such as altars and ablution basins stood. The temple proper or *ma'bed* is raised on a platform, and its entrance is reached by a couple of stairs. It consists of an antecella and a cella, where offering tables and cultic basins were found. Little is known about the building technique because of the bad preservation of the structures. There is also evidence that the tops of the walls were decorated with crenellations.

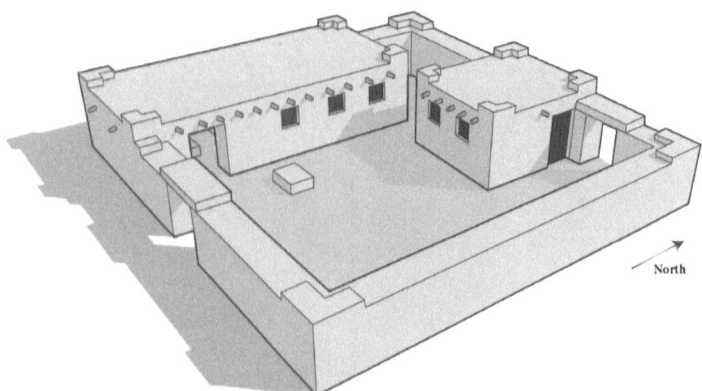

Fig. 5.5. 3-D reconstruction of the Persian period temples of Tell Sianu. Courtesy Michel Al-Maqdissi.

## 5.2.4. The 'Amrit Temples

One of the best-preserved examples of northern Phoenician sacred architecture is the Persian-period temples of 'Amrit, south of Ṭarṭūs (Al-Maqdissi and Ishaq 2016, fig. 1). The most famous, known as the *ma'bed* (Dunand and Saliby 1985), consists of a large basin cut in the rock, in the midst of which stood a *naos*, the so-called *ma'bed* (see fig. 5.6). The 46.7 m long, 38.5 m wide and 3.5 m deep basin is fed by a spring that seeps through its eastern sidewall. The temple's main entrance was on the north side, which was protected by two towers and had two altars. On the other three sides of the basin are quays with porticoes. The *naos* or shrine consisted of a small enclosure, partly built out of the bedrock. Two tiers of crenellations surmounting Egyptian-style cornices, one crowning its top, the other halfway through its height, decorated its outer façade. Crenellations decorated also the porticoes' roof.

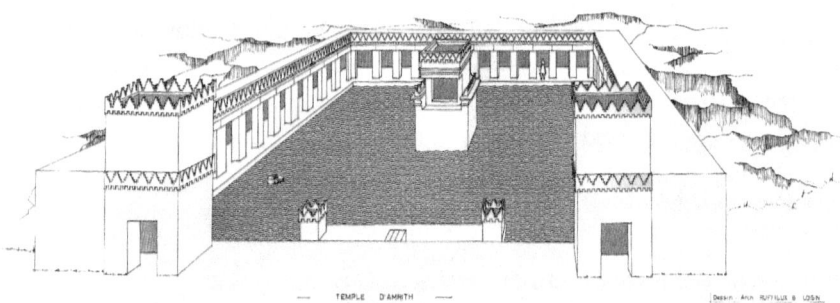

Fig. 5.6. A reconstruction of the *ma'bed* of 'Amrit, modeled after Dunand and Saliby 1985.

Two other sanctuaries were identified in the area of 'Ayn el-Ḥayyāt, and one in Area G, south of the harbor (Al-Maqdissi and Ishaq 2016, fig. 1). The former were already noted and illustrated by Renan: "The careful investigation we undertook of the Amrith area allowed us to discover in a swamp of oleanders located near the spring known as عين الحيات, 'Ayn el-Ḥayyāt, two other naoi that had been overlooked thus far."[7] The first

---

7. Renan 1864, 68–69, pl. IX: "L'exploration minutieuse que nous avons faite du sol d'Amrith nous a permis de découvrir, dans un marais de lauriers-roses situé près de la source appelée عين الحيات, Aïn el Hayât, 'La Fontaine des Serpents,' les débris de deux autres naos, restés jusqu'ici inaperçus."

is a 5.5 m high *naos* built inside a water pool on a cubic stone podium. It is characterized by an Egyptian cornice surmounted by a row of *uraei* (which gave its name to the water spring). On the vaulted ceiling of the cella a winged sun-disc protected by two cobras and an eagle with open wings is represented. On the north and south façade of the *naos* there are traces of a stairway leading to the cella platform. The second *naos* is similar to the first but was badly damaged and broken into several fragments. These 'Amrit temples display a very strong Egyptian influence and are all built inside a water pool. This may indicate that the temples were dedicated to healing gods and that healing cults and rituals were taking place there.

Two religious structures have been exposed recently at 'Amrit and presented summarily in an article written in Arabic by Al-Maqdissi and Eva Ishaq (2017). These excavations have revealed southeast of the main temple a monumental building dug in the rock with a main entrance and niches on its entrance façade, where votive offerings were placed (Al-Maqdissi and Ishaq 2017, fig. 4). The other structure is a huge altar located in the southern part of the site with a series of niches on its southern face to receive the people's offerings (Al-Maqdissi and Ishaq 2017, fig. 5). These structures are quite extraordinary and so far without parallels.

5.2.5. Tell Kazel

The site of Tell Kazel, south of Ṭarṭūs, has also yielded an Iron Age temple in Area IV (Badre and Gubel 1999–2000, fig. 30; see fig. 5.7 below). This temple, which was built in the Late Bronze Age, continued to be in use with several repairs in the Iron Age. The Level V temple is dated to the end of the Late Bronze Age around 1300 BCE (Badre and Gubel 1999–2000, 198). It is a rectangular structure built with fieldstones with ashlar blocks at the corners. It has a long cella and a back room separated from the former by a wall. The temple has a paved courtyard and two building complexes, with domestic installations surrounding it to the north and south. The cella and back room have floors made of beaten soil and covered with plaster. This Level V temple was destroyed by fire and it was replaced by the very poor and fragmentary remains of Level IV. In Level III the rebuilt cella clearly indicates that the site had revived: the cella is well preserved and is larger than the Level V one. The temples of Levels IV and III are dated to Iron Age I. The temple was burned around 850 BCE and abandoned during Iron Age II and III.

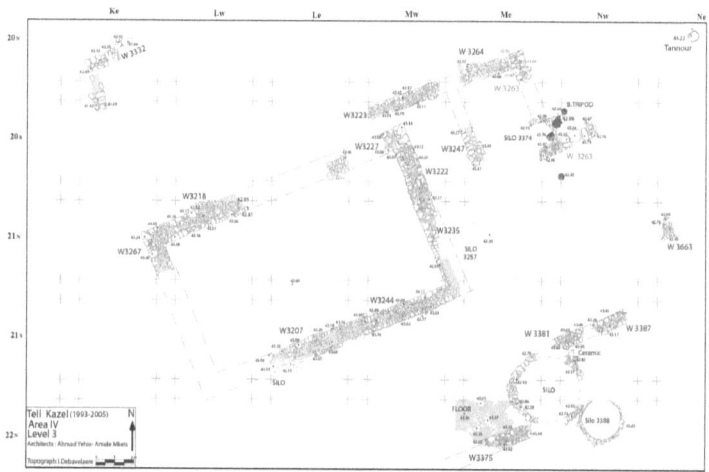

Fig. 5.7. The Iron Age temple of Tell Kazel in Area IV. Courtesy of Leila Badre.

5.2.6. Tell Arqa

In Tell Arqa a small sanctuary of the eighth century BCE was excavated, but it is still awaiting publication (Thalmann 1998: 132; see also Badre, Gubel, and Thalmann 2007; see fig. 5.8 below). The plan of the sanctuary is unfortunately incomplete. It was built next to the city wall and was bordered by a terrace wall to the northeast. It is a double sanctuary with an eastern and a western unit that did not communicate with each other. The former consists of a courtyard, a room with a basin for ablutions, and a brick platform on which a figurine was found in situ. It represents a goddess seated on a throne with astral symbols. The latter is formed by a courtyard, which may have been accessed from a street running along the fortification wall, and a square cella that contained a stone altar.

5.2.7. Beirut

In Beirut, Building U16, which was much larger than the other buildings and had multiple rooms, was interpreted as a temple (Elayi and Sayegh 2000, 153, 264, fig. 32; Wightman 2008; see fig. 5.9 below). In room 16.8 a *favissa* containing fragments of terra-cotta figurines with extended arms was found, as well as pits full of jar fragments and masks. A betyl was found in situ next to two lustration basins and a water channel. All these elements suggested to the excavator that the building was for religious use.

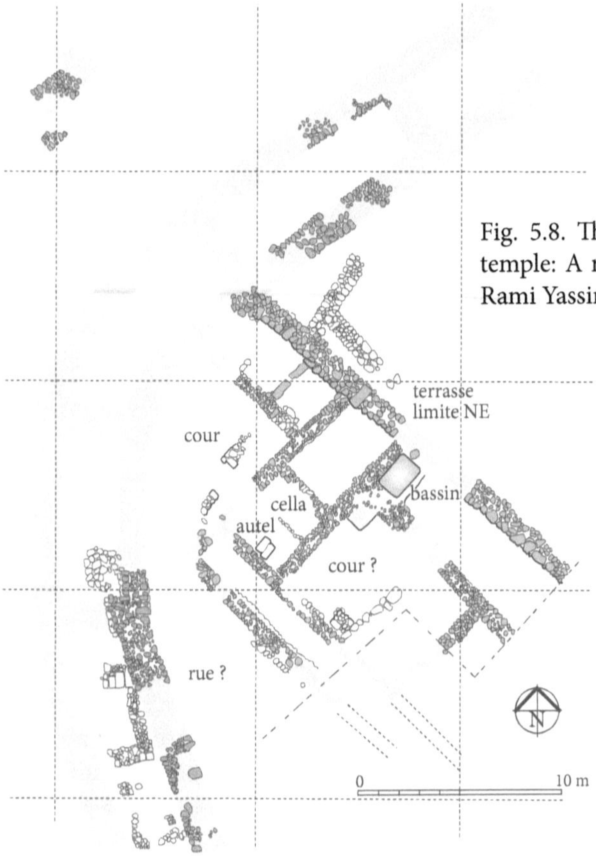

Fig. 5.8. The Tell Arqa Iron Age temple: A reconstruction. Source: Rami Yassine.

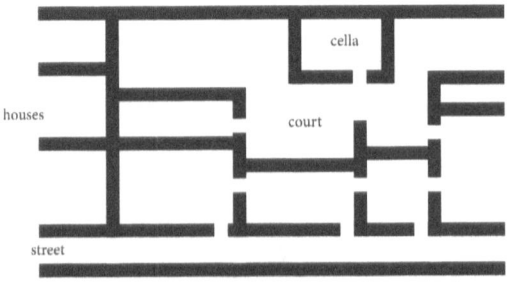

Fig. 5.9. The Iron Age Beirut temple: a reconstruction. Source: Rami Yassine.

## 5.2.8. Bustan esh-Sheikh

In Bustan esh-Sheikh, near Sidon, the only preserved remain of the Eshmun temple is a massive stone podium, which replaced a first one that had collapsed and of which only a corner is still visible today (Stucky 2005, fig. 1). The podium is 60 m long and 40.6 m wide and consisted originally of twenty-two courses of hewn blocks that were extensively robbed by the locals over the centuries (Stucky 2005, 25; see fig. 5.10 below). It was built around the natural cliff where probably a cave or a rock fissure existed, a natural phenomenon which was the original cult object on site. The existence of such a phenomenon is suggested by the fact that in one area of the podium the rock was not cut to receive the stone slabs but on the contrary, the stones were prepared to fit the natural cliff that was left untouched. In that same area too, several duplicate inscriptions of King Bod'aštart and his son, the crown prince Yatonmilk, were found, clearly making the former the builder of this new temple and dating it to the early fifth century BCE.

Fig. 5.10. A view of the Eshmun temple area at Bustan esh-Sheikh showing the corner of Podium 1 and behind it the remains of Podium 2. In the front is a retaining wall built in the pier-and-rubble technique. Source: Stucky 2005.

Stucky (2005, fig. 80) attempted a reconstruction of the temples that stood once on the podium based on the architectural remains that were retrieved on site. He identified the existence of a temple built with limestone, for which he assumed hypothetically a rectangular plan with two freestanding columns, the Syrian *in antis* type of temple. Outside the temple in the courtyard there was a stone altar, which was retrieved during the excavations. He dated the massive podium and this first temple to the reign of Bod'aštart I. The second temple he identified was built with marble and displayed Greek influence. It had ribbed columns with Ionian capitals, a triangular pediment at the front and rear of the building standing on four such columns. He assumed that the four Persian-type column bases that were retrieved onsite were placed inside the cella, thus combining Greek and Persian elements in the same temple. The lack of space on the podium area led him to this suggestion, since there was no room for two additional temples, one with Oriental and the other with Greek features. These reconstructions, although highly probable, remain nevertheless hypothetical, but the retrieved architectural elements betray the new influences that were progressively making their way into Phoenician architecture. It is interesting to note that the altar was built with a reused Egyptian cornice (Stucky 2005, insert 14).

5.2.9. Sidon

A recent and important discovery was made in Sidon on the so-called College Site, near the Crusader land castle (Doumet-Serhal 2013, 108, figs. 100, 100a; Doumet-Serhal forthcoming). There, an Iron Age temple was exposed. It is an impressive structure that was in use from the thirteenth until the eighth century BCE, with ten phases of occupation. It is built with ashlars and has eleven rooms with beaten-earth floors except for some spaces that are framed and paved with stones. Several cultic installations were recognized in it, such as hearths, stone pillars, freestanding stones, *tannurs*, benches, and niches. It has yielded a large number of offerings, which portray the foreign relations of Sidon mainly with Egypt and Cyprus. This building is important because it demonstrates continuity in both plan and cult from the Late Bronze into the Iron Age period.

5.2.10. Sarepta

South of Sidon, a shrine was exposed in Sarepta, modern Sarafand. The Sarepta shrine displayed two main and successive building phases, labeled Shrines I and II. The best preserved of the two is the older Shrine I, dated to the eighth/seventh century BCE (Pritchard 1975, 14, fig. 2), which is a very modest rectangular building circa 15 m$^2$ large. Its walls were built with ashlar blocks placed as headers and stretchers, a rare example of "pure" ashlar masonry from Lebanon. Along the walls were remains of benches built of fieldstones and covered with cement. At the west end was the altar or offering table, which was badly preserved, its stones having been robbed, leaving only the fill that was in the middle. In front of the altar was a depression in the floor, most probably a socket for a stone betyl or an incense altar (Pritchard 1975, 18).

Fig. 5.11a. The Sarepta shrine: plan of Shrine 1 showing the remains of the altar as well as the hole left by the removed cultic object. Source: University Museum, Pennsylvania.

Fig. 5.11b. The Sarepta Shrine 1: a reconstruction. Drawing Rami Yassine.

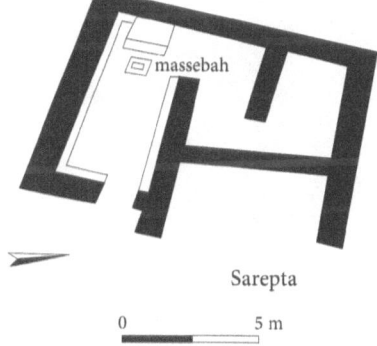

## 5.2.11. Kharayeb and Tyre

The site of Kharayeb, north of Tyre, has yielded a Persian-period sanctuary that continued to be used in the Hellenistic period (Kaoukabani 1973). Recent work at the site of Kharayeb has led Ida Oggiano (2018, 18–19) to suggest the existence of a temple of the Late Iron Age/Persian period as a predecessor of the Hellenistic temple. The existence of such a temple is suggested by various finds, mainly fragment of limestone statues.

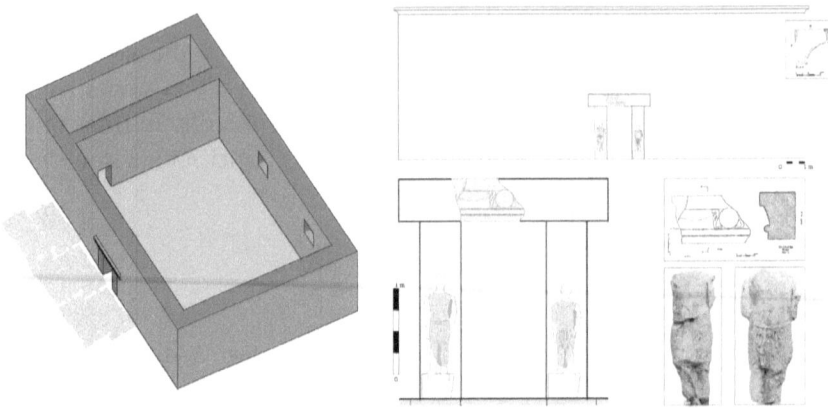

Fig. 5.12. Suggested reconstruction of the Kharayeb Persian-period temple and temple façade. Source: courtesy Ida Oggiano.

Recently a Persian-period temple was exposed in Tyre, west of the main basilica building and below the modern Shiite cemetery (Badre 2015). It is a rectangular building oriented west-east (see fig. 5.13). It is built with neatly cut ashlars laid as headers and stretchers and is an additional example of this characteristic Phoenician ashlar masonry. An Egyptian cornice runs on the outer face of its back wall. Against the latter is a podium, southeast of which stands a furnace filled with charred animal bones, a feature attested for the first time in a Phoenician temple. A stone altar consisting of a large monolithic square slab was also found. The ashlar foundation of what has been tentatively interpreted as a square tower, as well as several wells, were also part of the temple.

Fig. 5.13. Tyre Persian-period temple plan. Courtesy of Leila Badre.

## 5.2.12. The Tell el-Burak Cultic Installation

A cultic installation of a type found for the first time outside Palestine was recently exposed at Tell el-Burak (Kamlah, Sader, and Schmitt 2016b; see fig. 5.14 below). It was probably an open-air installation, but this assumption cannot be verified. It consists of a small circular enclosure made of a row of fieldstones, at the western edge of which stood a stone stela with a semicircular top. The stone is natural and does not show any trace of being cut with tools. Next to the stela was a smaller hewn rectangular stone, the top of which was covered by a grayish plaster. This cultic installation was erected when the site was founded toward the end of the eighth century BCE. It was located near the enclosure wall and remained in use for almost two centuries. Its stone enclosure underwent several rebuildings and was enlarged, but the stone stela was not moved. When the installation went out of use, it was not dismantled but rather covered up as it stood, which indicates the reverence and awe that the installation inspired to the settlers. No cultic object was found within the enclosure, but a faience female statuette of Egyptian manufacture was found nearby: it is believed to represent a female figure, probably a goddess. In 2018 another only partly preserved cultic installation was exposed in Area 3 west of House 3. Remains

Fig. 5.14. Tell el-Burak cultic installation seen from the south, showing the large natural stone and the smaller rectangular-cut stone 137 as well as the circular fieldstone enclosure 90. North of the stela is the second enclosure wall (II) with its double row of ashlars and ashlar-built buttresses. Source: Tell el-Burak Archaeological Project.

Fig. 5.15. Remains of a second cultic installation found in Area 3 at Tell el-Burak, west of the first one. View from the west. Preserved part of a paved floor, a fallen betyl, and a cultic stone vessel can be seen. Source: Tell el-Burak Archaeological Project.

of a stone-paved floor were found, on which a betyl had fallen. East of the fallen betyl was a stone vessel (see fig. 5.15).

Installations of this type were common in Palestine and were usually found inside or in front of one of the city gates (for a general presentation of sites with cultic features in or near gates, see Blomquist 1999; Jericke 2010, 121-77)—in other words, in close connection with the city wall in a more or less similar situation to the Tell el-Burak installation. The stelae found at these sites, like the Tell el-Burak stela, are aniconic and often unworked or crudely worked natural stones. The fact that most standing stones have a crude nature "may be understood in the light of the Biblical command of using 'unhewn stones' for religious purposes" (Mettinger 1995, 33). The size and natural shape of the stela indicate that it was the focal point of the installation, as is the case in other south Levantine sites. There can be no serious doubt that it should be considered a sacred stone. It is indeed generally assumed that standing stones represent a deity or a variety of idols (Graesser 1972, 36). Carl Graesser (36) is more inclined to see the standing stone as "a medium of power, as charged with a concentration of the divine power operative in the whole sacred area." Regarding the function of such stelae, four criteria were identified by Graesser (37) and summed up by Tryggve Mettinger (1995, 33) as "*memorial*, to mark the memory of a dead person; *legal*, to mark a legal relationship between two or more parties; *commemorative*, to commemorate an event; and *cultic*, to mark the sacred area or the point where the deity is cultically immanent." It is difficult to determine which of these four functions should be ascribed to the Tell el-Burak stela. The cultic function as defined by Mettinger seems to be the most appropriate in view of the available evidence (for the function of standing stones see also Doak 2015, 78).

5.2.13. Common Features and Regional Differences

The above evidence relating to Phoenician religious architecture shows that there is no common plan for Phoenician temples. The excavated examples do not all date to the same periods: some are dated to Iron Age I and cease to exist in the ninth/eighth century BCE, while very few examples are known from the eighth/seventh century BCE. The largest number of Phoenician shrines is attested during the Persian period.

Except for the problematic Tell Sukas temple, the archaeological evidence has clearly demonstrated that none of these Phoenician religious buildings is of the *in antis* type. This evidence corrects a long-standing tradition that the temple *in antis* represented the typical Phoenician temple plan. As previously mentioned, this tradition was based on Herodotus's description of the Tyrian Melqart temple and on the biblical description of the Solomonic temple, allegedly built by Hiram's masons.

In spite of the fact that the excavated examples vary in date and size and are thus difficult to compare and to classify, we can nevertheless identify some groups that are characteristic of either a region or a period.

The Ǧabla Plain temples, for example, form a homogeneous group characteristic of the northernmost Arwadian territory and share architectural features that are not found in southern Phoenicia. They form a clear regional group that shows more affinities with Late Bronze Age north Syrian buildings than with buildings from southern Phoenicia. Tell Kazel belongs also to this group.

The Persian-period temples from ʿAmrit, Sidon, and Tyre, all from the heartland of Phoenicia, form another group that can be identified by the strong Egyptian influence on their architecture. These temples display typical Egyptian elements such as lintels with Egyptian cornices, bands of *uraei*, winged sun-discs, and crenellations. These features are found not only on the excavated buildings but also on Persian-period *naiskoi* from Sidon (Sader 2005, figs. 61–68) and Burj aš-šamali near Tyre (Sader 2005, 67, fig. 44). These Egyptian features are attested also on shrines known from Phoenician iconography, such as, for example, the Sidonian stone mentioned by Renan (1864, 70) and the fifth-century BCE terra-cotta plaque from Byblos (Markoe 2000, fig. 43). Given the wide distribution of this Egyptianizing type of shrine in north and south Phoenicia, it would not be very far-fetched to assume the existence of a typical Phoenician temple during the Late Iron Age.

The 'Amrit shrines present a singular characteristic in that they were built in the midst of a water pool fed by a perennial spring. They can be compared to the later, Hellenistic-period Astarte pool in Bustan esh-Sheikh (Stucky 2005, 147–59). This characteristic was probably dictated only by the nature of the god worshiped and the healing cults associated with it.

The Tell el-Burak cultic installation revealed the existence in Phoenicia of a new type of religious structure that had been hitherto known only from Palestine. It also indicated that the cult of aniconic stones was well established in Phoenicia in the eighth century BCE. Since the Burak example is so far unique in Phoenicia and since the large majority of the Palestinian examples are earlier, one is entitled to question the origin of such religious structures: Were they typical of Phoenician religion, or were they imported from further south? The evidence does not allow a straightforward answer, and the question will remain open until further evidence is available.

Fig. 5.16. Stone monument representing a shrine or naos from Burj aš-šamali, near Tyre showing several Egyptian features: Egyptian cornice, winged sun disc with uraei, and row of uraei. Source Directorate General of Antiquities.

In spite of the fact that the Phoenician religious buildings do not offer the same plan at all periods, they nevertheless offer the same type of cultic installations: lustration basins for purification, altars for libations and sacrifices, cult statues or aniconic betyls representing divine presence, and benches to store offerings. Many had *favissae*, where the offerings made to the god were discarded. These features reveal that the cultic performances were the same and were independent of the temple plan. They are more revealing about communal religious belief and behavior than the architectural plan.

### 5.3. Cultic Artifacts

Since cultic installations are almost the same in all these Phoenician temples and seem to indicate similarities in the cultic performance, the next issue to clear is to see whether the artifacts that one finds inside a religious building are comparable in all Phoenician shrines. Several of the temples mentioned above have yielded such artifacts, and they seem to divide clearly into two groups: the first consists of the votive offerings and the second of the implements and vessels used to perform the cult.

#### 5.3.1. *Ex-votos*

Regarding the first group, the Sarepta shrine offers a good inventory of what the devotees offered to their god or goddess: "figurines of the human female, carved ivory pieces, amulets in human forms as well as the symbolic *wajet*, cosmetic equipment, beads, a cultic mask, gaming pieces, and a number of lamps" as well as handmade clay sphinx thrones (Pritchard 1978, 22). The most typical category of offering is the female terra-cotta statuettes, which are commonly believed to represent the female goddess Astarte. In Sarepta, the front part was cast in a mold and the back part added manually. A mold for casting such figurines was found in the Beirut Central District excavations (*La Méditerranée des Phéniciens* cat. no. 225), and another one displayed in the Beirut National Museum is said to come from Tyre. These figurines are represented holding a circular object that was interpreted either as a drum or as a cake, or a U-shaped object that seems to represent a dove, the animal symbol of Astarte (Pritchard 1978, figs. 41, 1 and 6; 42, 2). These female figures can be represented also nude, holding their breasts, or pregnant and as such are known as the *dea gravida* (for this type see Culican 1969, 35–50), or holding a child in their arms (Pritchard 1978, fig. 41, 1; 46, 3; 1988, fig. 12, 34; fig. 13, 54; see fig. 5.17 below). Examples of such terra-cotta figurines were found also in the Persian-period temple at Tell Tweini (Al-Maqdisi, Badawi, and Ishaq 2016, figs. 7, 9). One example from the Tell Arqa temple represents the goddess seated on a throne with star symbols. Dor has yielded also the same type of terra-cotta female figures: they were found in a Persian-period *favissa*, which suggests that a temple must have stood nearby. Like the Sarepta examples, they represent the deity nude holding her breasts, pregnant with a hand on her belly, or carrying a child (Stern 2000, 166, fig. 99). All these representations clearly indicate the fertility and life-giving powers of the deity. In the Persian period, a new type of female figurines represented with extended arms became predominant and is attested in several Phoenician sites such as the Beirut shrine (Elayi and Sayegh 1998, pls. XXIII, XXIV, 27–35) and the Tell Tweini temple (Al-Maqdisi, Badawi, and Ishaq 2016, 179). Other female faience statuettes of Egyptian manufacture, which are believed also to represent a deity, were found: one example was excavated in the Sarepta shrine (Pritchard 1988, fig. 13, 64), and one was found near the cultic installation of Tell el-Burak (Kamlah, Sader, and Schmitt 2016b, fig. 23).

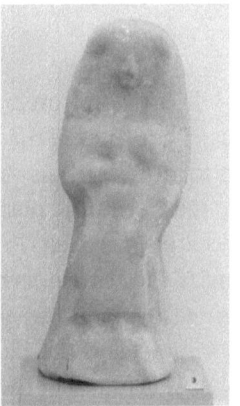

Fig. 5.17. Terra-cotta figurines representing the female fertility goddess Astarte from the AUB Museum. Source: AUB Museum.

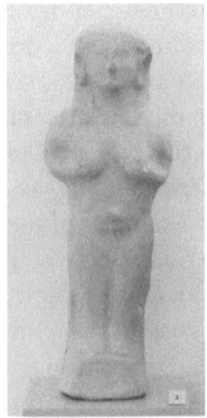

At Dor, male figures were also found in the *favissa* mentioned above, and some of them represented Heracles-Melqart. Male figures are also known from ʿAmrit. In a *favissa* located west of the main temple, male limestone statuettes were found. They fall into three categories: males dressed *à l'égyptienne*, statuettes representing Heracles-Melqart, and men holding a goat under their arm for offering (Saliby 1989, 24, fig. 5). Other male figures were found in the *ma'bed*: some represent the god Heracles-Melqart (Dunand and Saliby 1985, pls. XXXVIII, XXXIX, XL); one represents the god Shadrapa, whose identity is confirmed by the Phoenician inscription carved on its base (Dunand and Saliby 1985, pl. XLI; see fig. 5.2 above);[8] and some represent worshipers holding animals, mainly caprids but also birds. Some present a vase, a flower, a palmette, or a fruit (Dunand and Saliby 1985, 44, pls. XLIV, XLV, XLVI). So offering an image of the god or the goddess was a common practice in Phoenician temples and one of the most widely attested *ex-votos*.

In the Persian-period Eshmun temple at Bustan esh-Sheikh, statues of young children were offered as *ex-votos*. They were found in an abandoned channel (Stucky 1993). One of them was offered by Baalshillem II, son of the Sidonian king Baʿna (Mathys 2005, 277; see fig. 3.9 above). The meaning of this type of *ex-voto* representing children is still debated. Some believe that these children were vowed to the temple since their young age, while others prefer to see the accomplishment of a healing ritual or a ritual, the nature of which escapes us. In the ʿAmrit *ma'bed* two statues of adults guiding a young child were found. They probably symbolize also the accomplishment of a ritual, maybe a temple presentation or the dedication of a child to temple service.

The other most common type of offering is amulets that, in their overwhelming majority, are made of faience and represent Egyptian gods: Bes, Ptah Sokar, Bastet, Horus child (Pritchard 1978, 44, 6), animals such as cats and baboons (44, 4), and the *wajet* or Horus eye (Pritchard 1988, figs. 17, 18). All had holes or loops to be worn around the neck or to be tied around the wrist to repel evil. These amulets were found also outside the temples and were extremely common in all Persian-period settlements in Phoenicia. Three such amulets, one representing Anubis and two representing Bes, were found at Tell el-Burak (see fig. 5.18 below). Dor has

---

8. This stela was found near Tell Kazel but is believed to have come from the ʿAmrit temple (*La Méditerranée des Phéniciens* 2007, cat. 76).

also yielded faience amulets representing Egyptian gods and baboons as well as Horus eyes (Stern 2000, figs. 110, 112). The Tell Tweini temple has yielded a type of amulet in the shape of a terra-cotta leg with a hole for suspension, which has not been attested elsewhere in Phoenicia so far (Al-Maqdisi, Badawi, and Ishaq 2016, fig. 8). It has also yielded terra-cotta figurines representing horse riders, a type of find typical of the Late Iron Age. This type is well attested in all of Phoenicia, but examples from temples are rare.

Fig. 5.18. Anubis amulet from Area 2 and Bes amulet from Area 3 at Tell el-Burak. Source: Tell el-Burak Archaeological Project.

Sphinx thrones, *ks' krbm* (Lemaire 2014, 25–26), were found also in the Sarepta shrine (Pritchard 1978, fig. 42, 3). They are crude, handmade terra-cotta thrones. On one of them there was once a seated person, but only the lower part of the body survived (Pritchard 1978, 25). These sphinx thrones are common in the area of Sidon and Tyre. One was found also in the site of Umm el-Amed (Aliquot 2009, 97). Life-size examples were used in temples to replace the cult statue and to represent divine presence, as, for example, the still–in situ throne in the Astarte pool in Bustan esh-Sheikh and the life-size marble throne that stood probably in the Eshmun temple, which is displayed today in the Beirut National Museum (see fig. 5.19 below). These life-size sphinx thrones are the prototypes that inspired the throne of Yahweh described in the Bible. They became very popular in the Hellenistic era. In miniature models they were offered as *ex-votos*. Examples are known from Sidon and Byblos and are displayed today in the Beirut National Museum. Several other examples were found in the area of Tyre (*La Méditerranée des Phéniciens* 2007, cat. 70); unfortunately, however, almost all these thrones came from the antiquities market.

Fig. 5.19. Sphinx throne made of marble from the Eshmun temple in Bustan esh-Sheikh, Sidon. Source: Directorate General of Antiquities.

Ivory carvings are rare in Phoenicia in general and in temples in particular. Sarepta has yielded a few examples from the shrine: a couple of ivory figurine heads as well as a plaque bearing a Phoenician inscription dedicated to Tanit-Astarte (Pritchard 1982). A comb was offered in the temple in Sidon. Glass beads representing eyes and colored glass masks for apotropaic use were also found in the Sarepta shrine.

5.3.2. Cultic Tools and Vessels

Regarding the second group of objects used in the performance of the cult, the finds are very rare, except for pottery vessels. Storage jars to stock provisions for the temple, as well as pottery vessels such as jugs, plates, and bowls used for libation or food offerings, were a common find in Phoenician temples, as attested at Tell Kazel (Badre and Gubel 1999–2000, figs. 32–34, 43–44, 46), Sidon (Doumet-Serhal forthcoming), and Sarepta, for example. Several imported vessels were used in the cult. In the Sidonian temple they found also knives and *tannur*s inside the building, probably for the preparation of the food destined for the deity worshiped there. Astragalus bones, suggesting the existence of divination or magic cults, were also found. One common cultic object is the incense burner. A terracotta example was found in the Sarepta shrine (Pritchard 1978, 34, fig. 16, 6). Other types of incense altars made of stone were found in the Kharayeb temple area (Kaoukabani 1973), and one was found not in situ at Tell el-Burak (Sader 2016).

Incense burners from Phoenicia are known also from local iconography: they are either freestanding and placed in front of a seated divinity, as represented on the carved stone of a bracelet found in Mgharet Tablun near Sidon (Ghadban 1998, 148) and on a small bas-relief from the area of Tyre (*La Méditerranée des Phéniciens* cat. no. 152), or held by priests (for these thymiateria see Morstadt 2008).

One can conclude on the basis of the available evidence that the cult performed in honor of the gods was more or less the same in Phoenicia or, at least, that it required the same installations and implements. The cultic installations (basins, altars, benches, and *favissae*), as well as the tools and vessels used to perform the cult, when available, were more or less the same, indicating the performance of purification rituals as well as that of both animal and vegetal sacrifices: animal bones were found in large numbers inside the shrines or in their courtyards. All temples stored food and drink needed for the daily meals of the gods, for sacrifices, and for libations. Burning incense or other kinds of resins and herbs is also widely attested in the archaeological record as well as in the iconography.

On the other hand, the god or goddess received the same kind of offerings from the devotees: figurines and statuettes representing the deity, but also sometimes the worshiper himself or the persons vowed to the temple, amulets representing Egyptian gods, and apotropaic glass beads and masks, as well as other items of daily use such as cosmetic tools and lamps. Some offerings are known almost exclusively from either southern or northern Phoenicia, such as the sphinx thrones typical of the area of Sidon and Tyre, and the terra-cotta amulets in the shape of legs found only in a northern Phoenician temple at Tell Tweini (see fig. 5.20). Finally, important temples dedicated to the main city god or goddess had richer offerings, from the devotees who were mainly members of the local aristocracy or from rich merchant families, to the smaller, provincial temples visited mainly by craftsmen, farmers, and common people, who offered handmade clay copies of the limestone and marble thrones and statues.

## 5.4. Foreign Influence on Phoenician Religion

The Phoenicians came into contact with a large number of countries and were confronted with other cultures and other religious traditions. They were in trade relations with the Near Eastern kingdoms of Mesopotamia, Asia Minor, Syria, and Palestine, and they fared also with the countries of the eastern Mediterranean, such as Egypt, Greece, and Cyprus, and they may have been acquainted with some of their religious beliefs and practices. However, the Phoenicians appear to have been influenced mainly by Egyptian and, in the Late Iron Age, Greek culture. What is noteworthy is

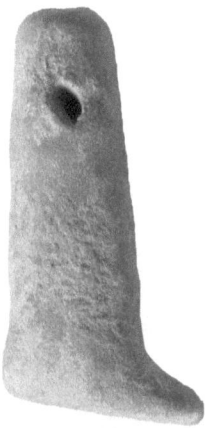

Fig. 5.20. Terra-cotta legs found in the sanctuary of Tell Tweini in northern Phoenicia. Courtesy Eva Ishaq.

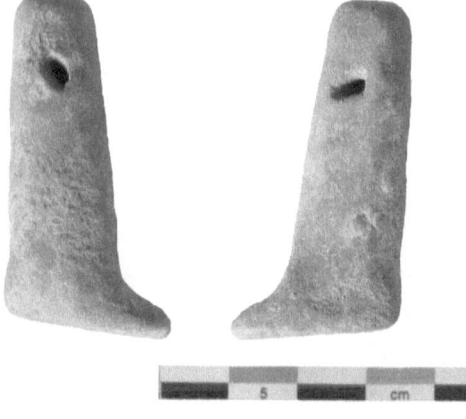

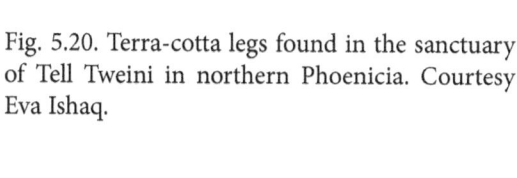

that they seem to have been rather impervious to others, more specifically to Assyrian religion in spite of centuries of contact (Sader 2017a). This is at least what the available evidence seems to suggest.

### 5.4.1. Egyptian Influence

Egyptian religion had a very strong influence on the beliefs and popular religion of the Phoenicians. This influence is obvious in all aspects of the religious life: in temple architecture; in the adoption of Egyptian gods, as attested in the onomastics and archaeological record; and in the adoption of Egyptian religious symbols such as the *ankh* sign, the lotus flower, and the *uraei*. The archaeological record betrays the widespread popularity of Egyptian gods, mainly during the Persian period. This is not surprising since contacts between Egypt and the Levantine coast are attested since the third millennium BCE in both the written and the archaeological records (Scandone 1994). They were uninterrupted for more than four millennia. The peak of these relations was reached in the second millennium BCE, as attested by the wealth of Egyptian and Egyptianizing artifacts found in Middle and Late Bronze Age sites. Abundant evidence came from Byblos (Jidejian 1977, figs. 75–115), Sidon (selected bibliography: Doumet-Serhal 2006b, 35–39; Bader 2003; Forstner-Müller, Kopetsky, and Doumet-Serhal 2006; Doumet-Serhal 2013, 31–45), and Tell el-Burak on the coast (Kamlah and Sader 2010a; 2010b; Sader 2015), and from Tell Hizzin (Genz and Sader 2010) and Kāmid el-Lōz, ancient Kumidi, the capital of the Egyptian province of Upe, in the Biqāʿ (Hachmann 1983; 1989), to mention only the most important sites.

In the first millennium BCE or Phoenician period, these contacts continued in spite of the constant threat from the Neo-Assyrian army. The Egyptians made several military incursions to try to restore their hegemony in the Levant and counter Assyrian presence, but without success. Abibaal and Elibaal, the tenth-century BCE Phoenician kings of Byblos, wrote their royal inscriptions on imported or offered statues of Sheshonq I (Dussaud 1924, pl. XLII) and Osorkon I (Dussaud 1925, pl. XXV), respectively. The Phoenician kings seem to have remained loyal to their former Egyptian overlords, and in the seventh century BCE the Tyrian king, Baal I, allied himself with Taharqa of Egypt against Esarhaddon of Assyria (Leichty 2011, 1, ii 65–82). Egyptian influence continued well beyond the fall of Assyria and regained its importance under the Persian Empire and persisted even stronger through the Hellenistic period.

All through these centuries, the Phoenicians adopted in their pantheon several Egyptian gods, as attested in Phoenician onomastics. Phoenician personal names built with Egyptian divine names such as Amon, Ptah, Osiris, Horus, and Isis betray this assimilation (Benz 1972, 269, 271, 272, 317, 396). According to Lipínski (1995, 321), the process of formation of some Phoenician divine figures such as Hathor, Shadrapa, and Ṣid was influenced by Egyptian deities. This author dedicates a whole chapter (Lipínski 1995, ch. 11) to deal with Phoenician deities of Egyptian origin. This adoption of Egyptian gods and beliefs is attested also by the large number of scarabs, figurines, and amulets representing Egyptian gods or apotropaic symbols that were found in Phoenician sites of the motherland. The most popular is Bes, an Egyptian god of fertility and protector of the family, who became omnipresent in the popular religion of the

Phoenicians (for example Mazar 2009–2010, figs. 34, 39, 44; Boschloos 2014; Pritchard 1988, figs. 17–18; Chéhab 1951–1952, 20; 1953–1954, pls. VI, VII: 1, 3). Horus eyes form a large group of Egyptianizing amulets. The Astarte of Byblos and the Astarte of Tyre were represented as the Egyptian Hathor as attested, respectively, on the Yeḥumilk stela (Parrot, Chéhab, and Moscati 1975, fig. 49) and on the Wadi Ashour rock relief (Dunand and Duru 1962, 178, pl. LXXV, 2). A funerary stela from Tyre bears the name of Matar, priest of Astarte-Isis, and witnesses the association of the Phoenician goddess with Isis (Abou Samra and Lemaire 2014, stele 40; 2013, 157). According to Xella (1990, 175), double theonyms reflect the association of deities that were perceived to be very close because of genealogical and functional links. Most female terra-cottas who are believed to represent Astarte, the main Phoenician goddess, wear an Egyptian wig. The same faience statuette of an Egyptian female goddess was found in Sarepta and in Tell el-Burak. Egyptian architectural elements were also adopted by the Phoenicians for their religious buildings (see 5.1.2).

The religious influence of Egypt can still be traced in Philo of Byblos's *Phoenician History*: the author says that he learned about the secrets of Phoenician religion from Sanchuniaton, who quite carefully searched the works of Taautos, the Egyptian god Thot, who was patron of scribes. This is a clear indication of the lasting theological influence of Egypt on Phoenician religion.

To sum up, evidence for Egyptian influence on Phoenician religion is tremendous mainly in southern Phoenicia, and Egyptian beliefs and practices became with time an inherent part of Phoenician religion.

5.4.2. Greek Influence

The other culture that had a strong but lesser influence on Phoenician religion is Greek culture. Its impact lasted and steadily increased until the early centuries of the Common Era. The Phoenicians developed with Greece peaceful trade connection since the second millennium BCE. These peaceful trade relations continued after the collapse of the Late Bronze Age and witnessed an intensive revival in the Late Iron Age, which opened the way for cultural interactions. It is obvious that the Phoenicians became particularly attracted by Greek art and architecture: the Sidonian king Straton I was referred to as a "Lover of Greek culture" (Elayi 2013a, 279). As early as the fifth century BCE, while Phoenicia was still under

Persian rule, Greek influence on Phoenician culture started to leave its marks and progressively competed with the long-lasting Egyptian influence. Greek influence is tangible not only on the material culture of Phoenicia, as attested in the imports of Athenian ceramics, for example, but also on Phoenician religion and art (Stucky 2012). A striking example is the famous late fourth-century BCE Eshmun tribune, where Greek mythological scenes are represented (Matoïan 1998, 138; see fig. 3.11 above). This monument testifies to the knowledge and appreciation the Phoenicians had of these religious symbols and how they attempted to integrate them into their own religious views. As pointed out by Martin (2017, 107), while the iconography of the tribune is clearly Greek, the fact that it was found next to a standing pillar and with a life-size marble Astarte throne standing on it "offers a fascinating window into the world of Sidonian art and religion in the early Hellenistic period."

The beautiful Hellenizing anthropoid marble sarcophagi as well as the marble sarcophagi unearthed in the royal necropolis of Ayaa in the suburbs of Sidon (Hamdy Bey and Reinach 1892), such as the Wailing Women and Alexander sarcophagi, all denote an increasing admiration for Greek culture. The former sarcophagus represents a Greek temple, and in his reconstruction of the second Eshmun temple in Bustan esh-Sheikh, Stucky (2005, 91) suggests that this temple must have been very similar to the one represented on the Wailing Women sarcophagus on the basis of the retrieved marble fragments. In other words, the Sidonian king who built it must have been greatly influenced by Greek religious architecture, for he built a Greek-style temple for his city god. The religious influence of Greece went even further than that of Egypt, since it led to a symbiosis between Phoenician and Greek gods: the Phoenicians accepted the identification of their main god Eshmun with Asclepius and/or Apollo, and their god Melqart with Heracles, and they represented them with the characteristic features of the Greek gods. Melqart, for example, was represented with the club and the lion skin that identified Heracles in Greek religion. The Phoenician educated elite started learning Greek, which opened wide the gates of Greek mythology and philosophy.

It is noteworthy that Phoenician religion in the motherland, while strongly attracted to Egyptian and later Greek religion, remained almost impervious to all others. This is particularly striking when considering Assyrian culture and religion, with which Phoenicia was in close contact for centuries but which left absolutely no trace in its religious culture. It is easy to understand why Phoenicia was attracted to Egyptian religion.

Egypt was perceived by the Phoenicians as having a culture superior to their own. The phenomenon known as elite emulation, "a theory that holds that the peripheries of prestigious cultures sometimes derive a legitimating function from the core culture" (Higginbotham 2000, 6), may be one good explanation: "Features of the 'great civilization' are adopted and adapted by local elites and their communities to provide an iconography of power which transfers some of the prestige of the distant center to the local rulers." To imitate Egyptian royal ways added to the prestige of the Phoenician royal families, a phenomenon known since the Middle Bronze Age, when the kings of Byblos represented themselves wearing the same emblems as the Egyptian pharaoh. The pharaoh was considered to be a symbol of power and wealth, and the monumentality of Egyptian buildings reflected his might. The divine powers supporting and protecting Egypt and granting its prosperity became also highly respected. Religious influence was exercised first at the level of the ruling class. This is not surprising, since it is at this level that contacts first occurred, through messengers, gifts, or trade. Only when foreign beliefs and symbols were adopted by the royal family did they begin to creep slowly into the life of the aristocracy who lived in close relation to the royal circle. It is with time and by emulation that it reached the people, who started imitating and producing all the objects that were popular among the rich and ended up adopting them. Egyptian religious traditions exercised an attraction over the Phoenicians and progressively infiltrated their religious world to the extent that they became part of their religious consciousness and their worldview. What made their impact so lasting is that they were known to and adopted by the common people: they became part of popular and not only the official Phoenician religion. According to Günther Hölbl (1989), the Phoenicians were familiar with Egyptian culture and understood its religious content perfectly well. The same opinion is shared by Othmar Keel and Christoph Uhlinger (1992), who strongly object to the opinion that the symbols used by the Phoenicians such as the winged sun-disc had a mere decorative purpose and carried no religious connotation.

The same must have happened with Greece as a result of a long and peaceful trade relationship. The royal family of Sidon was attracted by Greek culture and started imitating its monuments. Having mastered the language, they became acquainted with Greek mythology and represented its gods in their own local sanctuaries.

If elite emulation is the reason behind cultural transfer between a prestigious core and a peripheral state, why did the Phoenician elite simply ignore the Assyrian prestige markers, since Assyria was also a powerful empire that served as a model for several north Syrian kings who took pride in imitating Assyrian ways and borrowing Assyrian religious symbols? Assyria and Egypt were declared enemies, and the Phoenicians probably sided with Egypt, as attested by the alliance between Taharqa and Baal I of Tyre, and refused to be incorporated into the Assyrian cultural sphere. One important reason may be that the Assyrian encounters with the Phoenicians were based first and foremost on coercion, which probably generated rejection for anything that was Assyrian. Destroying cities and exacting heavy tribute did not make Assyria and its gods attractive to the Phoenicians. The latter may have opposed cultural resistance to the Assyrians by refusing to adopt Assyrian ways and by keeping their religious beliefs intact and free of any Assyrian influence.

## 5.5. Phoenician Mortuary Practices

Scholars dealing with funerary traditions in Iron Age Phoenicia are faced with several problems. The first is the total absence of ancient texts describing the beliefs the people had about life after death and the cultic performances required to secure the dead an eternal rest. From the scattered information that can be gleaned from the available written sources from Phoenicia proper, we may infer that the Phoenicians, like all other ancient Near Eastern people, believed in life after death (Bonnet and Niehr 2010, 117). They also believed in the existence and immortality of the soul, which survives the disintegration of the body. This may explain the presence of offerings and of religious symbols in the tombs (119). The "afterlife" was referred to as the "House of Eternity," *beth 'olam*, and the fact that the dead were believed to continue to live in the underworld is attested by the reference to the Rephaim, or "shades" (Ribichini 2004, 57–58). Details regarding the location and the description of the underworld as well as the fate awaiting the dead in the afterlife are, however, totally absent.

Concerning the funerary ritual, there is also hardly any indications about cultic performances in the texts. There is some information regarding the treatment of the dead body before interment: one Phoenician text from Byblos (Starcky 1969) refers specifically to the embalmment of the dead and mentions two products, myrrha and bdellium, which were used in this process. The inscription of the Phoenician queen Batnoam (*KAI* 11;

Fig. 5.21. The sarcophagus of the Phoenician queen Batnoam, mother of Ozzibaal, king of Byblos. Source: Directorate General of Antiquities.

see fig. 5.21) mentions a mouthpiece of gold that was placed on the face of the deceased. Terms relating to funerary practices in the Persian-period inscriptions from Phoenicia were listed and commented on by Gaby Abou Samra (2008).

In the absence of detailed written documentation, one has to turn to archaeology in order to find complementary information on funerary traditions. However, the archaeological evidence available is also highly problematic: first, the largest number of burials are dated to Iron Age II and III. Iron Age I tombs are rare. Those attested in the el-Baṣṣ cemetery at Tyre could not be excavated because they were enclosed in beach-rock formations, but retrieved ceramic sherds attested their existence. The documentation relating to the Early Iron Age tombs from Khaldeh was lost, and only photos and some ceramic vessels are available. Second, the data are unequally distributed over the territory; while many tombs are known from southern Phoenicia, only three cemeteries dated to the Persian period have been excavated north of Beirut: at Sheikh Zenad, ʿAmrit (for a location of the various parts of the necropolis, see al-Maqdisi and Ishaq 2016, fig. 1), and Tell Sukas (Riis 1979). Two seventh-century tombs were found at Tell Arqa (Thalmann 1978a; 1978b) and one at Byblos (Salles 1994). Finally, most of the evidence comes from accidental finds and from material bought on the antiquities market, all of them with no archaeological context. Well-excavated and well-documented material that allows the reconstruction of the funerary ritual is quite rare and so far restricted to a few sites, namely, Sukas, Khaldeh, Tyre, and Akhziv.

One thing archaeology teaches us is that great care was given to the "resting place" of the dead. In the Iron Age, the city of the dead was usually located outside the settlement. In Beirut, for example, "we observe that the cemeteries are located on the fringes of the contemporary habitation area" (Stuart 2001–2002, 105), and in Sarepta the tombs were located on the neighboring hills (Saidah 1969, 134; 1983, 216). The only evidence for intramural interment in the Iron Age comes from Tell Arqa and Tell el-Rašidiyye. Several tomb types are attested: simple earth pits, cist, rock-cut, shaft, and ashlar-built tombs.

### 5.5.1. Funerary Architecture: Phoenician Tombs

There are several types of tombs attested in Phoenicia. They range from simple earth pits to royal hypogea.

#### 5.5.1.1. Earth Pits

This type of tomb is very common and represented widely in all of Phoenicia. It is best represented in the Khaldeh cemetery, where large numbers of pits dug in the dunes were excavated. The pit borders were often lined with stones, which sometimes covered also the body. In Beirut ten pit burials were found in the remains built on top of the Iron Age glacis and ramp (Stuart 2001–2002, 88). In 'Amrit several pit graves were also found (al-Maqdisi and Ishaq 2016, 295). Pit graves were also used for cremation burials in Tell Arqa and Tyre al-Baṣṣ.

#### 5.5.1.2. Cist Tombs

Cist tombs built with neatly cut slabs are known from Khaldeh (Saidah 1967, 166–67) and from the site of Sidon-Dakerman (Saidah 1969, 122; see also Saidah 1983, 215–16, pl. LII, 3; Doumet-Serhal, Karageorghis, and Loffet 2008, 26). They date from the seventh/early sixth century BCE (Saidah 1983, 215–16; pl. LIII, 1–2; see also fig. 5.22 below). Cist tombs of the latter site were, unfortunately, not published. From the available information it seems that the Dakerman tomb walls were 0.5 m high and that they were built with cut stones placed without any mortar. The tomb was roofed with long slabs held together by a coarse limestone mortar.

Cist tombs seem to have been in use from the beginning of Iron Age III onward. Cist tombs were also found in the southern cemetery at Akhziv (Mazar 2001).

Fig. 5.22. Cist tombs from Sidon Dakerman. Source: Archives of R. Saidah. Courtesy of C. Doumet-Serhal.

5.5.1.3. Rock-Cut Tombs with or without a Shaft

A large number of Iron Age rock-cut tombs have been found in Lebanon. Rectangular tombs cut in the rock are known from Tell el-Rašidiyye (Macridy Bey 1904) and Beirut (Stuart 2001–2002, 88–90), where they are described as narrow shafts without a rock-cut chamber. They are also attested in ʿAmrit (Al-Maqdisi and Ishaq 2016, 295). Shaft tombs with one or more rock-cut chambers at the bottom are attested in Tell el-Rašidiyye (Chéhab 1983; Doumet 1982), Beirut (Stuart 2001–2002, 90), Byblos (Salles 1980; 1994), Tambourit (Saidah 1977, 135–36), Sarafand (Saidah 1983, 216), and Zibqin (Saidah 1967, 172). The use of natural or rock-cut caves as tombs is also attested in Byblos (Culican 1970, 10) and in several looted tombs in the hinterland of Tyre (Sader 1995, 23–25). Some of them, such as the Byblos example, may have been entered from the ceiling. Twenty-six tombs, all of them rock-cut chambers accessed by a shaft, were found in the Sheikh Zenad necropolis. In Sarepta forty tombs were explored. The published plans are those of rock-cut tombs with two burial caves, one accessed by a staircase and the other by a shaft (Saidah 1969, 135–36). According to the excavator, the great majority of these finds date to the Late Iron Age sixth/fifth century BCE. Several rock-cut tombs were also found at Akhziv (Dayagi-Mendels 2002, 3; Mazar 2001; 2004, 16).

The most beautiful examples of rock-cut and shaft tombs come from the Persian-period royal necropolis of Sidon, which extended southeast (Mgharet Tablun, Miye-w-Miye, Ayn el-Helwe) and northeast (Hlaliye, Bramiyeh, Ayaa, el-Mrah) of the settlement (see Frede 2000, maps 2 and 3; Lembke 2001, map 1). The accidental discovery of the Eshmunazar sarcophagus (fig. 3.8 above) in 1855 in the area known as Mgharet Ablun or Mgharet Tablun, "Apollo's cave," south of the settlement launched a series of investigations of the Sidonian necropolis. Renan (1864, 361–505) in his *Mission de Phénicie* was the first to explore that area, where he discovered royal hypogea. These are mainly shaft tombs with 3–4 m shafts and two rock-cut funerary chambers where the sarcophagi were placed. Others, usually later than the Persian period, consist of vaulted chambers accessed by a staircase with loculi on both sides, inside which sarcophagi were placed. These had an opening in the ceiling, and the large majority were looted before Renan's investigation. On the other hand, two royal shaft tombs A and B were excavated by Osman Hamdy Bey (Hamdy Bey and Reinach 1892), the then-Ottoman director of antiquities, in Ayaa, near the village of Hlaliye, east of Sidon. More royal tombs were excavated by Macridy Bey east of Sidon in Dahr el Aouq between Bramiyeh and Hlaliye. A shaft tomb with two rock-cut chambers, one looted and one filled with water, was found. In the locality of Ḥārah, Macridy Bey (1904, fig. 9) excavated three shaft tombs ending in a rock-cut chamber with multiple burials.

In 1963–1964, the archaeologists of the Lebanese Department of Antiquities discovered southeast of the city, in the area of Mgharet Tablun, several shaft tombs containing marble anthropoid sarcophagi and thecae as well as wooden coffins that had disintegrated. Hypogeum I had two funerary chambers; the western one contained two inhumation levels (Ghadban 1998).

In more recent times, the early 2000s, other shaft tombs with beautiful marble anthropoid sarcophagi were found southeast of Sidon during infrastructure works on the main street leading to Maghdouche, next to the Ayn el-Helwe camp, in the area known as Dakerman. No other information is available about these new finds.

Royal shaft tombs were also excavated at ʿAmrit: they are surmounted by funerary towers, the so-called *maghazel*s (al-Maqdisi and Ishaq 2016, 295 and fig. 5).

### 5.5.1.4. Ashlar-Built Tombs

The northern cemetery at Akhziv has yielded one example of an ashlar-built tomb with a gabled roof (Mazar 2004, photos 6, 10) accessed by a dromos. It had a hole in the ceiling in order to enable libations to be poured inside the tomb during the rituals remembering the dead. Other ashlar-built tombs were found in other parts of the necropolis. Ashlar-built tombs with slanting roofs are also known from the Ram ez-Zahab necropolis in Ṭarṭūs (Elayi and Haykal 1996, 49, pl. IV).

Inside these tombs, two types of funerary practices, inhumation and cremation, were attested, sometimes side by side in the same cemetery. Important information regarding the funerary ritual accompanying each practice was retrieved during the excavations.

### 5.5.2. Inhumation

Inhumation is the practice of burying the body of the dead intact. It was practiced since the Neolithic on the Levantine coast, and it continued to be widespread in the Iron Age. This type of interment is attested in both common and royal cemeteries.

Inhumed bodies were deposited in the tomb directly on the floor, on stone or wooden benches, in jars or in coffins. Most tombs had single burials, but multiple burials are also attested.

### 5.5.2.1. General Introduction

Inhumation was widespread in all the Phoenician area. It continues a millennia-old funerary practice and does not present substantial differences with the interments of the previous periods, and nor do the mortuary practices accompanying it, as attested by the available evidence. The Iron Age settlers continued to practice the same funerary traditions as previously, as can be expected in an area where the material culture witnessed continuity. The continuity in the funerary ritual is evinced in the Iron Age I temple of Sidon, where the same Late Bronze Age installations for the funerary cult were retrieved.

The evidence clearly shows that the inhumed bodies were treated more or less in the same manner. Before placing the body in the tomb, the general practice was to wrap it in a shroud or to bury it clothed. In spite of the fact that textiles are rarely preserved, the presence of fibulae, ancient safety pins, is good evidence for this practice. Remains of textiles were found in a clay sarcophagus from the area of ʿAmrit (Renan 1864, 78) and in an anthropoid sarcophagus found in Cadiz (Frede 2000, 63). While shrouding the body with a cloth seems to have been common practice, the body treatment is difficult to assert in the present state of the evidence. Except for the textual evidence mentioned above suggesting embalmment using myrrh and bdellium, no physical evidence allows us to conclude that it was generalized practice.

In the tombs the body was placed either on the floor, as in Khaldeh; in a rectangular cavity dug inside the chamber, as in Akhziv; on a bench or inside a wooden coffin, as in Beirut (Stuart 2001–2002, 88–90; the presence of iron nails in the Beirut tombs suggests the use of wooden coffins); or in a stone, marble, or clay sarcophagus, as in the Sidonian and ʿAmrit necropolis. Inside the stone and marble sarcophagi there is evidence that the dead was placed on a wooden plank, as is the case in Sidon and in Arwad: "Following an Egyptian tradition, the corpses inside the stone sarcophagi seemed to have been attached to sycamore planks, of which wooden remains and fixation rings were retrieved."[9] The same was observed in Sidon. In Sheikh Zenad, Tomb A had a stone sarcophagus (Brossé 1926, pls. 38–39), which presented the particularity of having a stone vessel carved at one end of the cover, indicating probably the existence of a libation or commemoration ritual in honor of the dead. A symbol representing the crescent and the disc was depicted on one of its short sides.

### 5.5.2.2. The Funerary Ritual: Evidence from Khaldeh

The Khaldeh necropolis is located south of Beirut to the west of Beirut International Airport. The building of the highway to south Lebanon exposed a large necropolis, which was in use from the eleventh century BCE (Mura 2015, 6 and n. 8) until the Roman period (Saidah 1966, 55 n. 1). The necropolis contained both inhumations and cremations: 422 buri-

---

9. Elayi and Haykal 1996, 121: "Dans les sarcophages en pierre, les corps étaient vraisemblablement attachés à la manière égyptienne sur des planches de sycamore dont on a retrouvé des restes en bois et des anneaux de fixation."

## 5. PHOENICIAN RELIGION 223

als were exposed, but only 178 inhumations were published (Saidah 1966; 1967; 1969), thus providing the most substantial evidence for the funerary practice relating to inhumations from the homeland. Cremations were mentioned but not published (for an analysis of the Khaldeh evidence see Dixon 2013, 495–519). Except for built Tomb 121, all the others are pits dug in the dunes in which the body was placed directly on the ground. The presence of bronze fibulae indicates that the dead were wrapped in a shroud: "We repeatedly found bronze fibulae on the chest of the skeleton, which led us to assume that the deceased upon inhumation was wrapped in a shroud or was wearing clothes."[10] The body was indifferently placed lying on the back, on the belly, or on the side, and no specific orientation was observed. The bodies were normally placed parallel to the coastline, but in some instances they were place in an east-west orientation with the head toward the west. The skeleton was surrounded by offerings consisting mainly of pottery vessels and, often, a scarab. It was then covered with fieldstones. Children were also inhumed in this adult cemetery (Shanklin and Ghantus 1966, 91; Saidah 1967, 167), while they are completely missing in the cremation cemetery of Tyre and Akhziv (see below).

Recently, Barbara Mura reviewed and studied the available Khaldeh documentation that has survived the destructions of the Department of Antiquities offices, among which was that of Roger Saidah, the site excavator. It consists of plans, unpublished photographs from Saidah's private collection, and the ceramic material preserved in the storage of the Beirut National Museum. In her PhD thesis, Mura (2015) studied the material from the 1961 and 1962 excavations. She was able to consult 529 pottery vessels and to reconsider the dates of the necropolis based on her comparative study of the Khaldeh ceramics with those of Tyre al-Baṣṣ and Akhziv. From her study it appears that inhumations and cremations coexisted in the cemetery, sometimes in very close connection (Mura 2015, tombs 3a, 3b). She was also able to identify the development of the funerary ceramic assemblage that accompanied both practices. In the Early Iron Age (eleventh–tenth century BCE) this assemblage consisted mainly of neck-ridge and bichrome-painted strainer jugs, amphoriskoi, pilgrim flasks, and plates (Mura 2015, 197, fig. 42). In the transitional phase (ninth century) the trefoil-mouth jug started replacing

---

10. Saidah 1966, 84: "À quelques reprises, nous trouvâmes des fibules de bronze sur la poitrine du squelette, ce qui laisse à penser que le mort était inhumé recouvert d'un suaire, ou de ses vêtements."

the strainer-spouted jug. In the later eighth century BCE, she observed that the assemblage accompanying the incinerations became standardized and was more or less the same as the one at Tyre al-Baṣṣ and that the assemblage of the inhumations was similar but generally poorer (Mura 2015, figs. 44, 45). It consisted of the cinerary urn accompanied by a neck-ridge, mushroom-lipped, and red-slipped wheel-burnished trefoil-mouth jug, a bowl, and a plate.

Solid food was placed in the plates. One of the most commonly offered foods at Khaldeh was fish, and excavators found "several plates containing a fish skeleton" (Saidah 1966, 85: "plusieurs plats contenant un squelette de poisson"; Mura 2015, 193 and fig. 38; see fig. 5.23 below). Drinks were placed in jugs: it is assumed that the mushroom-lipped jug probably contained precious liquids such as wine and honey (Mura 2015, 193; see also Aubet, Nuñez, and Tresilló 2014, 510). The intentional breaking of crockery, which suggests the existence of a funerary meal in honor of the dead, was attested only above Tomb 166; this is, at least, the only published example. This evidence may lead to the assumption that in inhumation ceremonies no funerary banquet took place in the cemetery, as is common in the cremation burials. These vessels and their content formed the only offerings given to the dead for his journey to the underworld. With the exception of an occasional scarab, almost no personal item is attested in the Khaldeh tombs.

Finally, it is important to note that eight dog burials were found in the Khaldeh cemetery. Only a short note mentions them (Saidah 1967, 166). They were carefully buried, suggesting a funerary ritual. The species was identified as greyhound, *lévriers du désert*, as specified by the excavator. As Helen Dixon (2013, 517) observes: "They represent the only dog burials of this kind known to be associated with a human burial area. However, the nature of the relationship between the eight dog burials and the human cemetery area at Khaldeh is not entirely clear from Saidah's publications. If these are contemporary, the Khaldé burials represent the only Phoenician dog burials of this kind known from before the Persian period."

5.5.2.3. The Funerary Ritual: Evidence from Sidon and ʿAmrit

Sidon and ʿAmrit are the only two Phoenician cities that have yielded royal cemeteries in which the inhumation mortuary practice was exclusively used. This is not surprising, since these royal tombs are all dated to the Persian period, when cremation ceased to be observed. Cemeteries for the

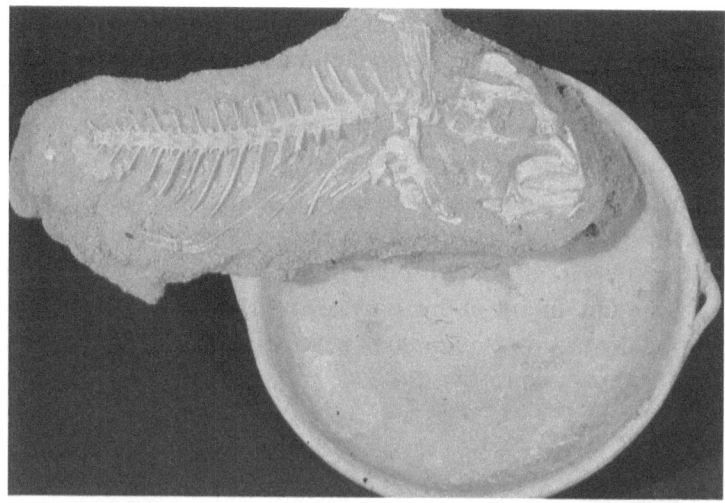

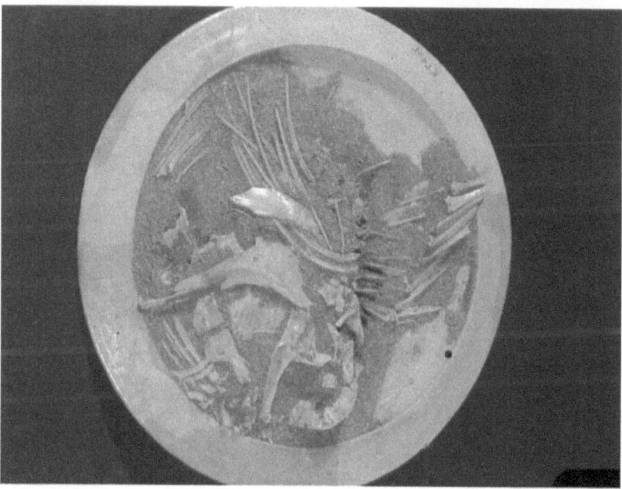

Fig. 5.23. Plates with complete fish skeletons placed in inhumation tombs in the Khaldeh cemetery. Archives Roger Saidah. Courtesy C. Doumet-Serhal.

common people where inhumation was practiced were also found in both cities, but they have not been published.

In the royal necropolis of Sidon, which surrounded the urban settlement on its southern and eastern edge, all the dead were placed in stone or marble sarcophagi (for a detailed description of these necropolises see Lembke 2001; Frede 2000). The large majority of these sarcophagi are of the so-called anthropoid type (Renan 1864, 411–12). They all bear traces of red paint (on the polychromy of the anthropoid sarcophagi, see Lembke 2001, 91ff.), and they were often found together with rectangular white marble sarcophagi of the *theca* type (Renan 1864, 422, 427). Toward the end of the nineteenth century twenty-five marble anthropoid sarcophagi were found by the American School of Jerusalem in Sidon in the area of Ayn el-Helwe. They are known as the Ford collection, after the name of the then–school director who donated them to the Lebanese authorities. They are displayed today in the lower gallery of the Beirut National Museum. In one of the tombs a lower jaw of a skull with a gold wire holding the teeth was found (Clawson 1934, fig. 5), one of the earliest examples of dental prostheses.

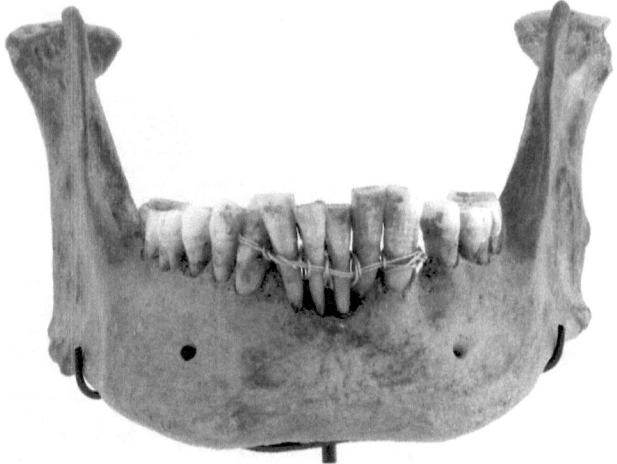

Fig. 5.24. Lower jaw with a golden wire holding the teeth from a Sidonian tomb from the Persian period. Source: AUB Museum.

In Hypogea A and B of the Ayaa royal necropolis (Hamdy Bey and Reinach 1892, pls. III, XLIII, 1), Hamdy Bey found a collection of beautiful marble sarcophagi, the most famous of which are the Tabnit, Alexander, Wailing Women, Satrap," and Lycian sarcophagi. They are all displayed in the Museum of Istanbul. Tabnit's was a reused Egyptian basalt mummy sarcophagus with a hieroglyphic and a Phoenician inscription identifying respectively its former and later owner.

What seems typical of the royal necropolis of Sidon in the Persian period is the widespread use of marble sarcophagi of the anthropoid, *theca*, and architectural type (Elayi 1989, 262–69). The Sidonian anthropoid sarcophagi are an imitation of Egyptian prototypes (Kukahn 1955; Buhl 1964; 1983b; 1991; Elayi 1989; Elayi and Haykal 1996; Lembke 2001; Frede 2000). The local imitation of Egyptian mummy sarcophagi is a typical Phoenician production of the late sixth to the end of the fourth century BCE (Lembke 2001, 117). They stopped being used after the invasion of Alexander the Great. They are found almost exclusively in the Arwadian and Sidonian necropolis, with a few scattered examples in other Phoenician cities and western colonies (Frede 2000, 36–63). At the beginning, the local Sidonian sarcophagi imitated the Egyptian prototypes, but as Greek influence started affecting Phoenician art and architecture, Greek features replaced the Egyptian faces. According to Katja Lembke, we owe this category of funerary items to both Egyptian and Greek influence: "Notwithstanding Persian rule, the anthropoid sarcophagi formed a new category of items which was equally influenced by Egyptian and Greek culture."[11] It has been suggested that Greek masters were brought to Sidon to produce them (Elayi 1989, 262; Lembke 1998, 145). Local sculptors learned from them how to cut marble, a technique with which the Phoenician stone cutters were not familiar (Lembke 2001, 91, 108). More than fifty marble anthropoid sarcophagi were found in Sidon. It is interesting to note that this type of sarcophagus was found almost exclusively in Sidon and in the Arwadian territory, mainly ʿAmrit and Ṭarṭūs, which indicates that the main production sites were established there. This raises the question as to why these sarcophagi were popular in the Arwadian and Sidonian kingdoms, where they were found in large numbers, and almost absent in the other two Phoenician kingdoms. No satisfactory answer can be given at present.

Fig. 5.25. The sarcophagus of the Sidonian king Tabnit, retrieved from a Persian-period hypogeum at the Ayaa royal necropolis. Source: Istanbul Classical Museum.

---

11. Lembke 2001, 117: "Unabhängig von der persischen Oberherrschaft bildete sich also mit den anthropoiden Sarkophagen in Phönizien eine neue Gattung heraus, die sich zu gleichen Teilen aus ägyptischen und griechichen Quellen speiste."

Greek influence on funerary monuments is attested also in the use of *thecae*. The *thecae* are Greek coffins of a very simple shape with a rounded or a triangular lid in the shape of a slanting roof that were copied in Asia Minor and in the Levant. The best example is Batnoam's sarcophagus (Dunand 1939, pl. XXVIII; see fig. 5.21 above), displayed today in the Beirut National Museum. The architectural sarcophagi found in Sidon—the Satrap, Lycian, Alexander, and Wailing Women sarcophagi (Lembke 1998, 145; Elayi 1989, 269, excludes the Alexander sarcophagus from this category)—are so called because they are cut in the shape of a monument and their sides are sculpted with reliefs.

The Sidonian funerary evidence indicates the strong Egyptian and Greek influence during the Late Iron Age in Lebanon. The finds attest to the wealth of the Sidonian royal house and aristocracy in the Persian period and to the skills of its artisans and goldsmiths, as appears from the jewelry that was retrieved in these coffins. The most spectacular examples of Phoenician jewelry from the motherland came from the royal tombs at Mgharet Tablun: a diadem with Medusa head (Ghadban 2008, 149); a silver bracelet with an inlaid amethyst representing the goddess Astarte with a worshiper; two golden rings, one representing a lion attacking a caprid and the other a ritual scene (148); and an amphora-shaped pendant (147). Another assemblage of Phoenician jewelry was recently found in a hypogeum exposed during infrastructure work in the area of Dakerman, south of Sidon (Seif 2012, 79). In one of the sarcophagi was a preserved female skeleton who wore a complete jewelry set: a golden necklace (Seif 2012, fig. 10), a pair of golden earrings with agate stones (fig. 12), a gold ring with a carnelian engraved with a fabulous animal (figs. 11, 13), and a gold ring representing a lion similar to those found in Mgharet Tablun (fig. 7). They attest to skilled Phoenician craftsmanship in using *repoussé*, filigree, and granulation techniques.[12] This technology was transferred to jewelers working in the Mediterranean area, examples of which were found mainly in Carthage, Sardinia, and southern Spain.

Some Sidonian royal tombs betray a funerary practice otherwise unknown in Phoenicia: mummification. This practice seems to have been restricted to the royal family. "The methods used by the Phoenicians to preserve their dead offers strong evidence that at the very least, some Per-

---

12. Filigree consists of producing fine gold or silver threads and soldering them together; granulation consists in producing little dots of precious metal and soldering them to form a motif.

sian period kings were prepared for burial in such a way as to attempt preservation of their soft tissues" (Dixon 2013, 553). While in Arwad there was only indirect evidence for this practice (Elayi and Haykal 1996, 121), three examples of mummification, all of them from the royal necropolis, are attested in Sidon. The most famous example is that of the Sidonian king Tabnit, whose corpse was lying in a liquid and attached to a sycamore plank. It had been mummified but was badly damaged as local workmen overturned the sarcophagus. According to Henry Jessup's account (Jessup 1910, 507), they "spilled all the precious fluid in the sand. The Bey's [i.e., Hamdy Bey] indignation knew no bounds but it was too late and the body could not be preserved and the secret of the wonderful fluid was again hidden in the Sidon sand."

In one of the shaft tombs excavated by Macridy Bey in Dahr el Aouq was a white, undecorated marble sarcophagus inside which was a young girl fastened to a sycamore plank floating in a fluid. In spite of the fact that the sarcophagus had been looted, Macridy Bey found it filled with liquid, bones, and a lump of hair still preserved on the skull (Macridy Bey1904, 556, fig. 5, pl. IV, 1). The skeleton presented the same evidence for mummification as that of Tabnit. Finally, one of the recently excavated royal tombs of Sidon contained a mummified body wrapped in a linen cloth (Ghadban 1998, 147). There has been unfortunately no analysis of the liquid in any of these cases. Mummification is additional evidence for Egyptian influence on the funerary customs of the Sidonian royal family.

In ʿAmrit the anthropoid sarcophagus was not used exclusively by the royal family, as in Sidon. People there used a variety of raw materials for the production of these sarcophagi, which reflects the provincial character of the ʿAmrit production (Lembke 2001, 49). Furthermore, the anthropoid sarcophagi were not found exclusively in hypogea, as is the case of Sidon, but in different types of tombs. Another characteristic of the Arwadian funerary practice is the building of a funerary tower or mausoleum on top of the tombs in the royal necropolis. These funerary towers are commonly referred to as *maghazil*. No such structure was found in Sidon. The clay anthropoid sarcophagi did not contain remains of wooden planks, as did the stone ones, and the dead was placed directly on the floor of the sarcophagus. Another characteristic of the clay sarcophagi is that some of them were covered on the inside with a whitish plaster. The covers were molded to represent the head of the deceased. Some hypogea containing clay anthropoid sarcophagi do not seem to have been for the ruling class but rather for common people. Still, these sarcophagi are informative about

Phoenician coroplasts. Most clay sarcophagi were molded to represent the figure of the dead. Some were worked in the traditional Phoenician way and represented the dead with clear Egyptian features and jewelry (Elayi and Haykal 1996, pl. XXIX), while others adopted Greek features (Elayi and Haykal 1996, pl. XXXVI).

Both Sidon and 'Amrit have yielded Persian-period tombs for the common people. In Sidon, in the area of Dakerman, one of the largest Late Iron Age cemeteries, dated to the end of the seventh century BCE, was exposed but unfortunately not published (Saidah 1969, 122). Two inscribed stone stelae and a funerary mask from this cemetery were published respectively by Teixidor (1982, 233–35) and William Culican (1975–1976, 55), who described the mask as a "bearded male mask from Sidon from Iron Age tombs discovered at Sheikh Abaroh."[13]

The cemeteries in the territory of Arwad were studied by Elayi and Haykal (1996). In 'Amrit, almost all the tombs were looted, and no information about the funerary ritual could be detected. What Elayi and Haykal say about the collective tomb of the chalets area could be applied to all the others: "It is difficult to reconstruct the ceremonies that took place upon the death and the interment of the occupants of this grave, as well as the rituals performed by the living after inhumation: if there were inscriptions painted on the sarcophagi, they were erased, and if offerings were deposited inside the sarcophagi, they have disappeared; we do not have parallels likely to shed light on this funerary ritual."[14]

Al-Maqdisi and Ishaq (2016, 295 and fig. 6), who undertook new excavations in 'Amrit, mention a common cemetery at al-Bayyada northeast of the royal necropolis. In this cemetery rock-cut tombs with carved stone stelae were found recently. They are the first funerary stelae to be found in northern Phoenicia. They are made of *ramleh* stone, the same material used also for the Tyrian and Akhziv stelae, and they are carved with motifs attested also in the south. Some of the published examples

---

13. Sheikh Abaroh is another name of the Dakerman area used also by Renan (1864, pl. LXVII).

14. Elayi and Haykal 1996: 114: "Il est difficile d'imaginer les cérémonies qui ont entouré le décès et la mise au tombeau des occupants de cette tombe, de même que les rites accomplis par les vivants après l'inhumation: s'il y avait des inscriptions peintes sur les sarcophages, elles sont effacées; si des objets avaient été déposés dans ces sarcophages, ils ont disparu; et l'on ne dispose pas non plus de parallèles susceptibles d'éclairer ce rituel funéraire."

have cavities, which represent most probably shrines, and one has the crescent and disc. These motifs are similar to the ones represented on Tyrian (Sader 2005, nos. 50 and 17, 20) and Akhziv stelae (Mazar 2009–2010, fig. 127, 27). One unpublished example from 'Amrit, made of basalt, was placed in a niche inside the tomb (see fig. 5.26). Its shape and its material indicate that is in the tradition of north Syrian rather than Phoenician tomb stones. Other cemeteries for the common people were excavated: the Azar and Tell Ghamqe tombs are located north and northeast of the royal necropolis (al-Maqdisi and Ishaq 2016, 295 and fig. 1). The evidence from the latter sites was presented by Elayi and Haykal (1996). However, little can be said about the funerary ritual, since most of these tombs had been emptied.

5.5.2.4. The Funerary Ritual: Evidence from the South and East Cemetery at Akhziv

The tombs excavated in the southern and eastern cemetery at Akhziv were used from the eleventh until the seventh century BCE (Dayagi-Mendels 2002, 163). These tombs were excavated in the 1940s by Ben Dor and published by Michal Dayagi-Mendels in 2002. New excavations by Moshe Prausnitz between 1958 and 1980 were presented mainly in short notes and in two articles (Prausnitz 1982; 1993). Finally, Eilat Mazar (2001) published her excavations in the southern cemetery as well as the inhumation shaft tomb 1 of the northern cemetery (Mazar 2004). Most of the documentation from the Ben Dor excavations had been lost, and nothing is known about the people who were buried in the tombs he excavated: no information regarding the skeletons, such as age and gender, is available (Dayagi-Mendels 2002, 163). Dayagi-Mendels's publication deals with the tombs and the finds.

The tombs are mainly shafts with rock-cut chambers, roofed sometimes with stone slabs. In the northern part of the southern cemetery there are rectangular pit graves for individual inhumations and oval pit graves for the incinerations. The large majority of the burials in the eastern cemetery are inhumations, with only very few incinerations. The tombs had multiple burials and may have served as family tombs. In such cases, previous interments were moved to the back of the chamber or placed in jars to make room for the new burials.

Mazar (2001) published the results of her recent excavations in the southern cemetery. The tombs were mainly shaft tombs, some with roofed

Fig. 5.26. Basalt funerary stela from 'Amrit in the tradition of north Syrian stelae. It is a rectangular monument with a geometrical motif in the shape of a triangle in its upper part. It was placed in a niche inside the tomb. Courtesy of M. Al-Maqdissi and E. Ishaq.

ceilings and some with burial "beds," which are rectangular pits inside the burial chamber where the dead was deposited. This feature is attested also at Tell el-Rašidiyye (Macridy Bey 1904, 564–70). Cist tombs and pit graves are also attested. The inhumations form the majority of the burials, but incinerations are also found.

The eastern and southern cemeteries at Akhziv present features that shed light on the funerary rituals relating to inhumations. The presence of offering tables above the tomb ceiling, found in Tombs 19 and 14 of the southern cemetery, suggest the existence of a cultic ritual in commemoration of the dead. Another interesting feature in these tombs in relation with that same ritual is the presence of an opening in the tomb ceiling, meant probably to pour libations inside the grave. So offering tables and ceiling openings are clear indications that a cult to honor the dead was regularly performed (Mazar 2001, 144).

The wealth and variety of the retrieved material inside the tombs contribute to shed light on the funerary practices. The dead was placed on the floor of the tomb, surrounded by funerary offerings (Dayagi-Mendels 2002, 164). These consist mainly of pottery vessels. The pottery assemblage is very rich and similar to that of the Khaldeh and Tyre al-Baṣṣ tombs. It reflects the same funerary ritual of offering solid food and liquids to the dead. According to Dayagi-Mendels (2002, 164): "There is no clear-cut evidence attesting the holding of banquets, or offering of funerary sacrifices at the cemeteries under discussion." The absence of funerary banquets in inhumation cemeteries is also attested at Khaldeh and seems to be a feature differentiating inhumation from cremation rituals. While indeed no banquets were detected, evidence for funerary sacrifices may be inferred from the occasional presence of offering tables.

In addition to the pottery vessels, the offerings included terra-cotta figurines representing female figures playing a tambourine or a flute, some pregnant and others holding a dove (Dayagi-Mendels 2002, figs. 7.1–7.3, 7.4–7.6; Mazar 2001, figs. 53, 54). These figures are similar to the ones found at other Phoenician sites of the motherland. There are also terra-cotta figures of horse riders (Dayagi-Mendels 2002, figs. 7.13–7.16; Mazar 2001, figs. 55–56), a shrine model (Dayagi-Mendels 2002, fig. 7.25) identical to one of the shrine models of Tyre al-Baṣṣ (Metzger 2004, fig. 280), and masks (Dayagi-Mendels 2002, figs. 7.20, 7.22–23). The most common and abundant find are amulets representing a variety of Egyptian gods and goddesses as well as those in the shape of a Horus eye (Dayagi-Mendels 2002, 4.11, 36–41; 4.21, 66–74). Another common find is the scarab, symbol of life regeneration, one of the most widespread finds in Phoenician tombs. It is indeed the only type of find that was retrieved from the Khaldeh tombs, which otherwise had no other offerings. Jewelry consisted mainly of earrings, rings, and bracelets, which were found in large numbers (Dayagi-Mendels 2002, fig. 4.20, 7–104.21, 42–52). Preserved fibulae attest the clothing of the dead. Some tools used by the dead person during his or her lifetime, such as fishing hooks, iron sickles, and axes (Mazar 2001, figs. 39–41), were also placed with the dead. Other finds such as beads, stamp seals, and weights were sometimes part of the offerings. All the finds mentioned above are attested also in Tomb 1 of the northern cemetery. It is a family tomb used over several generations from the eleventh until the sixth century BCE (Mazar 2004). Finally, one aspect of the funerary cult is betrayed by the presence of inscribed and uninscribed stelae, which were found above some of the tombs (Cross 2002, 169–73).

To sum up, from the archaeological evidence mentioned above one can reconstruct some aspects of the funerary ritual that accompanied inhumations. When a person died, the body was probably embalmed with perfumed oils and wrapped in a shroud or dressed. Richer people had gold pieces covering the eyes and mouth, as was the case with Batnoam, while the more common people could afford only terra-cotta masks to cover the dead's face (for a general review and typology of Phoenician masks see Orsingher 2018). Lamentations accompanied the interment ceremonies, as attested on the Ahiram and Wailing Women sarcophagi. There is no reason to assume that such scenes were restricted to royalty. The expression of grief in typical gestures such as beating one's chest, tearing one's clothes, and crying were normal behavior upon the death of a loved one and are still attested in villages of the Middle East. Wailing women, known in Arabic as *naddābe*, were hired to lament for the dead, enumerating his or her good deeds and virtues. The dead was then buried in a tomb either directly on the floor, or inside a coffin on a wooden plank, or on a bench. Offerings, consisting mainly of food and drink, were placed in ceramic containers in the tomb. Since the pottery assemblage is the same in the inhumation tombs known so far, it may be safely assumed that it was the expression of a common belief that the items they contain were necessary for the dead's safe journey to the underworld. It also appears that the dead needed divine protection in the afterlife or in the transition when the spirit traveled to the afterlife. Hence the presence of figurines and amulets representing deities, shrine models, scarabs, and masks, which secured the dead's protection against evil spirits. Some features, such as the opening

Fig. 5.27. The Ahiram Sarcophagus. Source: Directorate General of Antiquities.

in the tomb ceiling and the presence of offering tables, indicate that an ancestor cult probably existed. This cultic performance seems also implied by the iconography of the Ahiram sarcophagus representing the dead king seated on the throne while offerings are presented to him. The recently discovered Kuttamuwa stela (Pardee 2015) has shed some light on this ancestor cult, which was supposed to take place every year before the stela representing the dead person. It enumerates the offerings that should be brought during the cult. Noteworthy is the mention of wine and rams, which are attested on Ahiram's sarcophagus too.

For the common people who could not afford a stone monument, the cultic performance took place most probably in the burial place, where a stone stela indicated the tomb and sometimes betrayed the identity of the deceased. It seems also that there was no difference in the funerary ritual between rich and poor except that the royal family could afford richer coffins and had more precious personal belongings and better-built hypogea.

5.5.3. Incineration

5.5.3.1. General Introduction

Incineration of the dead is not attested in Phoenicia before the Iron Age. It consisted of burning the dead body on a pyre and placing the cremated remains in a pit or inside a shaft or built tomb, either directly on the floor or in an urn.

Evidence for cremation burials is attested mainly at Tell Sukas (Riis 1961–1962), Tell Arqa (Thalmann 1978b), Byblos (Salles 1994, 54), Khaldeh (Saidah 1966; 1967, 166), Tambourit (Saidah 1977, 135–46), Tyre al-Baṣṣ (Aubet 2004; 2014), Tell el-Rašidiyye (Macridy Bey 1904; Chéhab 1942–1943, 86; Doumet 1982), 'Athlit (Johns 1933; 1998), and Akhziv (Mazar 2009–2010). Renan (1864, 464, 485, pl. 63) mentions also the existence of a cremation tomb in Mgharet Tablun, east of Eshmunazar II's tomb. The existence of cremation tombs in the Sidonian kingdom is also supported by the Tambourit tomb and by the recent publication of two eighth-century BCE cinerary urns (Puech 1994), which were allegedly looted in the area of Sidon and sold on the market.

The question that arises here is the following: Was this new mortuary practice introduced in Phoenicia by newcomers, or was it a local religious development reflecting a new belief? Incineration (see Bienkowski 1982; Gasull 1993), which is alien to the funerary customs of the Levant, started to spread at the beginning of Iron Age I in northern Syria, where cremation tombs dated as early as the twelfth/eleventh century BCE are attested in Hama (Riis 1948) but also on the Phoenician coast at Tell Sukas (Riis 1961–1962). They are also attested on a large scale since Iron Age II in the southern kingdom of Tyre, where cremation cemeteries and tombs were excavated. Looking at the distribution of cremation burials, the present state of the evidence suggests that with the exception of Tell Sukas, this tradition was adopted mainly in southern Phoenicia. In the other parts of the Phoenician coast, only individual or occasional cremations have been attested.

The origin of incineration is still debated: it was first ascribed to the settling of the Sea Peoples (for a review of all these theories see Bienkowski 1982) who came from Asia Minor, where cremation was practiced in the Bronze Age. This theory, which had been abandoned for many years, finds renewed support today in recent archaeological and epigraphic evidence. Indeed, the existence of a Luwian kingdom in the Amuq Plain called Walistin or Palastin, which extended its dominion over large parts of north and central Syria, including Aleppo and Hama (Harrison 2009), strengthened the opinion that this tradition was brought by the Luwian people from Asia Minor and other parts of the former Hittite Empire. While cremation cemeteries at Tell Sukas and Hama may have resulted from the occupation of northern Syria by the kingdom of Palastin, which brought with it an influx of groups from southern Turkey, it is more difficult to explain its adoption by the southern Phoenicians. It is interesting to note that cremation disappeared at Tell Sukas at the end of the tenth century BCE (Bienkowski 1982, 82) at the same time as it appeared in southern Phoenicia. This mortuary practice became a major landmark of Tyrian culture and of all the Phoenician settlements that are believed to have been founded by that kingdom. There is to date no satisfactory explanation for its emergence in Iron Age I and its disappearance at the beginning of the Persian period.

Other theories regarding the origin of cremation were proposed: some have ascribed the origin of cremation to the exiguity of space or to the need of bringing back sailors or merchants who died during long-distance maritime journeys (Gras, Rouillard, and Teixidor 1989, 156). This theory of the narrowing of space cannot be held anymore, for "cremations occur at sites with no 'space problems'" (Dixon 2013, 491).

While the newly attested kingdom of Palastin might explain the existence of cremation in northern Syria, it does not explain how this tradition bridged all of northern Phoenicia to establish itself so strongly at Tyre. It would not be too far-fetched to assume that Phoenician presence in Cilicia and southern Anatolia, evinced by Phoenician inscriptions since the early ninth century BCE and which has always been presumed to be Tyrian, led the Phoenicians settled there to adopt some of the local funerary traditions and to bring them back to their homeland. On the other hand, it is possible that groups from Asia Minor, Cyprus, or northern Syria, who established themselves in Tyre for trade purposes, brought this tradition with them. The diversity of the imports in the southern Phoenician cities since Iron Age I may support this suggestion. The available evidence seems to imply that those practicing cremation were "culturally" not different from those practicing inhumation. They had the same belief in the afterlife, since they gave the dead the same type of food and drink offerings and placed with them the same pottery assemblage. They also offered the dead the same type of protective or apotropaic items such as the scarab, the amulets, and the masks, which also reflect the same belief in life after death. They even wrote their funerary inscriptions in Phoenician, and it seems that closely related individuals chose different burial traditions, since inhumations and cremations were found often in very close connection. The evidence seems to point to the same group of people opting, for reasons that still need to be clarified, for two different practices. If one may be allowed the comparison, the same situation is attested in many modern societies where individuals of the same community choose either cremation or inhumation as their burial practice. As pointed out by Mazar (2009–2010, 26–27): "Having appeared as suddenly as it disappeared, the origins of the Phoenician cremation cult remain a major unsolved question. There are no signs of any foreign cultural influence that would indicate that it was an imported practice of some kind; rather, accompanying the cremations are the same objects found altogether with 'regular' Phoenician burials from the same time, which indicates that cremation burial cult, including the Akhziv Tophet, comprised an integral part of the Phoenician culture and must be understood and studied as such." Today most scholars are of the opinion that the introduction of the new rite of cremation should not be associated with the coming of new populations and that "the adoption of cremation may not always have been a fundamental change. In many cases the idea was known in neighboring areas, and it may gradually have become acceptable" (Bienkowski 1982, 87). Pepa Gasull (1993, 82) also concluded her study of Phoenician burial practices by saying that the adoption of one or the other funerary practice does not imply necessarily differences in religious beliefs and reflects simply the population and cultural diversity of the Phoenician settlements.

5.5.3.2. The Funerary Ritual: The Evidence from Tell Arqa

Tell Arqa is situated in the Lebanese 'Akkār Valley, on the northern bank of Nahr 'Arqa (on Tell Arqa, see Thalmann 1978a; 1978b). Two incineration tombs, T1 and T2, were dug from the floor of Level 10 and are contemporary with it, as shown by the pottery. These tombs were dug in the area of the Iron Age II settlement after the houses had been razed and the area abandoned.

Tomb 1 is an oval pit with a bottom lined with stones. The cremated remains were not placed in an urn but directly on the pit floor, as attested in several Phoenician sites of the western Mediterranean (Gras, Rouillard, and Teixidor 1989, 156). Together with the offerings, they were placed in the eastern corner of the tomb (Thalmann 1978b, fig. 17). The offerings consist of amphorae, bowls, and a cooking pot, which were broken before being thrown inside the tomb, a ritual attesting the existence of a funerary meal. T1 contained also two bronze rings, an iron sword and blades, one red-slip hemispherical bowl, and five bored clay balls, which may have served as storage-jar stoppers (Thalmann 1978b, fig. 45). At least two complete amphorae were placed inside the tomb. One of them bears a painted Phoenician inscription (Bordreuil 1977; 1983, 751–53).

Tomb 2 was badly damaged by later structures, which left only its bottom intact, with some ashes and cremated bone remains. But it is clearly of the same type and contemporary with Tomb 1. A third tomb may be identified in Pit 20.64, which is partly destroyed. It yielded a large number of broken amphorae similar to those found in Tomb 1. Although no cremation remains survived because of the destruction, the excavator suggests that it is a third tomb given its location next to an incineration and burial ground.

An interesting feature is Pit 20.51 (Thalmann 1978a, 71), which shows traces of intense burning and which was filled with ashes and burnt ceramics and other materials. The amphorae it contained were of the same type as those found in Tomb 1. It is clear that it is the incineration pit that is associated with Tomb 1. Another incineration area was identified in Pit 10.68 (71, fig. 5), which was filled with ash and covered with a brick layer. This evidence indicates that the dead were cremated next to the spot where they were buried and not in a different place. It also suggests that a new pyre was built for each new cremation. The Tell Arqa tombs were dated to the seventh century BCE.

5.3.3. The Funerary Ritual: The Evidence from Tyre al-Baṣṣ

An Iron Age cremation cemetery was discovered accidentally in Tyre al-Baṣṣ, a district located on the main Tyre-Nāqūra highway, southeast of the island of Tyre, and in the immediate vicinity of the large Roman necropolis (Seeden 1991; Sader 1991; Ward 1991; Aubet 2004; Aubet, Nuñez, and Tresilló 2014). Regular excavations on the site started in 1997 by a Spanish team under the direction of M. E. Aubet and are still ongoing. They have exposed the largest Phoenician cremation cemetery in the motherland. Until 2008, 278 cremations had been exposed, with the "most numerous funerary assemblage from Iron Age II known so far in ancient Phoenicia" (Aubet, Nuñez, and Tresilló 2014, 507). The el-Baṣṣ cemetery was most probably the main urban cemetery of the island of Tyre (507). In Iron Age I (eleventh–tenth century BCE) inhumation was practiced, but in Iron Age II cremation became the only mortuary custom.

The careful excavations of this cemetery allowed clear insight into the mortuary practices of Iron Age Tyre (Aubet, Nuñez, and Tresilló 2014, 507–24). The tombs are all pits dug in the dune in which one, two, or a group of urns containing the cremated remains of the dead were deposited. The standardized ceramic assemblage consists of the ciner-

Fig. 5.28. Tyre al-Baṣṣ cemetery double-urn burial.
Courtesy of Maria Eugenia Aubet.

ary urn covered with a plate or a stone, accompanied by two jugs, one of the trefoil mouth and one of the mushroom-lipped type, and a fine ware bowl, usually found placed on the cinerary urn shoulder (see fig. 5.28). The latter could be a reused domestic pottery or a vessel especially made for the funerary purpose. As for the jugs, the analysis was not conclusive, but there is some evidence that the mushroom-lipped one may have contained honey or wine: "Only in one case have remains of wax or honey been identified in a mushroom-rimmed jug.… Nevertheless the bottom of the mushroom-rimmed jug from Tomb no 124/125 provided remains of grape seeds, which would seem to indicate the remains of wine" (Aubet, Nuñez, and Tresilló 2014, 509). The composition of the above assemblage clearly suggests that we are in the presence of a specific funerary libation ritual, different from the offering of solid food and of the funerary banquet performed by the living.

The ceramic assemblage described above is common to all tombs, and it was clearly separated from the personal belongings of the deceased, such as scarabs, amulets, and jewelry, which were deposited inside the cinerary urn (Aubet, Nuñez, and Tresilló 2014, 512). Sometimes miniature vessels, the ritual purpose of which is still debated, were placed also inside the urn. Food remains and burnt sherds of pottery were found also inside some cinerary urns, which indicates that sometimes a funerary banquet took placed during the cremation ceremony. Exceptionally, funerary offerings other than the ceramic assemblage were placed inside the tomb but outside the urn, as illustrated by the terra-cottas deposited in Tomb 8: two shrine models, a horse rider, and a mask, which had been placed in a wooden box (513). In some cases, before closing the tomb a fire was lit (512).

After the closure of the tomb, another ritual was performed. It was a funerary meal or banquet that took place after the interment on the burial site. It is attested by intentionally smashed pottery vessels found on some of the tombs. Bonnet and Niehr (2010, 121) interpret this tradition of breaking vessels as a marker to indicate the break between life and death. Aubet (Aubet, Nuñez, and Tresilló 2014, 515) understands it as a sort of "rite of passage" that is meant "to stress the rupture disappearance of the physical body of the deceased and construct social memory through the destruction of objects" (515). She considers this funerary banquet as a typically Phoenician practice that occurred at all Phoenician cremation cemeteries in the motherland and in the colonies. The last ritual performance in this mortuary practice was to offer animal sacrifices and to distribute "their meat in the name of the deceased" (516). The richer the sacrifices, the wealthier the deceased, and the larger the inheritance: "In the al-Bass necropolis, clear signs have been identified of the existence of rites of commensality … notable for its volume and importance is the spectacular assemblage of unburnt bones belonging to an adult bovine found in Sector II beside urn no. 80" (516). This practice of communal eating in remembrance of the dead is known from Mesopotamia as the *kispu* ritual, from the Old Testament as the *marzeah*, from the Iron Age funerary stelae from Syria that represent the funerary banquet, and, in Phoenicia, from the relief on the Ahiram sarcophagus and four Phoenician inscriptions (Lemaire 2014, 27–28; Amadasi-Guzzo and Zamora 2018, 195–214). In their review of the four occurrences of the term *marzeah* in Phoenician, Amadasi-Guzzo and Zamora (2018, 204) conclude,

> The word clearly denotes a feast in the Piraeus inscription and an association in the Marseille Tariff. It is related to gods (directly and indirectly in the Marseille Tariff and directly in the inscriptions on the phiale and from Idalion), to one or more divinities (*mrzḥ 'lm, mrzḥ šmš*). In the Idalion ostracon, the *marzeaḥ* was bound to the central administration, at least for its celebration, as it received food from the palace. Its role in the society is well demonstrated by the use of the adjectival form *mrzḥy* as a personal name in Cyprus and Carthage.

The final act in the ritual was at times to erect a stone stela above the tomb. Stone stelae were found associated with burials having exceptional grave goods, thus inferring that they may have belonged to individual with a higher social rank. The ratio of stone stelae to the number of tombs is very low, and not every tomb had such a monument (Aubet, Nuñez, and Tresilló 2014, 518). However, the ratio may have been higher, for it is not far-fetched to assume that several crudely hewn stones may have served as tomb markers but were discarded inadvertently. The case of Akhziv (Mazar 2009–2010), where a number of blank stones were collected, seems to support this assumption. The stelae are sometimes inscribed with the name of the deceased, his patronym, and at times his profession, while some bear religious or apotropaic symbols, and some are simply blank. The inscribed stelae were a means to transmit the memory of the deceased. Others could have served as the focus of commemorative rituals for the ancestor cult. Mathias Lange (2012) interpreted the stelae representing a human figure as an image of the deceased, his *nephesh*, which was necessary for the performance of the ancestor cult. The evidence suggests "that the stelae didn't just serve as a visual reminder of the sits [sic] of the burial, but at the foot of some of the stelae, ritual activities took place as a culmination of the funeral ceremonies in memory of the deceased" (Aubet, Nuñez, and Tresilló 2014, 520).

The cremation cemetery at Tyre did not yield any child burials. This is according to the excavator "the most obvious feature" of that burial site (Aubet, Nuñez, and Tresilló 2014, 523). The assumption is that children were not considered to be part of the community before a certain age and had therefore no right to be buried in the citizens' cemetery.

5.5.3.4. The Funerary Ritual: The Evidence from Akhziv

The excavations at the northern cemetery of Akhziv, which were started by Prausnitz and continued by Mazar, have exposed Phoenician cremation burials dated to Iron Age II (tenth–seventh century BCE). This cemetery, like the Tyrian one, is located on the seashore, 50 m north of the tell. Mazar uses the term *tophet* to refer to that cemetery, in spite of the fact that that term refers to a cemetery for adults. She justifies this designation by referring to the biblical use of that term: "Since it is customary in Phoenician/Punic studies that contained numerous cremation burials as *tophet* sites—in this way utilizing the biblical term for the burial ground in Jerusalem where cremations were practiced … —this term has been applied to the case of the Northern Cemetery of Akhziv" (Mazar 2009–2010, 21). Her definition fails to specify that in Phoenician and Punic studies only child cemeteries, and not any cremation cemeteries, are referred to as *tophet*s. Hence calling an adult cremation cemetery a *tophet* is misleading because it goes against the traditional scholarly use of the term.

The study of the funerary practices at Akhziv will focus mainly on Mazar's publication, which deals only with the results of the excavations undertaken from 1992 until 2004 (Mazar 2009–2010).

The northern cemetery of Akhziv stands out because of the presence in the burial ground of a complex circular structure identified as a crematorium. This building is located in the northern part of the excavated area and is surrounded by incineration tombs (Mazar 2009–2010, plans 3–4). The burial ground extended to the area south of the crematorium and encompassed the older built inhumation Tomb 1. This tomb, which existed before the building of the crematorium, continued to be used throughout Iron Age II and even later (Mazar 2009–2010, plan 6) and continued to receive inhumation burials. Contemporary with this tomb were two structures, a plastered pool and a plastered platform, which were destroyed by the crematorium. The pool had a plastered pit in its northwestern corner (Mazar 2009–2010, 186, photo 2.12), which indicates "that the liquid in the pool was worth being collected to its last drop" (184). The excavator believes that it may have contained oil that was emptied with jugs and jars, remains of which were found in the pool. This precious liquid was most probably used in the funerary cult associated with the inhumations and was not necessary for the practice of cremation, since the pool was sealed by the crematorium building. The plastered platform, which is associated with the pool, was partly incorporated in the entryway of the crematorium, while the other half was used for the burial of cinerary urns. This evidence clearly indicates that in the tenth century all the installations relating to the inhumation practice were covered by the crematorium and stopped being in use. It is to be noted in this context that the plastered pool and its associated platform at Akhziv compare closely with the plastered vat and its associated plastered platform that were recently discovered at Tell el-Burak (see 6.2.3 below). The latter have been interpreted as parts of a winepress, given the large number of pips of grapes that were found in the area. This may mean that the Akhziv pool also contained wine, unless botanical analysis proves otherwise. In her publication Mazar does not mention botanical evidence to determine the content.

Toward the end of the tenth century BCE, the crematorium was built (Mazar 2009–2010, 186–206). It consists of a 5 m long plastered entryway with a 2.50 m wide entrance to allow the bodies to be brought in. The entranceway narrows to become 1.5 m wide close to the round structure. The round structure where the bodies were cremated had plastered walls and an inner diameter ranging from 2.5 to 4.3 m. Its walls are slanting inwards, and on its floor is a sort of built tunnel that communicated with a window. The latter channeled and directed the air blowing from the chute to fuel the fire. The chute is a sort of passageway, the purpose of which was to harness the wind and activate the fire inside the round structure. It was preserved to a maximum length of 3.7 m. and ended at the window. It was thus in connection with the tunnel inside the round structure. This crematorium is so far the only building of its kind to be excavated in Phoenicia.

Regarding the funerary ritual, the cremated remains were placed in urns, which were buried in earth pits. Men and women were buried there, but no child cremations were found (Mazar 2009–2010, 209), as is the case in Tyre al-Baṣṣ. The ceramic assemblage that accompanied the cinerary urn is also very similar to that of Tyre al-Baṣṣ and consists of bowl, a trefoil-rimmed jug, and a mushroom-lipped jug. Sometimes two or even groups of urns share only one such set. Often a stela indicated the location of the urn or group of urns. Dozens of stelae were found at Akhziv (214), and the majority did not carry any inscriptions or symbols. They were simply plain (Mazar 2009–2010, photo 3.5) and served first and foremost to indicate the location of the tombs. They were all oriented to the west, toward the sea, because this direction represented death and the afterlife, according to the excavator (227). The symbols represented on the stelae, such as the disc, triangle, and cross, were interpreted as representing Baal and Astarte (214). Mazar (2009–2010, 214) inferred from the blank stelae, as well as from the almost total absence of personal belongings, that "personal identity did not seem to matter in the Tophet." She suggests that "the belief behind the cremation rite was to leave one's earthly identity behind. Because of this evidence, we assume that the afterlife of those cremated was apparently different than that of those interred in the family tombs" (Mazar 2009–2010, 228), a far-reaching conclusion that cannot be supported in the present state of the evidence, since inscribed stelae were also attested at Akhziv. There is also no evidence to support her theory that the absence of belongings may indicate that "this is a practice related to the cult of the first-born or some other group whose members belonged to the gods Baal and Ashtoret…, regardless of whether they were rich or poor, commoners or of the elite" (228). Another feature singles out the Akhziv cemetery: the presence of hearths next to the stelae. These structures had thick layers of ashes, indicating several reuses. They attest to the burning of food offerings, as evidenced by the burnt animal bones. The presence of hearths in the cemetery is attested in Middle and Late Bronze Age, as well as in Iron Age I Sidon, which indicates that such funerary animal offering ceremonies had a long history on the Phoenician coast. Among the cultic objects found inside the urn, scarabs (Keel 2009–2010, fig. 128) and amulets in the shape of Egyptian gods (Mazar 2009–2010, figs. 44, 83) are well represented.

## 5.5.3.5. Concluding Remarks

The introduction of cremation is a characteristic of Phoenician funerary practices. While cremation cemeteries of adults are attested, there is no evidence in Phoenicia for *tophet*s, the cemeteries dedicated to the burial of cremated infants, one of the markers of the Phoenician settlements in the central Mediterranean. This raises the issue of the origin of this tradition, which cannot be sought in the motherland, as the present state of the evidence seems to suggest. However, there is evidence that the children were not buried with adults in the cremation cemeteries of Phoenicia, which suggests that they were buried in a different place. The latter has not been identified yet. While in cremation cemeteries and tombs burials of children are not attested, they were found in inhumation cemeteries. This evidence seems to imply a difference in the treatment of child burial in both practices, the reasons for which remain to be explained.

The above evidence clearly suggests that the belief in an afterlife was the same in both cremations and inhumations. The care with which the dead were buried, along with the funerary assemblages and offerings, is a clear indication that a proper burial and the performance of specific rituals were prerequisites for securing the dead an eternal rest. The archaeological evidence from Tyre al-Baṣṣ and Akhziv has contributed in reconstructing aspects of this ancestor cult.

The archaeological evidence clearly shows that the influence of Egyptian religion was as important in cremation practices as in inhumations. The use of scarabs, Bes figures, Horus eyes, *ankh* signs, and lotus buds as amulets placed in the tomb for apotropaic purposes provide undeniable evidence that all Phoenicians had adopted some aspects of Egyptian religion.

To conclude this chapter, a further word must be said about the emergence of dog burials, a funerary practice that appears in the Persian

Fig. 5.29. Dog burial from Tell el-Burak. Source: Tell el-Burak Archaeological Project.

period in Phoenicia and disappears at the end of that period. It is another characteristic of the Phoenician mortuary practices that has not yet been explained satisfactorily. In Khaldeh (Saidah 1967, 166) eight dogs were found buried in the city's cemetery; in Beirut thirteen dog skeletons were found buried on the glacis in the sector Bey 020 (Finkbeiner and Sader 1997, 130–31, fig. 7); at Tell el-Burak (Kamlah and Sader 2003, 149, fig. 8; Çakırlar et al. 2014) three dog burials were found outside House 1 during the last phase of the site occupation in the mid-fourth century BCE (see fig. 5.29); at Akko several dog burials were found (Helzer 1998), as well as at Tel Dor, where twenty-five dog burials in total have been exposed (Sapir-Hen 2011, 137). Ashkelon, which belonged to Phoenicia in the Persian period, yielded a dog cemetery of more than one thousand burials, the largest known to date (Stager 1991). Other sites on the southern Palestinian coast provided also evidence of dog burials. In all these Phoenician sites, the absence of butcher marks implies that all the dogs died a natural death and hence were not sacrificed. Meir Edrey (2008, 275), however, seems to assume that they were ritually killed, maybe by poison, which did not leave traces in the bone remains. The evidence mainly from Ashkelon and Dor indicates that the burials took place over a long period of time and were not the result of one single event that led to their death. Dixon (2018, 29) reviewed all the interpretations proposed to explain dog burials and suggested that "these dog burials should be examined not according to how dogs were worshipped, sacrificed, traded, or otherwise used by humans but in light of how dogs were socially conceived." She observes that human mortuary practices were applied to dog burials, and she argues, "The extension of human mortuary rituals to canines over the course of the second half of the 1st millennium B.C.E. seems a plausible explanation for the dog burial phenomenon" (32).

It is to be noted that, in spite of the fact that occasional dog burials were found before the Iron Age in cultic contexts, this practice became widespread and reached its climax only with the arrival of the Persians and disappeared at the beginning of the Hellenistic period. Another noteworthy observation is that this practice is found mainly in Phoenician sites and seems to be a marker of Phoenician culture in the Persian period. The origin and meaning of this phenomenon, however, are still debated.

The first to offer an explanation to this phenomenon was Lawrence Stager (1991), who linked the dog burials in Ashkelon to a healing practice performed in a nearby temple. He argued that the same practice is attested at Kition, where a fifth-century inscription mentions dogs belonging to the temple of the goddess Astarte and the god Reshef-Mukol. The issue was discussed further by Edrey (2008), who mentioned additional examples linking a cult of the goddess Astarte involving dogs. One such healing cult involving dogs is attested in Mesopotamia, at the site of Isin, where the temple of the healing goddess Gula stood. The goddess herself had the dog as her animal symbol, and her temple produced a large number of dog figurines. Furthermore, a dog burial site was associated with her temple. Halpern (2000) argued that this cult was brought to the Levant during the Assyrian and Babylonian periods or later by exiles returning from Babylon. After reviewing all the possible foreign origins and influences relating to this practice, Edrey (2008, 276–77) suggests that maybe "Achaemennid rulers who held dogs in high esteem, encouraged the dog-related cult" and assumes that it is a Zoroastrian practice that was brought by the new rulers to the Levant. There cannot be a final answer to explain this new funerary practice of dog burials: whether it was connected to new religious ideas, or whether it was a newly introduced rite in honor of Eshmun, or whether it was a foreign tradition brought by the new rulers.

While available evidence allows some insight into Phoenician mortuary practices, a comprehensive assessment and a good understanding of these practices will have to await more epigraphic and archaeological discoveries.

# 6
# PHOENICIA'S ECONOMY

## 6.1. Phoenician Trade

The fame of the Phoenicians as daring navigators, shrewd merchants, and skilled traders has been established based on classical authors' accounts and on biblical narratives, which deal almost all with Tyrian trade. Foremost among the latter is the famous chapter 27 of the prophet Ezekiel's book, describing the trade network of Tyre. This text is always cited as a key source for Phoenician trade (Katzenstein 1997, 159–61, Diakonoff 1992; Liverani 1991; Aubet 2001, 120–26). Although written in the sixth century BCE, the text may reflect a situation that was prevailing before that period (Liverani 1991, 71). It identifies the trade partners of Tyre as well as the goods that were traded. Ezekiel 27 sheds light on the origin of the raw materials and other commodities imported by the Phoenicians: timber and linen from the inland mountains, Cyprus, and Egypt; agricultural products from Palestine and Damascus; horses, mules, sheep, and goats from Armenia and Arabia; metals, textiles, ropes, and slaves from southeast Turkey; and metals and luxury goods from Tarshish, Yemen, and Edom.

Mario Liverani reconstructed four trade belts or circuits: the innermost circuit supplied Phoenicia with agricultural products, the second with animals and animal products, the third with manufactured products, and the outer one with metals and luxury goods. According to Ezek 27, Tyrian trade extended from Spain to Assyria and from Anatolia to Yemen (Liverani 1991, 68–69, fig. 2). However, it is to be noted that Ezekiel's text focuses on the trade relations with countries east, north, and south of Phoenicia as well as the eastern Mediterranean, while it is almost mute regarding the western Mediterranean trade network and mentions only Tarshish. Liverani (68) had already noted that in this text "the relevance of the sea trade (Tarshish and Yawan) is quite secondary in comparison with land trade, which was presumably carried out by means of caravans."

Aubet (2001, 85–88) identified three trade circuits for Tyre, which developed chronologically as a result of the prevailing political situation. The first and oldest, dated to the tenth century BCE, was the network involving Israel, the Red Sea, and Ophir. The second, dated to the ninth century BCE, involved the expansion to northern Syria, Cilicia, and Cyprus. The latest and third stage of the expansion, dated to the eighth century BCE, involved the central and western Mediterranean. The chronological sequence of Aubet's Phoenician trade circuits seems to imply that only when one circuit was abandoned did the other start, which does not exactly match the reality, because these circuits certainly overlapped. Furthermore, as will be argued below, trade with Cyprus was almost uninterrupted since the Late Bronze Age, and evidence for it is attested abundantly as early as Iron Age I. Finally, these three circuits do not account for the privileged trade relations the Phoenician cities had with Egypt, Assyria, and Babylonia.

Based on the same biblical text, Frederick Fales (2017, 264) identified "at least five circuits … (a) an 'Egyptian' circuit … (b) the 'island' circuit, connecting the Phoenician littoral with Cyprus, perhaps Rhodes and/or Crete, and thence to Yawan/Ionia; (c) the Anatolian circuit … (d) the Transjordanian-Arab circuit … (e) the Mesopotamian circuit." This author understood the prophetic text as "meant to provide a sweeping bird's-eye view of the main foci of the universe of Phoenician commerce known to him, a view endowed with some points of geographical proximity, with some level of interarea hierarchical structure, with some differentiation between land- and sea-routes, but not necessarily forming at the end of the day, a fully organized and coherent pattern to be fitted on a geographical grid of the ancient Near East" (267).

Ezekiel's text lists in detail all the goods that Tyrians imported from each of the countries they traded with. As for the goods that Tyre gave in exchange, the prophet speaks only of "merchandise" and "wares," two vague and general terms that do not inform us about the traded Tyrian goods: "When your merchandise went out on the seas, you satisfied many nations. With your great wealth and your wares, you enriched the kings of the earth" (27:33 NIV).

So what did the Tyrians export in exchange of the goods they received? It is well established that the only raw material that Phoenicia could use in a trade exchange was the coveted timber and resins of its forests. One can only speculate about the other kinds of items exported by the Phoenicians. They may have consisted of finished luxury products made of imported raw materials such as metal and ivory, which are consistently mentioned as part of the tribute the Phoenicians paid to the Neo-Assyrian kings. In the western Mediterranean such items were offered sometimes as gifts to facilitate the acquisition of raw materials from native chieftains controlling the mines (Aubet 2001, 132–38), thus following an ancient tradition of gift exchange between rulers that was regulating international trade relations in the Mediterranean during the Late Bronze Age (Feldman 2006). All the luxury metal vessels and jewelry displaying "Orientalizing" motifs found in the central and western Mediterranean were ascribed traditionally to the Phoenicians (for a critical review of this tradition see Martin 2016). After tracing the history of the Sidonian crater given by Achilles as a prize for the winner of the funerary games in honor of Patroclus, Aubet (2001, 131) concluded, "The episode of Achilles' crater,... is clear evidence of an itinerant Phoenician trade in which merchants transported their goods and objects of great value from one port to another. These luxury products, consisting generally of craters, cauldrons, and tripods, passed from hand to hand as prizes, ransoms or ceremonial gifts to local kings or lords."

The same can be assumed also for the eastern Mediterranean and inland countries, since the text speaks of "kings" being enriched by the Phoenician merchandise. However, these luxury items were not the only goods traded by the Phoenicians: Homer speaks in the *Odyssey* (15.459) of *athyrmata*, cheap jewelry and charms of no value, given by the Phoenicians to the locals in exchange for raw materials. The recent archaeological evidence, on the other hand, has clearly shown that some of the main items traded by the Phoenicians were exotic spices, agricultural products such as oil and wine, and purple-dyed textiles (see below).

According to Herodotus (*Hist.* 1.1.1–2), after having settled the Phoenicians "began to make long sailing voyages. Among other places to which they carried Egyptian and Assyrian merchandise, they came to Argos." This passage seems to imply that the Phoenicians were mainly intermediaries selling to the western countries products from Egypt and Assyria, countries that had no established trading networks in the Mediterranean, together with their own. The luxury goods that have been traditionally assigned to them may have come from other countries and may have been produced by other craftsmen.

Peter van Alfen, in his 2002 PhD dissertation, investigated all the items traded between the Levant and the Aegean during the Persian period based on both literary and archaeological sources. He interestingly concluded that "the bulk of the items sent west were (high value) raw and semi-processed goods, including industrial commodities like ebony, ivory, and various pigments and chemicals. More than half of the raw goods heading west were spices, which were perhaps the most important component of the western trade. Only a limited number of metals, mostly copper and tin, and manufactured goods were traded west, which stands in significant contrast to the proportion of manufactured goods … traded east" (van Alfen 2002, 316).

### 6.1.1. The Nature and Organization of Phoenician Trade

There is hardly any evidence describing in detail the nature and organization of Phoenician trade: Was it a public, state-sponsored, monopolized activity? Or was it mainly in the hands of private individuals? Or was it a combination of both? To answer these questions, one must rely mainly on the scanty information from the written sources, but archaeology is now starting to contribute to the understanding of this issue.

It has been generally assumed that long-distance and overseas trade was organized by state agents because of the complexity and expenses of its organization. This assumption is supported by the fact that the Phoenician kings became extremely rich, as attested by the substantial amount of metal items listed in the tribute they paid to the Assyrian kings and by the words with which the prophet Ezekiel (28:4) addresses the king of Tyre: "By your wisdom and your intelligence you have amassed great wealth; you have piles of gold and silver inside your treasure-houses" (JB). It would not be far-fetched to assume that major trade enterprises were regulated by state agreements between the Phoenician king and rulers of foreign countries.

The sources clearly document the fact that "kings of Levantine city-states controlled production and exchange in their polities to some degree" (Bettles 2003, 38). There is clear textual evidence that the Phoenician kings were at the head of large trading enterprises, but they did not monopolize trade. This can be inferred mainly from the fact that the bargaining interlocutor of the royal Egyptian envoy, Wenamun, was the king of Byblos himself. The Wenamun text seems to suggest that the king was directly sponsoring trade activity: he had his own commercial ships and his own trade partners in Egypt. At the beginning of the first millennium BCE, Phoenician kings were using treaties with neighboring kings to control interregional trade (39). Next to the treaty between Solomon and Hiram of Tyre mentioned by Josephus and in the Old Testament, the Assyrian sources mention a treaty between the Assyrian king Esarhaddon and Baal I of Tyre (Borger 1982–1985; Parpola and Watanabe 1988), which fixed the landing places of Tyrian ships as well as the trade routes for Tyrian traders and established the rules concerning the wreck of Tyrian vessels. The treaty mentions the elders of Tyre, who probably were the merchant princes of the city. In the Persian period, the sources identify four actors active in Phoenician trade: the king of Persia, the satrap or governor of the province, the city, and private enterprise (Bettles 2003, 38).

However, "there must have been professionals, possibly members of some local trading elite … who had the mean, the skills, and especially the extensive know-how required for such maritime endeavours" (Gilboa 2015, 261): Urkatel, a merchant residing in Egypt, seems to have been at the head of a huge trading enterprise involving fifty ships in relationship with Sidonian merchants. So the written record seems to suggest that trade was partly in royal hands and partly in the hands of powerful merchants who were either actual members of the royal family or private individuals who became so rich that they had as much power as the princes and other members of the ruling class. This is what can be inferred from Isaiah's (23:8) oracle on Tyre: "Who took this decision against imperial Tyre, whose traders were princes, whose merchants, the great ones of the world?" (JB).

So, despite the fact that the royal house controlled important commercial areas such as cedarwood and metal trade, there is also evidence that individual merchants were very active and were harvesting substantial profits. We hear about the "merchants of Sidon whose goods travelled over the sea, over wide oceans" (Isa 23:2 JB). The existence of private trade enterprises is corroborated by the mention in two Assyrian tablets found in Uruk of a merchant who "was an agent of one of the big trading firms of Tyre" (Katzenstein 1997, 340), and also by the mention in the Assyrian administrative records of intense trading activity of the "people" in the harbor of Tyre: "All the wharves are occupied by the people. Its subjects (i.e., those of Tyre) who are within them (i.e., the wharves) enter (and) leave (the warehouses), give and receive (in barter), ascend (and) descend Mount Lebanon which is in front of it (i.e., of Tyre) as they will and they have timber brought down here" (Saggs 1955, 127 ). Recent archaeological evidence from Beirut indicates also that private households were active in trade, having large storerooms stacked with amphorae inside their dwellings (Elayi and Sayegh 2000, 161). The treaty of Esarhaddon with Baal I also refers to ships belonging to the king and others belonging to the people of Tyre. Finally, the Homeric epics (mainly *Od.* 15.455) refer often to individual Phoenician merchants selling their merchandise to locals. According to Aubet (2001, 118), "public trade and private initiative … were perfectly complementary. It was a synchronous process in which both the private sector and the palace were looking for profits and in which the palace needed the private merchant as much as the trader needed the protection of the palace."

No wonder, then, to see the Assyrians exacting taxes on this trade activity and encouraging it to raise their profit. Bettles (2003, 43) discusses the issue of whether foreign domination, Assyrian, Babylonian, or Persian, caused the impoverishment of the Phoenician city-states, as argued by some scholars, or whether foreign dominion was an incentive to increase their commercial potential. The evidence collected indicates that imperial dominion was rather an incentive for long-distance trade, and this is corroborated by the fact that the climax of the Phoenician expansion was in the eighth and seventh century BCE, the period of Assyrian rule. According to Bettles (44), Assyrian rule seems to have encouraged the development of techniques of mass production. The Neo-Babylonian and Persian empires furthered Phoenician trade because they found their own benefit in it. Under the Persian Empire, demands for food and drink necessary to feed the Persian elite and military must have resulted in an increase in the demand and production of liquid foodstuffs, and in the need to sustain the capability of food producers to meet this demand over two centuries (45 and relevant bibliography). This explains the development of amphorae production and agriculture-based industries in Phoenicia in the Iron Age since the Assyrian period. Joachim Bretschneider and Karel van Lerberghe (2008, 44) ascribe the establishment and development of olive oil and wine industry at Tell Tweini directly to the Assyrian domination of north Syria:

> At the end of the eighth century, an important change took place in the building architecture of the central tell area (Chantier A). The whole area developed new economic practices, relating mainly to olive-oil production…. Olive presses and large installations in the shape of a bulb appear in all the buildings….The architectural and functional changes may have resulted from the international politics of the eighth century,

when Assyrian hegemony was clearly established over the coastal cities of the Levant.[1]

The same situation may have been behind the development of an industrial olive oil production at Tell Miqne and of wine production at Ashkelon and Tell el-Burak in the seventh century BCE.

6.1.2. Metal Trade

The main item collected by the Assyrians from the Phoenician cities was metal, and among the most famous luxury objects ascribed to the Phoenicians are metal vessels. Metals were imported by the Phoenicians because they were not available on the Levantine coast and they were badly needed: silver was the international currency and "came to fulfill the function of a standard rate for commercial transactions" (Aubet 2001, 82). Copper and tin were used to make bronze implements, vessels, and tools, and later in the first millennium, iron progressively started to replace bronze.

Where did the Phoenicians get these raw materials? The question of the origin of the metals imported by the Phoenicians has been and still is debated by scholars. Little archaeological evidence for the origin of metals is available from the homeland area, and there is substantial evidence for Phoenician metal trade only from the western colonies. In the absence of analysis of Iron Age metal hoards from Phoenician sites, it is difficult to determine the origin of the raw material, which could have come from any of the eastern or western metal ores that are attested in Anatolia, Cyprus, and the central and western Mediterranean. Since Phoenician presence in Cyprus is attested as early as Iron Age I, and in Turkey since at least the ninth century BCE, and, finally, in Spain and Italy since the eighth century BCE and maybe earlier, metals could have been imported from any of these countries. Egypt may have been also a source for gold.

---

1. Bretschneider and van Lerberghe 2008, 44: "A la fin du 8e siècle apparait un changement important dans l'architecture des bâtiments de la partie centrale du tell (chantier A). Toute la région développe de nouvelles pratiques économiques, surtout concernant la production d'huile d'olive.... Des presses à olives et de grandes installations en forme de fanal apparaissent dans tous les bâtiments.... Les changements architecturaux et fonctionnels peuvent être la conséquence de la politique internationale au 8e siècle, lorsque la domination assyrienne s'établit clairement sur les villes côtières du Levant."

Notwithstanding the difficulties and the absence of substantial evidence, new light on the origin of Phoenician metals is progressively emerging. Recent investigations in the Faynan region, mainly the site of Khirbet en-Nahas, have demonstrated the existence of active copper mining in this area in the Early Iron Age, mainly the tenth and ninth century BCE (Levy, Ben-Yosef, and Najjar 2012, 212). These copper mines may have been an easily accessible source of metal used by the Phoenicians. This possibility is supported by the biblical account about joint trade ventures and foreign relations between Hiram of Tyre and Solomon (1 Kgs 9:26–28), as well as the mention of Edom as provider of metal for Tyre (Liverani 1991, 73). This possibility has been recently confirmed: analyses undertaken by Humbolt University in Berlin and the Bergbau Museum in Bochum on Phoenician copper objects from Sidon dated to the eleventh–ninth century BCE have clearly demonstrated that the origin of the copper was not Cyprus or Anatolia but rather the mines of Wadi Araba, "certainly Faynan and probably Timna" (Vaelske and Bode 2018–2019, 130). It is not surprising any more to hear Homer (*Od.* 15.415) refer to Sidon as a "city rich in bronze"! These results open a totally new direction in the study of metal-trade networks in the Mediterranean, since Faynan copper was also attested at Olympia and Delphi between 950 and 750 BCE (Kinderlen et al. 2016).

As for the origin of silver, the recent analysis of "six silver hoards hidden in ceramic jars at the sites of Akko, Dor, Ein Hofez and Tell Keisan, in contexts datable to between 1200 and 800 BC" (Thompson and Skaggs 2013), has provided evidence that the origin of the silver was Sardinia. This discovery has important implications for the origin of the metals imported by the Phoenicians, for the date of the Phoenician presence in the west, and also for the location of the controversial Tarshish of the biblical narratives: "Lead isotope analyses of silver hoards found in Phoenicia now provide the initial evidence for pre-colonial silver-trade with the west; ore-provenance data correlate with the ancient documents that indicate both Sardinia and Spain as suppliers, and Sardinia as the island of Tarshish" (Thompson and Skaggs 2013). However, a recent in-depth study of the same silver hoards from these Phoenician sites has warned against such hasty conclusions regarding the origin of silver: "So far, studies dealing analytically with the provenance of silver in the Levant … have not integrated chemical and isotopic data and show no awareness of the implications of all the difficulties mentioned above. Therefore, the identification of the origins of the silver requires reexamination" (Eschel et al. 2018, 222).

Another recent discovery is an iron-mining site in the central Jordan Valley. The archaeological excavations at Tell Hamme East, a small site on the north bank of the River Zarqa, have produced evidence for iron mining (Veldhuijzen 2003; Veldhuijzen and Rehren 2006; for identification and additional bibliography, see Zwickel forthcoming). In Phase 4, dated circa 910 BCE, large-scale iron production was attested there. The metal was mined in the nearby site of Mugharet el-Wardeh (Veldhuijzen and van der Steen 1999; al-Amri 2007), approximately 2.5 km northeast of the tell. It is thus far the only iron mine known in the southern Levant. Iron slags excavated at Akko proved to have come from there (see below).

### 6.1.3. Ivory Trade

Ivory, the raw material that adorned Phoenician furniture, was available in Syria at least until the eighth–seventh century BCE (Miller 1986, 29). Elephant ivory was used until the first centuries of the first millennium BCE, and the Assyrian kings often received the raw material, that is, elephant tusks, as royal gifts. This perhaps suggests that the Assyrians had ivory workshops, probably manned by Phoenician craftsmen who transferred their techniques to the local ivory cutters. Ivory may have come also from Africa via the Red Sea or from India via the Persian Gulf (Caubet et al. 2007, 206). Elephant ivory was not the only type of ivory used in Phoenicia; several other animals, mainly the hippopotamus, provided this raw material (205). Of particular interest is the discovery at Tell Tweini of hippopotamus ivory waste (Linseele 2010), which seems to indicate the presence of a small workshop for the production of ivory objects. There was evidence also for bone waste, indicating the existence of a workshop for the production of bone artifacts as well as objects produced from antlers.

### 6.1.4. Other Traded Goods

Other raw materials traded by the Phoenicians are attested in the Assyrian inscriptions. Regarding hard woods such as ebony and boxwood, which are always mentioned as part of the tribute imposed by the Assyrians on the Phoenician cities, they were imported from Egypt, which provided also linen. Precious stones such as lapis lazuli and carnelian were imported from Iran and Afghanistan via Mesopotamia. All these materials and their countries of origin testify to the wide trade network of the Phoenicians, which, contrary to common opinion, was as active in the east as it was in the west (see also van Alfen 2002, table 2). It seems clear today that the incentive behind the trade expeditions of the Phoenicians to the western Mediterranean was dictated by the pressing demand for metals, mainly silver, as well as other raw materials needed by the great Oriental empires, whose elites demanded luxury and exotic objects.

Furthermore, recent studies dealing with Phoenician trade have focused on a specific type of Phoenician vessel designed for the maritime transportation of liquids, which became the main marker of Phoenician trade in Iron Age II and during the Persian period (Demesticha and Knapp 2016; Schmitt et al. 2018). This container is the carinated-shoulder amphora, a typical Phoenician product that was used presumably for the transport of Phoenician olive oil and wine. Petrographic studies (Aznar 2005; Bettles 2003) have sampled amphorae that were found on several sites of coastal and inland Palestine and on the southern Lebanese coast. Their petrographic study has demonstrated that they were produced on the southern Lebanese and the northern Palestinian coast. Their distribution indicated the trade relations of the Israelite and Philistine cities with Phoenicia. These amphorae transported a merchandise produced by the Phoenicians and distributed to the neighboring kingdoms. This merchandise is assumed to have been mainly wine, because similar vessels found on the shipwrecks off the shore of Ashkelon contained wine, as attested by residue analyses (Ballard and Stager 2002; Stager 2003). These amphorae may have contained also olive oil, as attested by the residue analysis of amphorae found in a late seventh–early sixth century storeroom at the site of Tell el-Burak (more on this issue below). Aznar (2005, 210) concludes: "The petrographic study, therefore, revealed that all storage jars included as type 9—the 'thick' cylindrical jar, the cylindrical elongated jar, and the 'bullet'-shaped jar—were made on the Phoenician coast.... Since they are found far from the Phoenician coast, in inland sites such as Hazor and southern places such as Ashdod, their appearance at those sites seems to reveal foodstuff market exchange," which, she argues, consisted mainly of wine. The recent evidence from Tell el-Burak is in support of this conclusion.

### 6.1.5. Phoenicia's Trade Partners

### 6.1.5.1. Trade with Assyria

Phoenician foreign relations with Assyria are known to us from the annals of the Assyrian kings since the eleventh century BCE. The Phoenician texts of the homeland do not mention the Assyrians at all. As already presented in chapter 3, the Neo-Assyrian kings led repeated military campaigns against the Phoenician cities from the eleventh until the end of the seventh century BCE, and they exacted heavy tribute and took rich booty from them. As we have already seen, the listed booty and tribute are indicators used by scholars to identify the commodities that were traded by the Phoenician cities and the contacts Phoenicians had with the countries of origin of these commodities. There is hardly any information about regular trade activity between the Phoenician cities and Assyria. However, as already argued, there is evidence that the Assyrians did not only control but also protected the commercial activity of Tyre, from which they were obviously profiting. The incident involving Sargon II fighting Ionian pirates who were threatening the circulation of Tyrian boats is revealing (Fuchs 1994, 117–19). On the other hand, there may have been an agreement between the Assyrians and the Phoenician cities whereby Assyrians had their own quays in the Phoenician harbors of Tyre and Arwad, which were different from those of the city itself, thus implying that they had started their own trade network (Fales 2017, 243). This seems to imply that the trade activity of the Phoenicians coexisted with but was independent of the Assyrian one.

Next to this peaceful coexistence, the Assyrians often took what they wanted by coercion as tribute or booty. As for Assyrian goods imported by the Phoenicians, we have noted elsewhere that in spite of the long-lasting Assyrian presence in Phoenicia, there is hardly any evidence for Assyrian goods or imports in the Phoenician cities. This may be explained by the fact that the Phoenicians probably imported from Assyria perishable commodities such as wool, which did not survive in the archaeological record.

6.1.5.2. Trade with Babylonia

Little is known about the trade relations of the Neo-Babylonian empire with the Phoenician cities. We only know from the Nahr el-Kalb and Wadi Brisa inscriptions of Nebuchadnezzar II that the Babylonian king needed the cedar logs from the Lebanon Mountains to build temples and palaces. This commodity seems to have been taken also by coercion and not by regular trade agreements, as appears from the king's inscriptions, in which he does not mention any agreement or treaty with a local king.

The Babylonian inscriptions attest the presence of Phoenician craftsmen from Byblos, Arwad, and Tyre in Babylon (Weidner 1939, 928–29; Pritchard 1969, 308): in a list of oil rations we find among the recipients

126 men from Tyre, three carpenters from Arwad, and eight carpenters from Byblos. We also know from these texts that there were localities in Babylonia called Bīt Sūrāya and Arqā, which were located near Nippur. They may indicate the presence of Tyrian deportees or of small Phoenician merchant communities settled in this area (Katzenstein 1997, 323). Some commercial dealing with Tyre are also occasionally found in Babylonian tablets, such as a sale of sesame oil and a delivery of dates (Unger 1931, 36–37). We have already mentioned the two tablets found in Uruk in which "the merchant was an agent of one of the big trading firms of Tyre" (Katzenstein 1997, 340), which seems to imply that trade activity between Babylonia and Phoenicia did exist. Finally, the famous Ur box (Gibson 1982, 71; also Amadasi-Guzzo 1990) with its Phoenician inscription is additional evidence for contacts between Phoenicia and Babylonia.

6.1.5.3. Trade with Aramaean and Neo-Hittite Syria

Phoenicia had diplomatic and political relations with the Aramaean and Neo-Hittite kingdoms of Syria. The main sources for these relations are the annals of the Neo-Assyrian kings (Grayson 1991; 1996), the Aramaic stela of Breij (*KAI* 201), and bilingual inscriptions written in Phoenician and Luwian that were found in south Turkey (Hawkins 2000). (For an overview of the relations between Phoenicia and Aramaean and Neo-Hittite Syria, see Kestemont 1985; Lipínski 1985; Lebrun 1987).

Evidence for these relations appears mainly in the Neo-Assyrian inscriptions and is represented by the alliance of Syrian and Phoenician kingdoms against Assyrian attacks. At the Battle of Qarqar, for example, twelve kings of the sea coast, among which were the Phoenician cities of Byblos, Arqā, Arwad, Usnu, and Sianu, fought side by side with Hamath and Damascus against the Assyrian invader (Grayson 1996, 23).

Contacts between Phoenicia and the Syrian-Luwian states were, however, mainly economic. Phoenician interest in the area of Iskenderun could help explain the need of the Phoenicians to secure their presence in the gulf region because the latter controlled "access routes to the rich metal deposits in southeast Anatolia by way of the marts and trading posts of Tarsus, in Cilicia, of Sam'al (Zinjirli), Karatepe, Carchemish and Aleppo" (Aubet 2001, 49). For this purpose, the Phoenicians had a harbor installation at Myriandros, near modern Iskenderun (Kestemont 1985, 135). Phoenician presence is attested by the Phoenician materials, mainly pottery, retrieved in archaeological excavations in Syria and Cilicia. This is the case of Tarsus, for example, where Iron Age II Phoenician pottery was found in large quantities (Goldman 1963, 110, 122, 131). Lebrun (1987, 24) mentions six Phoenician seals from the Cilicia region. Hodos (2006) ascribes the expansion of the red-slipped pottery across Syria in Iron Age II to Phoenician influence.

The most striking evidence for a Phoenician presence in Cilicia and Anatolia in general is the Phoenician monumental inscriptions that were discovered at various sites in Turkey (Hodos 2006, 78–79). The Kilamuwa inscription (*KAI* 24) found at Sendjirli, ancient Sam'al, is written in the Phoenician language and dated to the ninth century BCE. It is the oldest Phoenician inscription found in this area and attests Phoenician presence in Cilicia as early as the ninth century BCE. Two bilingual Phoenician and Neo-Hittite royal inscriptions were found at Karatepe, in the Plain of Adana (Çambel 1999; Röllig 1999), and at Cineköy, south of Adana (Tekoğlu and Lemaire 2000). The first was written by Azitawadda, king of the Danuna, and the second is ascribed to Urikki, king of Que. Both are dated to the eighth century BCE. A third bilingual Phoenician-Luwian inscription was found at Ivriz, near Konya, and dated also to the eighth century BCE. It was commissioned by Muwaharna, son of King Warpala (Dinçol 1994, 119; Röllig 2013). Phoenician inscriptions were also found at Hassan Beyli, near Sendjirli (Lemaire 1983), and Cebel Ires Daği, 15 km east of Alanya (Mosca-Russel 1987). At Kinet Hüyük, a Luwian personal name, "To Sarmakaddmis," written in Phoenician letters, was found incised on a jar (Hodos 2006, fig. 2.31). In al-Mina, several Phoenician inscriptions were found (Bron and Lemaire 1983). According to Hodos (2006, 79), "the nature and locations of such inscriptions suggest that Phoenician served as regional, political language." Katzenstein (1997, 202) considers the widespread use of Phoenician inscriptions "a most interesting phenomenon.… It was a great advantage for the Phoenician trader and merchant to be able to use the Phoenician letters and language in Greater Syria." Additional evidence for the relations with northern Syria can be found in the inscription of Yariris, king of Carchemish, who claims to know the "Tyrian script" (Lipínski 1985, 82), which again testifies to the wide use of Phoenician among Luwians. Further evidence for Phoenician trade with the Luwian states is the tribute paid by the Neo-Hittite king Mutallu of Commagene, which included purple-dyed textiles, probably of Phoenician origin. After reviewing the main opinions regarding the reason for the use of Phoenician in Cilicia, Fales (2017, 194–95) found no satisfactory answer yet to the question whether the status of Phoenician derived "from an explicitly aimed socio-economic and/or cultural input proceeding from the heartland." Ilya Yakubovich (2015, 36) assumes the coming of new groups to Cilicia in Iron Age I and argues that "one possible interpretation of the written use of Phoenician would be the assertion of a separate cultural identity by the new elites, in contrast to the rulers of the neighbouring states."

Finally, the fact that Phoenician gods were worshiped by the Aramaeans is attested in several inscriptions, such as that of Kilamuwa (*KAI* 24), where the Tyrian god Baal Hammon is mentioned. The Breij stela (*KAI* 201), found near Aleppo, represents the Tyrian god Melqart and mentions his name, thus attesting not only to the influence of Phoenician religion on the Aramaeans of Syria but also to the presence in the area of Aleppo of a Phoenician merchant community and also a temple dedicated to Melqart, where the stela was presumably erected (Kestemont 1985, 137; Bonnet and Niehr 2014, 75). According to Aubet (2001, 50), "There can be no doubt that the use of Phoenician as an official language and the invocation of Melqart of Tyre by the rulers in northern Syria and Cilicia reflect a Phoenician political and cultural influence of some importance in this territory."

The contacts between the Phoenician cities and the Syrian inland are illustrated by Phoenician materials found in inland sites and Syrian imports in Phoenician cities. The latter are rather rare, maybe because they were not recognized or because of the limited number of excavations. Syrian materials at the site of Dor during the Early Iron Age led to the assumption that a small community of Syrian people was living at the site. Tell Sukas on the north Syrian coast, for example, has yielded pottery that has clear parallels with pottery found in Hama (Buhl 1983a, 124). The southern Phoenician sites have provided so far little or no evidence for Syrian imports.

### 6.1.5.4. Trade with the Israelite Kingdoms

The relations of Phoenicia with the kingdoms of Israel and Judah were studied by Briquel-Chatonnet (1992), who has reviewed all the written sources as well as the archaeological record dealing with the subject. While the epigraphic data, whether Phoenician, Hebrew, or Aramaic, do not contribute much to the study of these relations, literary sources, mainly the biblical record and Flavius Josephus's *Jewish Antiquities* and *Against Apion* provide the most substantial information (6–18). Several episodes of the relations between Hiram and Solomon are reported by Josephus from Menander's work.

The political and diplomatic relations between the two kingdoms were the result of their economic cooperation. The best-known episodes of these relations are concealed in the books of Kings, Samuel, and Chronicles. They deal with the relations of David and Solomon with Hiram of Tyre, which took place—according to the conventional chronology—in the tenth century BCE. The building of the Jerusalem palace and temple and the joint commercial expeditions to Ophir are the highlights of these relations. The famous Solomonic "house of the forest of Lebanon," in reference to the four rows of cedar beams used in its building (1 Kgs 7:1–11), indicates the import of cedarwood from Lebanon by the Israelites. In return for the technological skills and assistance of the Phoenician builders, sailors, traders, and providers of cedarwood for the monumental buildings, Phoenicia received what it needed most for the survival of its population: staple food such as cereals and olive oil, as well as agricultural land, such as the villages from the territory of Cabul that were given by Solomon to Hiram in payment for his services (1 Kgs 9:10–14; Briquel-Chatonnet 1992, 47–51). The agricultural importance of these villages as producers of cereals was confirmed by the archaeology (Lemaire 1991b), and Phoenician presence is clearly attested in their material culture.

These economic relations between Phoenicia and the kingdom of Israel were sealed under the reign of Ahab by his diplomatic marriage with the Tyrian princess Jezebel, daughter of King Ittobaal (1 Kgs 16:31). According to the biblical record, the Phoenician princess encouraged the worship of the Tyrian Baal (1 Kgs 16:32), which caused the anger of the Israelites, who destroyed the temple of Baal (2 Kgs 10:26–27) after the murder of the Tyrian princess (2 Kgs 9:30–37). These events may have caused a drastic change in the friendly relations between Tyre and the kings of Israel.

From the account of the joint expeditions undertaken in the Red Sea, we know that the Phoenicians came into contact with the land of Ophir (1 Kgs 9:26–28; 10:11, 22; 2 Chr 8:17–18; 9:10, 21), the identity of which remains debated. For some it indicates India, for others the western and southern coast of the Arabian Peninsula, and for yet other scholars Sudan or Ethiopia (Briquel-Chatonnet 1992, 277–83). This account raised also the problem of the meaning and location of Tarshish. This term has been variously interpreted: first it was understood to be a geographical term. For some it indicates southern Spain, the Tartessos of the classical texts, while for others it refers to Tarsus in Cilicia. Tarshish was also interpreted as a type of ship, namely, the kind that was used for sailing the high seas en route to southern Spain (273–77). As we have already mentioned, recent evidence seems to have helped solve this issue and indicated that Tarshish may be identified with Sardinia (Thompson and Skaggs 2013).

As for the archaeological data, Phoenician products are found mainly in the cities of the northern kingdom, such as Samaria, Tel Dan, Megiddo, and Tell Rehov (Waiman-Barak and Gilboa 2016), where Phoenician containers were found since the Early Iron Age, as attested by the presence of Phoenician bichrome ware at some sites such as Megiddo, Kinneret, and Yoqneam (Gilboa and Goren 2015, 79), but also in cities of the kingdom of Judah, such as Ramat Raḥel, where architectural elements such as ashlar masonry and proto-aeolic capitals traditionally considered to be Phoenician were found (Mazar 1992, 474–75).

Next to architecture, contacts with Phoenicia are attested by the presence of Phoenician pottery on Israelite and Judean sites. The recent discovery of a large number of Phoenician amphorae in Beersheba together with cedar beams from the Lebanon attest to the trade relations between Phoenicia and Judah in Iron Age IIB (Singer-Avitz 2010). The presence of Phoenician goods in Beersheba at that specific period only is explained by the excavators by the opening of the "Sealed Kāru of Egypt" by Sargon II, who had lifted the ban imposed by his predecessor regarding trade with Egypt (Singer-Avitz 2010, 195–96). Petrographic analysis has confirmed the origin of most jars to the southern Lebanese coast, while others imitating them were produced locally. Imported Phoenician pottery dated to Iron Age IIB–C is also attested at Tell en-Nasbeh (Brody 2014). According to Aaron Brody (63), "The Iron Age IIB shows numerous connections between Phoenicia and Israel/Judah" in pottery, glyptic, carved ivories, eye beads, ashlar masonry, and cedarwood. At Hazor, Phoenician carinated-shoulder amphorae as well as ovoid jars were found in a storeroom (Yadin et al. 1958, pls. LXXIIl 9; LXXIII 12, 14) together with red-slip-ware bowls. The excavators speculated that perhaps the cylindrical jars were used for wine and the ovoid ones for oil (Yadin et al. 1958, 24). The typical Phoenician repertoire found in Israelite and Judean sites was either imported or produced locally. It is, however, difficult to know the nature of the goods that were traded in these containers, since no organic-residue analysis is available.

Another typical Phoenician find in the Israelite kingdom is ivory. Carved ivories, mainly those found in Samaria (Crowfoot, Crowfoot, and Sukenik 1938), are believed to be of Phoenician, more specifically Tyrian, manufacture. Ahab's "ivory house" in that city is mentioned in 1 Kgs 22:39. The Bible often ascribes a Phoenician origin to ivory products. For example, Solomon's ivory throne is said to have been made by Tyrian craftsmen

(1 Kgs 10:18). Cedarwood, the main import from Phoenicia, was used for monumental buildings, and fragments have been occasionally recovered in Palestinian sites.

As for Palestinian finds in Phoenicia, they are more difficult to trace because they consisted mainly in foodstuffs such as cereals, olives, and olive oil. It is also difficult to trace the origin of the ceramic vessels that served for the transport of these products in the absence of analyses. Some so-called sausage jars were found in both Palestinian and Phoenician sites (Briquel-Chatonnet 1992, 246–47). The examples found in Bikai's sounding in Tyre were assumed to be Palestinian imports based on neutron activation analysis (Geva 1982), a conclusion that was adopted by some scholars (Aubet 2001, 48) and doubted by others for lack of decisive evidence (Briquel-Chatonnet 1992, 248–49).

### 6.1.5.5. Trade with Philistia

There is hardly any historical information dealing with the relations between the Phoenician cities and Philistia. The most relevant information comes from the *Periplus* of Pseudo-Scylax, which says that Ashkelon, one of the cities of the Philistine Pentapolis, was a Tyrian city in the Persian period. Nothing is known, however, about the circumstances that led to the incorporation of Ashkelon into the territory of Tyre. Even before the Persian period there is evidence for trade contacts between Phoenicia and Ashkelon, as attested by Phoenician amphorae as well as other forms unearthed there (Stager et al. 2011, 97–102).

Other evidence for Philistine-Phoenician contacts is the fact that the Phoenician script played an influential role in the Philistine area between the sixth and the second century BCE because of the political and commercial importance of the Phoenicians in this region during that period:

> On the other hand, the role played by the Phoenician script in the Philistine plain from the sixth until the second century BCE can perhaps be explained by the political and commercial importance of the Phoenicians in this region but also by the cultural proximity in script, language, and religion that the Philistine culture of Iron Age II had with the Phoenician culture.[2]

---

2. Lemaire 2000, 249: "D'autre part, le rôle joué par l'écriture phénicienne dans la plaine philistine du VIe au IIe s. av. n.è. s'explique sans doute par l'importance poli-

The presence at Tell Qasile of Phoenician amphorae produced on the northern Palestinian coast (Aznar 2005, 204) in large quantities indicates strong trade relations with Phoenicia: "The finds from Tell Qasile are particularly significant, as they reveal longstanding relations between the Philistine city and the (Israeli) northern coast, probably by means of the Phoenicians.... The Phoenician connection is not a surprise, as Tell Qasile Stratum X yielded Phoenician Bichrome ware."

According to David Ben-Shlomo (2013, 724), Phoenician pottery was rare in Philistia, but the locally made Iron Age IIA pottery "shows certain 'Phoenician' attributes." However, the emergence of cremation burials in several Philistine sites, such as Azor, Tell Ruqeish, and Tell el-Far'ah South, and "The rising popularity of this practice during Iron IIB-C could be strongly influenced by the Phoenician culture" (726). Mazar (1985, 127) had already suggested that "the population at Tell Qasile was of Canaanite-Phoenician origin, living together with Philistines."

6.1.5.6. Trade with Cyprus

The island of Cyprus had close relations with Phoenicia since the second millennium BCE. These contacts were not interrupted after the great collapse of the Late Bronze Age culture but continued through Iron Age I. These relations witnessed a drastic change in the first millennium BCE, when Cyprus and Phoenicia developed stronger ties, characterized by the foundation of Phoenician settlements on the island (for a detailed evidence for Cypriot-Phoenician trade see Gilboa, Sharon, and Boaretto 2008). Aubet (2001, 54) believes that the foundation of Kition was instrumental in giving Phoenician trade "the first impulse towards establishing commercial exchanges with the west by sea."

Contacts between Cyprus and Phoenicia are confirmed by both the epigraphic (Masson-Sznycer 1972; Amadasi-Guzzo and Karageorghis 1977; Reyes 1994) and the archaeological record (Reyes 1994; Karageorghis 2002), and they are attested as early as the mid-eleventh century BCE in the funerary assemblages of Palaepaphos-*Skales* (Karageorghis 1983), where Phoenician ceramics dated to the Cypro-Geometric I period were found (Karageorghis 2002, 132, figs. 278–80; see also Bikai 1987a;

---

tique et commerciale des Phéniciens dans cette region, mais aussi par la proximité culturelle, d'écriture, de langue et de religion, de la culture philistienne du Fer II avec la culture phénicienne."

1987b). Phoenician interest in expanding to Cyprus was most probably the search for metals (Karageorghis 2002, 141).

Phoenician settlement in Cyprus took place in Iron Age II toward the end of the ninth century BCE. The Phoenicians settled first in Kition, where they built a temple to their goddess Astarte on top of the older Late Bronze Age temple (Karageorghis 1976, ch. 5; 2002, fig. 306). In it, Phoenician red-and-black-slip pottery dated to circa 800 BCE was found. A dedication to Astarte inscribed on a votive bowl secured the identification of the divinity worshiped in this temple (Amadasi-Guzzo and Karageorghis 1977, 149–60). The presence of a large number of terra-cotta figurines of the *dea gravida* type brought additional evidence for such identification. Phoenician settlement in Cyprus is also attested by the inscription mentioning *qarthadasht*, the "New City," and its governor, who is said to be the servant of Hiram king of Tyre. This inscription, which is of unknown provenance, is dated to the eighth century BCE (Karageorghis 2002, 149). Some scholars identify *qarthadasht* with Kition, while others think that it refers to the city of Amathus or Limassol (Masson and Sznycer 1972, 77–78; Karageorghis 2002, 151; Kastzenstein 1997, 207). That Lulî, the Sidonian king, fled to Cyprus before the army of Esarhaddon and stayed there until he died may be considered as additional evidence for the existence of Phoenician settlements on the island.

Archaeological evidence for Phoenician presence is represented also by the recent discovery of a Phoenician cremation cemetery dated to the Cypro-archaic period (eighth–seventh century BCE) in Amathus (Karageorghis 2002, 153). It is very similar to the cemetery that was recently discovered in Tyre al-Baṣṣ (Aubet 2004; Aubet, Nuñez, and Trellisó 2014). Gold objects representing the Phoenician goddess Astarte were found, and they were dated to the Cypro-Geometric II period, tenth–ninth century BCE (Karageorghis 2002, 133, figs. 283–84). The Phoenicians settled in Tamassos around 800 BCE, as attested by the epigraphic evidence. Several Cypriot sites, such as Salamis, have yielded a variety of items generally considered to be Phoenician, such as ivories and metal bowls (Karageorghis 2002, figs. 343–52, 365–66).

More importantly, Phoenician trade with Cyprus is attested by the presence of Phoenician containers in several Cypriot sites (Culican 1984, 47–70; Bikai 1987a). Evidence for Phoenician trade with Cyprus is attested as early as Iron Age I by the presence of several types of Phoenician pottery, such as Phoenician bichrome ware, found mainly south and southwest of the island and represented by ring-based and strainer jugs, by unpainted small flasks that form the majority of imports from the Levant, and by red-ware containers as well as by a small number of jars (Gilboa and Goren 2015, 76–78, fig. 3; for the distribution of Phoenician bichrome ware in Cyprus see Gilboa, Sharon, and Boaretto 2008; Gilboa and Goren 2015, 80–81). Of the forty-eight containers analyzed, thirteen were of Cypriot fabric and thirty-five were imports. Fifteen of the latter came from the Tyre-Sidon area and fifteen from the Carmel coast (Gilboa and Goren 2015, 86). Trade relations between Cyprus and Phoenicia went both ways, and Cypriot pottery is found in large numbers in Phoenician sites (Gilboa, Sharon, and Boaretto 2008, 134–41). The sites where most Cypriot pottery is attested in Iron Age I are Dor and Tyre. According to Gilboa and Yuval Goren (2015, 88), "This convergence does not seem to be accidental. It points to exchange networks operating specifically between Tyre (and Sidon?) and Dor with Cyprus." Gilboa assumes the presence of a Cypriot community at Dor in Iron Age I. In the Tyrian cremation cemetery at el-Baṣṣ, Cypriot ceramics formed 56.1 percent of the imports (Nuñez 2014, 264, fig. 3.4).

The oldest examples of Cypriot pottery found in Phoenician sites are White Painted I wheel-made wares dated between 1050 and 850 BCE (Koehl 1985, 45–46; Bikai 1978a, pls. 23.10, 28.3, 9.34, 9 and 12) and bichrome I wheel-made wares, dated to the tenth century BCE (Koehl 1985, 45–46). Cypro-geometric white-painted wheel made ware I (tenth/ninth century), III (eighth/seventh century), and IV (seventh century), and bichrome wheel-made I (tenth century), III (ninth/seventh century), and IV (seventh century) are attested mainly in Sarepta (Koehl 1985, figs. 9–10), Tyre (Núñez 2004, figs. 153–54, 245; Bikai 1978a, pls. XXI, XXIIa; Aubet and Núñez 2008), and Khaldeh (Doumet-Serhal, Karageorghis, and Loffet 2008, figs. 78–80). The basket-handled Cypriot jar is found in most Phoenician sites. Good examples were found at Tell el-Burak. These jars were also made in the northern Levantine coast.

Finally, Cypriot objects were found also from the Iron Age II in Phoenicia, such as the horse rider and terra-cotta mask that were found in Tomb 8 of the el-Baṣṣ cremation cemetery (Lehmann-Jericke 2004; Karageorghis 2004).

6.1.5.7. Trade with the Greek World

The emblematic source relating to contacts between Greece and Phoenicia, and by extension between East and West, is the myth of Cadmos (from

Semitic *qdm* = East), searching for his kidnapped sister Europe (from Semitic *'rb* = West; Herodotus, *Hist.* 5.58). The Phoenician prince is said to have taught the alphabet to the Hellenes and to have founded the city of Thebes. That the Greeks have kept the Semitic names of the letters adds to the historicity of the transfer. The earliest Greek inscriptions written with the Phoenician alphabet are dated to the eighth century BCE (Naveh 1982, 176; Kourou 2007, 138).

Archaeological evidence for Phoenician contacts with the Greek world is widely attested for the eighth and seventh century BCE but may have started earlier (Baurain and Bonnet 1992, 119–26; Le Meaux 2007, 281–82; Kourou 2007, 137–39; 2009, 39–42). A Phoenician inscription from Tekke near Knossos was dated to the tenth century BCE. Early contacts with Phoenicia are attested in Euboa, where a metal bowl dated to the tenth century BCE and pieces of jewelry dated to the eleventh and tenth century BCE have been retrieved from tombs. From these early sporadic contacts, Phoenician presence in the Greek islands became permanent in the eighth century BCE. Encounters between Greeks and Phoenicians became very frequent in the eighth century BCE, as attested by the large number of incidents involving Phoenicians in the Homeric epics. They are presented as sailors infesting the Mediterranean, as merchants and skilled craftsmen, but also as pirates and kidnappers.

Regarding the archaeological evidence, recent excavations at Kommos have exposed a sanctuary that yielded from its Phase A Floor 2 Phoenician pottery dated to the "mid-ninth century B.C. and most of it probably dates to its second half. There is no evidence to support a date in the tenth century B.C." (Gilboa, Waiman-Barak, and Jones 2015, 78). The Phase B (800–600 BCE) of the sanctuary yielded also Phoenician pottery from Level 2 dated circa 760–650 BCE (Gilboa, Waiman-Barak, and Jones 2015, 80). From this Phase B betyls or standing stones associated with Phoenician pottery and Aegyptiaca were retrieved, indicating clearly Phoenician presence in the island in the eighth century BCE (Le Meaux 2007, 282). Petrographic analysis of the Phoenician pottery found at Kommos was done on twenty samples, and "the first result of our study is that we can now demonstrate clearly that most of the vessels at Kommos ... are indisputably 'Phoenician' in the sense that they were produced on the southern Lebanese coast, specifically in the region between Tyre and Sidon" (Gilboa, Waiman-Barak, and Jones 2015, 89).

An often-mentioned example of coexistence between Phoenicians and Greeks was found in Pithecussai (Baurain and Bonnet 1992, 122; Gras,

Rouillard, and Teixidor 1989). Phoenician pottery, objects, and inscriptions were found in Athens, Samos, Cos, and Rhodes.

Greek presence is, in turn, attested on the Phoenician coast as early as Iron Age I at Sukas, Tell Kazel, Byblos, Sarepta, and Tyre, as evidenced by Greek pottery identified at these sites (Lehmann 2013; see also Coldstream 2008, 168–88; Hodos 2006, 86; Baurain and Bonnet 1992, 126–31). Aubet (2001, 41) mentions the discovery of a proto-geometric Greek vase dated to the tenth century BCE, which is "one of the earliest Greek imports discovered in Phoenicia and would coincide with the beginning of Tyre's commercial expansion in the period of Hiram I." Aubet mentions also a Cycladic plate found in the Tyrian cemetery and dated to 850 BCE. The most common import from Greece in Iron Age II is the Sub-Proto-Geometric skyphos, examples of which were found in Tyre (Núñez 2004, fig. 234; 2014, 264, fig. 3.4), Sarepta (Koehl 1985, fig. 12, 248–49), Khaldeh (Saidah 1971, 197a–b; Doumet-Serhal, Karageorghis, and Loffet 2008, figs. 59–60), and Sidon (Doumet-Serhal 2003, 16, fig. 19; Doumet-Serhal, Karageorghis, and Loffet 2008, 61–62). They are dated to the ninth/eighth century BCE. Ionian cups and pyxis are also attested (Saidah 1977, 141; 1983, pl. LIII, 1). The tenth- and ninth-century Greek pottery found in Tyre is among the earliest Greek imports in the Levant (Aubet 2001, 41).

It is difficult to identify the goods traded in the absence of textual evidence and organic-residue analysis of the imported vessels. The content of some of the jars is well-known from the Greek homeland. Hence, the so-called Chios jars, examples of which were found in Beirut and Tell el-Burak (Kamlah, Sader, and Schmitt 2016a, fig. 35; see fig. 6.1 below) were used to store wine, which suggests that this commodity was imported by the Phoenicians in spite of the fact that there is evidence for industrial Phoenician wine production at the latter site (see below).

Recent petrographic analysis of fifth–fourth century so-called East Greek imports from southern Phoenicia have provided evidence for a Cretan origin of these vessels (Gilboa et al. 2017). Several samples from coastal settlements such as Dor, Shiqmona, and Akko were Cretan imports. These analyses have provided the first tangible evidence for trade contacts with Crete in the fifth–fourth century BCE. The smaller containers, such as jugs, may have contained perfumed oils, while the larger ones, such as the *hydriai*, may have been imported for the vessels themselves. The suggestion that these table amphorae and *hydriai* may have been used to complete the symposium set would have an important implication on

Fig. 6.1. Chios amphora found in room 3.3 of House 3 at Tell el-Burak. Source: Tell el-Burak Archaeological Project.

Phoenician cultural traditions if verified, but this remains hypothetical (Gilboa et al. 2017, 585). These Cretan vessels were also locally produced in the northern Levant and Cyprus and thus indicate the participation of Crete in a "ceramic koine": this evidence "implies economic and perhaps broader cultural connections. Fundamentally, it indicates information exchange and knowledge of foreign markets" (586).

Finally, one has to mention the recent discovery of East Greek ceramics at Tell el-Burak. The study of these imports as well as their petrographic analysis is in preparation.

Finally, it is important to mention here again the community of Phoenician merchants active in Attica and whose presence is attested by several Phoenician inscriptions from Athens, as previously mentioned. The massive presence of Attic wares in Phoenician cities during the Persian period testifies to the commercial activity between Athens and Phoenicia.

6.1.5.8. Trade with the Arabian Peninsula

The prophet Ezekiel (27:20–22) mentions the connections Tyre had with Dedan, Qedar, Sheba, and Raamah, countries that provided the Phoenician city with small cattle, spices, precious stones, and gold. Trade in spices has been archaeologically attested, as some containers yielded evidence for cinnamon, as previously mentioned. One inscription from Main in south Arabia mentions the cities of Tyre and Sidon (Robin 1990, 139–41). Van Alfen (2002, 32–61) discusses Arabian trade in detail and lists all the commodities that came from there, mainly frankincense, myrrh, bdellium, cassia, and cinnamon.

6.1.5.9. Trade with Egypt

The country that had the strongest ties with Phoenicia across the millennia was Egypt. Trade relations between the two countries led to substantial Egyptian influence on Phoenician culture, as early as the third millennium BCE. These connections reached their climax in the Middle and New Kingdom period, when Phoenician cities came under the Egyptian political sphere of influence (Helck 1962). These relations seem to have witnessed a drawback in the first millennium BCE with the weakening of Egyptian power, but trade relations continued to prosper between the two countries (Leclant 1968).

According to the Wenamun text, the harbors of Tyre, Sidon, and Byblos had important merchant fleets that were active in trade with Egypt at the end of the tenth century BCE. Phoenician wood was traded for precious metals, mainly gold and silver, as well as many other Egyptian items, such as linen, papyrus, ropes, ox hides, and foodstuff, mainly lentils and salted fish. It is interesting to note that the only commodity requested by the Egyptian envoy was cedarwood.

Phoenician and Egyptian trade relations are also attested during the Persian period in Herodotus's *Histories*. The Greek historian mentions the presence of Tyrians dwelling around a sacred precinct in Memphis dating to the reign of Psammetic I, known as the Tyrian camp (*Hist.* 2.112). As already mentioned, Katzenstein (1979, 30) rightly suggested that this camp existed probably before the Persian period and that it was not the only one in Egypt. He also believes that since the camp was built around a temple dedicated to Hephaistos, the Tyrian craftsmen established there may have produced some of the metal bowls with Egyptian motifs.

The fragments of the statues of three Egyptian pharaohs, Sheshonq I, Osorkon I, and Osorkon II (Jidejian 1977, 66–67; Leclant 1968, 13, pl. VIIIb), found in Lebanon are evidence for a revival of cordial foreign and trade relations with Egypt. These relations reached their climax under the reign of Neco I, who may have counted the Phoenician cities as part of his dominion for a very short time (Katzenstein 1997, 304; Leclant 1968, 17). He is also the pharaoh who, according to Herodotus (*Hist.* 4.2), commissioned the Phoenicians to circumnavigate Africa. This was a sponsored Phoenician trade expedition to seek new sources of raw materials.

New evidence from the site of Dor has yielded evidence for trade contacts with Egypt in Iron Age I (Waiman-Barak, Gilboa, and Goren 2014; Gilboa 2015). According to the Dor excavators, this is the largest assemblage of Egyptian vessels from that period found so far outside Egypt (Gilboa 2015, 247). It consists of some 750 ceramic sherds, including partly or completely preserved vessels dating to Iron Age I (251). Egyptian vessels were identified also at ʿAthlit and Shiqmona (253), but in much smaller quantities. In all the other northern Palestinian coastal sites as well as in the main Lebanese and Syrian sites, there is hardly any evidence of Egyptian vessels, but this may be due to the fact that such Egyptian imports were not recognized earlier. Sidon in the south and Tell Mirhan in the north are yielding substantial amounts of Egyptian imports.[3] South of Dor, there is some evidence only from Ashkelon (253). Petrographic analysis confirmed that they were made of Nile clays. All belong to large containers, indicating commercial exchange. Relations with Egypt completely stopped after the ninth century BCE, when Dor came under Israelite dominion. Regarding the goods traded in these jars, there is no direct evidence from residue analysis, but it can be assumed, based on evidence from the faunal remains, that the Nile perch may have been one of the traded goods (255).

While Egyptian imports such as scarabs, amulets, and figurines are clearly attested in the Phoenician cities all through the Iron Age, with a clear increase in the Persian period, evidence for Phoenician-traded items is difficult to find in first-millennium BCE Egypt. We know from the historical sources that the Egyptians imported not only wood but also resins, agricultural products, wine, and oil, as well as purple-dyed textiles. Direct evidence for contacts in the Iron Age is scanty; however, Iron Age I jars were found in the royal tombs of Ramesses VI and VII (Aston, Aston, and Brock 1998, 161, 163). Other Phoenician vessels such as lentoid flasks and Phoenician bichrome jugs were also found (Aston 1996). At Dor these small containers were filled with liquids containing cinnamon, and the same product may have been exported to Egypt (Gilboa 2015, 258). Except for ceramics vaguely referred to as Syro-Palestinian (Maeir 2002, 237–40, fig. 1), south Levantine presence in general, and Phoenician presence in particular, is rarely attested in the Egyptian archaeological record (235 and n. 3). Storage jars form the largest number of the excavated Levantine ceramics, and some of them may have been imported from Phoenicia (239–40), but no petrographic analysis is available. One has to mention in this context the discovery of the remains of sixty carinated-shoulder amphorae that were discovered at site K at Elephantine. They probably originate from Phoenicia, but no petrographic analysis is available (Bettles 2003, 268). They may have contained wine, since Aramaic papyri from that southern island mention Sidonian wine. The discovered Phoenician

---

3. Personal communication of Hermann Genz and Karin Kopetsky.

shipwrecks off the shore of Ashkelon (Ballard and Stager 2002), which, according to their investigators, were heading to Egypt with a cargo consisting of eighth–seventh century BCE amphorae transporting wine, resin, or oil, provide some clue as to what these jars may have contained. A large number of such jar fragments from Elephantine and Abydos bore Phoenician inscriptions (Röllig 2013; Lidzbarski 1915). Röllig (2013, 199) concluded from this evidence that most fragments with Phoenician letters were imports and belong to a type known as "Phoenician" or "Levantine" amphora: "Still, there is a high probability that the vessels bearing Phoenician inscriptions were imports. There are often amphorae of the so-called Phoenician or Levantine type that, in any event, do not seem to be of local Egyptian manufacture."[4] Next to Sidonian wine, one of the Elephantine papyri mentions for the year 475 BCE various types of Phoenician ships loaded with different sorts of wood, namely, cedar, as well as iron, copper, tin, clay, and wool (Yardeni 1994, 70).

Finally, Phoenician trade contacts are clearly evidenced in Sudan (Lohwasser 2002, 233 and n. 47). Examples of such finds are a Phoenician metal bowl of the "bull-bowls" type, which was found in a tomb of the Sanam cemetery (Lohwasser 2002, fig. 1a–b), as well as two Phoenician mushroom-lipped and one black-on-red jugs (Lohwasser 2002, fig. 6-9). This type of bowl has been variously dated to the late ninth or early or mid-eighth century BCE (Lohwasser 2002, 228) and the jugs to the eighth/seventh century BCE. Evidence for Phoenician-traded goods in Egypt will certainly increase if more attention is given by Egyptologists to imported ceramics.

6.1.5.9. Trade with the Central and Western Mediterranean

The Phoenician expansion in the Mediterranean has been intensively investigated and is beyond the scope of this book. The textual sources relating to this expansion were collected and discussed by Bunnens (1979), while the archaeological evidence for the Phoenician settlement was most recently updated in the general study of Aubet (2001) as well as in individual regional studies relating to some of the major Phoenician settlements:

---

4. Röllig 2013, 199: "Dennoch besteht eine hohe Wahrscheinlichkeit, dass die Gefässe mit phönizischen Inschriften Importstücke sind. Es sind ja auch häufig Amphoren eines Typs, der als 'phönizisch' oder 'levantinisch' bezeichnet wird, der jedenfalls nicht einheimisch ägyptisch zu sein scheint."

Carthage (Lancel 1992), Sicily (Tusa 1982; Bondì 1985), Sardinia (Barreca 1974; Acquaro 1985), Spain (Bierling and Gitin 2002), and the Atlantic coast of Africa (Marzoli 2012).

The date of the first contacts between Phoenicians and the central and western Mediterranean is still debated. The information provided by the classical authors about the founding of the oldest colonies, Lixus, Cadiz, and Utica, at the end of the twelfth century BCE is clearly contradicted by the archaeological evidence. No remains earlier than the eighth century have been found so far. However, recent evidence from Huelva indicates earlier contacts (for a discussion of the ceramic evidence from Huelva, see Gilboa, Sharon, and Boaretto 2008, 168–73). The earliest types of Phoenician pottery found in the west are similar to those of Tyre Strata IV–I and dated to the second half of the eighth century BCE (Aubet 2001, 41). Because of the discrepancy between the classical sources and the archaeological evidence, scholars are today divided into two groups: those who want to bridge this discrepancy favor the existence of a precolonial stage (twelfth–eighth century BCE) followed by a colonial stage proper (eighth–sixth century BCE; Aubet 2001, 199), while those who deny the existence of a precolonial stage base their dating exclusively on the archaeological evidence. The latter confirm that "almost all the southern coasts and islands of the western Mediterranean were under Phoenician dominion, a dominion that seems to have been consolidated during the eighth and seventh centuries" (Aubet 2001, 165). However, evidence for a precolonial stage is slowly emerging. The above-mentioned imports of Sardinian hacksilber from the tenth century BCE may illustrate this phase.

To sum up, Phoenician trade, which was almost unknown for the Early Iron Age period except for the controversial information in the Wenamun Report, is now evidenced to have been quite active in the eastern Mediterranean. Archaeological discoveries, and mainly petrographic analyses of Phoenician pottery from several sites of the eastern Mediterranean, have proven to be instrumental in tracing Phoenician contacts and in defining the place of origin of the traded items. Organic-residue analyses also contributed at times to identify areas of contact and goods traded by the Phoenicians. They were able to prove, for instance, contacts between Phoenicia and Southeast Asia by identifying cinnamon contained in the small flasks at Dor that were exported also to Cyprus and Egypt. Archaeological finds in the Phoenician homeland are another indicator of the trade networks Phoenicia had established with its neighboring countries as well as with the eastern Mediterranean. This evidence brought new light on the extent of Phoenician trade as early as the end of the second millennium BCE. The recent and abundant documentation from Iron Age I Tel Dor yielded evidence for thriving contacts with Cyprus, Egypt, and Syria, which was interpreted by the Dor excavators as being maybe the result of the presence of Cypriot and maybe also Syrian expatriates in the city. They also argued that Dor, which had preeminence in Phoenician trade in Iron Age I, was eclipsed by Tyre only when it came under Israelite dominion in the ninth century BCE, which put an end to its foreign contacts and opened the way to Tyre to take the lead of Phoenician trade and to become the main metropolis and mother of most colonies in the east and west Mediterranean. Such a conclusion, which may very well be correct in the present state of the evidence, may be perhaps biased by the fact that little is known about Iron Age Tyre and Sidon. It is indeed unfortunate that the ancient sites of these cities are hidden by the modern towns. Our sole information about these two important Phoenician cities comes from the little sounding made by Bikai at Tyre, whereas the Dor evidence comes from several extended areas on the site, which have demonstrated that the Iron Age I city extended over the whole 8 ha large mound. The amount of information collected from Dor is very substantial, while evidence from Tyre and Sidon is either minimal or nonexistent. In my opinion, in the absence of substantial information about the Iron Age settlements of the latter cities, any final conclusions about the economic preeminence of a city over the other would be premature. Recent excavations at Tyre next to the Bikai sounding seem promising and may yield more substantial information about the role of the Phoenician metropolis in Mediterranean trade in the Early Iron Age.

Another conclusion arises from this review of Phoenician trade, namely, that northern Phoenicia does not seem to have played an active role in Mediterranean trade in the early and even later Iron Age. The archaeological evidence seems to indicate that Phoenician trade was mainly in the hand of the southern Phoenician cities, which is in line with the evidence from the historical sources. Here, again, no hasty conclusions should be drawn. However, the available evidence seems to suggest a difference in trade activity between northern and southern Phoenicia.

## 6.2. Phoenician Agriculture

The Phoenician coastal plain is narrow, and in several places it tends to disappear because the mountains jut directly into the sea, mainly north of Beirut and south of Tyre. The Iron Age inhabitants of the Lebanese and Arwadian coast probably tried to gain more arable land by terracing the deforested and easily accessible lower mountain slopes. However, this assumption has not been verified by archaeological research for the Iron Age. Nevertheless, in spite of the limited arable land, Phoenicia's coastal plain was fertile and well irrigated, and various kinds of crops were cultivated.

We often hear since the Late Bronze Age that Phoenician cities were in dire need of staple food. The letters of Rib-Adda, king of Byblos, are a striking example in this context: the city, according to the claim of its king, had to sell the sons and daughters of its citizens as slaves, and its people had to give all their possessions to buy food from Yarimuta, an unidentified city located probably on the southern Phoenician coast (Belmonte-Marín 2001, 343), in order not to starve: "(Our) sons and daughters, and the furnishings of the houses are gone, since they have been sold {in} the land of Yarimuta for our provisions to keep us alive" (Moran 1987, EA 75.13). However, this famine may have been caused by years of drought, which have been attested by recent studies around the Mediterranean (e.g., Kaniewski et al. 2010; 2013) and which may have been one of the factors favoring the collapse of the Late Bronze Age culture.

The need for staple food is attested again in the Iron Age, when the king of Tyre received as payment twenty villages in the upper Galilee: "King Solomon gave Hiram twenty towns in the land of Galilee" (1 Kgs 9:11–14). The archaeological evidence from these towns, such as Tell Keisan, indicated that the latter site was producing large quantities of cereals in Iron Age I, as attested by the presence of numerous silos and storage jars (Briend and Humbert 1980, 200–201). The Bible speaks also of large quantities of wheat and olive oil delivered annually to Tyre as payment for the cedar wood: "So Hiram provided Solomon with all the cedar wood and juniper he wanted, while Solomon gave Hiram twenty thousand kors of wheat to feed his household, and twenty thousand kors of pure oil. Solomon gave Hiram this every year" (1 Kgs 5:25 JB). We have already seen that Ezekiel's book mentions the import by the Tyrians of grain, honey, wine, lambs, rams, and he-goats. It seems clear that the heartland of Phoenicia, that is, the Lebanese coast, did not produce enough staple food for its densely settled cities and always needed to import additional quantities of them. The above information has led some scholars to consider that Phoenicia suffered regularly from agricultural deficit, and the latter coupled with overpopulation have been given as causes, among others, for Phoenician colonization. According to Aubet (2001, 79), "the whole of Tyre's political strategy ... is dictated by territorial ambitions arising largely from ... limited space for agriculture, overpopulation and a shortfall in food supplies."

Such statements have led to the assumption that Phoenicia had a poor agricultural sector and was in bad need of basic staple food. The archaeological evidence does not lend much support to such an assumption. Indeed, notwithstanding the above evidence, agriculture formed an important sector of Phoenician economy, and certainly most people made a living from it. While long-distance trade aiming mainly at the import of metals and other raw materials was sponsored by the royal family or other powerful members of urban society who harvested the profits for their own welfare, the large majority of the population lived outside the cities. It is not very far-fetched to assume that they were overwhelmingly peasants making a living by producing agricultural goods for their own, or landlord, consumption. Some of the planted crops served in developing local agro-industries such as wine and olive oil, which became with time one of the main traded goods by the Phoenicians, as will be argued below. The presence of all sorts of tools and installations for the storing and processing of crops in most excavated sites, such as silos, *tannur*s, storage jars, *mortaria*, pestles, grinders, olive presses, and winepresses, indicates that processing agricultural products at both a private and industrial level was one of the main sectors of Phoenician economy.

6.2.1. What Did the Phoenicians Plant, and What Did They Eat?

The archaeological evidence has produced ample information from Phoenician sites about cooking and food processing: the presence of cooking pots, grinders, pestles, and *mortaria* as well as knives and *tannur*s at almost every site indicates that the Phoenicians were producing all sorts of food, mainly bread, as well as animal stew. Until recently, however, little was known about the main components of their diet.

Since agriculture was an important sector of Phoenician economy, it is legitimate to ask what they planted, what they ate, and what type of agricultural produce they exported. There is little evidence from the Phoenician motherland to answer these questions thoroughly. As already noted by Andrea Orendi and Katleen Deckers (2018, 718), "Studies dealing with Phoenician agriculture and archaeological excavations of Phoenician rural settlements are, however, very rare.... Whereas recent studies cover the rural landscapes of the later Punic or Carthaginian world…, the Phoenician core country has not been taken into account."

Antonella Spanò Giammellaro (1999), in one of the earliest studies on the subject, summed up the main types of food that were produced and consumed by the Phoenicians. However, she based her study on biblical, Egyptian, and Ugaritic texts, which are for the larger part earlier or later than the Iron Age and which she often fails to reference. She summarizes the information gleaned from these texts and concludes that the Phoenicians grew cereals, mainly wheat and barley; pulses and vegetables such as peas, lentils, chickpeas, broad beans, and olives; and fruits such as grapes, figs, pomegranate, and dates. She also sums up the evidence relating to the types of consumed meat, which consisted of both domesticated and wild species as well as fish. Unfortunately, her lists are not always evidence based, for she does not refer to botanical and faunal analyses from the homeland, most probably because these analyses in the Phoenician homeland were still in their infancy when her article was written.

6.2.1.1. The Results of Botanical Analyses

In the last decades, substantial evidence regarding the plant and faunal species attested in the Phoenician settlements of the homeland has started to emerge. The evidence comes mainly from southern Phoenicia, and the picture is far from being complete. However, we have some relevant information for northern Phoenicia from the earlier Bronze Age periods as well as the Early Iron Age. For example, the evidence from Tell Fadous-Kfarabida, north of Byblos, provides a good example of the crops that were grown on the northern Lebanese coast. "There almost all the seeds and fruits represent crop species with olive and emmer chaff dominating the assemblage" (Riehl and Deckers 2009, 111), but there was also evidence for grape pips, barley, and lentils. It would not be far-fetched to assume that the same crops continued to be planted in the Iron Age since climatic and geographical conditions in the area did not undergo drastic changes over time. This assumption was proposed and substantiated in the case of Sidon (see below).

Further north, Tell Tweini has also produced botanical evidence for the Early Iron Age, but the results obtained indicated a change in the climate during that period: "Recently published results of palynological, sedimentary, and paleo-ecological research at Tell Tweini linked to a pollen-based reconstruction of the eco-system have convincingly suggested an abrupt climate change in the period between 1200 and 850 B.C.E., and especially during the Early Iron Age levels at Tell Tweini" (Bretschneider et al. 2011, 84). Still, it is very unfortunate not to have results from other sites further south in the territory of Aradus, from Tell Arqa, or from Beirut in spite of recent excavations in these areas.

Regarding southern Phoenicia, paleo-botanical analyses from Iron Age levels are available mainly from Sidon, Tell el-Burak, Tyre al-Baṣṣ, Horbat Rosh Zayit, and Tell Keisan. Tel Dor's botanical remains have not yet been published.

6.2.1.2. The Evidence from Sidon College Site

Recent analyses from the College Site excavations in Sidon have yielded important information on the crops available during the Iron Age and have demonstrated that there was no substantial change in the diet of the people since the Early Bronze Age. "The assemblages of all periods indicate that the plant diet of the people who occupied the site at all periods was a very Mediterranean diet" (de Moulins 2015, 38). The assemblages ascribed to the Iron Age were fairly uniform and contained mainly emmer wheat, barley, and olive stones (38 and table 1). There is also evidence for some legumes such as lentils, and fruits such as pips of grapes. Dominique de Moulins (40) concludes her study of the Sidonian botanical remains saying, "The usual modern Mediterranean plant diet of the inhabitants can be confirmed for the Middle Bronze Age to the Iron Age periods as far as the ingredients are concerned. The use of olives is particularly of note and may increase in the Iron Age."

6.2.1.3. The Evidence from Tell el-Burak

At Tell el-Burak the diet of the Iron Age people could be followed over the four hundred years of the Iron Age occupation. The careful stratigraphic sequence has allowed the study of the changes or fluctuations in the agricultural habits of the settlers. Orendi and Deckers (2018; see also Orendi 2016 and a summary in Kamlah 2016) have identified 141 taxa, and their study has shown that pips of grape formed 41.7 percent of the botanical material. This taxon was by far the largest group identified in the seeds and fruits group. Cereals consisting of barley and wheat formed the second largest group (33.8 percent), large-seeded legumes formed the third (14.52 percent), and olives the fourth most frequent taxon (8.46 percent; Orendi and Deckers 2018, table 2). In spite of the diversity of the archaeo-botanical remains, *Vitis vinifera* was the most frequent crop in all the phases of the Phoenician settlement. As noted by Orendi and Deckers, this is a very unusual pattern for archaeo-botanical remains from Bronze or Iron Age settlements in the Levant.

Looking more specifically at House 3, which is ascribed to Phase D (seventh century BCE), and at the two-room building associated with Structure II and ascribed to Phase C (sixth century BCE; for these architectural remains, see Kamlah, Sader, and Schmitt 2016a), the archaeo-botanical samples gave the following results: In House 3 the distribution of the taxa did not differ from the general trend of the site, with grape seeds being the most frequent remains, mainly in the front room 3.3, where a small plastered vat was found (Kamlah, Sader, and Schmitt forthcoming). *Vitis vinifera* remains and *vitis* charcoal have a higher presence in this front room than in the other two back rooms of House 3, which seems to suggest that some grape processing was taking place there. Moreover, inside the vat was a broken vessel still in situ, showing traces of fire. The pips of grape inside the vat were all charred, which seems to suggest that the grapes were processed into a product that has not been identified yet, maybe a sort of molasses used as sweetener.

The archaeo-botanical analysis of the samples from the two-room structure dated to Phase C are more significant since *vitis vinifera* formed 86.9 percent of the whole assemblage. From the five hundred identified charred seeds, 420 were grape pips. Together with pips, other grape parts were found, including undeveloped pips, undeveloped fruits, and pedicels. Since the charred grape pips were found in the ashes of the two-room building, which was probably a kitchen, Kamlah (2016, 46) suggested that they probably belong to the marc resulting from the treading of the grapes that was then dried and used as fuel.

In the samples taken from the fill of the large plastered vat in Area 4 (for the vat see below) *vitis vinifera* represented 31 percent of the cultivated taxa. The charcoal in the samples from the basin fill was dominated by *vitis* species, about 37 percent, and this is the only context from the site so far with such huge proportions of grapevine. The results of the archaeo-botanical analysis strongly suggest that the high ubiquity of grape pips in all phases points to wine making as a major economic activity. According to Orendi and Deckers (2018), sites where such high percentages of *vitis vinifera* were obtained allowed the interpretation of the specific structures, the plastered vat and platform in the case of Tell el-Burak, as winepresses.

Grapes were grown in large quantities in the area of Tell el-Burak and may have been used for the production of wine at that site. The presence of two nearby harbors, Sarepta and Sidon, would have secured the export of the production.

In spite of the fact that olives did not form a high proportion of the cultivated taxa, there is nevertheless some evidence that olive oil was stored, if not also produced, at Tell el-Burak. Indeed, the organic residue of twenty amphora samples from House 3 was analyzed,[5] and preliminary results from the analysis of fourteen amphorae and soil samples from House 3 were reported in an unpublished internal summary by Evgenia Tachatou after a first assessment (see also Schmitt et al. 2019). The analysis of the extracted material showed that except for one, which definitely contained wine acid, all other samples showed high amounts of fat acids. The majority of samples from House 3 yielded evidence for fats. Two samples so far have yielded more specific results, and they contained probably plant oil. Given the abundance of olive wood in the charred remains dating to the Iron Age, the plant oil could have been olive oil, though more evidence is needed for verification. Based on the botanical evidence as well as on the residue analysis of the amphorae, it can be concluded that "Olive oil was probably also pressed and stored at Tell el-Burak" (Orendi and Deckers 2018, 734), but the production of olive oil probably took place elsewhere because thus far no evidence for olive presses has been identified on site.

6.2.1.4. The Evidence from Tyre al-Baṣṣ

At the Tyre al-Baṣṣ cemetery, between 2002 and 2005 twenty-four samples were collected from the Iron Age tombs. Predominant among the cultivated taxa found inside the urns were grape pips. There was little evidence for cereals, and only one olive stone was found (Rovira 2014, fig. 10.3). The presence of botanical remains in general and of grape pips in particular could be accidental, but they could also have come from the offered goods that were placed in the jugs near the cinerary urn. These probably contained precious liquids such as wine (Rovira 2014, 499). It is obvious that vegetal food remains are not expected to be found in large quantity

---

5. The samples were sent to Mainz in spring 2015. They were divided into two sets, which were given to the Department of Microbiology and Wine Research, headed by Prof. Dr. König, and to the Department of Soil Sciences, headed by Prof. Dr. Fiedler. There content analyses were carried out using different methods by Evgenia Tachatou.

and variety in a cemetery. These results do not reflect the diet of the Tyrians but may hint at the nature of some funerary offerings.

6.2.1.5. The Evidence from Tell Keisan

At Tell Keisan there was no systematic collection of botanical samples. The content of one silo was analyzed, which gives only a partial picture of the botanical specimens found at that site. The analysis of the content of that eleventh-century BCE silo demonstrated that 70 percent of the botanical remains were wheat of the *triticum durum* variety (Kislev 1980, 361). The analyses have also identified the presence of emmer, barley, bitter vetch, and darnel. This evidence showed that cereals, mainly wheat, were a major agriculture produce in Tell Keisan in Iron Age I.

6.2.1.6. The Evidence from Horbat Rosh Zayit

Analysis of botanical remains from Horbat Rosh Zayit from levels dated to the tenth–ninth century BCE has yielded evidence for the culture of grains. The largest collection of crop plants consisted of naked wheat mixed with smaller quantities of barley, horsebean, and pips of grapes (Kislev and Melamed 2000 and table app.3.1). Among the weeds, darnel formed the largest collection. Insects that infested wheat were also identified (Kislev and Melamed 2000, table app.3.9).

Olive wood was found dispersed all over the site and formed the largest collection of charred wood remains (Baruch and Lipschitz 2000, 203). Moreover, seeds found in a sealed jar in the storehouse consisted of olive stones, peas, and cultivated *Vicia* (Baruch and Lipschitz 2000, table app.2.2). This evidence combined with the archaeological discovery of oil presses led Uri Baruch and Lipschitz (204) to suggest, "As the site seems to have served as a regional center, olives could have been brought from elsewhere, or cultivated locally. The relative abundance of olive wood fragments at Horbat Rosh Zayit favours the second possibility."

6.2.2. The Results of Faunal Analysis

The protein-bearing diet of the Phoenicians was provided mainly by domesticated animals and fish. Wild animals were also consumed, but always in very small quantities. Most sites being located in the immediate vicinity of the seashore, the high presence of fish and mollusks is not surprising. Several sites have provided evidence for the types of faunal remains present in Phoenician settlements. The evidence is here too more substantial for southern Phoenicia. In northern Phoenicia results of faunal analyses from Iron Age layers are available so far only from Tell Tweini (Linseele 2010). From Tell Kazel, only Late Bronze Age remains were analyzed and published (Chahoud 2015). From southern Phoenicia there is evidence from Sidon, but so far only the Bronze Age remains have been published (Chahoud and Vila 2011–2012), and the Iron Age faunal material is still under study[6] from Tell el-Burak (Çakırlar forthcoming), from Tyre al-Baṣṣ (Montero 2014), from Horbat Rosh Zayit (Horwitz 2000), and Tel Dor (Raban-Gerstel et al. 2008; Sapir-Hen et al. 2014). There is also mention of faunal results from Akko and Tell Abu Hawam relating only to marine fauna. Regarding the faunal material from Sarepta, it was entrusted by the excavators to David Reese (2010, 114), who has published so far only the shells, the first of several planned studies to be published.

6.2.2.1. The Evidence from Tell Tweini

At Tell Tweini the large majority of the assemblage comes from Late Bronze and Iron Age contexts. Not all the faunal remains belonged to animals brought by the people to be consumed. Many came with sediments or clay, others with the fishing nets, such as crabs and corals, and others were intrusive animals, such as small insectivorous and rodent mammals. The people of Tweini ate mainly sheep, goat, and cattle, with the first two prevailing with 68 percent and the third forming 31 percent of the consumed domestic animals: "Il est clair que la chèvre, le mouton et le boeuf étaient les principaux pourvoyeurs de protéines animales" (Linseele 2010, 154–55). The ratio of wild animals such as gazelles, wild boars, and wild goats did not exceed 2 percent of the consumed animals. Remains of birds were also very few. In the Iron Age the ratio of cattle increased, and their remains were found mainly in the public buildings, while sheep and goats were found in domestic dwellings. This may reflect the consumption of cattle by people of a higher social status (155). It is interesting to note that pig remains represented only 1 percent of the assemblage. The pig is very rare in all the strata of Tell Tweini, thus indicating that its quasi-absence had nothing to do with ethnic groups or religious taboos and that it was

---

6. Personal communication with Claude Doumet-Serhal.

simply never part of the regular diet of the people there. This absence is not surprising, since pig is not represented at all at Ugarit during the Late Bronze Age. Furthermore, fish, of which fifteen taxa were identified, were an important part of the people's diet. Shells and mollusks were also found.

### 6.2.2.2. The Evidence from Tell el-Burak

The faunal remains of Iron Age Tell el-Burak are still under study. In a short internal report dated October 10, 2018, Canan Çakırlar, who had studied only part of the collections, was able to make some preliminary observations. First she observes, "Despite its location right on the coast, it is clear that Tell el-Burak was oriented towards an agricultural economy. Remains of cattle, sheep and goat are abundant, in contrast to a dearth of fish bones or even shells." Mixed economy is indicated by the fact that all age groups of cattle and caprines are attested. Pigs are also very rare and form 2 percent of the whole assemblage in spite of the abundance of water in the area required for pig husbandry. Çakırlar is of the opinion "that there is a general scarcity of pigs in the Levant during the Iron Age, and this seems to be a cultural trend, for whatever the reasons might be." The inhabitants of Iron Age Tell el-Burak seem to have avoided shellfish consumption, but mollusk shells are abundant and belong, in their majority, to the Nasa shell species, which are traditionally used as beads. *Hexaplex trunculus* shells used in the purple-dye industry were also common. On the basis of the study of the 2011 collection, it was concluded that "most of the shells do not represent animals that were eaten, except perhaps some limpets."

To sum up, "The taxonomic spectrum shows that the animal sector of the subsistence at LIA Tell el-Burak depended largely on domestic animal husbandry. Wild resources, excluding perhaps fish, played an insignificant role in activities involving food procurement.... In this regard the general character of the subsistence economy of the settlement does not deviate substantially from its known contemporaries along the southern coast of the Levant, e.g. Tel Dor and Ashkelon" (Çakırlar et al. 2014, 247–48).

### 6.2.2.3. The Evidence from Tyre al-Baṣṣ

Faunal remains from the 2002 and 2004 seasons of excavations at Tyre al-Baṣṣ were analyzed (Montero 2014). The studied assemblage was rather small and limited to those species related to funerary ceremonies. Since they do not stem from the settlement but rather from a funerary context, they play an important role in understanding cultic ceremonies but are less relevant regarding the economy and regular diet of the Tyrians. The analysis shed light on the species represented and established that ox, goat, and pig appear in all strata. Stratum 4 had the largest spectrum of species represented. Only domesticated animals are represented, and cattle and ovicaprids were the best documented.

### 6.2.2.4. The Evidence from Dor

A first study of the Dor faunal remains indicated that sheep and goat formed 76 percent of the assemblage and that fish were a substantial part of the Dorians' diet (Raban-Gerstel et al. 2008, fig. 4 and table 2). They formed a "major food resource in the economy of the site" (42). The importance of fish is illustrated by the fact that Dor has also yielded evidence for fish industry. Some species, among which are the Nile perch and the Nile catfish, were imported from Egypt (41). "The Egyptian fish at Dor thus complements the picture obtained by ceramic analysis. As mentioned, to date Dor is the only early Iron Age site in the southern Levant where extensive contacts with Egypt are attested by hundreds of Egyptian store jar fragments (and some complete vessels) at least from the Late Bronze Age II until Ir I/II and possibly Ir IIa" (49 with relevant bibliography).

Furthermore, 6,500 bones of mammals from Dor were studied in detail (Sapir-Hen et al. 2014) in order to obtain more information about the site's economy. Dominant were sheep, goat, and cattle (Sapir-Hen et al. 2014, table 1), with the frequency of cattle increasing during the Iron Age, while pig bones are almost absent in that period, representing only 1 percent of the assemblage (Raban Gerstel et al. 2008, 38). Wild fauna, consisting mainly of wild game, had a minimal representation at Dor. One interesting observation is that with the increase of cattle, which formed a new and substantial source of meat, sheep and goat started to be used mainly for secondary products such as milk and wool (Sapir-Hen et al. 2014, 90). The study of the fauna over the years at Dor has demonstrated that "The people at Tel Dor raised their own food throughout the periods … and did so in a similar manner. For the Iron Age, this conclusion gains support from geoarchaeological studies, which demonstrated, using phytolith and spherulite analysis, that livestock were frequently kept, probably penned on the tell" (Sapir-Hen et al. 2014, 91; see also Gilboa and Sharon 2008, 151). So Dor was in all periods and mainly in the Early Iron Age a "productive-consumptive" site (Sapir-Hen et al. 2014, 91).

### 6.2.2.5. The Evidence from Tell Abu Hawam

Only the mollusk remains of Tell Abu Hawam were studied (Baruch et al. 2005). Seventy-three species of shell were identified, the overwhelming majority being Mediterranean marine shells. Most results are from Late Bronze Age strata. In addition, a few specimens came from the Red Sea, with a few sweet-water shells from the Nile River, which suggests trade contacts with these two areas. A deposit of *Hexaplex Trunculus* shells was interpreted as evidence for purple-dye industry.

### 6.2.2.6. The Evidence from Horbat Rosh Zayit

The faunal remains at Horbat Rosh Zayit display a clear domination of sheep and goats over cattle in Stratum II, which is the oldest occupation stratum of the site, dated to the late tenth century BCE (Horwitz 2000, table app. 4.1, fig. 4.1a), as well in the other strata of the fort and in the other excavation areas. Wild mammals, bird, and fish are hardly represented, while camels, equids, and pigs are totally absent. The absence of the latter was explained by lack of freshwater sources near the site, since pigs need regular access to fresh water (Horwitz 2000, 230), though others prefer to ascribe this absence to ethnic or religious reasons.

Regarding bone distribution in Area B, where Building 100 was exposed, the lowest density was found in the courtyard where olive presses were found, while the highest concentration was found in the rooms leading off from the courtyard (Horwitz 2000, 226–27). Liora Horwitz also noted "a greater concentration of bone in the cultic area than in the domestic area," but in both, sheep and goat predominate. That 60 percent of the sheep and goat group were kept into maturity "is consistent with economies aimed at secondary product exploitation (milk, wool) rather than meat production" (229). The same was observed at Tel Dor. The limited number of species at Horbat Rosh Zayit is unusual and is probably due to the absence of water sources nearby.

The fish bone assemblage at Horbat Rosh Zayit was studied in depth in spite of the small number of retrieved samples, which amounted to twenty-two (Lernau 2000). They belonged to both marine and freshwater specimens. Interesting is the presence of Nile perch and catfish in the assemblage, probably imported from Egypt, together with other local species such as sea bass and sea bream. The assemblage collected is refuse of food consumption. Omri Lernau noted the absence of fishing gear and deduced that the fish at Horbat Rosh Zayit were bought on the market, probably from Akko.

In his study of the Horbat Rosh Zayit fish remains, Lernau listed all the sites on the Phoenician coast of Israel where Nile fish were found. As previously mentioned, a more exhaustive study (Van Neer et al. 2004) established ancient trade relations in the Mediterranean based on excavated fish remains. The coastal Phoenician sites where evidence for Nilotic fish is attested are Tell Kabri, Dor, Akko, and Horbat Rosh Zayit (Van Neer et al. 2004, table 3).

6.2.2.7. The Evidence from Tell Kabri

The analysis of faunal remains from the Iron Age levels at Tell Kabri was based on a small assemblage from the fortress in Area E (Horwitz 2002, 399). Sheep and goat formed 75 percent of the assemblage, with a majority of adults, thus suggesting secondary production of milk and wool, as is the case at Dor and Horbat Rosh Zayit. Cattle formed 20 percent of the assemblage, while wild species had a low frequency. Equids, birds, and pigs were here too hardly represented. No mention was made of fish remains for the Iron Age.

To sum up: The evidence for faunal and botanical remains is far more abundant for southern than for northern Phoenicia. With the exception of Tell Tweini, there is hardly any evidence for Phoenician diet north of Sidon unless we want to extrapolate the evidence from the Bronze Age to the first millennium BCE.

When and where available, the botanical analyses have demonstrated that the Phoenicians had a typical Mediterranean diet, in which wheat and barley, olive oil, and grapevine dominated. Legumes such as chickpeas, peas, and lentils as well as figs and dates complemented this diet, which did not change since the Bronze Age in southern Phoenicia. The distribution of plant remains varies from one site to another, depending both on its environment and its function: while olives and wheat predominate at Tell Tweini, Sidon, and Horbat Rosh Zayit, cereals and grapevine predominate at Tell el-Burak, and wheat farther south at Keisan. The evidence shows clearly that in southern Phoenicia the people shared the same diet and exchanged between them the staple crops that they did not produce in sufficient quantity. That Tyre had to import wheat and olive oil does not mean that the cultivation of these crops did not occur there but that it was maybe not enough for the need of the population or that of the royal court and retinue. The evidence from Tell el-Burak, Horbat Rosh Zayit, and Tell Tweini (see below) shows that olive oil was produced locally. The seventh-century BCE industrial production of olive oil at nearby Tell Miqne-Ekron as well as other sites farther south (Gal and Frankel 1993) may have also supplied the Phoenician cities with this produce, although no direct evidence is available for such an exchange. The situation in Phoenicia regarding olive oil production progressively developed in the Persian-Hellenistic period to reach its climax in the Roman-Byzantine period, when almost all the coastal settlements specialized in this industry, as indicated by the oil presses that were found in almost every excavated site, such as Byblos, Khaldeh, Jiyye, Chhim, Sarepta, and Umm el-Amed, to name but a few.

Regarding faunal remains, the evidence shows that the Phoenicians consumed mainly sheep and goat meat. However, these were slaughtered at maturity, thus suggesting an economy based on secondary production of milk and wool. Cattle seem to have increased during the Iron Age, and they were penned sometimes on site, as suggested by the Dor evidence. The absence of pigs in almost all these sites except Tyre's cemetery has to be noted. This dietary tradition is long-lived on the Levantine coast, where pigs were hardly ever part of the protein diet of the inhabitants. The evidence from the Tyrian cemetery is therefore rather puzzling since, in spite of the small assemblage, pig appeared in all strata. It is difficult to draw conclusions about this fact in the present state of the evidence. Wild animals such as the fallow dear and the gazelle were only occasionally hunted and consumed, which seems to be characteristic of the highly urbanized population of Phoenicia.

Another main element of the Phoenician diet are the fish species from both marine and fresh waters. This is only normal since most of these sites are located directly on the shore, and among their artifacts one finds commonly fish-net weights and fishing hooks. Some of the fish species were not local and were imported. This is the case of the Nile perch and catfish, which are indicators of trade contact with Egypt. However, the import of Egyptian fish is still debated, and some scholars argue that in the quaternary this species may have reached the Levant and may have continued to live in the rivers on the Levantine coast (Lernau 2000).

In short, the inhabitants of the Phoenician coast had the same ingredients for their diet and shared most probably the same culinary traditions. This can be ascertained for the south, and more evidence from northern Phoenicia is needed to see whether there were regional differences in the grown crops or whether the diet was the same as in the south. So far the only available evidence from Iron Age Tell Tweini seems to indicate similarity rather than differences.

### 6.2.3. Phoenician Wine Production: The Winepress Installation at Tell el-Burak

Phoenician wine was famed in antiquity. Echoes of its fine quality are found in the Bible and in the writings of classical authors. The eighth-century BCE prophet Hosea (14:7) praises the fragrance of the wine of Lebanon, and Hesiod (*Op.* 589) says that Byblinus, the wine of Byblos, is famous for its bouquet. Highly interesting is the mention in a papyrus from Elephantine of a Sidonian wine *ḥmr ṣydn* (C3.12; Cowley 1923, text 72, lines 2 and 17). This papyrus from southern Egypt dating to the end of the fifth century BCE lists the inventory of an Egyptian household on the Nile island of Elephantine and mentions, among other things, wine from Sidon.

In the Iron Age, Phoenician amphorae were always assumed to have served for the transport and export of wine and/or olive oil, thus implying the existence of these two industries in Phoenicia. The retrieved amphorae from the Ashkelon shipwreck, which is believed to have sailed from Phoenicia to Egypt, contained wine, as indicated by the content analysis of some of them (Stager 2003). So far, however, no direct and explicit archaeological evidence confirmed the existence of wine production or wine industry in Phoenicia proper. Several examples are known from the Bronze and Iron Age Israelite sites, such as the winery at Gibeon (Pritchard 1964), as well as several examples from the classical and Byzantine periods. From the Iron Age, examples are known mainly from the Philistine sites of Ashkelon, Ashdod, and Tell Michal north of Tell Qasile. The Phoenician site of Akhziv has yielded also an installation from the Iron Age, which seems to have served as a winepress, but this cannot be ascertained. While oil presses are attested since the eighth century at Horbat Rosh Zayit and in northern Phoenicia at Tell Tweini, little is known about Phoenician wine production in general and wine presses in particular. The recent findings at Tell el-Burak may be a first step toward filling the gap left by the archaeological evidence on this issue.

Before describing the wine press of Tell el-Burak, one should mention briefly all the studies that were concerned with wine production in the ancient Levant. Several authors have addressed this issue, including Walsh (2000), Walsh and Zorn (1998), Ahlström (1978), McGovern, Fleming, and Katz (1996), and Brun (2003; 2004). They discuss the origin of viticulture, winepress installations, the process of wine making from the treading to the storage, and export in amphorae. However, the archaeological examples that are cited are either earlier or later than the Iron Age or outside the Phoenician area and are therefore not directly relevant to our purpose.

The winepress at Tell el-Burak is the first well preserved example from Phoenicia (see fig. 6.2). The installation is located at the foot of the southern slope of the tell in Area 4, outside the enclosure wall. It was exposed partially in 2005, but it was left unexcavated until 2015, when work in the area resumed. A 2.3 m high leveling dump made of horizontal layers of pottery sherds and soil, which were retained to the south by a stone wall, had to be removed before reaching the vat. This leveling must have occurred after the vat went out of use, but its purpose remains unexplained. What remains also unexplained is where this huge amount of pottery came from. When exposed in 2015, this structure appeared to be a wide semicircular basin with a straight wall as its southeastern edge. In 2017, the vat structure was completely exposed. Northeast of it and associated with it is a wide rectangular plastered platform, which was exposed entirely in 2018.

The winepress consists of a large treading platform roughly 5 m long, where the grapes were crushed, and a huge vat associated with it, where the juice was collected and fermented. The excavations allowed a good under-

Fig. 6.2. Winepress consisting of a treading floor and a vat at Tell el-Burak. It was exposed in Area 4 at the foot of the site's southern slope. Source: Tell el-Burak Archaeological Project.

standing of the platform-building technique. A foundation made of ashlar stones between 5 and 12 cm thick and about 50 cm wide was laid under the plaster or cement that covered it. There is a 3–5 cm thick leveling layer of cement on top of the stones and, above the latter, a circa 8 cm thick smooth layer of plaster, which formed the actual treading floor of the platform. Its back side was preserved to a height of 70 cm, while its western and eastern edges were preserved only a few centimeters high. The plaster covered also a row of ashlar stones, which formed a strengthening belt around the platform. It seems that the plaster of the treading platform was painted red, because traces of red paint were preserved on the back side.

The vat had an original height of 1.5 m (indicated by its preserved northern edge), a wall thickness of 32 cm, and a maximum width of 2.5 m. The basin's content capacity is estimated at circa 5.5 liters, which clearly indicates production far beyond private need and points toward industrial production. Against its northeast wall, a semicircular depression to collect the dregs was cut into the floor. It is 89 cm wide at the top, 58 cm wide at the bottom, and 24 cm deep. Standing in situ on the floor was an almost intact amphora leaning against the vat's wall. Other broken amphorae were found outside the structure, which indicates that the vat was emptied by filling amphorae directly from it. Regarding the date of the winepress, recently recovered evidence has indicated that it was built in the late eighth century BCE, probably upon the resettlement of the site. It may be not far-fetched to assume that the settlement was designed and used for the purpose of meeting an increasing demand for such products. It remained in use probably all through the Late Iron Age. The geo-physical survey has revealed the existence of another winepress west of this one, but it has not been exposed yet.

There is a close but older Phoenician parallel to the installation of Tell el-Burak at the northern cemetery of Akhziv (Mazar 2013, figs. 2.4, 2.12). There a plastered platform associated with a plastered basin has been unearthed. The basin also had a depression in its southwestern corner, like the Tell el-Burak vat. The Akhziv structures were dated to the tenth century BCE, and they were in use before the inhumation cemetery was turned into a cremation burial ground and before the crematorium was built. The latter covered almost all the above-mentioned installation except part of the platform. When discussing the nature of these installations, the excavator suggested, "The existence of a small plastered pit hewn in the southeastern corner of the floor of the pool seems to indicate that the liquid in the pool was worth being collected to its last drop, and the high quality of the lime plaster and the red paint signifies that it was not merely an industrial or agricultural installation but that it had a cultic function" (Mazar 2013, 184). Mazar suggests that the pool was filled with some type of oil, but it could very well have been wine, given the similarity with the Tell el-Burak structures. In any case, it is very difficult to decide on the nature of the content of the Akhziv vat in the absence of paleo-botanical analyses, which have not been published yet. Notwithstanding this difficulty, the installation at Akhziv is most probably our oldest example of what seems to be a Phoenician winepress, dated to the tenth century BCE.

The Tell el-Burak winepress has several other and more contemporary parallels, mainly from the southern and central coast of Palestine. As previously mentioned, four seventh-century wine presses were discovered at Ashkelon (Stager, Master, and Schloen 2011) in Building 776. They are very similar to the Tell el-Burak example, and they consist also of plastered vats with associated plastered treading platforms. One of the vats displayed a depression in its southeastern corner (Stager, Master, and Schloen 2011, fig. 2.8). Four winepress installations were found at Tell Michal: they were exposed 180 m away from the Iron Age IIA settlement (Herzog 1989). A further example very similar to the Tell el-Burak installation is known from Jaffa, which became a Phoenician possession in the Persian period (Fantalkin 2005).

The presence of the winepress at Tell el-Burak shed light on the economy of the site, which was based on wine and also probably on olive oil production. The presence of another winepress west of the previous one was evidenced during a recent electric resistivity tomography survey of Area 4, and its planned excavation will bring additional evidence for the role and economy of Tell el-Burak. Other installations were also visible in the surveyed area, and maybe other industrial installations related to agricultural production will be exposed in the future. It is certainly not far-fetched to suggest that the famous wine of Sidon mentioned in the Elephantine papyrus referred to wine produced at Tell el-Burak.

6.2.4. Phoenician Olive Oil Production

There is little evidence for olive oil production from the Phoenician sites in spite of the fact that available botanical analyses have demonstrated that olives were found at almost every site. Only three settlements to date have yielded evidence for olive oil production: one in northern and two in southern Phoenicia. The sites are Tell Tweini, Horbat Rosh Zayit, and Shiqmona. On the other hand, content analyses of jars from Tell el-Burak have indicated that olive oil was stored probably in the amphorae found in House 3. Moreover, based on their analysis of the Tell el-Burak remains, Orendi and Deckers (2018) noted that "the ubiquity of olive remains nearly reached the values shown by *Vitis vinifera* and *Olea* sp. charcoal, which dominated these remains in the overall records of all periods, indicating the importance of olive for the economy of the site." However, as previously mentioned, no olive press installations have been found on the site.

The archaeological evidence from Tell Tweini has clearly shown the existence of olive oil presses. Unfortunately, these installations are simply mentioned but are not yet published. The excavators (Bretschneider, Van Vyve, and Jans 2011, 84) mention that "by the end of the 8th century BCE, a significant architectural renewal occurred at the center of Tell Tweini. Production of olive oil and wine became the main economic activity of the town and oil presses and refining installations were found in every house." However, nowhere are these oil presses and winepresses illustrated. In one of the publications (Bretschneider and van Lerberghe 2008, fig. 3.63) an artistic drawing with the caption "industrial installation" seems to represent the grooved press bed of an oil press. The only infor-

Fig. 6.3. Oil press from Tell Tweini in the shape of a bulb. Eighth century BCE. Courtesy Michel Al-Maqdissi. Source: Photograph Massoud Badawi (DGAM – Jablé)

mation available is that the public building in Area A was reused and replaced by a series of small rooms dedicated to various industries, among which is also a metal workshop (Al-Maqdissi et al. 2010, 45).

The other Phoenician site that has yielded evidence for oil presses is Horbat Rosh Zayit (Gal and Frankel 1993; Gal and Alexandre 2000, 164–67). In Area B, west of the fort, oil-press elements could be seen on the area before the excavations (Gal and Alexandre 2000, 161). In this area a large building, Building 100, dated to the eighth century BCE (Gal and Frankel 1993, 130), was exposed. Inside the building were three olive presses, and in the open area in front of it was only one. In the building's inner courtyard stood Press 103, which was entirely preserved. It consisted of a crushing mortar, a round press bed with a circular groove, and a hewn vat (Gal and Alexandre 2000, fig. 6.3). Later on a rock-cut vat replaced the previous one. From the second press, labeled 184, only the crushing mortar was preserved. Stone weights with a hole for suspension were found inside the building. They weigh 20, 29, and 45 kg (Gal and Alexandre 2000, 164). In the outer courtyard, labeled 101, was Press 132, which had all its elements preserved (Gal and Alexandre 2000, fig. 6.4). The fourth press, labeled 120, was found in the open in front of the building. It was very well preserved, and all its elements were hewn in the rock. This press had a niche above the press bed in which the press beam was anchored (Gal and Alexandre 2000, 164 and fig. 6.6). Four weights were found in the crushing mortar, and two of them are heavier, 60 and 62 kg, than the ones found inside the building. A complete jar with a capacity of 40 liters was found in situ to collect the oil dripping from the circular press bed.

Several other press elements were scattered in Area B, suggesting the existence of additional olive presses (Gal and Alexandre 2000, 165–66). The extraction method attested at Horbat Rosh Zayit remained unchanged until the Byzantine period, as attested by the oil presses at Chhim, a site northeast of Sidon (Walizsewski et al. 2002). The extraction started with the crushing of the olives, either by pounding them in a circular crushing vat or by using cylindrical rollers in a rectangular one. Then the pulp was placed in sacks piled on top of each other on the press bed, and the wooden beam was anchored on one end while weights were hung on the other. The oil ran into a stone vat or a pithos placed nearby. The oil was separated then from the lees by overflow decantation.

Three oil presses were discovered at the Phoenician site of Shiqmona (Elgavish 1978, 1103; 1993). They consisted of round crushing mortars, and oil was collected laterally in jars. The press beds are round and freestanding with a circular groove. The weights, like those of Horbat Rosh Zayit, were fieldstones with a natural bore. These installations are dated to the ninth–eighth century BCE. In both sites, too, the press bed is uniform: round and freestanding with a circular groove (Gal and Frankel 1993, 137). Zvi Gal and Rafael Frankel (138) stated after their review of oil presses in Palestine: "The oil presses of Horbat Rosh Zayit exemplify the techniques of oil production prevalent in Galilee in the late Iron Age, which were different from those found in the south.… This technological differentiation largely coincides with the cultural and ethnic differentiation between the Phoenician presence in the north and that of Judah in the south. This means that the oil presses of Horbat Rosh Zayit can, therefore, be defined as Phoenician in character." This conclusion was adopted in the final report by the excavators (Gal and Alexandre 2000, 167).

The above evidence indicates clearly that agriculture played an instrumental role in Phoenician economy and that agriculture based or related industries formed an important part of the Phoenician exports. "The evidence suggests that agricultural production played an important role in Phoenician economy, in contrast to suggestions that Phoenicians relied largely on far flung trade networks to supply their settlements with agricultural produce" (Schmitt et al. 2018, 84). This aspect of the Phoenician economy will be highlighted further in the section dealing with ceramic production.

## 6.3. Phoenician Industries

Next to industries based on agricultural products, Phoenician settlements have yielded evidence for other industries, some of which have contributed to their fame. The evidence for these industries is scarce, but nevertheless some remains hint at their existence. In this section the evidence related to purple dye, pottery, and metallurgy will be presented. As for ship building, we shall briefly review the scanty evidence from shipwrecks as well as the available textual and iconographic evidence.

### 6.3.1. Phoenician Purple-Dye Industry: The Archaeological Evidence

Phoenicians were famed for their purple-dyed textiles, which form a constant item in the list of tribute paid to the Assyrian kings. It has always been assumed that purple dye was a Phoenician discovery. This widely spread idea was anchored in the mind of the people for centuries, first because of the Greek legend that ascribed the discovery of the purple dye to the Tyrian god Melqart. According to this legend, the god was walking on the beach of Tyre with the nymph Tyros when his dog chewed a murex shell and had its mouth colored purple. The nymph loved the color and requested a cloth dyed with it. The god answered her request by collecting the shells and producing the dye. This legend was so vivid in the consciousness of the Tyrians that they represented it on their coins, on the obverse of some of which a dog munching on a murex shell or a murex shell alone is represented (Hill 1910, cxli, plate XLIV, no. 7; see fig. 3.12 above). In addition to the Greek legend and the iconography of Tyrian coins, the description by Pliny the Elder of the production process of the famous Tyrian purple dye (*Hist. nat.* 9.63) has contributed to associate this industry with the Phoenicians and more particularly with the Tyrians, an association that remained unchallenged for centuries. Finally, "The production of this dye has been so closely associated with the Phoenicians that there is an oft-repeated axiom in popular and scholarly publications alike that the ethnic designator 'Phoenician' (a Greek label—Phoinikes—decidedly not what the Phoenicians called themselves) finds its origins in the Greek word *phoinix*, meaning crimson or purple" (Nitschke, Martin, and Shalev 2011, 136).

However, contrary to common opinion, the Phoenicians did not invent the purple dye. It is well established today that the purple dye was discovered in the Aegean as early as the second millennium BCE (see Reese 1987; 2010 with relevant bibliography). Purple dye from shells is attested for the first time at Palaepaphos-*Skales* in Crete during the Middle Minoan period. Heaps of crushed murex found at this site were dated to the Middle and Late Minoan period (Reese 1987, 204). A century later, ancient Near Eastern texts start mentioning purple-dyed textiles. For example, the fifteenth-century BCE Nuzi texts speak of blue-purple dye, *kinaḫḫu* in Akkadian, and the Amarna letters (Moran 1987, EA 22) mention purple-dyed textiles sent by the Ḫurrian king Tushratta to Amenhotep III. Furthermore, heaps of murex shells were found in Minet el-Beida, the harbor of Ugarit (*PRU* 2:26), attesting that this industry was already known in the Levant in the Late Bronze Age. In short, "The archaeological evidence available to date suggests that the purple dye industry began in the Middle and Late MM (c. 1700–1600 BC) in Eastern Crete.... The earliest evidence in the Levant is about a century later, suggesting that the Minoans developed the industry later to be associated more with Tyre and the Phoenicians" (Reese 1987, 206).

Several experiments have been undertaken in order to reproduce the extraction and dying process used by the ancients. Three major species of shells were utilized to produce the purple dye: *Murex trunculus, Murex brandaris,* and *Thais haemastoma,* which produced slightly different colors. The dye is made from the hypobranchial gland, which is extracted by crushing or piercing the shell. Before being exposed to sun and air, the gland was mixed with salt and boiled for several days (Reese 1987, 203), after which textiles were dipped in this yet-colorless solution. A wide range of colors could be obtained when the textiles were exposed to sun and air. These experiments have also shown that a huge number of *Murex trunculus, Murex brandaris,* or *Thais haemastoma* are required to produce the dye (Reese 1987, 203–4; 2010, 118). While Pliny says that the dye was boiled in a lead container, archaeological evidence has proven that in the Phoenician period it was boiled in ceramic vats.

In a recent article Reese (2010) has studied the shell remains of Sarepta and has reviewed the available archaeological evidence relating to purple dye in the eastern Mediterranean, including the sites on the Phoenician coast. Nira Karmon and Ehud Spanier (1987) had also previously reviewed all the evidence from Palestine. Both articles provide a good summary of the evidence.

In Phoenicia, an unpublished fifth–sixth century CE Greek inscription from Beirut mentions a purple dyer (Reese 2010, 119) and suggests the existence of the industry in that city in spite of the fact that the recent excavations in the Beirut Central District did not spot—or maybe overlooked?—evidence relating to such industry.

Remains of crushed shells were spotted by ancient travelers at Sidon and Tyre (for a full bibliography see Reese 2010, 119–20). In Sidon a huge heap of crushed murex shells is mentioned by several early travelers south of the city, a clear indication that Sidon produced the precious dye. This area was called Sheikh Abaroh, but it is known today as Dakerman. However, in spite of the fact that this location was known since the eighteenth century and is still visible partly today under the Shiite cemetery of the city, it was never properly investigated. Regarding Tyre, next to mentions by travelers who had visited the area and spotted shell heaps there, the only archaeological evidence was retrieved by Chéhab (1965, 114) in Roman and Byzantine levels. To my knowledge, there is no evidence for earlier archaeological data regarding purple-dye industry from Tyre.

South of Sidon, the city of Sarepta was the first Phoenician settlement to have yielded evidence for purple-dye production from excavations. The site has produced 501 shells found in various deposits dating from the Late Bronze II until the later classical period (Reese 2010, 114). Several shell species were recognized, among which predominated *Murex trunculus* (297) and *Thais Haemastoma*, used to extract the purple dye. The excavators also found there fourteenth/thirteenth century jar or vat sherds that had a purple deposit on their interiors (218). However, no installations were found.

The sites of Akko (Karmon and Spanier 1987), Abu Hawam (Baruch et al. 2005), Shiqmona (Karmon and Spanier 1988), and Dor (Karmon and Spanier 1987; Nitschke, Martin, and Shalev 2011) have also provided evidence for purple-dye industry. This was evidenced by deposits of crushed shells as well as traces of purple color on jar sherds. However, when the crushed murex deposits were very small, they were considered to be the result of consumption refuse because all the species were edible. Regarding the traces of color on jar sherds, an eleventh-century BCE large vessel with a purple-colored stripe was found at Tell Keisan, and several such jar sherds with stripes of color were found at Tell Shiqmona. The color stripe appears only on the upper part of the vessel: "These two examples show that the colour was used for dyeing in its reduced (leuco) form (colourless), as required for a proper dyeing procedure with the indigoid colours. The reduced dye in the inner part of the vessel did not leave any traces of colour on its walls. However, the upper part of the liquid, which was in contact with air, could not have been kept in its reduced form and was oxidized by the air, and thus the colour appeared" (Karmon and Spanier 1988, 185–86).

Only four sites, Tel Dor, Tel Mor, and possibly Akko and Tel Mevorakh, have yielded installations for dye industry. At Tel Mor the installation is dated to the Hellenistic period: "A probable dyeing workshop was found in 1959. It consisted of a deep well … full of thousands of *M. brandaris* and next to it a large rectangular plastered basin … and a small semi-circular plastered basin" (Reese 2010, 123). In Persian-period levels at Dor there was abundant evidence for purple-dye industry, represented not only by layers of crushed shells and pits filled with crushed murex but also by very well-preserved installations associated with them (Nitschke, Martin, and Shalev 2011, 135–36). These installations consist of two pits: a southern one lined with stone and filled with murex shells, and a northern one that was not stone lined but contained lime stained with purple color, which was tested as purple-dye residue. The function of the latter remains unclear, however. A rectangular, stone-lined basin was attached to the southern pit, maybe for the crushing of the shells, which were then thrown into the nearby pit. A drain ran from the basin into the second pit.

To sum up, there is ample evidence that the Phoenician cities were familiar with purple-dye production since the Late Bronze Age and that this industry continued to develop until the Persian and later classical periods, when the process was perfected by the Tyrians, who produced, according to Pliny the Elder, "the best purple in Asia" (*Hist. nat.* 9.60).

6.3.2. Ceramics Industry

Pottery is one of the main markers of Phoenician culture. Its presence at any site indicates trade contacts with Phoenicia. As previously discussed, the Phoenicians produced a wide range of characteristic shapes and area decoration. Typology and petrographic studies are today key to determine the origin and the center where these vessels were produced. These studies have to be complemented by archaeological excavations providing evidence for kilns as well as other installations denoting industrial production of pottery. To date, one such center was discovered on the southern Phoenician coast at the site of Sarepta. It is the only site that has yielded substantial and continuous evidence for mass production of pottery from the Late Bronze Age until the end of the Persian period. The only other site on the Phoenician coast to have produced evidence for pottery kilns is Akko. Other sites, such as Ashdod, Tell Michal, and Megiddo, further inland were also producing pottery in the Iron Age.

We shall first look at the Sarepta evidence as an example of a pottery-production center, and then we shall briefly survey the contribution of petrographic analysis of amphorae to the study of Phoenician economy and trade.

6.3.2.1. Sarepta: A Pottery-Production Center

The University of Pennsylvania excavations at the site of Sarepta under the direction of Pritchard have exposed no fewer than twenty-four pottery kilns, twenty-two of which were discovered in sounding II, X, and two in sounding II, Y (Anderson 1987; 1988; 1989; 1990; Pritchard 1978; Khalifeh 1988). The excavators identified fifteen pottery workshops dating from the beginning of the Late Bronze Age II down to the Persian period.

The kilns were found built on top of each other or partly overlapping. The earlier kilns were elliptical in form, while the later ones were more rounded. They were preserved only to the level of the firing chamber and, except for one, had all the same plan and the same building technique. The kilns had two stories: a firing chamber and a stacking chamber. The firing chamber was built underground to retain the heat. A pit was dug for this purpose and was then lined with stones. The firing chamber had a bilobate shape and was divided into two kidney-shaped halves by a wall extending from the rear of the chamber from one-half to two-thirds the distance of the longer axis. The purpose of this wall was probably to support the platform on which the vessels were placed. The firing pit was coated with a thick layer of clay for insulation and sealed by several layers of clay or baked bricks. The roof of the firing chamber formed the floor of the stacking chamber. It had several flue holes to allow the heat to circulate around the pots. The stacking chamber had an open roof in order to provide a draft. These kilns showed clear evidence of several rebuildings and repairs, which cut eventually "the interior dimensions of a kiln to an inefficient size, necessitating the reconstruction of a new kiln" (Anderson 1987, 43).

Next to the kilns, the excavators found various installations for the preparation of the clay (Pritchard 1978, fig. 116): these were areas surrounded by a low wall where the clay was prepared and stocked. In the center was a pit, which either was used for blending the clay or indicates the emplacement of the potter's wheel. Rooms 67/68 presented a well-preserved example of a pottery workshop (Anderson 1987, 45, figs. 3, 5), which consisted of two parallel rectangular rooms: one was used to place the vessels to dry and gave access to the second room, which contained two basins. The basins may have contained either water or slip. Between the basins, a stone-lined area and a stone cylindrical support indicated the emplacement of the potter's bench. "One of the more significant parts of the potter's workshops excavated at Sarepta were the wheel pits, or remains of wheel emplacements. This feature was found in a number of locations, all in a definable ceramic workshop" (Anderson 1987, 48). Several settling basins for the preparation of the clay were also exposed.

The archaeological evidence from Sarepta clearly indicates the presence of an industrial ceramic production, which continued to develop from the Late Bronze through the whole Iron Age period. It is so far the only Phoenician site to have provided evidence for large-scale production of ceramics. It is also an instrumental site to understand the "historical and cultural aspects of pot making in the Phoenician homeland" (Anderson 1987, 49).

In a recent article, Schmitt and colleagues (2018) have reexamined the evidence from Sarepta relating to pottery production. They have concluded that in spite of the continuous presence of kilns since the Late Bronze Age, no more than two kilns were active at the same time. Even in the Late Iron Age, when there was a notable increase in the production of amphorae, only two kilns were active at the site. This evidence indicates that the capacity of pottery production at Sarepta was overestimated, and it was certainly not "a primary pottery production center." The authors assumed that several such pottery-production centers must have existed in the various harbor cities, the presence of which could be corroborated only by future excavations. Nevertheless, the available evidence already hints in that direction, since pottery workshops are attested at Tyre and Akko. At Tyre, according to Bikai (1978a, 13), there may have been in Strata III and II a pottery workshop, which was unfortunately not excavated. Its existence was indicated, however, by the presence of wasters and unfired clay balls. Pottery kilns were discovered also at the Phoenician site of Akko (Dothan and Conrad 1978; 1984). Some were dated to the transition period from the Late Bronze to the Iron Age, one from IA–IIA, and one from Iron Age IIB (Dothan 1993, 21–22). In Areas A and AB, Moshe Dothan and Diethelm Conrad write, "The excavation of Iron Age strata also provided surprises: a pottery kiln in a badly eroded oven (Stratum 7) dating from the eighth century B.C. The kiln is oval, plastered inside and supported from without by a course of stones and within by a central column" (1978, 265); in Area K, "In the western part of this area was found a living quarter with various installations; to its east was a spacious courtyard. Among the installations were identified pottery kilns and what seems to be a metal-working furnace" (Dothan and Conrad 1984, 190). In that same area, Dothan (1993, 22) mentions the existence of an Iron Age IIB "oval mud-brick kiln, plastered on the outside, with a central brick column supporting it." So there is evidence that at least three pottery production centers were active in southern Phoenicia in the Iron Age. Unfortunately, no such centers are attested to date in northern Phoenicia, and no petrographic studies are available.

6.3.2.2. Recent Results of Petrographic Analyses from Phoenician Sites

Optical mineralogy analysis or ceramic petrography is the study of the composition and structure of rocks and minerals. Petrography is particularly used for pottery to identify inclusions, such as particles of minerals or rock fragments that may be characteristic of a specific source (Renfrew and Bahn 2004, 366).

Petrographic analysis has become a standard procedure in the study of ceramics in order to determine their provenance and, eventually, the centers where they were produced. Petrography has become absolutely crucial in identifying the movements of traded goods by analyzing the containers that transported them and by establishing their origin. This type of analysis was and still is used to identify trade connections between Phoenicia and the various areas of the Levant as well as between Phoenicia and the eastern Mediterranean. These containers are overwhelmingly transport amphorae suited mainly for maritime but also for land transport. However, smaller containers with more precious and valuable items can also be indicators of trade connections.

Petrography requires a good knowledge of the geology of the investigated areas and their characteristics in order to determine the exact origin of the clays used in the manufacturing of the pottery vessels. The geology of the Syro-Palestinian coast is rather well documented (Bettles 2003, 128, 134–36). One of the identifiers of the clays used on coastal sites is the composition of the sand, which was often used as temper. In every stretch of coast from Gaza to Ugarit, the morphology of the composition of the sand particles changes and indicates the area of provenance. This is mainly based on the size and percentage of the quartz particles in the composition of the clay. "By combining the data retrieved from the composition of the sand and the soil types, it is possible to slice the Levantine coast into segments, each representing a different combination of sand and soil" (Gilboa and Goren 2015, 84).

The importance of petrography in the study of Phoenician trade and economy in general was the incentive behind several recent studies. Bettles (2003) was one of the first scholars to study Persian-period carinated-shoulder amphorae, the maritime transport amphora par excellence, in order to determine their origin, their distribution, and their modes of production. She assumed that these amphorae transported mainly wine based on several clues: first, some of them had inscriptions indicating their content (Bettles 2003, 37), and others, such as the amphorae retrieved from shipwrecks (Ballard and Stager 2002), had their organic residue analyzed and were proven to have contained wine. However, some of these amphorae may have been used to transport oil, as attested at Tell el-Burak. Bettles's (2003, 26) primary aim with this project was "to examine evidence (archaeological, artefactual and literary) which may indicate patterns of commodity production and distribution of the Phoenicians in their homeland region." She collected samples from twenty-one sites on the south Levantine coast from Sarepta to Ashkelon (Bettles 2003, 22, table 1.307). The available data suggested that the six identified amphora fabrics with raw materials consistent with a provenance in southern Phoenicia represented five separate manufacturing centers (Bettles 2003, 202).

In her PhD dissertation, Aznar (2005) used petrography to determine the relations between Phoenicians, Israelites, and Philistines during the Iron Age by sampling mainly the various types of Iron Age II common storage jars likely to have transported foodstuffs, mainly olive oil and wine, which were retrieved in Phoenician, Israelite, and Philistine sites (2). For example, all the storage jars of her type 9 originated from the Lebanese coast, and her study led to their identification in Philistine and Israelite sites. Aznar (210) also assumed that these jars contained wine and not olive oil, first because the Israelite were exporting oil to Tyre according to the Bible and, second, because the amphorae of the shipwrecks off the coast of Ashkelon included amphorae of this type and contained wine. This storage-jar type "reveal[s] large-scale industry in the second half of the 8th century BCE–beginning of the 6th c. BCE" (212) at Sarepta and Tyre, and from the seventh and sixth century at Sarepta and "probably" Tyre.

A major study aiming to determine the extent of Phoenician exchanges, mainly maritime trade, within the boundaries of Phoenicia and beyond based mainly on optical mineralogy, has been designed and is ongoing (Waiman-Barak and Gilboa 2016, 169). Some results of this study have already been published and have demonstrated that contrary to common opinion the southern Lebanese coast was not the only area where Phoenician pottery was produced but that areas further south, the Akko Plain and the Carmel coast, were also producers of Phoenician ceramic vessels exported to the eastern Mediterranean. As we have previously seen, in section 6.1.10, petrographic analyses of Phoenician vessels found in Cyprus and in Crete have determined their area of origin as well as the likely centers of production in these areas. For Phoenician bichrome vessels in Cyprus, for example, two areas of origin were defined: the Tyre-Sidon area, with a production center probably at Tyre, and the Carmel coast, with a production center probably at Dor (Gilboa and Goren 2015, 86). Not only did petrography provide the origin of the imported vessels in Cyprus, but it has also corrected the identification of ten samples that were considered to be Phoenician and were proven to be locally produced.

Petrography is thus instrumental in identifying imports from local imitations of prototype vessels.

A most recent study analyzed the carinated-shoulder amphorae from Tell el-Burak. It was possible to follow their development over four hundred years, from the Late Iron Age II until the end of the Persian period, which is the time span during which the Iron Age settlement of Tell el-Burak existed. This type of amphora forms the most widespread maritime transport container in Phoenicia during these periods. The study used an original approach combining morphometric analysis together with petrographic, geochemical, and organic-residue analysis (Schmitt et al. 2018). The morphometric analysis has shown that the amphorae shapes did not drastically change over the years: they were mass-produced and highly standardized, indicating centralized modes of production. Between the end of the eighth century and the end of the Persian period, their proportion increased from 37 to 75 percent of the locally produced pottery. Various sizes coexisted: small amphorae had a content ranging from five to eleven liters, while the larger ones could contain seventeen to twenty-four liters. The petrography indicated that, with the exception of four imports from coastal Palestine or Cyprus, all carinated-shoulder amphorae were made locally in centers located on the southern Lebanese coast, Sarepta being probably one of them, thus "indicating a strong regional orientation for the trade in the commodities held by the CSA from Tell el-Burak, which were presumably mostly agricultural." The organic-residue analysis, as previously stated, yielded evidence for fat acids, probably from plants, suggesting olive oil. Only one sample has yielded so far evidence for wine. These results are of extreme importance for the economy of Phoenicia and indicate that, contrary to widespread opinion, agriculture played a very important role in the economy of the motherland.

### 6.3.3. Metallurgy

In spite of the fact that none of the famous Phoenician bowls, cauldrons, or tripods found scattered all over the Mediterranean were retrieved in the homeland, there is yet evidence for metallurgic activity in a few sites of Phoenicia. One of the most substantial pieces of evidence for metallurgy was excavated at Akko. Dor has also yielded some evidence for metal work, and at a much smaller scale is the evidence from Sarepta. Metallurgic workshops are also mentioned at Tell Tweini, but, unfortunately, they have not been published. Sidon, the city "rich in bronze," is the place where the famous bronze crater mentioned by Homer was made. This city has produced metal slags from the tenth–ninth century BCE as well as evidence for a small metal workshop.

The written sources seem to suggest that metallurgy was attached directly to the royal palace. This evidence comes mainly from the Old Testament. The account of 1 Kgs 7:13–14 mentions that Hiram of Tyre sent to Solomon one of his most skilled metal workers. We also know that it was one of these Tyrian craftsmen sent by Hiram who produced the famous "Sea of Bronze" of the Yahweh temple. Evidence that this industry continued to be controlled by the palace relates to the minting of coins (Bettles 2003, 39), which started to be used as the normal currency in Phoenicia in the Persian period (for Phoenician coinage see Elayi and Elayi 2004; 2009; 2014; 2015).

At Dor metal industry is attested in Iron Age I, in Area G Level 10. In the so-called courtyard house, evidence for metalwork is represented by the presence of small pits in which the fuel was stocked. Broken pieces of bronze or copper were placed in a small crucible, and the crucible in the pit where a fire was lit. Air bellows activated the fire by pipes and clay tuyères to bring it to a heat of over 1300°C. The molten metal was then cast into a mold to form a new implement (Gilboa and Sharon 2008, 154–55). Concentrations of metal were found at the bottom of these crucibles. This metal industry was abandoned after a generation and disappeared completely in Phase G/9.

The old excavations of Akko, which were undertaken in the 1970s and 1980s, have exposed metallurgical installations. Dothan (1993, 21) summed up the findings relating to the metal workshop installations from Areas A and AB, which he dated to the transition period from the Late Bronze to the Early Iron Age: "Numerous fragments of bronze and copper vessels on a charred flagstone pavement, alongside two burned and charred clay smelting crucibles that still had remains of copper adhering to their inner walls; fragments of the clay blast pipes (tuyères) through which air was forced into the furnace in the smelting process; and copper slag and fragments of flawed metal vessels that were apparently destined for recycling." A mold for the casting of jewelry was also found (21). This industry continued to prosper in the Hellenistic period. In Area K several building units from that period were exposed. "It seems that most of the area was an industrial zone specializing in metallurgy, particularly iron and lead" (Dothan 1979, 228). So Akko was a center of metalworking since the end of the Late Bronze Age and until the Hellenistic period. While copper smelting is attested in the Early Iron Age, as was the case at Dor, in the Persian period the evidence indicates large-scale iron tool production. Indeed, a new archaeological project began on the site in 2010, and the excavators started by reassessing the results of the previous excavations and by publishing them. In a paper delivered at the International Congress on the Archaeology of the Ancient Near East in Munich on April 6, 2018, Ann Killebrew presented the results of the new project relating to metal work at Akko. She mentioned that some 321 kg of iron slags were found together with crucibles and tuyères and a lamb burial connected with the slag production area. Iron production started before the Persian period but flourished during the Late Iron Age. The slags are homogeneous and denote smithing, thus indicating that iron objects were produced at Akko. The origin of the metal was traced to the iron mines of Magharet al-Wardeh in Jordan (Veldhuijzen and van der Steen 1999). One has to mention in this context the fifth-century BCE Phoenician ostracon that was found in a pit in the same building together with cultic objects (Dothan 1985). According to Dothan's translation, the ostracon speaks of an order issued, probably by the governor or another administrative authority, to the guild of metalworkers to provide the temple with a variety of metal vessels. It is interesting to see that the craftsmen were united in a guild, a sort of corporation already attested at Ugarit. The inscription infers the existence of a temple at Akko. In his first publication of the inscription, Dothan (86) interpreted the term $šrt$ to mean simply "temple" or "shrine." Later, however, he interpreted it as the name of the goddess Asherah (Dothan 1993, 22). Xella (2017) adopted the 1985 translation by Dothan, thus clearly opting for the meaning "shrine" (see also Cross 2009; Lipínski 2009).

In Sarepta Sounding II, Y, remains attesting metalwork were retrieved from Stratum G, dated to the thirteenth century BCE. Crucible fragments as well as five bins probably used in the metallurgical process were excavated. The best preserved of the three was built by digging a pit, lining it with stones, and covering it partly with a stone slab. Over the slab was an extended cement platform. This bin "was actually a sump designed to provide underground drainage" (Pritchard 1978, 78). Pritchard (79) and Anderson (1988, 380) are uncertain as to the exact function of the bins but say that one of the possibilities is that they may have been associated with foundries, based on their similarity to metallurgical installations found at Enkomi: the cement platform was used to crush and wash the metal and the nearby pit to drain the resulting water. Anderson (1988, 381) concluded, "The evidence is inconclusive, although some doubt must be expressed that Room 41 and the bins in Stratum G were part of a foundry comparable to those at Enkomi." There is no evidence that this industry continued in Sounding II, Y, in the Iron Age.

In Sounding II, X, which "had been given over to industry for about a millennium of its archaeological history" (Pritchard 1978, 111), there is scant evidence for metallurgy. Fragments of slags, crucibles, and shapeless metal objects together with a steatite mold for jewelry (128 and fig. 123) are indications that small-scale metalwork was taking place at Sarepta in the Iron Age.

The presence of jewelry molds in Sarepta and Akko hints at the existence of workshops for jewelry production. Not only is there evidence for their manufacture, but there are a few but very beautiful examples of the finished products from the royal necropolis of Sidon at Mgharet Tablun (see above). They attest to skilled Phoenician craftsmanship in using repoussé, filigree, and granulation techniques.[7] This technology was transferred to jewelers working in the Mediterranean area, examples of which were found mainly in Carthage, Sardinia, and southern Spain.

6.3.4. Ship Building

The Phoenicians are known to have been experienced seafarers and navigators. Almost all scholars agree that the location of the Phoenician cities on the Mediterranean shore led them naturally to turn westward to discover and explore new countries. They identified through repeated experience and a series of trials and errors the emplacement and the movement of the maritime currents, and, with time, based on their observation of the stars, they trusted themselves to sail the high seas by night. We know today that they depended on Ursa Minor to travel by night and that the ancients named it the "Phoenician star" after them. That the Phoenicians were believed to be experts in astronomy is acknowledged by classical writers, such as Strabo (*Geog.* 16.2.24). Scholars have long assumed that the Phoenicians were sailing only along the coast, not losing sight of the land. But it is well known today that they also sailed the high seas without

---

7. Filigree consists of producing fine gold or silver threads and soldering them together; granulation consists in producing little dots of precious metal and soldering them to form a motif.

having land in sight. This is attested by the Phoenician shipwrecks off the coast of Ashkelon, which "were most likely not hugging the coast" (Ballard and Stager 2002, 167).

In order to sail, the Phoenicians needed boats and ships. The raw material for ship building was abundant and available in the Lebanon Mountains, where all sorts of coniferous trees, such as pine, cypress, and, more importantly, cedar, could be felled and transported to the building areas on the shore. There is no archaeological evidence relating to these ship-building sites and no evidence for this industry. While there is ample information about Late Bronze Age Levantine ships, there is hardly any relating to Phoenician vessels. The only shipwrecks that can be certainly dated to the Phoenician period and known to have sailed from a Phoenician harbor carrying typical Phoenician maritime containers are the two shipwrecks found off the shore of Ashkelon, nicknamed Tanit and Elissa. They give an idea about the size of the cargo ships: according to estimations based on the size of their cargo, Tanit was 6.5 m wide and 14 m long, while Elissa was slightly larger, being 7 m wide and 14.5 m. long. This may give an idea about the average size of Phoenician cargo ships. But since their hulls had long disappeared, no information could be gathered about their building technique.

Scholars who have studied Phoenician ships relied mainly on written sources and iconography. Looking at Syrian boats from the Late Bronze Age, which are better documented in the representations depicted in Egyptian tombs, the most often cited being that of Kenamun in Thebes, and from the two shipwrecks of Uluburun and Cape Gelidonya, scholars all agree that the Phoenician cargo ship is their descendant. The iconographic representations used to study Phoenician ships are those depicted in contemporary sources. The most informative and the most cited are the eighth-century BCE bronze gates of Balawat representing the payment of the tribute of Tyre, the eighth-century BCE Assyrian relief from Sargon II's palace at Khorsabad depicting the transport of wood, the seventh-century BCE scene from Sennacherib's palace depicting the flight of Lulî king of Sidon, the Karatepe monument representing a Phoenician warship (de Graeve 1981, 132), and the representations of war galleys on the coinage of the Phoenician cities from the Persian and Hellenistic period. Several boat models were also found, but they are too small to give details of the construction technique.

Based on the available evidence, scholars were able to reconstruct the building technique of the Phoenician ships and to describe their various types and functions. Regarding the building technique, it has been established that the hull was built first with wooden planks, which were linked together by pegged tenon and mortise joints. This technique is attested in the two Late Bronze Age shipwrecks (Bass 1961, 269–71; 1967; Pulak 1998, 210) mentioned above and continued to be in use in the Iron Age, as attested by a seventh-century BCE Phoenician shipwreck off the coast of Spain: "The keel has been discovered, together with a good part of the planking which is held together by a system of mortises, tabs and wooden tenons ... as well as cylindrical frames ... which are sewn with ropes to the hull of the boat" (Negueruela et al. 1995, 195, figs. 11–12; Negueruela 2005).

Several types of transport boat and ships are known. The first are the *hippoi* boats, so called because of the horse head decorating their prow. The best examples are those depicted on the Assyrian reliefs mentioned above. As for the origin and meaning of the horse head, it is still debated, but it might symbolize the horse's speed. This type of boat was used for the transportation of goods. They were usually small, used for short-distance transportation, but larger ships of that type are also attested.

The typical Phoenician transport ship was the *gaulos*, so called by the Greeks because of its rounded hull. Its length was three times its width, and the Ashkelon shipwrecks were most probably of that type. Both stern and prow were rounded, the former in the form of a fish tail and the second often with the horse-head decoration (for the religious meaning of these figures see Woolmer 2012). They had one rectangular or square sail hung on the mast and a steering rudder at the back near the stern. Some scholars believe that this is the type of ship referred to in the Bible as the "ship of Tarshish."

Next to transport ships used for trade, which could be loaded with cargos up to 250 tons, the Phoenicians developed a type of ship that was better fit for maritime battles and transport of troops. One representation of warships is found on Sennacherib's palace relief. Characteristic of this ship was its rapidity, which was obtained by having rows of rowers on board and by not relying only on the wind sail. This made it also possible to maneuver the vessel to escape enemy attack. Finally, these ships are characterized by the presence of a conical ram covered with a metal sheet at the stern of the boat, which was believed to have been used in frontal attacks to break the hull of enemy ships. However, Samuel Mark (2008) and Woolmer (2012) have argued that these devices were not rams but cutwaters because they could not have been structurally strong enough to damage

Fig. 6.3. Stone anchor retrieved during the marine survey of the Tell el-Burak site. Source: Tell el-Burak Archaeological Project.

the hull of a ship: "According to Mark it is not until the sixth century that Phoenician ships were first outfitted with a ram, an innovation which he convincingly demonstrates was inspired by the Greeks" (Woolmer 2012, 15). Although they kept the rounded form of the *gaulos*, they were thinner and longer for a more efficient ramming. This invention is dated to the Early Iron Age (Casson 1994, 51). This type of ship is depicted on the Karatepe stela (de Graeve 1981, 132). At the beginning there was only one row of rowers, but as the ships became larger and heavier, a second deck with a second row of rowers was added on top of the lower one. The space above the rowers was roofed for protection. This type of ship is known as the bireme. During the Persian wars in the fifth century BCE, another type of warship was developed. It is the trireme, which was characterized by the addition of a third row of rowers. It is represented on Phoenician coins of the Persian and Hellenistic periods.

All these Phoenician boats used anchors. Smaller *hippoi* must have used simple rocks with a hole, like the ones retrieved next to the Tell el-Burak and Beirut shores. The Burak example (see fig. 6.3 below) weighed only 20 kg. More elaborate trapezoidal or apsidal anchors made of hewn stones and known since the Bronze Age at Byblos and Ugarit continued to be used in the Iron Age, as attested by the examples found in the two shipwrecks off the shore of Ashkelon: "These anchors are of the most common ancient type, an apsidal stone with a single hole bored through it, a type found from the Bronze Age through modern times" (Ballard and Stager 2002, 163). They could not be lifted off the sea floor because they were too heavy. Their weight could not be evaluated; similar anchors had weights that varied from 80 to 400 kg.

# Conclusion

This study has demonstrated that the Phoenicia of the Greeks is a geographical designation encompassing the territories of four different Iron Age kingdoms: Arwad, Byblos, Sidon, and Tyre, which reached their largest extension during the Persian period and occupied the Levantine coast from Tell Sukas to Jaffa. These four kingdoms never united to form one unified polity, and there is no evidence that their inhabitants ever identified themselves as belonging to one people or one nation. Finally, there is nowhere an equivalent in Phoenician or in other Near Eastern sources for the concept of Phoenicia and Phoenicians as coined and understood by the Greeks.

Another conclusion suggested by the available evidence is that the Phoenician homeland's southern and northern parts seem to have witnessed different developments. The former stretches from Beirut to the Sharon Plain and the latter from Nahr el-Kalb to Tell Sukas. Northern Phoenicia was dominated by the kingdoms of Byblos and Arwad, while southern Phoenicia was dominated by the kingdoms of Sidon and Tyre. The geographical regions followed different paths in their development, which led to regional differences in some aspects of their material culture and economy. The northern kingdoms seem to have suffered from the growth of the Aramaean city-state of Hamath, which occupied coastal areas traditionally under the hegemony of Byblos and which encircled the territory of Arwad, thus preventing its extension until the coming of the Persians. On the other hand, the Neo-Assyrian expansion to the west weighed more heavily on the situation of the northern kingdoms, with the creation of Assyrian provinces in northern Syria as early as the eighth century BCE, mainly that of Ṣimirra, which occupied the Eleutherus Valley as well as several cities on the northern coast of Lebanon. Preliminary results of surveys of coastal areas in northern Lebanon have shown a scarcity of Iron Age settlements in that region.

Furthermore, the written record relating to the Iron Age focused almost exclusively on Tyre and Sidon and yielded hardly any information about the northern kingdoms of Byblos and Arwad before the Late Iron Age. In addition, most of the archaeological evidence available for Phoenicia to date has come from the southern cities. This major discrepancy in the available evidence between southern and northern Phoenicia may lead to the assumption that the northern cities did not play a major role in the development of the Phoenician trade network and that the Phoenicians owed their fame and reputation to the achievements of the southern cities alone. Indeed, so far, all the evidence relating to the presence of Phoenicians abroad has come from the southern cities. The preeminence of Sidon and Tyre in the written sources is another indication of the dominant role they played. The situation seems to have changed in the Late Iron Age, when Arwad appeared as a major maritime power that was able to expand its territory and to increase its wealth to the extent that it was able to threaten Assyrian interests. However, one should be careful not to draw hasty conclusions from the current discrepancy in both the written and the archaeological record. The wealth of new data relating to southern Phoenicia as opposed to the rare information from the northern kingdoms seems to support the above assumption, but future evidence may contribute to a more balanced understanding.

Notwithstanding this geographical dichotomy and the fragmentation of this area into four kingdoms, the evidence clearly suggests that northern and southern Phoenicia shared basically the same culture. They spoke the same language, had the same onomastics, the same religion, the same type of monarchic rule, and the same reliance on maritime power with both commercial and war fleets. In addition, they had the same territorial organization, with a capital built on an island or a peninsula on which the main harbor was located, and a series of fortified settlements scattered across the territory with access to nearby mountains. In terms of regional differences, the most obvious can be seen in the funerary practices: While cremation became a highly popular practice in the kingdom of Tyre, it remained almost totally absent in the northern kingdoms if we except Tell Sukas. The use of anthropoid sarcophagi was widespread at Sidon and Arwad but remained absent at Tyre and Byblos. Finally, one can notice a stronger Egyptian influence in the south versus a Syrian influence in the north. It is only during the Persian period that Egyptian influence on sacred and funerary architecture developed equally in all the

Phoenician kingdoms as a result of the Phoenician kingdoms' help in the Persian campaigns against Egypt.

Recently discovered Sardinian silver in southern Phoenician cities attests to the existence of Phoenician expeditions to the central Mediterranean already in Iron Age I, that is, unless the metal reached Phoenicia through another eastern Mediterranean country. It has also shown that the Phoenicians had access to new and closer sources of copper and iron from nearby sources in Wadi Araba and Jordan, respectively, and that they may have played an important role in exporting the mined copper to the Greek mainland. The wealth of imported vessels from the eastern Mediterranean and Egypt, as well as the presence of exotic items, such as cinnamon found in Phoenician containers, has shed new light on the scope and extent of Phoenician inland trade, which reached Southeast Asia, with the use of intermediaries, and Arabia.

The recent archaeological evidence has also indicated that agriculture formed a major sector of Phoenician economy in the Late Assyrian and Persian periods. The production of agricultural goods, mainly olive oil and wine, formed the main items traded by the Phoenicians next to imported spices. These products are among the few that can be directly connected to the Phoenician homeland, as shown by the petrography of the transport amphorae.

The purple-dye industry, which made the fame of the Phoenicians according to the written sources, is represented in the archaeological record of the homeland, but so far only in the southern cities and often from the later Iron Age.

As for the cultural achievements traditionally ascribed to the Phoenicians, such as the invention of the alphabet and of the purple-dye and glass industry, which are all based on later Greek and Latin myths and legends, modern research has proven that they are not historically correct. The alphabet was developed in Egypt all through the second millennium BCE under the influence of the Egyptian hieroglyphic script by groups of Semitic-speaking people working or trading with the Egyptians—in other words, much earlier than the Phoenician period. Moreover, the role of the inhabitants of the various Levantine coastal cities in this developmental process remains unknown. However, what is widely accepted is that Iron Age Phoenicians were responsible for the transmission of this script to the Mediterranean countries and to the Atlantic coast of Europe and Africa.

The purple-dye industry developed in Crete in the second millennium BCE and not in Phoenicia. However, the Phoenicians were able to improve some of its techniques in the late first millennium BCE and produced a color known as Tyrian purple. The same goes for the invention of glass, which originated in Mesopotamia, but its production techniques were later developed by the Phoenicians, whose colored glass objects such as colored beads and containers became a hallmark of their material culture.

A final important conclusion of this study is that it stresses the importance of archaeological research, which is the only means we have today to improve our understanding of the area the Greeks called Phoenicia. The more we know about the situation in the homeland, the less elusive the Phoenicians become. So far the scarce information from the heartland of Phoenicia, that is, Lebanon, has encouraged the reliance on mythical and legendary accounts. Developing archaeological research has contributed in giving a reliable picture of the Levantine coast in the Iron Age and in identifying the achievements and characteristics of the daily life of the inhabitants of these four kingdoms based on facts and not on myths. The Phoenicians were not a nation in the modern sense of the term, but they were the inhabitants of different coastal polities who shared the same language and culture but whose allegiance was devoted to their own cities. Not one of these kingdoms can claim sole paternity of this culture, and none of the three modern states on the territory of which these kingdoms are located today, namely, Syria, Lebanon, and Palestine, can appropriate this culture for itself. Furthermore, Phoenician culture is not exclusive to any of these modern states, since their territories were occupied during the same period by other polities belonging to other cultural and political spheres.

If there is a lesson to be drawn from this study, it is the necessity to develop archaeological research in historical Phoenicia to gain more concrete information about its inhabitants and their living conditions, and to protect it from modern political interests and nationalist feelings. History cannot be built on false claims and false information but rather must be built on solid factual evidence. Phoenician culture is part of the historical heritage of the Levantine coast, and all its inhabitants should take pride in it.

# Bibliography

Abou Abdallah, Marc. 2018. *Histoire du royaume de Byblos à l'âge du Fer (1080–333)*. Leuven: Peeters.
Abou-Assaf, Ali. 1990. *Der Tempel von ʿAin Dārā*. Mainz: von Zabern.
Abou Samra, Gaby. 2008. "Le vocabulaire funéraire dans les inscriptions phéniciennes d'époque perse." *Transeu* 36:25–35.
———. 2009. "Un nouveau cratère avec une inscription phénicienne." *KUSATU* 10:173–96.
———. 2014. "Cinq nouvelles pointes de flèche inscrites." *Transeu* 44:47–56.
———. 2018. "Huit stèles funéraires phéniciennes inédites." *Sem* 60:105–29.
Abou Samra, Gaby, and André Lemaire. 2013. "Astarte in Tyre according to New Iron Age Funerary Stelae." *DWO* 43:153–57.
———. 2014. *Nouvelles stèles funéraires phéniciennes*. Beirut: Kutub.
Acquaro, Enrico. 1985. "La Sardegna fenicia e punica: Fra storia e archeologia." *BolA* 31–32:49–56.
Acquaro, Enrico, Federico Mazza, Sergio Ribichini, Gabriella Scandone, and Paolo Xella, eds. 1994. *Biblo, una città e la sua cultura*. Rome: Consiglio Nazionale delle Ricerche.
Aharoni, Yohanan. 1967. *The Land of the Bible: A Historical Geography*. London: Burns & Oates.
Ahlström, G. W. 1978. "Wine Presses and Cup-Marks of the Jenin-Megiddo Survey." *BASOR* 231:19–49.
Al-Amri, Yosha Abdel Salam. 2007. "The Role of the Iron Deposit of Mugharet el-Wardeh/Jordan in the Development of the Use of Iron in Southern Bilad el-Sham." PhD diss., University of Bochum.
Alexandre, Yardenna. 2006. "A Canaanite-Early Phoenician Inscribed Bronze Bowl in an Iron Age IIA–B Burial Cave at Kefar Veradim, Northern Israel." *Maarav* 13:7–41.

Alfen, Peter Gerritt van. 2002. *Pant'agatha Commodities in Levantine-Aegean Trade during the Persian Period, Sixth–Fourth c. B.C.* Austin: University of Texas.

Aliquot, Julien. 2009. *La vie religieuse au Liban.* BAH 189. Beirut: Presses de l'IFPO.

Allen, James P. 2008. "The Historical Inscription of Khnumhotep at Dahshur: Preliminary Report." *BASOR* 352:29–39.

Al-Maqdissi, Michel. 1993. "Chronique des activités archéologiques en Syrie." *Syria* 70:448–53.

———. 2007. "Les nouvelles découvertes à Amrith." Pages 60–61 in *La Méditerranée des Phéniciens: De Tyr à Carthage.* Paris: Institut du monde arabe.

———. 2016a. "Bilan provisoire de la séquence stratigraphique à Tell Iris." Pages 229–40 in *Mille et une empreintes: Un Alsacien en Orient; Mélanges en l'honneur du 65e anniversaire de Dominique Beyer.* Edited by Julie Patrier, Philippe Quenet, and Pascal Butterlin. Subartu 36. Brepols: Turnhout.

———. 2016b. "Tell Sianu (Lattakia)." Pages 181–83 in *A History of Syria in One Hundred Sites.* Edited by Youssef Kanjou and Akira Tsuneki. Oxford: Archaeopress.

Al-Maqdissi, Michel, Massoud Badawi, and Eva Ishaq. 2016. "Tell Tweini (Lattakia)." Pages 174–80 in *A History of Syria in One Hundred Sites.* Edited by Youssef Kanjou and Akira Tsuneki. Oxford: Archaeopress.

Al-Maqdissi, Michel, and Eva Ishaq. 2016. "Amrith/Marathos (Tartous)." Pages 293–96 in *A History of Syria in One Hundred Sites.* Edited by Youssef Kanjou and Akira Tsuneki. Oxford: Archaeopress.

———. 2017. "Amrith in the Late Phoenician Period." *Ash-Sharq* 1:1–8.

Al-Maqdissi, Michel, Karel van Lerberghe, Joachim Bretschneider, and Massoud Badawi, eds. 2010. *Tell Tweini: Onze campagnes de fouilles syro-belges (1999–2010).* Edited by Michel al-Maqdissi, Karel van Lerberghe, Joachim Bretschneider, and Massoud Badawi. Damas: Ministère de la Culture: Direction Générale des Antiquités et des Musées.

Amadasi-Guzzo, Maria Giulia. 1990. "Two Phoenician Inscriptions Carved in Ivory: Again the Ur Box and the Sarepta Plaque." *Or* 59:58–66.

Amadasi-Guzzo, Maria Giulia, and Vassos Karageorghis. 1977. *Fouilles de Kition III. Inscriptions phéniciennes.* Nicosia: Zavallis.

———. 2013. "Re dei Sidonii?" Pages 257–65 in *Ritual, Religion, and Reason: Studies in the Ancient World in Honour of Paolo Xella.* Edited by Oswald Loretz, Sergio Ribichini, Wilfred G. E. Watson, and José Á. Zamora. Münster: Ugarit-Verlag.

Amadasi-Guzzo, Maria Giulia, and José Á. Zamora. 2018. "The Phoenician Marzeah: New Evidence from Cyprus in the Fourth BC." *StEb* 4:187–214.

Anderson, William P. 1987. "The Kilns and Workshops of Sarepta (Sarafand, Lebanon): Remnants of a Phoenician Ceramic Workshop." *Berytus* 25:41–66.

———. 1988. *Sarepta I: The Late Bronze and Iron Age Strata of Area II, Y*. Beirut: Lebanese University Publications.

———. 1989. "The Pottery Industry at Phoenician Sarepta (Sarafand, Lebanon), with Parallels to Kilns from Other East Mediterranean Sites." Pages 197–215 in *Cross-Craft and Cross-Cultural Interactions in Ceramics*. Edited by Patrick McGovern and William David Kingery. Westerville, OH: American Ceramic Society.

———. 1990. "The Beginnings of Phoenician Pottery: Vessel Shape, Style, and Ceramic Technology in the Early Phases of the Phoenician Iron Age." *BASOR* 279:35–54.

Archi, Alfonso. 1981. *Archives of Ebla: An Empire Inscribed in Clay*. Garden City, NY: Doubleday.

———. 1993. *ARES II: I nomi di luogo dei testi di Ebla (Aret I–IV, VII–X e altri documenti editi e inediti)*. Rome: Missione archeologica italiana in Siria.

Arnaud, Daniel. 1992. "Les ports de la Phénicie." *SMEA* 30:179–94.

Artin, Gassia. 2009. *La nécropole "énéolithique de Byblos": Nouvelles interprétations*. Oxford: Archaeopress.

Aruz, Joan, and Jean-François de Lapérouse. 2014. "Nimrud Ivories." Pages 141–51 in *Assyria to Iberia at the Dawn of the Classical Age*. Edited by Joan Aruz, Sarah B. Graff, and Yelena Rakic. New York: Metropolitan Musem of Art.

Aston, David. 1996. *Egyptian Pottery in the Late New Kingdom and Third Intermediate Period (Twelfth to Seventh Centuries BC)*. SAGA 13. Heidelberg: Heidelberger Orientverlag.

Aston, David, Barbara Aston, and Edwin C. Brock. 1998. "Pottery from the Valley of the Kings—Tombs of Merenptah: Ramses III, Ramses IV and Ramses VII." *AeL* 8:137–214.

Astour, Michael C. 1975. "Place Names." Pages 262–343 in vol. 2 of *Ras Shamra Parallels: The Texts from Ugarit and the Hebrew Bible*. Edited by Loren R. Fischer. Rome: Pontificium Institutum Biblicum.

Attridge, Harold W., and Robert A. Oden Jr. 1981. *Philo of Byblos: "The Phoenician History," Introduction, Critical Text, Translation, Notes.* Washington: Catholic Biblical Association of America.

Aubet, María Eugènia. 2001. *The Phoenicians and the West: Politics, Colonies, and Trade.* 2nd ed. Cambridge: Cambridge University Press.

———. 2004. "The Iron Age Cemetery." *BAAL* NS 1:9–62, 449–66.

Aubet, María Eugenia, and Francisco Jesús Nuñez. 2008. "Tyre." Pages 71–104 in *Networking Patterns of the Bronze and Iron Age Levant: The Lebanon and Its Mediterranean Connections.* Edited by Claude Doumet-Serhal, Anne Rabate, and Andrea Resek. London: Lebanese British Friends of the National Museum.

Aubet, María Eugenia, Francisco Jesús Nuñez, and Laura Trellisó. 2014. *The Phoenician Cemetery of Tyre-al Bass II: Archaeological Seasons 2002–2005. BAAL* NS 9.

Avigad, Nahman, and Benjamin Sass. 1997. *Corpus of West Semitic Stamp Seals.* 2nd ed. Jerusalem: Institute of Archaeology, the Hebrew University of Jerusalem.

Aznar, Carolina Ana. 2005. "Exchange Networks in the Southern Levant during the Iron Age II: A Study of Pottery Origin and Distribution." PhD diss., Harvard University.

Bader, Bettina. 2003. "The Egyptian Jars from Sidon in Their Egyptian Context." *AHL* 18:31–37.

Badre, Leila. 1997. "BEY 003 Preliminary Report: Excavations of the American University of Beirut Museum." *BAAL* 2:6–94.

———. 2006. "Tell Kazel-Simyra: A Contribution to a Relative Chronological History in the Eastern Mediterranean during the Late Bronze Age." *BASOR* 343:65–95.

———. 2013. "Tell Kazel—Sumur et le royaume d'Amourrou." *CRAI*: 737–56.

———. 2015. "A Phoenician Sanctuary in Tyre." *BAAL* NS 10:59–82.

Badre, Leila, and Eric Gubel. 1999–2000. "Tell Kazel (Syria): Excavations of the AUB Museum, 1993–1998; Third Preliminary Report." *Berytus* 44:123–204.

Badre, Leila, Éric Gubel, Emmanuelle Capet, and Nadine Panayot. 1994. "Tell Kazel (Syrie), Rapport préliminaire sur les 4e–8e campagnes de fouilles (1988–1992)." *Syria* 71:259–359.

Badre, Leila, Eric Gubel, and Jean-Paul Thalmann. 2007. *La Méditerranée des Phéniciens: De Tyr à Carthage.* Paris: Institut du monde arabe.

Badreshany, Kamel, and Aaron Schmitt. 2019. "The Middle Bronze Age Remains in Area 2." Pages 275–82 in *Tell el-Burak I, the Middle Bronze Age: With Chapters Related to the Site and to the Mamluk-Ottoman Periods*. Edited by Jens Kamlah and Hélène Sader. ADPV 45.1. Wiesbaden: Harrassowitz.

Bagg, Ariel M. 2007. *Die Levante*. Vol. 1 of *Die Orts–und Gewässernamen der neuassyrischen Zeit*. RGTC 7.1. Wiesbaden: Reichert.

———. 2011. *Die Assyrer und das Westland: Studien zur historischen Geographie unf Herrschaftspraxis in der Levante im 1. Jt. v.u. Z*. Leuven: Peeters.

Balensi, Jacqueline. 1985. "Revising Tell Abu Hawam." *BASOR* 257:65–74.

Balensi, Jacqueline, Maria D. Herrera, and Michael Artzy. 1993. "Tell Abu Hawam." *NEAEHL* 1:7–14.

Ballard, Robert D., and Lawrence E. Stager. 2002. "Iron Age Shipwrecks in Deep Water off Ashkelon, Israel." *AJA* 106:151–68.

Baramki, Dimitri. 1961. *Phoenicia and the Phoenicians*. Beirut: Khayats.

Barclay, John M. G., trans. 2007. *Against Apion: Translation and Commentary*. Flavius Josephus Translation and Commentary 10. Leiden: Brill.

Barnett, Richard. 1975. *A Catalogue of the Nimrud Ivories: With Other Examples of Ancient Near Eastern Ivories in the British Museum*. London: British Museum.

Barnett, Richard David, John Curtis, and Nigel Tallis. 2008. *The Balawat Gates of Ashurnasirpal II*. London: British Museum Press.

Barreca, Ferrucio. 1974. *La Sardegna Fenicia e Punica*. Sassari: Chiarella.

Baruch, Inbar, Michal Artzy, Joseph Heller, Jacqueline Balensi, and Maria D. Herrera. 2005. "The Mollusc Fauna from the Late Bronze and Iron Age Strata of Tell Abu Hawam." Pages 132–47 in *Archaeomalacology: Molluscs in Former Environments of Human Behaviour (Proceedings of the Ninth Conference of the International Council of Archaeozoology, Durham, August 2002)*. Edited by Daniella E. Bar-Yosef Mayer. Oxford: Oxbow Books.

Baruch, Uri, and N. Lipschitz. 2000. "Charred Wood Remains." Pages 203–5 in *Horbat Rosh Zayit: An Iron Age Storage Fort and Village*. Edited by Zvi Gal and Yardenna Alexandre. Jerusalem: Israel Antiquities Authority.

Bass, George F. 1961. "The Cape Gelidonya Wreck: Preliminary Report." *AJA* 65:267–76.

———. 1967. "Cape Gelidonya: A Bronze Age Shipwreck." *TAPS* 57.8:1–177.

Baumgarten, Albert I. 1981. *"The Phoenician History" of Philo of Byblos: A Commentary.* Leiden: Brill.

Baurain, Claude, and Corrine Bonnet. 1992. *Les Phéniciens: Marins des trois continents.* Paris: Colin.

Belmonte-Marín, Juan Antonio. 2001. *Die Orts–und Gewässernamen der Texte aus Syrien im 2. Jt. V. Chr.* RGTC 12.2. Wiesbaden: Reichert.

———. 2003. "Cuatro estudios sobre los dominios territoriales de las ciudades-estado fenicias." *CAM* 9:15–178.

Bennett, W. J., and Jeffrey A. Blakely. 1989. *Tell el-Hesi: The Persian Period (Stratum V).* Winona Lake, IN: Eisenbrauns.

Ben-Shlomo, David. 2013. "Philistia during the Iron Age II Period." Pages 717–29 in *The Oxford Handbook of the Archaeology of the Levant, c. 8000–332 BCE.* Edited by Ann E. Killbrew and Margreet Steiner. Oxford: Oxford University Press.

Benz, Frank L. 1972. *Personal Names in the Phoenician and Punic Inscriptions.* StPohl 8. Rome: Biblical Institute Press.

Bertsch, Julia. 2019. "Preliminary Report on the Wall Paintings of Tell el-Burak: Iconography." Pages in *Tell el-Burak I: The Middle Bronze Age.* Edited by Jens Kamlah and Hélène Sader. ADPV 45.1. Wiesbaden: Harrassowitz.

Bettles, Elizabeth. 2003. *Phoenician Amphora Production and Distribution in the Southern Levant: A Multidisciplinary Investigation into Carinated-Shoulder Amphorae of the Persian Period (539–332 BC).* BARIS 1183. Oxford: Archaeopress.

Bienkowski, Piotr. 1982. "Some Remarks on the Practice of Cremation in the Levant." *Levant* 14:80–88.

Bierling, Marilyn, and Seymour Gitin, eds. 2002. *The Phoenicians in Spain.* Winona Lake, IN: Eisenbrauns.

Bikai, Patricia Maynor. 1978a. *The Pottery of Tyre.* Warminster, UK: Aris & Phillips.

———. 1978b. "The Late Phoenician Pottery Complex and Chronology." *BASOR* 229:47–56.

———. 1987a. *The Phoenician Pottery of Cyprus.* Nicosia: AG Levantis Foundation.

———. 1987b. "Trade Networks in the Early Iron Age the Phoenicians at Palaepaphos." Pages 125–28 in *Western Cyprus Connections.* Edited by David William Rupp. SMA 77. Göteborg: Åström.

———. 1992. *The Site: Rencontres sur Tyr et la formation des civilisations méditerranéennes (1990)*. Paris: Association Internationale pour la sauvegarde de Tyr, UNESCO.

Biran, Avraham, and Joseph Naveh. 1995. "The Tel Dan Inscription: A New Fragment." *IEJ* 45:1–18.

Blomquist, Tina Haettner. 1999. *Gates and Gods: Cult in the City Gate of Iron Age Palestine; An Investigation of the Archaeological and Biblical Sources*. Stockholm: Almqvist & Wiksell.

Bondì, Sandro Filippo. 1985. "La Sicilia fenicio-punica il quadro storico e la documentazione archeologica." *BolA* 31–32:13–32.

Bonechi, Marco. 1993. *I Nomi geografici dei testi di Ebla*. RGTC 12.1. Wiesbaden: Reichert.

Bonnet, Corinne. 1988. *Melqart: Cultes et mythes de l'Héraclès tyrien en Méditerranée*. Leuven: Peeters.

———. 1996. *Astarté: Données documentaires et perspectives historiques*. Rome: CNR.

Bonnet, Corinne, and Herbert Niehr. 2010. *Religionen in der Umwelt des Alten Testaments II: Phönizier, Punier, Aramäer*. Stuttgart: Kohlhammer.

———. 2014. *La religion des Phéniciens et des Araméens*. Genève: Labor et Fides.

Bordreuil, Pierre. 1977. "Une inscription phénicienne sur jarre provenant des fouilles de Tell 'Arqa." *Syria* 54:25–30.

———. 1982. "Deux épigraphes phéniciennes provenant des fouilles de Tell Rachidieh." *AHA*: 137–40.

———. 1983. "Nouveaux apports de l'archéologie et de la glyptique à l'onomastique phénicienne." Pages 751–57 in vol. 3 of *Atti del I Congresso Internazionale di Studi Fenici e Punici 1979: Roma, 5–10 novembre 1979*. Rome: Consiglio Nazionale delle Ricerche.

———. 1985. "Le dieu Echmoun dans la région d'Amrith." Pages 221–30 in *Phoenicia and Its Neighbors*. StPhoe 3. Leuven: Peeters.

———. 1986. *Catalogue des sceaux ouest-sémitiques inscrits de la Bibliothèque Nationale, du Musée du Louvre et du Musée biblique de Bible et Terre sainte*. Paris: Bibliothèque Nationale.

———. 1992a. "Tyr et Ougarit au IIe millénaire." Pages 105–13 in *Tyr et la formation des civilisations méditerranéennes 1990*. Paris: UNESCO.

———. 1992b. "Les flèches phéniciennes inscrites: 1981–1991." *RB* 99:205–13.

———. 2003. "À propos des amphores inscrites de Tell Rachidieh." *AHL* 17:52–57.

———. 2007. "L'alphabet phénicien: Legs, héritages, adaptation, diffusion, transmission." Pages 72–81 in *La Méditerranée des Phéniciens: De Tyr à Carthage*. Paris: Institut du monde arabe.

———. 2011. "Tesson de céramique à inscription phénicienne du VIIIe siècle." *BAAL* 15:236–37.

Borger, Rykle. 1982–1985. "Der Vertrag Asarhaddons mit Baal von Tyros." Pages 158–59 in *Rechts—und Wirtschaftsurkunden: Historisch-chronologische Texte*. Vol. 1 of *Texte aus der Umwelt des Alten Testaments*. Gütersloh: Gütersloher.

Boschloos, Vanessa. 2014. "Scarabs and Seals from the 2002–2005 Seasons at Tyre el-Bass." *BAAL* NS 9:381–404.

Bordreuil, Pierre. 2003. "Two Inscribed Sherds of Sidon." *Archaeology and History in Lebanon* 18:70.

Bounni, Adnan, E. Lagarce, and Jacques Lagarce. 1979. "Rapport préliminaire sur la troisième campagne de fouilles (1977) à Ibn Hani (Syrie)." *Syria* 56:215–97.

Boyes, Philip J. 2012. "'The King of the Sidonians': Phoenician Ideologies and the Myth of the Kingdom of Tyre-Sidon." *BASOR* 365:33–44.

Braemer, Frank. 1982. *L'architecture domestique du Levant à l'âge du Fer*. Paris: Éditions Recherche sur les Civilisations.

Braidwood, Robert John. 1940. "Report on Two Sondages on the Coast of Syria, South of Tartous." *Syria* 21:183–221.

Bretschneider, Joachim, Greta Jans, and Anne-Sophie Van Vyve. 2010. "Les fouilles du chantier A en 2009 et 2010: Une analyse préliminaire de l'architecture de la transition du bronze récent et l'âge du fer I." Pages 131–46 in *Tell Tweini: Onze campagnes de fouilles syro-belges (1999–2010)*. Edited by Michel al-Maqdissi, Karel van Lerberghe, Joachim Bretschneider, and Massoud Badawi. Damas: Ministère de la Culture: Direction Générale des Antiquités et des Musées.

Bretschneider, Joachim, and Karel van Lerberghe, eds. 2008. *In Search of Gibala: An Archaeological and Historical Study Based on Eight Seasons of Excavations at Tell Tweini (Syria) in the A and C Fields (1999–2007)*. Barcelona: AUSA.

Bretschneider, Joachim, Anne-Sophie Van Vyve, and Greta Jans. 2011. "Tell Tweini: A Multi-Period Harbour Town at the Syrian Coast." Pages 73–87 in *Egypt and the Near East—The Crossroads: Proceedings of an International Conference on the Relations of Egypt and the Near*

*East in the Bronze Age; Prague, September 1–3, 2010*. Edited by Jana Mynářová. Prague: Czech Institute of Egyptology.

Briend, Jacques, and Jean-Baptiste Humbert. 1980. *Tell Keisan (1971–1976): Une cité phénicienne en Galilée*. OBO.SA 1. Fribourg: Editions Universitaires.

Briquel-Chatonnet, Françoise. 1991. "Les derniers témoignages sur la Langue phénicienne en orient." *RSF* 19:3–21.

———. 1992. *Les relations entre les cités de la côte phénicienne et les royaumes d'Israël et de Judah*. StPhoe 12. Leuven: Peeters.

———. 1996. "Arwad cité phénicienne." Pages 63–72 in *E Alle Soglie della classicità il Mediterraneo tra tradizione e innovazione*. Edited by Enrico Acquaro. StMosc. Rome: Istituti editoriali e poligrafici internazionali.

———. 1997. "Arwad et l'empire assyrien." Pages 57–68 in *Ana shadî Labnani lū allik: Beiträge zur altorientalischen und mittlemeerischen Kulturen; Festschrift für Wolfgang Röllig*. Edited by Beate Ponkratz-Leisten, Hartmut Kühne, and Paola Xella. VBBK. Neukirchen-Vluyn: Neukirchner Verlag.

———. 2000. "Le statut politique d'Arwad au IIe millénaire." Pages 129–33 in *Actas del IV Congresso Internazionale di Studi Fenici e Punici*. Vol. 1. Cadiz: Università degli Studi di Palermo, Facoltà di Lettere e Filosifia.

———. 2005. "Arwad et Simirra: Problèmes géostratégiques dela Phénicie du nord." Pages 23–26 in vol. 1 of *Atti del VII Congresso Internazionale di Studi Fenici e Punici*. Edited by A. Spanò. Palermo: Università degli Studi di Palermo, Facoltà di Lettere e Filosifia.

Brody, Aaron Jed. 2014. "Interregional Interaction in the Late Iron Age: Phoenician and Other Foreign Goods from Tell en-Nasbeh." Pages 56–69 in *Material Culture Matters: Essays on the Archaeology of the Southern Levant in Honor of Seymour Gitin*. Edited by John R. Spencer, Robert A. Mullins, and Aaron Jed Brody. Winona Lake, IN: Eisenbrauns.

Bron, François, and André Lemaire. 1983. "Inscriptions d'Al-Mina." Pages 677–86 in vol. 1 of *Atti del I congresso internazionale di studi fenici e punici: Roma, 5–10 novembre 1979*. Rome: Consiglio nazionale delle ricerche.

Brossé, C.-L. 1926. "La nécropole de Sheikh Zenad." *Syria* 7:193–208.

Brun, Jean-Pierre. 2003. *Le vin et l'huile dans la Mediterranée antique: Viticulture, oléiculture et procédés de transformation*. Paris: Errance.

———. 2004. *Archéologie du vin et de l'huile dela préhistoire à l'époque hellénistique*. Paris: Errance.

Brunt, P. A., trans. 1976. *Arrian. Anabasis of Alexander*. 2 vols. LCL. Cambridge: Harvard University Press.

Buccianti-Barakat, Liliane, and Henri Chamussy. 2012. *Le Liban: Géographie d'un pays paradoxal*. Paris: Belin.

Buhl, Marie-Louise. 1964. "Anfang, Verbreitung und Dauer der Phönikischen Anthropodien Steinsarkophage." *ActAr* 35:61–80.

———. 1983a. *Sukas VII: The Near Eastern Pottery and Objects of Other Materials from the Upper Strata*. Copenhagen: Munksgaard.

———. 1983b. "L'origine des sarcophages anthropoïdes phéniciens en pierre." Pages 199–202 in vol. 1 of *Atti del I Congresso Internazionale di Studi Fenici e Punici: Roma, 5–10 novembre 1979*. Rome: Consiglio nazionale delle ricerche.

———. 1991. "Les sarcophages anthropoïdes phéniciens trouves en dehors de la Phénicie." Pages 675–81 in *Atti del II Congresso internazionale di studi fenici e punici: Roma, 9–14 novembre 1987*. Rome: Consiglio nazionale delle ricerche.

Bunnens, Guy. 1979. *L'expansion phénicienne en Méditerranée: Essai d'interprétation fondé sur une analyse des traditions littéraires*. Rome: Institut historique belge de Rome.

Çakırlar, Canan. Forthcoming. The Faunal Remains of Iron Age Tell el-Burak.

Çakırlar, Canan, Verena Amer, Jens Kamlah, and Hélène Sader. 2014. "Persian Period Dog Burials in the Levant: New Evidence from Tell el-Burak (Lebanon) and a Reconsideration of the Phenomenon." Pages 243–64 in *Archaeozoology of Southwestern Asia and Adjacent Areas (ASWA) IX*. ANESSup. Edited by Veerle Linselee, Bea De Cupere, and Sheila Hamilton-Dyer. Leuven: Peeters.

Çakırlar, V. 2018. Internal report on Tell el-Burak. October 10.

Çambel, Halet. 1999. *Karatepe-Aslantaş, Corpus of Hieroglyphic Luwian Inscriptions*. Vol. 2. Berlin: de Gruyter.

Capet, Emmanuelle. 2003. "Tell Kazel (Syrie): Rapport préliminaire sur les 9e–17e campagnes de fouilles (1993–2001) du musée de l'Université Americaine de Beyrouth. Chantier II." *Berytus* 47:63–121.

———. 2008. "Les peuples des céramiques 'barbares' à Tell Kazel (Syrie)." Pages 187–208 in *Cyprus, the Sea Peoples and the Eastern Mediterranean: Regional Perspectives of Continuity and Change*. Edited by Timothy P. Harrison. Toronto: Canadian Institute for Mediterranean Studies.

Carayon, Nicolas. 2003. "L'île de Ziré à Saida: Nouvelles données archéologiques." *AHL* 18:95–113.

———. 2005. "Contribution historique, archéologique et géomorphologique à l'étude des ports antiques de Tyr." *BAAL* NS 2:53–60.

———. Forthcoming. "Les ports de Byblos, Sidon et Tyr. Étude comparative diachronique des caractéristiques physiques et structurelles." *BAAL*.

Carmona, Pilar, and Jose Miguel Ruiz. 2004. "Geomorphological and Geoarchaeological Evolution of the Coastline of the Tyre Tombolo: Preliminary Results." *BAAL* NS 1:207–19.

Casson, Lionel. 1994. *Travel in the Ancient World*. Baltimore: Johns Hopkins University Press.

Caubet, Annie. 2007. "Les oeufs d'autruche." Pages 225–27 in *La Méditerranée des Phéniciens: De Tyr à Carthage*. Paris: Somogy. Institut du Monde Arabe.

Caubet, Annie, Élisabeth Fontan, Georgina Herrmann, and Hélène Le Meaux. 2007. "L'âge de l'ivoire." Pages 205–15 in *La Méditerranée des Phéniciens: De Tyr à Carthage*. Paris: Institut du monde arabe.

Chahoud, Jwana. 2015. "Reconstruire les pratiques alimentaires liées aux animaux dans les lieux de cultes levantins au Bronze Récent." *BAAL* 10:373–92.

Chahoud, Jwana, and Emmanuelle Vila. 2011–2012. "The Role of Animals in Ancient Sidon: An Overview of Ongoing Zooarchaeological Studies." *AHL* 34–35:259–84.

Chéhab, Maurice. 1942–1943. "Chronique." *BMB* 6:81–87.

———. 1951–1952. "Les terres cuites de Kharayeb: Texte." *BMB* 10:5–184.

———. 1953–1954. "Les terres cuites de Kharayeb: Planches." *BMB* 11:v–xxviii.

———. 1965. "Chronique." *BMB* 18:111–25.

———. 1983. "Découvertes phéniciennes au Liban." Pages 165–72 in vol. 1 of *Atti del I Congresso Internazionale di Studi Fenici e Punici 1979: Roma, 5–10 novembre 1979*. Rome: Consiglio Nazionale delle Ricerche.

Chirpanlieva, Iva. 2010. "La Céramique attique dans le contexte religieux phénicien—Une nouvelle approche (matériel inédit des fouilles du site de Kition-Bamboula)." *RDAC*: 339–61.

———. 2015. "Byblos à l'Époque Perse. Étude des céramiques grecques de Byblos." *AHL* 42–43:55–94.

Clawson, M. Don. 1934. "Phoenician Dental Art." *Berytus* 1:23–31.

Coldstream, Nicholas. 2008. "Early Greek Export to Phoenicia and the East Mediterranean." Pages 167–88 in *Networking Patterns of the*

*Bronze and Iron Age Levant, The Lebanon and its Mediterranean Connections*. Edited by Claude Doumet-Serhal, Anne Rabate, and Andrea Resek. London: Lebanese British Friends of the National Museum.

Counts, Derek B., and Maria Iacovou. 2013. "New Approaches to the Elusive Iron Age Polities of Ancient Cyprus: An Introduction." *BASOR* 370:1–13.

Cowley, Arthur E. 1923. *Aramaic Papyri of the Fifth Century B.C.* Oxford: Clarendon.

Cross, Frank Moore. 2002. "Phoenician Tomb Stelae from Achziv." Pages 169–73 in *The Akhziv Cemeteries: The Ben-Dor Excavations, 1941–1944*. Edited by Mikhal Dayagi-Mendels. Jerusalem: Israel Antiquities Authority.

———. 2009. "The Phoenician Ostracon from Acco, the Ekron Inscriptions and 'ŠRH." *ErIsr* 29:2–32.

Crowfoot, John Winter, Grace M. Crowfoot, and E. L. Sukenik. 1938. *Early Ivories from Samaria*. London: Palestine Exploration Fund.

Culican, William. 1969. "Dea Tyria Gravida." *Australian Journal of Biblical Archaeology* 1.2:35–50.

———. 1970. "Phoenician Oil Bottles and Tripod Bowls." *Berytus* 19:5–18.

———. 1975–1976. "Some Phoenician Masks and Other Terracottas." *Berytus* 24:47–87.

———. 1982. "The Repertoire of Phoenician Pottery." Pages 45–77 in *Phönizier im Westen*. Edited by Hans Georg Niemeyer. Mainz: von Zabern.

Curvers, Hans H. 2001–2002. "The Lower Town of Beirut (1200–300): A Preliminary Synthesis." *Aram* 13–14:51–72.

Curvers, Hans, and Barbara Stuart. 2005. "The BCD Archaeology Project, 2000–2006." *BAAL* 9:189–222.

Da Riva, Rocío. 2008. "The Nebuchadnezzar Twin Inscriptions of Brisa (Wadi esh-Sharbin, Lebanon): Transliteration and Translation." *BAAL* 12:299–332.

———. 2009. "The Nebuchadnezzar Rock Inscription at Nahr el-Kalb." *BAAL NS* 4:255–302.

Darnell, John Coleman, F. W. Dobbs-Allsopp, Marilyn J. Lundberg, P. Kyle McCarter, Bruce Zuckerman, and Colleen Manassa. 2005. "Two Early Alphabetic Inscriptions from the Wadi el-Ḥôl: New Evidence for the Origin of the Alphabet from the Western Desert of Egypt." *BASOR* 59:67–124.

Davie, Michael F., and Hassan Salamé-Sarkis. 1986. "Le Théouprosopon-Ras as-Saq'a (Liban): Étude géo-historique." *MUSJ* 41:2–48.
Dayagi-Mendels, Mikhal. 2002. *The Akhziv Cemeteries: The Ben-Dor Excavations, 1941–1944*. Jerusalem: Israel Antiquities Authority.
De Bertou, Jules. 1843. *Essai sur la topographie de Tyr*. Paris.
Delavault, Bernard, and André Lemaire. 1979. "Les inscriptions phéniciennes de Palestine." *RSF* 7:1–40.
Demesticha, Stella, and A. Bernard Knapp. 2016. *Maritime Transport Containers in the Bronze-Iron Age Aegean and Eastern Mediterranean*. Uppsala: Åström Förlag.
Deutsch, Robert, and André Lemaire. 2000. *Biblical Period Personal Seals in the Shlomo Moussaieff Collection*. Tel Aviv: Archaeological Center Publications.
Diakonoff, Igor M. 1992. "The Naval Power and Trade of Tyre." *IEJ* 42:168–93.
Dils, Peter. 1992. "Fenkhu." Page 170 in *Dictionnaire de la civilisation phénicienne et punique*. Edited by Edouard Lipiński. Paris: Brepols.
Dinçol, Belkis. 1994. "New Archaeological and Epigraphical Finds from Ivriz: A Preliminary Report." *TAJA* 21:117–28.
Dixon, Helen. 2013. "Phoenician Mortuary Practices in Iron Age I–III (ca 1200–300 BC) Levantine Homeland." PhD diss., University of Michigan.
———. 2018. "Late First-Millennium B.C.E. Levantine Dog Burials as an Extension of Human Mortuary Behavior." *BASOR* 379:19–41.
Doak, Brian. 2015. *Aniconism in the Mediterranean and Ancient Near Eastern Contexts*. Atlanta: SBL Press.
Dongen, Erik van. 2010. "'Phoenicia': Naming and Defining a Region in Syria-Palestine." Pages 471–88 in *Interkulturalität in der Alten Welt: Vorderasien, Hellas, Ägypten und die vielfältigen Ebenen des Kontakts*. Edited by Robert Rollinger et al. Wiesbaden: Harrassowitz.
Donner, Herbert, and Wolfgang Röllig. 1973. *Kanaanäische und aramäische Inschriften*. Wiesbaden: Harrassowitz.
Dothan, Moshe. 1976. "Akko: Interim Excavation Report First Season 1973/4." *BASOR* 224:1–48.
———. 1979. "Akko. Notes and News." *IEJ* 29:227–28.
———. 1985. "A Phoenician Inscription from Akko." *IEJ* 35:81–94.
———. 1993. "Akko." *NEAEHL* 1:16–24.
Dothan, Moshe, and Diethelm Conrad. 1978. "Akko, 1978." *IEJ* 28:264–66.
———. 1984. "Akko, 1983." *IEJ* 34:189–90.

Doumet, Claude. 1982. "Les tombes IV et V de Rachidieh." *AHA* 1:89–136.
Doumet-Serhal, Claude. 2003. "Excavating Sidon." *AHL* 18:2–19.
———. 2006a. *The Early Bronze Age in Sidon: "College Site" Excavations (1998-2000-2001)*. BAH 178. Beirut: Institut Français du Proche-Orient.
———. 2006b. "Sidon: Mediterranean Contacts in the Early and Middle Bronze Age, Preliminary Report." *AHL* 24:34–47.
———. 2013. *Sidon: Fifteen Years of Excavations*. Beirut: Lebanese British Friends of the National Museum.
———. Forthcoming. "Sidon in Iron Age I: A Haven of Continuity." *BAAL*.
Doumet-Serhal, Claude, Vassos Karageorghis, and Henri Charles Loffet. 2008. "South Lebanon." Pages 1–70 in *Networking Patterns of the Bronze and Iron Age Levant: The Lebanon and Its Mediterranean Connections*. Edited by Claude Doumet-Serhal, Anne Rabate, and Andrea Resek. London: Lebanese British Friends of the National Museum.
Dunand, Maurice. 1939. *Fouilles de Byblos I*. Paris: Geuthner.
———. 1960. "Histoire d'une source." *MUSJ* 37:39–53.
———. 1963. *Byblos: Son histoire, ses ruines, ses legends*. Beirut.
———. 1966. "Rapport préliminaire sur les fouilles de Sidon en 1963–1964." *BMB* 19:103–6.
———. 1967. "Rapport préliminaire sur les fouilles de Sidon en 1964–1965." *BMB* 20:27–46.
———. 1969. L'architecture à Byblos au temps des Achéménides." *BMB* 22:93–99.
———. 1973. "Le temple d'Echmoun à Sidon: Essai de Chronologie." *BMB* 26:7–53.
Dunand, Maurice, and Raymond Duru. 1962. *Oumm el Amed: Une ville de l'époque hellénistique aux Echelles de Tyr*. Paris: Maisonneuve.
Dunand, Maurice, and Nessib Saliby. 1985. *Le temple d'Amrith dans la Pérée d'Aradus*. Paris: Geuthner.
Durand, Jean Marie. 1999. "La façade occidentale du Proche-Orient d'après les textes de Mari." Pages 149–64 in *L'acrobate au taureau: Les découvertes de Tell Daba'a et l'archéologie de la Méditerranée Orientale*. Edited by Annie Caubet. Paris: La Documentation française.
Dussaud, M. René. 1924. "Les Inscriptions phéniciennes du tombeau d'Ahiram, roi de Byblos." *Syria* 5:135–57.
———. 1925. "Dédicace d'une statue d'Osorkon I par Eliba'al, roi de Byblos." *Syria* 6:101–17.

———. 1927. *Topographie historique de la Syrie antique et médiévale*. Paris: Geuthner.
Duyrat, Frédérique. 2005. *Arados hellénistique: Étude historique et monétaire*. Beirut: Institut Français du Proche-Orient.
Edrey, Meir. 2008. "The Dog Burials at Achaemenid Ashkelon Revisited." *Tel Aviv* 35:267–82.
El-Amouri, M., et al. 2005. "Mission d'expertise archéologique du port sud de Tyr: Résultats préliminaires." *BAAL* NS 2:91–110.
Elayi, Josette. 1982. "Studies in Phoenician Geography during the Persian Period." *JNES* 41:83–110.
———. 1985. "Byblos et la domination assyro-babylonienne." *BaM* 16:393–97.
———. 1989. *Sidon, cité autonome de l'empire perse*. Paris: Éditions Idéaphane.
———. 2000. "Les sites phéniciens de Syrie au Fer III/Perse: Bilan et perspectives de recherche." Pages 327–48 in *Essays on Syria in the Iron Age*. Edited by Guy Bunnens. Leuven: Peeters.
———. 2005. *'Abd'aštart Ier/Straton de Sidon: Un roi phénicien entre Orient et Occident*. Paris: Gabalda.
———. 2007. "Gerashtart, King of the Phoenician City of Arwad in the Fourth cent. BC." *NumC* 167:99–104.
———. 2008. "Byblos et Sidon. Deux modèles de cités phéniciennes à l'époque perse." *Transeu* 35:97–122.
———. 2009. *Byblos, cite sacrée (8e–4e s. av. J.-C.)*. Paris: Gabalda.
———. 2013a. *Histoire de la Phénicie*. Paris: Perrin.
———. 2013b. "Un nouveau sceau phénicien inscrit." Pages 271–75 in *Ritual, Religion and Reason: Studies in the Ancient World in Honour of Paolo Xella*. Edited by Owald Loretz et al. Münster: Ugarit-Verlag.
———. 2018. *The History of Phoenicia*. Atlanta: Lockwood.
Elayi, Josette, and Alain G. Elayi. 1997. *Recherches sur les poids phéniciens*. SupTranseu 5. Paris: Gabalda.
———. 2004. *Le monnayage de la cité phénicienne de Sidon à l'époque perse (Ve–IVe s. av. J.-C.)*. 2 vols. Paris: Gabalda.
———. 2009. *The Coinage of the Phoenician City of Tyre in the Persian Period (Fifth–Fourth cent. BCE)*. Leuven: Peeters.
———. 2014. *A Monetary and Political History of the Phoenician City of Byblos in the Fifth and Fourth Centuries B.C.E.* HACL 6. Winona Lake, IN: Eisenbrauns.

———. 2015. *Arwad, cité phénicienne du nord.* SupTranseu 19. Paris: Gabalda.

Elayi, Josette, and Mohammed R. Haykal. 1996. *Nouvelles découvertes sur les usages funéraires des Phéniciens d'Arwad.* SupTranseu 4. Paris: Gabalda.

Elayi, Josette, and Hala Sayegh. 1998. *Un quartier du port phénicien de Beyrouth au Fer III/Perse: Les objets.* Paris: Gabalda.

———. 2000. *Un quartier du port phénicien de Beyrouth au Fer III/Perse: Archéologie et Histoire.* Paris: Gabalda.

Elgavish, Joseph. 1978. "Shiqmona, Tel." Pages 1101–8 in vol. 4 of *Encyclopedia of Archaeological Excavations in the Holy Land.* Edited by Michael Avi-Yonah and Ephraim Stern. Jerusalem: Massada.

———. 1993. "Shiqmona." *NEAEHL* 4:1373–78.

Eschel, Tzilla, Naama Yahalom-Mack, Sariel Shalev, Ofir Tirosh, Yigal Erel, and Ayelet Gilboa. 2018. "Four Iron Age Silver Hoards from Southern Phoenicia: From Bundles to Hacksilber." *BASOR* 379:197–228.

Faber, Alice. 1997. "Genetic Subgrouping of the Semitic Languages." Pages 3–15 in *The Semitic Languages.* Edited by Robert Hetzron. London: Routledge.

Fales, Frederick Mario. 2017. "Phoenicia in the Neo-Assyrian Period: An Updated Overview." *SAAB* 23:181–295.

Fantalkin, Alexander. 2005. "A Group of Iron Age Wineries from Ancient Jaffa (Joppa)." *SER* 2:3–26.

Feldman, Marian. 2006. *Diplomacy by Design: Luxury Arts and an "International Style" in the Ancient Near East.* Chicago: University of Chicago Press.

Finkbeiner, Uwe. 2001–2002. "BEY 020. The Iron Age Fortification." *Aram* 13/14:27–36.

Finkbeiner, Uwe, and Hélène Sader. 1997. "Bey 020 Preliminary Report of the Excavations 1995." *BAAL* 2:114–66.

Finkelstein, Israel, and Neil Asher Silberman. 2001. *The Bible Unearthed: Archaeology's New Vision of Ancient Israel and the Origin of Its Stories.* London: Simon & Schuster.

Finkelstein, Israel, and Benjamin Sass. 2013. "The West Semitic Alphabetic Inscriptions, Late Bronze II to Iron IIA: Archeological Context, Distribution and Chronology." *HBAI* 2:149–220.

Fischer-Elfert, Hans-Werner. 1986. *Die satirische Streitschrift des Papyrus Anastasi I: Übersetzung und Kommentar.* Wiesbaden: Harrassowitz.

Fleming, Wallace Bruce. 1966. *The History of Tyre.* New York: AMS.

Fontan, Elisabeth. 2018. *Les ivoires d'Arslan Tash: Décor de mobilier syrien, IXe–VIIIe siècles avant J.-C.* Paris: Coédition Louvre/Picard.
Forstner-Müller, Irene, Karin Kopetsky, and Claude Doumet-Serhal. 2006. "Egyptian Pottery from the Late Twelfth and Early Thirteenth Dynasty from Sidon." *AHL* 24:52–59.
Frede, Simone. 2000. *Fundgruppen und Bestattungskontexte.* Vol. 1 of *Die phönizischen anthropoiden Sarkophage.* Mainz: von Zabern.
Friedrich, Johannes, Wolfgang Röllig, and Maria Giulia Amadasi-Guzzo. 1999. *Phönizisch-Punische Grammatik.* 3rd ed. AnOr 55. Rome: Pontifical Biblical Institute.
Frost, Honor. 1964. "Rouad, ses récifs et mouillages." *AAAS* 14:67–74.
———. 1971. "Observations on the Submerged Harbourworks at Tyre." *BMB* 24:103–11.
———. 1973a. "Ancient Harbors and Anchorages in the Eastern Mediterranean." Pages 95–114 in *Underwater Archaeology: A Nascent Discipline.* Paris: UNESCO.
———. 1973b. "The Offshore Island Harbour at Sidon and Other Phoenician Sites in the Light of New Dating Evidence." *IJNA* 2:75–94.
———. 1998–1999. "Marine Prospection at Byblos." *BAAL* 3:245–59.
———. 2001. "The Necropolis, the Trench and Other Ancient Remains: A Survey of the Byblian Sea-Front." *BAAL* 5:195–217.
———. 2002. "Fourth Season of Marine Investigation: Preliminary Charting of the Offshore Shallows." *BAAL* 6:309–16.
———. 2005. "Archaeology, History and the History of Archaeology Connected with Tyre's Harbours." *BAAL* NS 2:45–52.
Frost, Honor, and Christophe Morhange. 2000. "Proposition de localisation des ports antiques de Byblos (Liban)." *Méd* 1–2:101–4.
Fuchs, Andreas. 1994. *Die Inschriften Sargons II aus Khorsabad.* Göttingen: Cuvillier.
Gal, Zvi, and Yardenna Alexandre. 2000. *Horbat Rosh Zayit: An Iron Age Storage Fort and Village.* Jerusalem: Israel Antiquities Authority.
Gal, Zvi, and Rafael Frankel. 1993. "An Olive Oil Press Complex at Hurvat Rosh Zayit (Ras ez-Zetun) in Lower Galilee." *ZDPV* 109:128–40.
Garbini, Giuseppe. 1977. "I dialetti del Fenicio." *AION* 37:283–94.
———. 1979. "Fenici in Palestina." *AION* 39:325–30.
Gardiner, Alan H. 1916. "The Egyptian Origin of the Semitic Alphabet." *JEA* 3:1–16.
Gasull, Pepa. 1993. "El sistema ritual fenicio: Inhumación e incineración." *MadMit* 34:71–82.

Genz, Hermann. 2013. "'No Land Could Stand before Their Arms, from Ḫatti … on …'? New Light on the End of Hittite Empire and the Early Iron Age in Central Anatolia." Pages 469–78 in *The Philistines and Other "Sea Peoples" in Texts and Archaeology*. Edited by Ann Killbrew and Gunnar Lehmann. Atlanta: Society of Biblical Literature.

Genz, Hermann, and Hélène Sader. 2010. "Tell Hizzin: Digging Up New Material from an Old Excavation." *BAAL* 12:183–202.

Geva, Shulamit. 1982. "Archaeological Evidence for the Trade between Israel and Tyre?" *BASOR* 248:69–72.

Ghadban, Ch. 1998. "La nécropole d'époque perse de Magharat Tabloun à Sidon." Pages 147–49 in *Liban, L'autre Rive*. Edited by Valérie Matoïan. Paris: Institut du monde arabe.

Gibson, John Clark Love. 1982. *Phoenician Inscriptions*. Vol. 3 of *Textbook of Syrian Semitic Inscriptions*. Oxford: Clarendon.

Gilboa, Ayelet. 2005. "Sea Peoples and Phoenicians along the Southern Phoenician Coast: A Reconciliation; An Interpretation of Šikila (*SKL*) Material Culture." *BASOR* 337:47–78.

———. 2013. "The Southern Levant (Cisjordan) during the Iron Age I Period." Pages 624–48 in *The Oxford Handbook of the Archaeology of the Levant c. 8000–332 BCE*. Edited by Ann Killbrew and Margreet Steiner. Oxford. Oxford University Press.

———. 2015. "Dor and Egypt in the Early Iron Age: An Archaeological Perspective of (Part of) the Wenamun Report." *AeL* 25:247–74.

Gilboa, Ayelet, and Yuval Goren. 2015. "Early Iron Age Networks: An Optical Mineralogy Study of Phoenician Bichrome Ware and Related Wares in Cyprus." *AWE* 14:73–110.

Gilboa, Ayelet, Yiftah Shalev, Gunnar Lehmann, Hans Mommsen, Brice Erikson, Eleni Nodarou, and David Ben-Shlomo. 2017. "Cretan Pottery in the Levant in the Fifth and Fourth Centuries B.C.E. and Its Historical Implications." *AJA* 121:559–93.

Gilboa, Ayelet, and Ilan Sharon. 2001. "Early Iron Age Radiometric Dates from Tel Dor: Preliminary Implications for Phoenicia and Beyond." *Radiocarbon* 43:1343.

———. 2003. "An Archaeological Contribution to the Early Iron Age Chronological Debate: Alternative Chronologies for Phoenicia and Their Effects on the Levant, Cyprus, and Greece." *BASOR* 332:7–80.

———. 2008. "Between the Carmel and the Sea: Tel Dor's Iron Age Reconsidered." *NEA* 71:146–70.

Gilboa, Ayelet, Ilan Sharon, and Elizabeth Bloch-Smith. 2015. "Capital of Solomon's Fourth District? Israelite Dor." *Levant* 47:51–74.

Gilboa, Ayelet, Ilan Sharon, and Elisabetta Boaretto. 2008. "Tel Dor and the Chronology of Phoenician 'Pre-Colonisation' Stages." Pages 113–204 in *Beyond the Homeland: Markers in Phoenician Chronology*. Edited by Claudia Sagona. Leuven: Peeters.

Gilboa, Ayelet, Paula Waiman-Barak, and Richard Jones. 2015. "On the Origin of Iron Age Phoenician Ceramics at Kommos, Crete: Regional and Diachronic Perspectives across the Bronze Age to Iron Age Transition." *BASOR* 374:75–102.

Goedicke, Hans. 1975. *The Report of Wenamon*. Baltimore: Johns Hopkins University Press.

Goldman, Hans. 1963. *Excavations at Gözlü Kule, Tarsus III*. Princeton: Princeton University Press.

Goldwasser, Orly. 2010. "How the Alphabet Was Born from Hieroglyphs." *BAR* 36.2:40–53.

———. 2012. "The Miners Who Invented the Alphabet—A Response to Christopher Rollston." *JAEI* 4:9–22.

———. 2015. "The Invention of the Alphabet: On 'Lost Papyri' and the 'Egyptiamn Alphabet.'" Pages 124–41 in *Origins of the Alphabet: Proceedings of the First Polis Institute Interdisciplinary Conference*. Edited by Christophe Attucci and Claudia Roico. Newcastle-upon-Tyne, UK: Cambridge Scholars Publications.

Graesser, Carl F. 1972. "Standing Stones in Palestine." *BA* 35.2:33–63.

Graeve, Marie-Christine de. 1981. *The Ships of the Ancient Near East (c. 2000–500 BC)*. Leuven: Departement Oriëntalistiek.

Gras, Michel, Pierre Rouillard, and Javier Teixidor. 1989. *L'univers phénicien*. Paris: Arthaud.

Grayson, Albert Kirk. 1991. *Assyrian Rulers of the Early First Millennium BC, I (1114–859)*. RIMA 2. Toronto: University of Toronto Press.

———. 1996. *Assyrian Rulers of the Early First Millennium BC, II (858–745)*. RIMA 3. Toronto: University of Toronto Press.

Grayson, Albert Kirk, and Jamie R. Novotny. 2012. *The Royal Inscriptions of Sennacherib, King of Assyria (704–681 BC)*. RIMA 3/1. Winona Lake, IN: Eisenbrauns.

Grimal, Nicolas, and Martine Francis-Allouche. 2012. "Nouvelles recherches archéologiques à Byblos." *CRAI*: 279–302.

Gubel, Eric, ed. 1986. *Les Phéniciens et le monde méditerranéen*. Bruxelles: Générale de Banque.

———. 1987. *Phoenician Furniture: A Typology Based on Iron Age Representations with Reference to the Iconographical Context*. Leuven: Peeters.

———. 2018. "Desperately Seeking Kašpuna … Notes on the Historical Topography of the 'Akkar Plain.'" *Akkadica* 139:109–26.

Guigues, Paul-Émile. 1926. "Pointe de flèche en bronze à inscription phénicienne." *MUSJ* 11:323–28.

Hachmann, Rolf. 1983. *Frühe Phöniker im Libanon: 20 Jahre deutsche Ausgrabungen in Kamid el-Loz*. Mainz: von Zabern.

———. 1989. "Kāmid el-Lōz 1963–1981: German Excavations in Lebanon, Part I." *Berytus* 37:11–187.

Haggi, Arad. 2006. "Phoenician Atlit and Its Newly Excavated Harbour: A Reassessment." *Tel Aviv* 33:43–60.

Haggi, Arad, and Michal Artzy. 2007. "The Harbor of Atlit in Northern Canaanite/Phoenician Context." *NEA* 70:75–84.

Haidar, M. 2012. *Greek Pottery Coming from the British Museum Excavations (The College Site) in Sidon: Some Aspects of Greek Influences on the Phoenician Culture and Society through the Pottery Importation*. Rome: University of Rome La Sapienza.

Haines, Richard C. 1971. *The Structural Remains of the Later Phases: Chatal Hüyük, Tell al-Judahidah, and Tell Ta'yinat*. Vol. 2 of *Excavations in the Plain of Antioch*. Chicago: University of Chicago Press.

Halpern, Baruch. 2000. "The Canine Conundrum of Ashkelon: A Classical Connection?" Pages 133–44 in *The Archaeology of Jordan and Beyond: Essays in Honor of James A. Sauer*. Edited by Lawrence E. Stager, Joseph A. Greene, and Michael D. Coogan. Winona Lake, IN: Eisenbrauns.

———. 2008. "The Sea-Peoples and Identity." Pages 15–32 in *Cyprus, the Sea Peoples and the Eastern Mediterranean: Regional Perspectives of Continuity and Change*. Edited by Timothy P. Harrison. Toronto: Canadian Institute for Mediterranean Studies.

Hamdy Bey, Osman, and Théodore Reinach. 1892. *Une nécropole royale a Sidon*. Istanbul: Archaeology and Art Publications.

Hamilton, Robert. 1934. "Tell Abu Hawam: Interim Report." *Quarterly of the Department of Antiquities in Palestine* 3:74–80.

Harden, Donald. 1962. *The Phoenicians*. London: Thames and Hudson.

Harrison, Timothy P., ed. 2008. *Cyprus, the Sea Peoples and the Eastern Mediterranean: Regional Perspectives of Continuity and Change*. Toronto: Canadian Institute for Mediterranean Studies.

———. 2009. "Neo-Hittites in the 'Land of Palistin': Renewed Investigations at Tell Ta'yinat on the Plain of Antioch." *NEA* 72:174–89.

Hawkins, John David. 2000. *Inscriptions of the Iron Age*. Vol. 1 of *Corpus of Hieroglyphic Luwian Inscriptions*. Berlin: de Gruyter.

———. 2009. "Cilicia, the Amuq, and Aleppo: New Light in a Dark Age." *NEA* 72.4: 164–73.

Helck, Wolfgang. 1962. *Die Beziehungen Agyptens zu Vorderasien im 3. und 2. Jahrtausend v. Chr.* Wiesbaden: Harrassowitz.

———. 1994. "Byblos und Ägypten." Pages 105–12 in *Biblo: Una città e la sua cultura*. Edited by Enrico Acquaro et al. Roma: Consiglio Nazionale delle Ricerche.

Helzer, Michael. 1998. "On the Fifth Century BCE Dogs from Ashkelon." *Transeu* 15:149–52.

Herrmann, Georgina. 1992. *The Small Collections from Fort Shalmaneser*. London: British School of Archaeology in Iraq.

Herrmann, Georgina, and Stuart Laidlaw. 2015. *Syro-Phoenician Ivories at Nimrud*. Leiden: Brill.

Herrmann, Georgina, Stuart Laidlaw, and Helena Coffey. 2008. *Ivories from the North West Palace (1845–1992)*. IN 6. London: British Institute for the Study of Iraq.

Herzog, Ze'ev. 1989. "A Complex of Iron Age Winepresses (Strata XIVXIII)." Pages 73–75 in *Excavations at Tel Michal, Israel*. Edited by Ze'ev Herzog, George Robert Rapp, and Ora Negbi. Minneapolis: University of Minnesota Press.

Higginbotham, Carolyn R. 2000. *Egyptianization and Elite Emulation in Ramesside Palestine: Governance and Accommodation on the Imperial Periphery*. Leiden: Brill.

Hill, George Francis. 1910. *A Catalogue of the Greek Coins in the British Museum: Phoenicia*. London.

Hodder, Ian. 1991. *Reading the Past*. 2nd ed. Cambridge: Cambridge University Press.

Hodos, Tamar. 2006. *Local Responses to Colonization in the Iron Age Mediterranean*. London: Routledge.

Hoftijzer, Jacob, and Karen Jongeling. *Dictionary of the North-West Semitic Inscriptions*. 2 vols. Leiden: Brill, 1995.

Hölbl, Günther. 1989. "Ägyptische Kunstelemente im phönikischen Kulturkreis des 1. Jahrtausends v. Chr.: Zur Methodik ihrer Verwendung." *Or* 58:318–24.

Horn, Siegfried H. 1963. "Byblos in the Ancient Records." *AUSS* 1:52–61.

Horwitz, Liora K. 2000. "Animal Exploitation—Archaeozoological Analysis." Pages 221–32 in *Horbat Rosh Zayit: An Iron Age Storage Fort and*

*Village*. Edited by Zvi Gal and Yardenna Alexandre. Jerusalem: Israel Antiquities Authority.

———. 2002. "Archaeozoological Remains." Pages 395–401 in *Tel Kabri: The 1986–1993 Excavation Seasons*. By Aharon Kempinski. Tel Aviv: Emery and Claire Yass Publications in Archaeology.

Houghton, Arthur, Catharine C. Lorber, and Oliver D. Hoover. 2008. *Seleucid Coins, A Comprehensive Catalogue: Part 2, Seleucus IV through Antiochus XIII*. New York: American Numismatic Society.

Huehnergard, John. 1996. "New Directions in the Study of Semitic Languages." Pages 251–72 in *The Study of the Ancient Near East in the Twenty-First Century*. Edited by Jerrold S. Cooper and Glenn M. Schwartz. Winona Lake, IN: Eisenbrauns.

Humbert, J.-B. 1993. "Keisan, Tell." *NEAEHL* 3:862–67.

Hvidberg-Hansen, F. O. 1979. *La déesse TNT: Une étude sur la religion cananéo-punique*. Copenhagen.

Jabak, S., J. Sapin, J. Elayi, and H. Sayegh. 1998. "Les jarres et amphores du Locus 130." Pages 25–44 in *Un quartier du port phénicien de Beyrouth au Fer III/Perse: Les objets*. Edited by Josette Elayi and H. Sayegh. Paris: Gabalda.

Jablonka, P. 1997. "Stratigraphy and Architecture." *BAAL* 2:124–34.

Jean, Charles-François, and Jacob Hoftijzer. 1965. *Dictionnaire des inscriptions sémitiques de l'ouest*. Leiden: Brill.

Jericke, Detlef. 2010. *Regionaler Kult und Lokaler Kult: Studien zur Kult— und Religionsgeschchte Israels und Judah im 9. und 8. Jahrhundert v. Chr.* Wiesbaden: Harrassowitz.

Jessup, Henry Harris. 1910. *Fifty-Three Years in Syria II*. New York: Revell.

Jidejian, Nina. 1977. *Byblos through the Ages*. Rev. ed. Beirut: Dar al-Machreq.

Johns, C. N. 1933. "Excavations at Atlit (1930–31): The South-Eastern Cemetery." *QDAP* 2:41–104.

———. 1938. "Excavations at the Pilgrim's Castle, Atlit (1933): Cremated Burials of Phoenician Origin." *QDAP* 6:121–52.

Jones, Horace Leonard, trans. 1932. *The Geography of Strabo*. LCL. Cambridge: Harvard University Press.

Kahrstedt, Ulrich. 1926. *Syrische Territorien in hellenistischer Zeit*. Göttingen: Weidmannsche Buchhandlung.

Kamlah, Jens. 1999. "Zwei nordpalästinische 'Heiligtümer' der persischen Zeit und ihre epigraphischen Funde." *ZDPV* 115:163–90.

———. 2007. "Sakraler Baumund mythische Jagd: Zur Ikonographischen Verbindung zwischen zweier mythologischer Motive auf einem eisenzeitlichen Rollsiegel aus Phönizien." *BaM* 37:549–64.

———. 2016. "Südlich von Sidon: Forschungen zu regionalen Ressourcen einer phönizischen Hafenmetropole." *AW* 4:40–48.

Kamlah, Jens, and Hélène Sader. 2003. "The Tell el-Burak Archaeological Project: Preliminary Report on the 2002 and 2003 Seasons." *BAAL* 7:145–73.

———. 2010a. "Deutsch-libanesische Ausgrabungen auf Tell el-Burak südlich von Sidon Vorbericht nach Abschluss der siebten Kampagne 2010." *ZDPV* 126:93–115.

———. 2010b. "Tell el-Burak: A New Middle Bronze Age Site from Lebanon." *NEA* 73:130–41.

Kamlah, Jens, Hélène Sader, and Aaron Schmitt. 2016a. "The Tell el-Burak Archaeological Project: Preliminary Report on the 2011, 2013, and 2014 Seasons in Area 3." *BAAL* 16:79–130.

———. 2016b. "A Cultic Installation with a Standing Stone from the Phoenician Settlement at Tell el-Burak." *Berytus* 55:135–68.

———. Forthcoming. "The Tell el-Burak Archaeological Project: Preliminary Report on the 2015, 2017 and 2018 Excavation Seasons." *BAAL*.

Kaniewski, David, Etienne Paulissen, Elise Van Campo, Michel Al-Maqdissi, Joachim Bretschneider, and Karel Van Lerberghe. 2008. "Middle Coastal Ecosystem Response to Middle-to-Late Holocene Abrupt Climate Changes." *PNAS* 105.37: 13941–46.

Kaniewski, David, Etienne Paulissen, Elise Van Campo, Harvey Weiss, Thierry Otto, Joachim Bretschneider, and Karel Van Lerberghe. 2010. "Late Second–Early First Millennium BC Abrupt Climate Changes in Coastal Syria and Their Possible Significance for the History of the Ancient Mediterranean." *QR* 74:207–15.

Kaniewski, David, Elise Van Campo, Joël Guiot, Sabine le Burel, Thierry Otto, and Cecile Baeteman. 2013. "Environmental Roots of the Late Bronze Age Crisis." *PLoS ONE* 8(8): e71004. https://doi.org/10.1371/journal.pone.0071004.

Kaoukabani, Ibrahim. 1973. "Rapport préliminaire sur les fouilles de Kharayeb, 1969–1970." *BMB* 26:41–59.

———. 2005. "Les estampilles phéniciennes de Tyr." *AHL* 21:3–79.

Karageorghis, Vassos. 1976. *Kition: Mycenaean and Phoenician Discoveries in Cyprus*. London: Thames & Hudson.

———. 1983. *Palaepaphos-Skales: An Iron Age Cemetery in Cyprus*. Ausgrabungen in Alt-Paphos auf Zypern 3. Konstanz: Universitätsverlag.

———. 2002. *Early Cyprus: Crossroads of the Mediterranean*. Los Angeles: Getty Museum.

———. 2004. "The Terracottas from Urn 8." *BAAL* NS 1:414–16.

Karmon, Nira, and Ehud Spanier. 1987. "Archaeological Evidence of the Purple Dye Industry from Israel." Pages 147–58 in *The Royal Purple and the Biblical Blue: Argaman and Tekhelet*. Edited by Ehud Spanier. Jerusalem: Keter.

———. 1988. "Remains of Purple Dye Industry Found at Tel Shiqmona." *IEJ* 38:184–86.

Katzenstein, H. Jacob. 1973. *The History of Tyre*. Jerusalem: Schocken Institute for Jewish Research of the Jewish Theological Seminary of America.

———. 1979. "Tyre in the Early Persian Period (539–486 B.C.E.)." *BA* 42:23–34.

———. 1997. *The History of Tyre*. 2nd rev. ed. Jerusalem: Ben Gurion University of the Negev Press.

Kaufmann, Asher. 2014. *Reviving Phoenicia: In Search of Identity in Lebanon*. London: Tauris.

Keel, Othmar. 2009–2010. "The Scarabs." *Cuadernos de Arqueología Meditrránea* 19–20:233–37.

Keel, Othmar, and Christoph Uehlinger. 1992. *Göttinnen, Götter und Gottessymbole: Neue Erkenntnisse zur Religionsgeschichte Kanaans und Israels aufgrund bislang unerschlossener ikonographischer Quellen*. Freiburg: Herder.

Kessler, Karlheinz. 1975–1976. "Die Anzahl der assyrischen Provinzen des Jahres 738 v. Chr. in Nordsyrien." *DWO* 8:49–63.

Kestemont, Guy. 1983. "Tyr et les Assyriens." Pages 53–78 in *Redt Tyrus/ Sauvons Tyr: Histoire Phénicienne/Fenicische Geschiedenis*. Edited by Eric Gubel, Edward Lipiński, and Bridgette Servais-Soyez. StPhoe 1. Leuven: Peeters.

———. 1985. "Les Phéniciens en Syrie du Nord." Pages 135–61 in *Phoenicia and Its Neighbours*. Edited by Eric Gubel and Edouard Lipiński. Studia Phoenicia 3. Leuven: Peeters.

Khalifeh, Issam. 1988. *Sarepta II. The Late Bronze and Iron Age Periods of Area II, X*. Beirut: Lebanese University Publications.

Killebrew, Ann E. 2005. *Biblical Peoples and Ethnicity: An Archaeological Study of Egyptians, Canaanites, Philistines, and Early Israel 1300–1100 B.C.E.* Atlanta: Society of Biblical Literature.

———. 2018. "Reconstructing Phoenician Iron Production at Tell Akko, Israel." Paper presented at International Congress on the Archaeology of the Ancient Near East. April 6. Munich.

Killebrew, Ann E., and Gunnar Lehmann, eds. 2013. *The Philistines and Other "Sea Peoples" in Text and Archaeology*. Atlanta: Society of Biblical Literature.

Kinderlen, Moritz, et al. 2016. "Tripod Cauldrons Produced at Olympia Give Evidence for Trade with Copper from Faynan (Jordan) to South West Greece, c. 950–750 BCE." *JASR* 8:303–13.

Kislev, M. E. 1980. "Contenu d'un silo a blé de l'époque du ferancien." Pages 361–79 in *Tell Keisan (1971–1976): Une cité phénicienne en Galilée*. Edited by Jacques Briend and Jean-Baptiste Humbert. Fribourg: Éditions universitaires; Göttingen: Vandenhœck & Ruprecht; Paris: Gabalda.

Kislev, M. E., and Y. Melamed. 2000. "Ancient Infested Weed and Horsebean from Ḥorbat Rosh Zayit." Pages 206–20 in *Horbat Rosh Zayit: An Iron Age Storage Fort and Village*. Edited by Zvi Gal and Yardenna Alexandre. Jerusalem: Israel Antiquities Authority.

Kitchen, Kenneth A. 2000. *Ramesside Inscriptions Translated and Annotated, Notes and Comments*. London: Blackwell.

Klengel, Horst. 2000. "Qatna-ein historischer Überblick." *MDOG* 132:239–52.

Kletter, Raz. 1994. "Phoenician (?) Weights from Horvat Rosh Zayit." *Atiqot* 25:33–43.

———. 2000. "Phoenician Weights from Horbat Rosh Zayit." Pages 129–33 in *Horbat Rosh Zayit: An Iron Age Storage Fort and Village*. Edited by Zvi Gal and Yardenna Alexandre. Jerusalem: Israel Antiquities Authority.

Koehl, Robert B. 1985. *The Imported Bronze and Iron Age Wares from Area II, X*. Beirut: Université Libanaise.

Kourou, Nota. 2007. "Les Phéniciens en Mer Égée." Pages 136–39 in *La Méditerranée des Phéniciens: De Tyr à Carthage*. Paris: Institut du monde arabe.

———. 2009. "Phoenicia, Cyprus and the Aegean in the Early Iron Age: J. N. Coldstream's Contribution and the Current State of Research." Pages 33–51 in *E Galenotate kai e Eugenestate: E Benetia sten Kypro kai e Kypros ste Benetia; Proceedings of the symposium "La Serenissima" and "La Nobilissima": Venice in Cyprus and Cyprus in Venice*. Edited by Angel Nikolau-Konnare. Leukosia, Cyprus: Politistiko Idryma Trapezēs Kypru.

Krings, Véronique, ed. 1995. *La civilisation phénicienne et punique: Manuel de recherche*. Leiden: Brill.

Kukahn, E. 1955. *Anthropoide Sarkophage in Beyrouth und die Geschichte dieser sidonischen Sarkophagkunst*. Berlin: Mann.

Kuschke, A. 1977. "Sidons Hinterland und der Paß von Ǧezzin." *ZDPV* 93:178–97.

Lancel, Serge. 1992. *Carthage*. Paris: Fayard.

Lange, Matthias. 2012. "The Role of Some Stelae in Phoenician Burial Customs." Pages 281–90 in *(Re-)Constructing Funerary Rituals in the Ancient Near East: Proceedings of the First International Symposium of the Tübingen Post-Graduate School "Symbols of the Dead" in May 2009*. Edited by Herbert Niehr, Peter Pfälzner, and Ernst Pernicka. QSS 1. Wiesbaden: Harrassowitz.

Lebrun, René. 1987. "L'Anatolie et le Monde phénicien du Xe au IVe siècle Av. J.-C." Pages 23–33 in *Phoenicia and the East Mediterranean in the First Millennium B.C.* Edited by Edward Lipiński. StPhoe 5. Leuven: Peeters.

Leclant, Jean. 1968. "Les relations entre l'Egypte et la Phénicie du voyage d'Ounamon à l'expédition d'Alexandre." Pages 9–31 in *The Role of the Phoenicians in the Interaction of Mediterranean Civilizations*. Edited by William A. Ward. Beirut: American University of Beirut.

Lehmann, Gunnar. 1996. *Untersuchungen zur späten Eisenzeit in Syrien und Libanon*. Münster: Ugarit-Verlag.

———. 1998. "Trends in the Local Pottery Development of the Late Iron Age and Persian Period in Syria and Lebanon, ca. 700 to 300 BC." *BASOR* 311:7–37.

———. 2013. "Aegean Style Pottery in Syria and Lebanon during Iron Age I." Pages 265–328 in *The Philistines and Other "Sea Peoples" in Text and Archaeology*. Edited by Ann E. Killbrew and Gunnar Lehmann. Atlanta: Society of Biblical Literature.

Lehmann, Reinhard G. 2005. *Die Inschrift(en) des Ahīrōm-Sarkophags und die Schachtinschrift des Grabes V in Jbeil (Byblos)*. DRBZ 1.2. Mainz: von Zabern.

Lehmann-Jericke, K. 2004. "The Terracotta Horseman." *BAAL* NS 1:417–19.

Leichty, Erle. 2011. *The Royal Inscriptions of Esarhaddon, King of Assyria (680–669 BC)*. RINAP 4. Winona Lake, IN: Eisenbrauns.

Le Lasseur, Denyse. 1922. "Mission archéologique à Tyr." *Syria* 3:1–26, 116–33.

Lemaire, André. 1976. "Milkiram, nouveau roi phénicien de Tyr?" *Syria* 53:85–93.

———. 1980. "Notes d'épigraphie nord-ouest sémitique." *Sem* 30:17–19.

———. 1981. *Les écoles et la formation de la Bible dans l'ancien Israël.* OBO 39. Fribourg: Universitätsverlag; Göttingen: Vandenhoeck & Ruprecht.

———. 1983. "L'inscription phénicienne de Hassan-Beyli reconsidérée." *RSF* 11:9–19.

———. 1991a. "Le royaume de Tyr dans la second moitié du VIe siècle av. J.C." Pages 131–50 in *Atti del II Congresso Internazionale di Studi Fenici e Punici: Roma, 9–14 novembre 1987.* Rome: Consiglio nazionale delle ricerche.

———. 1991b. "Asher et le royaume de Tyr." Pages 135–52 in *Phoenicia and the Bible.* Edited by Edward Lipiński. StPhoe 11. Leuven: Peeters.

———. 1991c. "Hazaël de Damas, roi d'Aram." Pages 91–108 in *Marchands, diplomates et empereurs: Études sur la civilization mésopotamienne.* Edited by Dominique Charpin and Francis Joannès. Paris: Éditions Recherche sur les Civilisations.

———. 1994. "Histoire et administration de la palestine à l'époque perse." Pages 11–53 in *La Palestine à l'époque perse.* Edited by Ernest-Marie Laperousaz and André Lemaire. Paris: Cerf.

———. 2000. "Phénicien et Philistien: Paléographie et dialectologie." Pages 243–49 in vol. 1 of *Actas del IV Congreso Internacional de Estudios Fenicios y Punicos.* Cadiz: Università degli Studi di Palermo, Facoltà di Lettere e Filosifia.

———. 2001. "Phoenician Funerary Stelae in the Hecht Museum Collection." *Mishmanim* 15:7–23.

———. 2006. "La datation des rois de Byblos Abibaal et Élibaal et les relations entre l'Égypte et le Levant au X$^e$ siècle av. notre ère." *CRAI*: 1697–1716.

———. 2012. "West Semitic Epigraphy and the History of the Levant during the Twelfth–Tenth Centuries BCE." Pages 291–307 in *The Ancient Near East in the Twelfth–Tenth Centuries BCE.* Edited by Gershon Galil et al. Münster: Ugarit-Verlag.

———. 2013a. "Levantine Epigraphy and Phoenicia: The Kingdoms of Aradus, Byblos, Sidon and Tyre during the Achaemenid Period."

Pages in 1–36 *The Schweich Lectures of the British Academy*. Oxford: Oxford University Press.

———. 2013b. "Ozibaal de Byblos? (XI$^e$ s. av. n. è.)." Pages 289–96 in *Ritual, Religion and Reason: Studies in the Ancient World in Honour of Paolo Xella*. Edited by Oswald Loretz et al. Münster: Ugarit-Verlag.

———. 2014. "Trône à kéroubs avec inscription phénicienne." Pages 127–45 in *Phéniciens d'Orient et d'Occident: Mélanges Josette Elayi*. Edited by André Lemaire, Bertrand Dufour, and Fabian Pfitzmann. Paris: Maisonneuve.

———. 2017. "Alphabetic Writing in the Mediterranean World: Transmission and Appropriation." Pages 103–15 in *Cultural Contact and Appropriation in the Axial-Age Mediterranean World*. Edited by Baruch Halpern and Kenneth Sacks. CHANE 86. Leiden: Brill.

Lembke, Katja. 1998. "Les sarcophages phéniciens." Pages 143–45 in *Liban, l'autre Rive*. Edited by Valérie Matoïan. Paris: Institut du monde arabe.

———. 2001. *Phönizische anthropoide Sarkophage*. Mainz: von Zabern.

Le Meaux, Hélène. 2007. "Le monde grec." Pages 281–82 in *La Méditerranée des Phéniciens: De Tyr à Carthage*. Paris: Institut du monde arabe.

Lernau, Omri. 2000. "Fish Bones." Pages 233–37 in *Horbat Rosh Zayit: An Iron Age Storage Fort and Village*. Edited by Zvi Gal and Yardenna Alexandre. Jerusalem: Israel Antiquities Authority.

Levy, Thomas Evan. 2010. *Historical Biblical Archaeology and the Future: The New Pragmatism*. New York: Routledge.

Levy, Thomas Evan, Erez Ben-Yosef, and Mohammad Najjar. 2012. "New Perspectives on Iron Age Copper Production and Society in the Faynan Region, Jordan." Pages 197–214 in *Eastern Mediterranean Metallurgy and Metalwork in the Second Millennium BC: A Conference in Honor of James D. Muhly*. Edited by Vasiliki Kassianidou and George Papasavvas. Oxford: Oxbow.

Lidzbarski, Mark. 1915. *Ephemeris für semitische Epigraphik III*. Giesen: Ricker.

Linseele, Veerle. 2010. "Etude faunique sur le site de Tell Tweini." Pages 153–60 in *Tell Tweini: Onze campagnes de fouilles syro-belges (1999–2010)*. Edited by Michel al-Maqdissi, Karel van Lerberghe, Joachim Bretschneider, and Massoud Badawi. Damas: Ministère de la Culture: Direction Générale des Antiquités et des Musées.

Lipiński, Édouard. 1983. "Notes d'épigraphie phénicienne et punique." *Orientalia Lovaniensia Periodica* 14:129–65.

———. 1985. "Phoenicians in Anatolia and Assyria Ninth–Sixth Centuries B.C." *OLP* 16:81–90.

———. 1991. "The Territory of Tyre and the Tribe of Asher." Pages 153–66 in *Phoenicia and the Bible*. Edited by Edward Lipiński. StPhoe 11. Leuven: Peeters.

———. 1995. *Dieux et déesses de l'univers phénicien et punique*. Leuven: Peeters.

———. 2004. *Itineraria Phoenicia*. Leuven: Peeters.

———. 2009. "Wares Ordered from Ben-Harash at Akko." *ErIsr* 29:105–10.

Lipiński, Edward, and Wolfgang Röllig. 1992. "Phénicie." Pages 348–51 in *Dictionnaire de la civilisation phénicienne et punique*. Edited by Edward Lipiński. Paris: Brepols.

Liverani, Mario. 1991. "The Trade Network of Tyre according to Ezek. 27." Pages 65–79 in *Ah, Assyria ... Studies in Assyrian History and Ancient Near Eastern Historiography Presented to Hayim Tadmor*. ScrHier 33. Jerusalem: Magnes.

Lohwasser, Angelika. 2002. "Eine Phönizische Bronzeschale aus dem Sudan." *AeL* 12:221–34.

Lopriano, Antonio. 2005. "Ein neues äagyptisches Inschriften-Fragment aus Sidon." Pages 271–72 in *Das Eschmun-Heiligtum von Sidon: Architektur und Inschriften*. Edited by Rolf A. Stucky. Basel: Vereinigung der Freunde antiker Kunst.

Lund, John. 1986. *Sukas VIII: The Habitation Quarters*. Copenhagen: Munksgaard.

Macridy Bey, Theodor. 1904. "A travers les nécropoles sidoniennes." *RB* 13:547–72.

Maeir, Aren M. 2002. "The Relations between Egypt and the Southern Levant during the Late Iron Age: The Material Evidence from Egypt." *AeL* 12:235–46.

Maïla-Afeiche, Anne-Marie. 2009. "Le Site de Nahr el-Kab." *BAAL* NS 5:11–17.

Mainberger, Martin. 2001. "The 'Seven Captains' Reef—An Archaeological Underwater Survey off the Coast of Tell el-Burak." *BAAL* 5:191–93.

Malbrant-Labat, Florence. 1991. "Les textes accadiens: Lettres." Pages 27–66 in *Une bibliothèque au sud de la ville*. Edited by Pierre Bordreuil. RS 7. Paris: Éditions Recherches sur les Civilisations.

Marcus, Ezra. 2007. "Amenemhet and the Sea Maritime Aspects of the Mit Rahina (Memphis) Inscription." *AeL* 17:137–90.

Mark, Samuel. 2008. "The Earliest Naval Ram." *The International Journal of Nautical Archaeology* 37:253–72.
Margueron, Jean-Claude. 1994. "L'urbanisme de Byblos: certitudes et problèmes." Pages 13–36 in *Biblo: Una città e la sua cultura*. Edited by Enrico Acquaro et al. Rome: Consiglio Nazionale delle Ricerche.
Markoe, Glenn E. 1985. *Phoenician Bronze and Silver Bowls from Cyprus, with Stamped Decoration and the Mediterranean*. Berkeley: University of California Press.
———. 2000. *Phoenicians*. London: British Museum Press.
Marriner, Nick, Christophe Morhange, Ysabeau Rycx, Marcelle Boudagher-Fadel, Michel Bourcier, Pierre Carbonel, J.-P. Goiran, and Germaine Noujaim-Clark. 2005a. "Holocene Coastal Dynamics along the Tyrian Peninsula: Palaeogeography of the Northern Harbour." *BAAL* NS 2:61–90.
Marriner, Nick, Christophe Morhange, Marcelle Boudagher-Fadel, Michel Bourcier, and Pierre Carbonel. 2005b. "Geoarchaeology of Tyre's Ancient Northern Harbour, Phoenicia." *JArSci* 32:1302–27.
Marriner, Nick, Christophe Morhange, and Nicolas Carayon. 2008. "Ancient Tyre and Its Harbours: 5000 Years of Human-Environment Interactions." *JarSci* 35:1281–1310.
Marriner, Nick, Christophe Morhange, and Claude Doumet-Serhal. 2006. "Geoarchaeology of Sidon's Ancient Harbours, Phoenicia." *JArSci* 33:1514–35.
Marti, Lionel. 2014. "Deux têtes coupées en cinq mois: La prise de Sidon par Assarhaddon." Pages 13–30 in *Phéniciens d'Orient et d'Occident: Mélanges Josette Elayi*. Edited by André Lemaire. Paris: Maisonneuve.
Martin, Robert. 2016. "The Development of Canaanite and Phoenician Style Maritime Transport Containers and Their Role in Reconstructing Maritime Exchange Networks." Pages 111–28 in *Maritime Transport Containers in the Bronze-Iron Age Aegean and Eastern Mediterranean*. Edited by Stella Demesticha and A. Bernard Knapp. Uppsala: Aströms Förlag.
———. 2017. *The Art of Contact: Comparative Approaches to Greek and Phoenician Art*. Philadelphia: University of Philadelphia Press.
Marzoli, Dirce. 2012. "Neugründungen im phönizischen Westen, los Castillejos de Alcorrín, Morro de Mezquitilla und Mogador." *AA* 2:29–64.
Masson, Olivier, and Maurice Sznycer. 1972. *Recherches sur les Phéniciens à Chypre*. Geneva: Droz.

Mathys, H.-P. 2005. "Die phonizischen inschriften." Pages 273–318 in *Das Eschmun-Heiligtum von Sidon: Architektur und Inschriften*. Edited by Rolf A. Stucky. Basel: Vereinigung der Freunde antiker Kunst.

Matoïan, Valérie, ed. 1998. *Liban, L'autre Rive*. Paris: Institut du monde arabe.

Matthiae, Paolo. 2013. *Studies on the Archaeology of Ebla 1980–2010*. Wiesbaden: Harrassowitz.

Mazar, Amihai. 1985. *The Philistine Sanctuary: Various Finds, the Pottery, Conclusions, Appendixes*. Part 2 of *Excavations at Tell Qasile*. Jerusalem: Institute of Archaeology, Hebrew University of Jerusalem.

———. 1992. *Archaeology of the Land of the Bible, 10,000–586 B.C.E.* New York: Doubleday.

Mazar, Eliat. 2001. *The Phoenicians in Akhziv: The Southern Cemetery; Jerome L. Joss Expedition; Final Report of the Excavations 1988–1990*. CAM 7. Barcelona: Bellaterra.

———. 2004. *The Phoenician Family Tomb Nr. 1 at the Northern Cemetery of Achziv (Tenth–Sixth Centuries BCE)*. CAM 10. Barcelona: Bellaterra.

———. 2009–2010. *The Northern Cemetery of Akhziv (Tenth–Sixth Centuries BCE): The Tophet Site*. 2 vols. CAM 19–20. Barcelona: Bellaterra.

McGovern, Patrick, Stuart Fleming, and Solomon Katz, eds. 1996. *The Origins and Ancient History of Wine*. London: Routledge.

Mettinger, Tryggve N. D. 1995. *No Graven Image? Israelite Aniconism in Its Ancient Near Eastern Context*. Stockholm: Almqvist & Wiksell.

Metzger, Martin. 2004. "Two Architectural Models in Terracotta." *BAAL* NS 1:420–36.

Miller, Robert. 1986. "Elephants, Ivory, and Charcoal: An Ecological Perspective." *BASOR* 264:29–43.

Monchambert, Jean-Yves. 2011. "Yanouh, un site dans l'arrière-pays montagneux de Byblos." *LT* 15:15.

Monchambert, Jean-Yves, J. Bargman, J. Beaudouz, A. Cuny, and Eric Morvillez. 2010. "Une campagne de sondages sur le tell Kharayeb à Yanouh (Printemps 2006)." *BAAL* NS 12:35–147.

Montero, Mabel. 2014. Analysis of Fauna Remains. Pages 479–85 in *The Phoenician Cemetery of Tyre-Al Bass II Archaeological Seasons 2002–2005*. Edited by María Eugenia Aubet, Francisco J. Núñez, and Laura Trellisó. Beirut: Ministère de la Culture, Direction Générale des Antiquités.

Moran, William L. 1987. *The Amarna Letters*. Baltimore: Johns Hopkins University Press.

Morhange, Christophe. 1998–1999. "Etude géomorphologique du littoral de Byblos: Résultats de la mission de terrain de 1998." *BAAL* 3:261–65.

———. 2005. "Le littoral de Tyr: Un patrimoine archéologique et naturel à sauvegarder." *BAAL* NS 2:129–31.

Morhange, Christophe, Olivier Dubuquoy, Nicolas Prunet, Jacques-Louis de Beauliu, Michel Bourcier, Pierre Carbonel, Christine Oberlin, and Honor Frost. 2000. "Nouvelles données paléoenvironnementales sur le port antique de Sidon: Proposition de datation." *NMN* 10:42–48.

Morhange, Christophe, Kathia Espic, Marcelle Boudagher-Fadel, and Claude L. Doubet-Serhal. 2005. "Les paléoenvironnements du port nord de Sidon: Tentative de synthèse." *BAAL* NS 2:135–46.

Morstadt, Bärbel. 2008. *Phönizische Thymiateria: Zeugnisse des Orienbtalisierungsprozesses im Mittelmeerraum; Originale Funde, bildliche Quellen, originaler Kontext*. Münster: Ugarit-Verlag.

———. 2015. *Die Phönizier*. Darmstadt: von Zabern.

Mosca, Paul G., and James Russel. 1987. "A Phoenician Inscription from Cebel Ires Daği in Rough Cilicia." *EpAn* 9:1–28.

Moscati, Sabatino, ed. 1988. *I Fenici*. Milan: Bompiani.

Moulins, Dominque de. 2015. "Plant Remains from Middle Bronze Age to Iron Age: Samples of the College Site, Sidon." *AHL* 42:32–54.

"Mount Carmel." N.d. Britannica.com. https://tinyurl.com/SBL1724b.

Mouterde, René. 1932. *Le Nahr el Kelb, guide archéologique*. Beirut: Imprimerie Catholique.

Mura, Barbara. 2015. "La necropoli fenicia di Khaldé (Beirut, Libano): Analisi della documentazione inedita degli scavi di Roger Saidah, campagne del 1961 e 1962." PhD diss., Universitat Pompeu Fabra.

Nashef, Khaked. 1982. *Die Orts—und Gewässernamen der mittelbabylonischen und mittelassyrischen Zeit*. RGTC 5. Wiesbaden: Reichert.

National Geographic. 2004. *The Quest for the Phoenicians*. Documentary.

Naveh, Joseph. 1982. *Early History of the Alphabet*. Leiden: Brill.

Negueruela, Iván. 2005 "Coagmenta punicana e bagli: La costruzione navale a fasciame portante tra i Fenici del VIIe s. a.C." Pages 22–41 in *mare, uomini e merci nel Mediterraneo antico: Atti del Convegno Internazionale, Genova, 9–10 dicembre 2004*. Edited by B. M. Giannattasio, C. Canepa, L. Grasso, and E. Piccardi. Firenze: All'insegna del giglio.

Negueruela, Iván, J. Pinedo, M. Gómez, A. Miñano, I. Arellano, and J. S. Barba. 1995. "Seventh-Century Phoenician Vessel Discovered at Playa de la Isla, Mazarron, Spain." *IJNA* 24.3:189–97.

Nibbi, Alessandra. 1986. "Phoenician from 'Carpenter' like *fnh(w)*?: A New Approach to an Old Problem." *DE* 6:11–20.

Niehr, Herbert. 1998. *Religionen in Israels Umwelt*. Würzburg: Echter.

———. 2003. *Ba'alšamem: Studien zu Herkunft, Geschichte und Rezeptionsgeschichte eines phönizischen Gottes*. Leuven: Peeters.

Nitschke, Jessica, S. Rebecca Martin, and Yiftah Shalev. 2011. "Between Carmel and the Sea: The Late Periods." *NEA* 74:132–54.

Noureddine, Ibrahim, and Michel El-Hélou. 2005. "Tyre's Ancient Harbor(s): Report of the 2001 Underwater Survey in Tyre's Northern Harbor." *BAAL* NS 2:111–28.

Novotny, Jamie R. 2016. "Inscriptions of Ashurbanipal." In *The Royal Inscriptions of Ashurbanipal, Aššur-etel-ilāni, and Sîn-šarra-iškun*. RINAP 5. http://oracc.museum.upenn.edu/rinap/rinap5/.

Nuñez, Francisco J. 2004. "Preliminary Report on Ceramics." *BAAL* NS 1:281–373.

———. 2014. "The Ceramic Repertoire." *BAAL* NS 9:261–372.

Nunn, Astrid. 2014. "Attic Pottery Imports and Their Impact on 'Identity Discourses': A Reassessment." Pages 391–428 in *A "Religious Revolution" in Yehûd? The Material Culture of the Persian Period as a Test Case*. Edited by Christian Frevel. OBO 267. Fribourg: Academic Press.

Oggiano, Ida. 2018. "Collecting *disiecta membra*: What Did the Cult Place of Kharayeb Look Like?" Pages 17–36 in *Cercando con zelo di conoscere la Storia Fenicia*. Edited by Giuseppe Garbati. CSF 47. Rome: CNR.

Orendi, Andrea. 2016. "Agricultural Resources of the Phoenician Settlement at Tell el-Burak: A Preliminary Report on the Archaeobotanical Investigations." *BAAL* 16:123–30.

Orendi, Andrea, and Katleen Deckers. 2018. "Agricultural Resources on the Coastal Plain of Sidon during the Late Iron Age: Archaeobotanical Investigations at Phoenician Tell el-Burak, Lebanon." *VHA* 27:717–36.

Orsingher, Adriano. 2018. "Ritualized Faces: The Masks of the Phoenicians." Pages 263–303 in *The Physicality of the Other: Masks from the Ancient Near East and the Eastern Mediterranean*. Edited by Angelika Berlejung and Judith Filitz. Tübingen: Mohr Siebeck.

Pardee, Dennis. 2015. "The Katumuwa Inscription." Pages 45–48 in *In Remembrance of Me: Feasting with the Dead in the Ancient Near East*.

Edited by Virgina Herrmann and J. David Schloen. Chicago: Oriental Institute of the University of Chicago.

Parpola, Simo, and Kazuko Watanabe. 1988. "Esarhaddon's Treaty with Baal, King of Tyre." Pages 24–27 in *Neo-Assyrian Treaties and Loyalty Oaths*. SAA 2. Helsinki: Helsinki University Press.

Parrot, André, Maurice Chéhab, and Sabatino Moscati. 1975. *Les Phéniciens, l'expansion phénicienne, Carthage*. Paris: L'Univers des Formes.

Peckham, Brian. 2014. *Phoenicia: Episodes and Anecdotes from the Ancient Mediterranean*. Winona Lake, IN: Eisenbrauns.

Petrie, William Matthew Flinders. 2009. *Researches in Sinai: Ancient Egypt and Palestine*. Electronic ed. London: Routledge.

Pettinato, Giovanni. 1983. "Le città fenicie e Byblos in particolare nella documentazione epigrafica di Ebla." Pages 107–18 in *Atti del Primo Congresso Internazionale di Studi Fenici e Punici*. Edited by Piero Bartoloni et al. Collezione di Studi Fenici 16. Rome: Consiglio nazionale delle ricerche.

Pfeiffer, Robert H. 1935. *State Letters of Assyria: A Translation and Transliteration of 355 Official Assyrian Letters Dating from the Sargonid Period (722–625 B.C.)*. New Haven: American Oriental Society.

Poidebard, Antoine. 1939. *Tyr, un grand port disparu*. Paris: Geuthner.

Poidebard, Antoine, and Jean Lauffray. 1951. *Sidon, aménagements antiques du port de Saïda, étude aérienne, au sol et sous-marine (1946–1950)*. Beirut: Ministère des travaux publics.

Porada, Edith. 1978. "The Cylinder Seal." Pages 77–82 in Patricia Bikai, *The Pottery of Tyre*. Warminster: Aris & Phillips.

Prausnitz, Moshe W. 1982. "Die Nekropolen von Akhziv und die Entwicklung der Keramik vom 10. Bis zum 7. Jh. V. Chr. in Akhziv, Samaria und Ashdod." Pages 31–44 in *Phönizier im Westen*. Edited by Hans Georg Niemeyer. Madrider Beiträge 8. Mainz: von Zabern.

———. 1993. "Achzib." *NEAEHL* 1:32–35.

Pritchard, James B. 1954. *The Ancient Near East in Pictures Relating to the Old Testament*. Princeton: Princeton University Press.

———. 1964. *Winery, Defenses, and Soundings at Gibeon*. Philadelphia: University Museum, University of Pennsylvania.

———, ed. 1969. *Ancient Near Eastern Texts Relating to the Old Testament*. 3rd rev. ed. Princeton: Princeton University Press.

———. 1975. *Sarepta: A Preliminary Report on the Iron Age*. Philadelphia: University Museum, University of Pennsylvania.

———. 1978. *Recovering Sarepta: A Phoenician City*. Princeton: Princeton University Press.

———. 1982. "The Tanit Inscription from Sarepta." Pages 83–92 in *Phönizier im Westen*. Edited by Hans Georg Niemeyer. MadBeit 8. Mainz: von Zabern.

———. 1988. *Sarepta IV: The Objects from Area II, X*. Beirut: Lebanese University Publications.

Puech, Émile. 1994. "Un cratère phénicien inscrit: Rites et croyances." *Transeu* 8:47–74.

Pulak, Cemal. 1998. "The Uluburun Shipwreck: An Overview." *IJNA* 27:188–224.

Quinn, Josephine. 2018. *In Search of the Phoenicians*. Princeton: Princeton University Press.

Quinn, Josephine, Neil McLynn, Robert M. Kerr, and Daniel Hadas. 2014. "Augustine's Canaanites." *PBSR* 82:175–97.

Raban-Gerstel, Noa, Irit Zohar, Guy Bar-Oz, Ilan Sharon, and Ayelet Gilboa. 2008. "Early Iron Age Dor (Israel): A Faunal Perspective." *BASOR* 349:25–59.

Reese, David. 1987. "Palaikastro Shells and Bronze Age Purple-Dye Production in the Mediterranean Basin." *ABSA* 82:201–6.

———. 2010. "Shells from Sarepta (Lebanon) and East Mediterranean Purple-Dye Production." *MAA* 10:113–41.

Rehm, Ellen. 2004. *Der Ahiram-Sarkophag*. DRBZ 1.1. Mainz: von Zabern.

Renan, Ernest. 1864. *Mission de Phénicie*. Paris: Imprimerie impériale.

Renfrew, Colin, and Paul Bahn. 2004. *Archaeology: Theories, Methods and Practice*. London: Thames & Hudson.

Rey-Coquais, Jean-Paul. 1974. *Arados et sa pérée aux époques grecque, romaine et byzantine: Recueil des témoignages littéraires anciens, suivi de recherches sur les sites, l'histoire, la civilisation*. Paris: Geuthner.

———. 1982. "Inscriptions grecques inédites découvertes par Roger Saidah." Pages 394–408 in *Archéologie au Levant: Recueil publié à la mémoire de Roger Saidah*. Lyon: Maison de l'Orient Méditerranéen.

Reyes, A. T. 1994. *Archaic Cyprus: A Study of the Textual and Archaeological Evidence*. Oxford: Clarendon.

Ribichini, Sergio. 2004. "Sui riti funerari fenici e punici: Tra Archeologia e storia delle religioni." Pages 43–75 in *El mundo funerario: Actas del III Seminario Internacional sobre Temas Fenicios; Guardamar del Sigura, 3–5 mayo de 2002; homenaje al Prof. D. Manuel Pellicer Catalán*. Edited by Alfredo González Prats. Alicante: Universidad de Alicante.

Riehl, Simone, and Katleen Deckers. 2009. "The Botanical Finds." *BAAL* 13:110–16.

Riis, P. J. 1948. *Hama: Fouilles et recherches de la fondation Carlsberg 1931–1938; Les cimetières à cremation*. Vol. 2.3. Copenhagen: Nationalmuseet.

———. 1961–1962. "L'activité de la Mission archéologique danoise sur la côte phénicienne en 1960." *AAAS* 11–12:133–44.

———. 1979. *The Graeco-Phoenician Cemetery and Sanctuary at the Southern Harbor*. Copenhagen: Nationalmuseet.

Robin, Christian. 1990. "Première mention de Tyr chez les Minéens d'Arabie du Sud." *Sem* 39:135–47.

Röllig, Wolfgang. 1983a. "On the Origin of the Phoenicians." *Berytus* 31:79–93.

———. 1983b. "The Phoenician Language: Remarks on the Present State of Research." Pages 375–85 in vol. 2 of *Atti del I Congresso Internazionale di Studi Fenici e Punici: Roma, 5–10 novembre 1979*. Rome: Consiglio Nazionale delle Ricerche.

———. 1992. "Die phönizische Sprache." Pages 76–94 in *Karthago*. Edited by Werner Huss. WF 654. Darmstadt: Wissenschaftliche Buchgesellschaft.

———. 1999. "The Phoenician Inscriptions." Pages 50–81 in vol. 2 of *Karatepe-Aslantaş, Corpus of Hieroglyphic Luwian Inscriptions*. Edited by Halet Çambel. Berlin: de Gruyter.

———. 2013. "Die phönikische Inschrift der Reliefstele von Ivriz, Turkei." Pages 311–20 in *Ritual, Religion and Reason: Studies in the Ancient World in Honour of Paolo Xella*. Edited by Oswald Loret, Wilfred G. E. Watson, and José Á. Xamora. Münster.

Rovira, N. 2014. "Les grains et les fruits." *BAAL* NS 9:487–501.

Sader, Hélène. 1990. "An Epigraphic Note on a Phoenician Inscription from Tell Kazel." *Berytus* 38:94–98.

———. 1991. "Phoenician Stelae from Tyre." *Berytus* 39:101–26.

———. 1995. "Nécropoles et tombes phéniciennes du Liban." *CAM* 1:15–33.

———. 1997. "Tell el Burak: An Unidentified City of Phoenician Sidon." Pages 363–77 in *Ana shadî Labnani lū allik: Beiträge zur altorientalischen und mittlemeerischen Kulturen; Festschrift für Wolfgang Röllig*. Edited by Beate Ponkratz-Leisten, Hartmut Kühne, and Paola Xella. VBBK. Neukirchen-Vluyn: Neukirchner Verlag.

———. 2000a. "Le territoire des villes phéniciennes: Reliefs accidentés, modèles unifies." Pages 227–61 in *Fenicios y territorio*. Edited by Alfredo González Prats. Alicante: Instituto Alicantino de Cultura Juan Gil-Albert.

———. 2000b. "Une pointe de flèche phénicienne inédite du Musée National de Beyrouth." Pages 271–79 in vol. 1 of *Actas del IV Congreso Internacional de Estudios Fenicios y Punicos*. Cadiz: Università degli Studi di Palermo, Facoltà di Lettere e Filosifia.

———. 2000c. "La 'route de la mer' en Phénicie." Pages 67–85 in *Les routes du Proche-Orient: Des séjours d'Abraham aux caravanes de l'encens*. Edited by André. Lemaire. Paris: Le Monde de la Bible-Desclée de Brouwer.

———. 2001. "Lebanon's Heritage: Will the Past Be Part of the Future?" Pages 217–31 in *Crisis and Memory in Islamic Societies*. Edited by Angelika Neuwirth and Andreas Pflitsch. BeirTS 77. Würzburg: Ergon Verlag.

———. 2005. *Iron Age Funerary Stelae from Lebanon*. CAM 11. Barcelona: Publicaciones del Laboratorio de Arqueología de la Universidad Pompeu Fabra de Barcelona.

———. 2010. "The Aramaeans of Syria: Some Considerations on Their Origin and Material Culture." Pages 257–84 in *The Books of Kings: Sources, Composition, Historiography and Reception*. Edited by André Lemaire, Baruch Halpern, and Matthew J. Adams. VTSup 129. Leiden: Brill.

———. 2014a. "The Stelae." *BAAL* NS 9:373–80.

———. 2014b. "Trois poids phéniciens inédits de la Collection de la Direction Générale des Antiquités du Liban." Pages 37–50 in *Bible et Orient: Mélanges André Lemaire*. Edited by Josette Elayi and Jean-Marie Durand. SupTranseu 46. Paris: Gabalda.

———. 2015. "Intertwined History: Lebanon's Role in the Transmission of Egyptian Culture to Inland Syria in the Middle Bronze Age." Pages 117–26 in *Qatna and the Networks of Bronze Age Globalism: Proceedings of an International Conference in Stuttgart and Tübingen in October 2009*. Edited by Peter Pfälzner and Michel al-Maqdisi. Wiesbaden: Harrassowitz.

———. 2016. "A Phoenician 'Incense Altar' from Tell el-Burak, Lebanon." *RSF* 44:61–66.

———. 2017a. "The Assyrian Empire and Phoenicia's Cultural Resistance." *RSF* 65:37–48.

———. 2017b. "Inscriptions phéniciennes inédites du Liban." Pages 1–8 in *Proceedings of the Seventh International Congress of Phoenician and Punic Studies*. Tunis: Institut National du Patrimoine.

———. Forthcoming. "The History of Phoenician Epigraphic Discoveries in the Lebanon." *Studi Epigrafici e Linguistici*.

———. N.d. "Orthosia." In *Dizionario Enciclopedico dell Civiltà Fenica*. decf-cnr.org. Accessed April 17, 2019.

Saggs, Henry W. F. 1955. "The Nimrud Letters, 1952: Part II." *Iraq* 17:126–60.

———. 2001. *The Nimrud Letters 1952*. London: Oxbow.

Saidah, Roger. 1966. "Fouilles de Khaldé: Rapport préliminaire sur la première et deuxième campagne." *BMB* 19:51–90.

———. 1967. "Chronique." *BMB* 20:155–80.

———. 1969. "Archaeology in the Lebanon 1968–1969." *Berytus* 18:119–42.

———. 1971. "Objets grecs géométriques découverts récemment sur le littoral libanais (à Khaldé près de Beyrouth)." *AAAS* 21:193–98.

———. 1977. "Une tombe de l'Âge du Fer à Tambourit (région de Sidon)." *Berytus* 25:135–46.

———. 1979. "Les fouilles de Sidon-Dakerman: L'agglomération chalcolithique." *Berytus* 27:29–55.

———. 1983. "Nouveaux éléments de datation de la céramique de l'âge du Fer au Levant." Pages 213–16 in vol. 1 of *Atti del I Congresso Internazionale di Studi Fenici e Punici: Roma, 5–10 novembre 1979*. Rome: Consiglio Nazionale delle Ricerche.

Saliby, Nassib. 1970–1971. "Hypogée de la nécropole de 'Azar." *MUSJ* 46:271–83.

———. 1989. "Amrith." Pages 19–30 in *Archéologie et Histoire de la Syrie II: La Syrie de l'époque achéménide à l'avènement de l'islam*. Edited by Jean-Marie Dentzer and Winfried Orthmann. Saarbrücken: Saarbrücker und Verlag.

Salles, Jean-François. 1980. *La Nécropole "K" de Byblos*. Paris: Editions ADPF.

———. 1994. "La mort à Byblos: Les nécropoles." Pages 49–71 in *Biblo: Una città e la sua cultura*. Edited by Enrico Acquaro et al. Rome: Consiglio nazionale delle ricerche.

Salskov Roberts, Helle. 2015. *The Attic Pottery and Commentary on the Greek Inscriptions Found on Tall Sūkās*. PCEP. Copenhagen: Det Kongelige danske videnskabernes selskab.

Sapin, J. 1989. "Les transformations d'un domaine de la couronne dans la trouée de Homs (Syrie) de Tiglat-Pileser III à Auguste." *Transeu* 1:21–54.

Sapir-Hen, Lidar. 2011. "Dog Burials at Dor." *NEA* 74.3: 132–54.

Sapir-Hen, Lidar, Guy Bar-Oz, Ilan Sharon, Ayelet Gilboa, and Tamar Dayan. 2014. "Food, Economy, and Culture at Tel Dor, Israel: A Diachronic Study of Faunal Remains from 15 Centuries of Occupation." *BASOR* 371:83–101.

Sass, Benjamin, and Christoph Uehlinger, eds. 1993. *Studies in the Iconography of Northwest Semitic Inscribed Seals*. OBO 125. Fribourg: Universitätsverlag; Göttingen: Vandenhoeck & Ruprecht.

Sartre, Maurice. 2001. *D'Alexandre à Zénobie: Histoire du Levant antique, IVe siècle avant J.-C.-IIIe siècle après J.-C*. Paris: Fayard.

Sass, Benjamin. 2002. "Wenamun and His Levant—1075 BC or 925 BC?" *AeL* 12:247–55.

Satzinger, Helut. 2002. "Syllabic and Alphabetic Script, or the Egyptian Origin of the Alphabet." *Aegyptus* 82:15–26.

Scandone, Matthiae Gabriella. 1994. "La cultura egiziana a Biblo attraverso le testimonianze materiali." Pages 37–48 in *Biblo: Una città e la sua cultura*. Edited by Enrico Acquaro et al. Rome: Consiglio Nazionale delle Ricerche.

Schmitt, Aaron, Kamal Badreshany, Evgenia Tachatou, and Hélène Sader. 2019. "Insights into the Economic Organization of the Phoenician Homeland: A Multidisciplinary Investigation of the Later Iron Age II and Persian Period Phoenician Amphorae from Tell el-Burak. *Levant* 51:1–39.

Schmitz, Philip C. 2014. "Phoenician Seal Script." Pages 141–74 in *"An Eye for Form": Epigraphic Essays in Honor of Frank Moore Cross*. Edited by Jo Ann Hackett and Walter E. Aufrecht. Winona Lake, IN: Eisenbrauns.

Schreiber, Nicola. 2003. *The Cypro-Phoenician Pottery of the Iron Age*. CHANE 13. Leiden: Brill.

Seeden, Helga. 1991. "A *Tophet* in Tyre?" *Berytus* 39:39–82.

Seif, A. 2012. "Nouvelle découverte de tombes à Dakerman." Pages 79–82 in *Fascination du Liban: Soixante siècles d'histoire, de religions, d'art et d'archéologie*. Geneva: Skira.

Shanklin, W., and M. Ghantus. 1966. "A Preliminary Report on the Anthropology of the Phoenicians." *BMB* 19:91–94.

Sharon, Ilan. 1987. "Phoenician and Greek Ashlar Construction Techniques at Tel Dor, Israel." *BASOR* 267:21–42.

——. 2013. "Levantine Chronology." Pages 44–68 in *The Oxford Handbook of the Archaeology of the Levant c. 8000–332 BCE*. Edited by Ann E. Killbrew and Magreet Steiner. Oxford: Oxford University Press.

Sharon, Ilan, and Ayelet Gilboa. 2013. "The SKL Town: Dor in the Early Iron Age." Pages 393–468 in *The Philistines and Other "Sea Peoples" in Texts and Archaeology*. Edited by Ann E. Killbrew and Guunar Lehmann. Atlanta: Society of Biblical Literature.

Shipley, Graham. 2011. *Pseudo-Skylax's "Periplous": The Circumnavigation of the Inhabited World; Text, Translation and Commentary*. Croydon: Bristol Phoenix.

Singer-Avitz, Lily. 2010. "A Group of Ceramic Vessels from Tel Beersheba." *Tel Aviv* 37:188–99.

Sollberger, Edmond. 1959–1960. "Byblos sous les rois d'Ur." *AfO* 19:120–22.

Sommer, Michael. 2008. *Die Phönizier: Geschichte und Kultur*. München: Beck.

Spanò Giammellaro, Antonella. 1999. "The Phoenicians and the Carthaginians." Pages 55–65 in *Food: A Culinary History from Antiquity to the Present*. Edited by Jean Louis Flandrin and Massimo Montanari. New York: Columbia University Press.

Stager, Lawrence. 1991. "Why Were Hundreds of Dogs Buried at Ashkelon?" *BAR* 17.3:26–42.

——. 2003. "Phoenician Shipwrecks in the Deep Sea." Pages 233–48 in *Sea Routes: From Sidon to Huelva; Interconnections in the Mediterranean Sixteenth–Sixth c. BC*. Edited by Nikolaos C. Stampolidis and V. Karagheorgis. Athens: Museum of Cycladic Art.

Stager, Lawrence E., Daniel M. Master, and J. David Schloen. 2011. *Ashkelon 3: The Seventh Century B.C.* Winona Lake, IN: Eisenbrauns.

Stampolidis, Nikolaos C., and V. Karagheorgis, eds. 2003. *Sea Routes: From Sidon to Huelva; Interconnections in the Mediterranean Sixteenth–Sixth c. BC*. Athens: Museum of Cycladic Art.

Starcky, Jean. 1969. "Une inscription phénicienne de Byblos." *MUSJ* 45:257–73.

——. 1982. "La flèche de Zakarba'al Roi d'Amurru." Pages 179–86 in *Archéologie au Levant: Recueil Roger Saidah*. Lyon: Maison de l'Orient.

Starr, Ivan. 1990. *Queries to the Sungod: Divination and Politics in Sargonid Assyria*. SAA 4. Helsinki: Helsinki University Press.

Stefaniuk, Lise, Christophe Morhange, Muntaha Saghieh-Beydoun, Honor Frost, Marcelle K. BouDagher-Fadel, Michel Bourcier, and Germaine Noujaim-Clark. 2005. "Localisation et etude paléoenvironnementale des ports antiques de Byblos." *BAAL* NS 2:19–44.

Stern, Ephraim. 1990. "New Evidence from Dor for the First Appearance of the Phoenicians along the Northern Coast of Israel." *BASOR* 279:27–34.

———. 2000. *Dor: Ruler of the Seas; Nineteen Years of Excavations at the Israelite-Phoenician Harbor Town on the Carmel Coast.* Jerusalem: Israel Exploration Society.

———. 2015. "Iron Age I–II Phoenician Pottery." Pages 435–82 in *The Ancient Pottery of Israel and Its Neighbors: From the Iron Age through the Hellenistic Period II.* Edited by Seymour Gitin. Jerusalem: Israel Exploration Society.

Stewart, Andrew, and S. Rebecca Martin. 2005. "Attic Imported Pottery at Tel Dor, Israel: An Overview." *BASOR* 337: 79–94.

Stuart, Barbara. 2001–2002. "Cemeteries in Beirut." *Aram* 13/14:87–112.

Stucky, Rolf A. 1993. *Die Skulpturen aus dem Eschmun-Heiligtum bei Sidon: Grieschiche, römische, kyprische und phönizische Statuen und Reliefs vom 6. Jahrhundert vor Chr. bis zum 3. Jahrhundert nach Chr.* Basel: Vereinigung der Freunde Antiker Kunst.

———. 2005. *Das Eschmun-Heiligtum von Sidon: Architektur und Inschriften.* Basel: Vereinigung der Freunde antiker Kunst.

———. 2007. "Lesstridacnes à décor gravé." Pages 218–23 in *La Méditerranée des Phéniciens: De Tyr à Carthage.* Paris: Institut du monde arabe.

———. 2012. "Du marbre grec en Phénicie: Grandeur et décadence de Sidon aux époques perse et hellénistique." *CRAI*: 1177–1203.

Suleiman, Antoine, and Massoud al-Maqdissi. 2016. "Tell Iris (Lattakia)." Pages 171–73 in *A History of Syria in One Hundred Sites.* Edited by Youssef Kanjou and Akira Tsuneki. Oxford: Archaeopress.

Suriano, Matthew J. 2013. "Historical Geography of the Ancient Levant." Pages 9–23 in *The Oxford Handbook of the Archaeology of the Levant c. 8000–332 BCE.* Edited by Ann E. Killbrew and Margreet Steiner. Oxford: Oxford University Press.

Sznycer, Maurice. 1994. "Les inscriptions 'pseudo-hiéroglyphiques' de Byblos." Pages 167–78 in *Biblo: Una città e la sua cultura.* Edited by Enrico Acquaro et al. Rome: Consiglio Nazionale delle Ricerche.

Tadmor, Hayim. 1994. *The Inscriptions of Tiglath-Pileser III King of Assyria*. Jerusalem: Israel Academy of Sciences and Humanities.

Taraqji, Ahmed Ferzat. 1999. "Nouvelles découvertes sur les relations avec l'Egypte à Tel Sakka et à Keswé, dans la région de Damas." *BSFE* 144:27–43.

Teixidor, Javier. 1975. "Selected Inscriptions." Pages 96–104 in *Sarepta: A Preliminary Report on the Iron Age*. Edited by James B. Pritchard. Philadelphia: University Museum, University of Pennsylvania.

———. 1979. "La fonction de *rab* et de suffète en Phénicie." *Sem* 29:9–17.

———. 1982. "Deux inscriptions phéniciennes de Sidon." Pages 233–36 in *Archéologie au Levant: Recueil Roger Saidah*. Lyon: Maison de l'Orient.

———. 1986. *Bulletin d'épigraphie sémitique (1964–1980)*. Paris: Geuthner.

Tekoğlu, Recai, and André Lemaire. 2000. *La bilingue royale louvito-phénicienne de Çineköy*. Paris: CRAIBL.

Thalmann, Jean-Paul. 1978a. "Tell 'Arqa 1978–1979: Rapport proviso ire." *BMB* 30:61–75.

———. 1978b. "Tell 'Arqa (Liban nord): Campagnes I–III (1972–1974): Chantier I: Rapport préliminaire." *Syria* 55:1–151.

———. 1990. "Byblos." Pages 99–104 in *Naissance des Cités*. Edited by Jean-Louis Huot, Jean-Paul Thalmann, and Dominque Valbelle. Paris: Nathan.

———. 1998. "Deux sanctuaires phéniciens: Arqa et Sarepta." Page 132 in *Liban, l'autre rive: Exposition présentée à l'Institut du monde arabe du 27 octobre 1998 au 2 mai 1999*. Edited by Valérie Matoian. Paris: Flammarion.

———. 2000. "Tell Arqa." *BAAL* 4:5–74.

———. 2006. *Tell Arqa-1: Les niveaux de l'âge du bronze*. BAH 177. Beirut: Institut français d'archéologie du Proche Orient.

Thompson, Christine, and Sheldon Skaggs. 2013. "King Solomon's Silver? Southern Phoenician Hacksilber Hoards and the Location of Tarshish." *IA* 35. https://doi.org/10.11141/ia.35.6.

Thureau-Dangin, François, Augustin-Georges Barrois Dossin, and Maurice Dunand. 1931. *Arslan-Tash*. 2 vols. Paris.

Thureau-Dangin, François, and Maurice Dunand. 1936. *Til Barsip*. Paris: Geuthner.

Tropper, Josef. 2001. "Entstehung und Frühgeschichte des Alphabets." *AW* 32:353–58.

Tusa, Vincenzo. 1982. "La presenza fenicio-punica in Sicilia." Pages 95–108 in *Phönizier im Westen*. Edited by Hans G. Niemeyer. Mainz: von Zabern.

Unger, Eckhard. 1926. "Nabuchadnesar II. und sein *Šandabakku* (Oberkommissar) in Tyrus." *ZAW* 44:314–17.

———. 1931. *Babylon: Die heilige Stadt nach der Beschreibung der Babylonier*. Berlin: de Gruyter.

University of Cambridge, Research News. 2017. "Genetic Study Suggests Present-Day Lebanese Descend from Biblical Canaanites." July 27. http://www.cam.ac.uk/research/news/genetic-study-suggests-present-day-lebanese-descend-from-biblical-canaanites.

Vaelske, Veit, and Michael Bode. 2018–2019. "Early Iron Age Copper Trails: First Results of a Pilot Study at Sidon." *AHL* 48–49:130–33.

Vanel, Antoine. 1967. "Six ostraca pheniciens trouvés au temple d'Echmoun, près de Saïda." *BMB* 20:46–95.

———. 1969. "Le septième ostracon phénicien trouvé au temple d'Echmoun, près de Saïda." *MUSJ* 45:345–66.

Van Neer, Wim, Omri Lernau, Renée Friedman, Gregory Mumford, Jeoroen Poblome, and Marc Waelkens. 2004. "Fish Remains from Archaeological Sites as Indicators of Former Trade Connections in the Eastern Mediterranean." *Paléorient* 30:101–47.

Veldhuijzen, Xander. 2003. "'Slag Fun'—A New Tool for Archaeometallurgy: Development of an Analytical (P)ED-XRF Method for Iron-Rich Materials. *Papers from the Institute of Archaeology* 14:102–18.

Veldhuijzen, Xander, and Th. Rehren. 2006. "Iron Smelting Slag Formation at Tell Hammeh (az-Zarqa), Jordan." Pages 245–50 in *Thirty-Fourth International Symposium on Archaeometry 3–7 May 2004*. Zaragoza, Spain: Institución "Fernando el Católico."

Veldhuijzen, Xander, and Eveline van der Steen. 1999. "Iron Production Center Found in the Jordan Valley." *NEA* 62:195–99.

Venturi, Fabrizio. 2000. "Le premier âge du Fer à Tell Afis et en Syrie Septentrionale." Pages 505–36 in *Essays on Syria in the Iron Age*. Edited by Guy Bunnens. ANESSup 7. Leuven: Peeters.

———. 2005. "Area E4b sud: Bronzo Tardo II–Ferro I." Pages 69–75 in *Tell Afis, Syria 2002–2004*. Pisa: ETS.

Vidal, Jordi. 2008. "The Men of Arwad, Mercenaries of the Sea." *BO* 65:6–16.

Volney, Constantin-François. 1787. *Voyage en Egypte et en Syrie*. Paris: Dugour et Durand.

Waiman-Barak, Paula, and Ayelet Gilboa. 2016. "Maritime Transport Containers: The View from Phoenician Tell Keisan (Israel) in the Early Iron Age." Pages 169–93 in *Maritime Transport Containers in the Bronze–Iron Age Aegean and Eastern Mediterranean*. Edited by Stella Demesticha and A. Bernard Knapp. Uppsala: Aströms Förlag.

Waiman-Barak, Paula, Ayelet Gilboa, and Yuval Goren 2014. "A Stratified Sequence of Early Iron Age Egyptian Ceramics at Tel Dor, Israel." *AeL* 24:317–41.

Waliszewski, Tomasz, et al. 2002. *Chhim. 2000 ans d'histoire au coeur d'un village antique du Liban*. Beirut: Centre polonais d'archéologie méditerranéenne, Varsovie-Direction Générale des Antiquités.

Waliszewski, Tomasz, et al. 2015. "Preliminary Report on the 2012 and 2013 Excavation Seasons at Jiyeh (Porphyreon): Work in Sector D (Residential Quarter)." *PAM* 24:453–74.

Walsh, Carey Ellen. 2000. *The Fruit of Vine: Viticulture in Ancient Israel*. Winona Lake, IN: Eisenbrauns.

Walsh, Carey Ellen, and Jeffrey Zorn. 1998. "New Insights from Old Wine Presses." *PEQ* 130:154–61.

Ward, William A. 1991. "The Scarabs, Scaraboid and Amulet-Plaque from Tyrian Cinerary Urns." *Berytus* 39:89–100.

Wartke, Ralf-Bernhard. 2005. *Samʾal: Ein aramäischer Stadtstaat des 10. bis 8. Jhs. v. Chr. und die Geschichte seiner Erforschung*. Mainz: von Zabern.

Waterfield, Robin. 1998. *Herodotus: The Histories*. Oxford: Oxford University Press.

Weidner, Ernst. 1939. "Jojachin, König von Judah, in babylonischen Keilschrifttexten." Pages 923–35 in vol. 2 of *Mélanges Syriens offerts à Monsieur René Dussaud*. Paris: Geuthner.

Wein, Erwin J., and Ruth Opificius. 1963. *7000 Jahre Byblos*. Nuremberg: Carl.

Weissbach, Franz Heinrich. 1922. *Die Denkmäler und Inschriften an der Mündung des Nahr-el-Kelb*. Berlin: de Gruyter.

Wightman, G. J. 2008. *Sacred Spaces: Religious Architecture in the Ancient World*. Leuven: Peeters.

Wiseman, Donald J. 1953. *The Alalakh Tablets*. London: British Institute of Archaeology at Ankara.

Woolmer, Mark. 2012. "'Ornamental' Horns on Phoenician Warships." *Levant* 44:238–52.

———. 2017. *A Short History of the Phoenicians*. London: Tauris.

———. Forthcoming. "Phoenician Communities in Fourth Century Athens."

Xella, Paolo. 1990. "Divinités doubles' dans le monde phénico-punique." *Semítica* 39:167–75.

———. 1995. "Ugarit et les Phéniciens: Identité culturelle et rapports historiques." Pages 239–66 in *Ugarit: Ein ostmediterranes Kulturzentrum im Alten Orient; Ergebnisse und Perspektiven der Forschung*. Edited by Manfried Dietrich and Oswald Loretz. Münster: Ugarit-Verlag.

———. 2017. "Phoenician Inscriptions in Palestine." Pages 153–70 in *Sprachen in Palästina im 2. Und 1. Jahrtausen v. Chr*. Edited by Ulrich Hübner and Herbert Niehr. Wiesbaden: Harrassowitz.

Xella, Paolo, and José-Ángel Zamora. 2004. "Une nouvelle inscription de Bodashtart, roi de Sidon, sur la rive du Nahr el-Awwali près de Bustan eš-Šeḫ." *BAAL* 8:273–300.

Xella, Paolo, José-Ángel Zamora, Maria Giulla Amadasi-Guzzo, Ida Oggiano, and Hélène Sader. 2005. "Prospection épigraphique et archéologique dans la région du Nahr el-Awwali (Saida/Sidon)." *BAAL* 9:269–90.

Yadin, Yigael, Yohanan Aharoni, Ruth Amiran, Trude Dothan, Immanuel Dunayevsky, and Jean Perrot. 1958. *Hazor II: An Account of the Second Excavations, 1956*. Jerusalem: Hebrew University of Jerusalem, Magnes Press.

Yakubovich, Ilya. 2015. "Phoenician and Luwian in Early Iron Age Cilicia." *AnSt* 65:35–53.

Yamada, Shigeo. 2000. *The Construction of the Assyrian Empire*. Leiden: Brill.

Yardeni, Ada. 1994. "Maritime Trade and Royal Accountancy in an Erased Customs Account from 475 B.C.E. on the Ahiqar Scroll from Elephantine." *BASOR* 293:67–78.

Yon, Marguerite. 2006. *The City of Ugarit at Tell Ras Shamra*. Winona Lake, IN: Eisenbrauns.

Yon, Marguerite, and Annie Caubet. 1993. "Aroud et Amrith. VIIIe-Ier siècles av. J.-C." *Transeu* 6:47–66.

Younger, K. Lawson, Jr. 2016. *A Political History of the Arameans: From Their Origins to the End of Their Polities*. ABS 13. Atlanta: SBL Press.

Zamora, José Á. 2008. "Epigrafía e historia fenicias: Las inscripciones reales de Sidón." Pages 211–28 in *Las culturas del Próximo Oriente Antiguo y su expansión mediterránea: Textos y materiales de los cursos de postgrado del CSIC en el Instituto de Estudios Islámicos y del Oriente

*Próximo (2003–2005).* Edited by Josué J. Justel, Juan Pablo Vita, and Jose Ángel Zamora. Zaragoza: Instituto de Estudios Islámicos y del Oriente Próximo.

Zernecke, Anna. 2013. "The Lady of the Titles: The Lady of Byblos and the Search for Her 'True Name.'" *DWO* 43:226–42.

Zwickel, Wolfgang. Forthcoming. "Pnuel." *Encycopedia of the Bible and Its Reception.*

# Ancient Sources Index

Hebrew Bible/Old Testament

Numbers
- 34:1–5 — 2

Joshua
- 11:8 — 92
- 14:28 — 92

1 Kings
- 4–11 — 6
- 5:2 — 13
- 5:24–25 — 128
- 5:25 — 277
- 7:13–14 — 306
- 9:10–14 — 263
- 9:11 — 120
- 9:11–14 — 277
- 9:26–28 — 256, 263
- 10:11 — 263
- 10:18 — 265
- 10:22 — 263
- 16:31 — 128, 263
- 16:32 — 263
- 22:39 — 264

2 Kings
- 10:26–27 — 263
- 25:22 — 135

Isaiah
- 23:2 — 253
- 23:8 — 253

Ezekiel
- 27 — 12, 72, 249
- 27:20–22 — 271
- 27:27 — 145
- 27:33 — 250
- 28:4 — 252

Hosea
- 14:7 — 290

2 Chronicles
- 8:17–18 — 263
- 9:10 — 263
- 9:21 — 263

Classical Sources

Arrian, *Anabasis*
- 2.13.7–8 — 58, 70
- 2.15.6 — 86
- 2.16–24 — 137
- 2.20.9–10 — 116
- 2.24 — 145
- 2.24.3–5 — 137

Diodorus Siculus, *Bibliotheca historica*
- 14.41.1 — 96
- 14.45.1–6 — 113
- 14.45.2 — 145

Herodotus, *Histories*
- — 27
- 1.1.1–2 — 251
- 2.44 — 100, 122, 189
- 2.112 — 136, 272
- 4.2 — 272

*Herodotus, Histories (cont.)*
| | |
|---|---|
| 4.42 | 103 |
| 5.58 | 151, 269 |
| 7.98 | 58, 69 |
| 8.67–68 | 108 |
| 8.98 | 108 |

Homer, *Iliad* — 1
| | |
|---|---|
| 23.65 | 176 |

Homer, *Odyssey* — 1
| | |
|---|---|
| 15.415 | 256 |
| 15.455 | 254 |
| 15.459 | 251 |

Josephus, *Contra Apionem* — 262
| | |
|---|---|
| 1.111 | 127 |
| 1.113 | 115 |
| 1.121–125 | 128 |
| 1.125 | 129 |
| 1.156–159 | 134 |
| 8.55 | 127 |

Josephus, *Jewish Antiquities* — 262
| | |
|---|---|
| 8.5.3 | 27 |
| 8.324 | 77, 82 |

Pliny the Elder, *Naturalis historia*
| | |
|---|---|
| 5.19 | 8 |

Ptolemy, *Geographia*
| | |
|---|---|
| 5.14.3 | 8 |

Strabo, *Geographica*
| | |
|---|---|
| 16.2.12 | 59 |

# Personal Names Index

## People

Abbalos 134
Abdaeos 134
'Abdalonim 23
Abdalonymos 114
Abdamun 109, 114
'Abd'aštart of Arwad (Straton) 72
Abd'aštart of Tyre 137–38
'Abd'aštart I (= Straton I) 114
'Abd'aštart II (= Straton II) 114
Abdastratos 138
Abdelimos 134
'Abdi-'Aširta 75
Abdi-Li'ti 67, 71
Abdi-Milkūti 93–94, 101, 102, 121, 131, 145
'Abdisis 72
Abibaal 35, 69, 81, 82, 86, 138, 212
Abī-Ba'al. See Abibaal
Abimilku 91, 98, 114, 119, 124–25
Achilles 251
Adad-nērārī III 66, 99, 129, 131
Adad Yašma' 98
Addūmu 98
Adonbaal 135
Adūnī-Ba'al 57, 69
Adunu-ba'al. See Adūnī-Ba'al
Agbalos. See Azi-Ba'al
Agbalus. See Azi-Ba'al
Ahab 57, 100, 128–29, 263–64
Ahiram 35, 82, 86, 142–43, 152, 234–35, 241
Ahirom 81
Akbar 138

Akhenaten 124
Alexander the Great 2, 23, 58, 70–71, 86, 103, 107, 111, 114–16, 120–21, 137, 145, 226–28
Amanappa 75
Amenhotep III 124, 297
Amoashtart 114
Anni-Wa 98
Anysus 70, 108, 114
Apries 103
Arrian 59, 65, 137, 145
Artaxerxes II 109, 113, 136
Aššurbanipal 55, 57, 67–69, 83, 132–33
Aššur-bēl-kala 65
Aššurnaṣirpal II 56, 65, 76, 82, 99, 126
Astharymos 138
'Augustine 2
Aynel 85–86
Azemilcus 137
'Azi-Ba'al 69–70
Azitawadda 261
Baal I (= Ba'alu) 131–33, 138, 142, 183, 185, 212, 216, 253–54
Baal II 134–35, 138
Baalazor I 129
Baalazor II 129
Ba'ali-Manzēri 120, 129
Baalshillem I 109
Baalshillem II 91, 96, 108, 109–10, 114, 207
Ba'alu (= Baal I) 94, 121, 131–33
Balatoros 134–35
Balazor 138
Balbazer. See Baalazor I
Baleazoros 138

| | | | |
|---|---|---|---|
| Balezor. *See* Baalazor II | 129 | Iakinlû | 55, 57, 67–69 |
| Balezoros | 138 | Iakīn-Lû. *See* Iakinlû | |
| Baʻlu (= Baal I) | 77, 83, 101–2 | Ikausu | 132 |
| Baʻna | 109, 114, 207 | Ikkalû. *See* Iakinlû | |
| Baslechos | 134 | Ikkilu. *See* Iakinlû | |
| Batnoam | 85, 216, 217, 228, 234 | Imtu | 98 |
| Bodʻaštart | 87, 91, 96, 10–8, 114, 143–44, 197–98 | Ithobalos. *See* Ittobaal III | |
| | | Itti-Šamaš-Balaṭu | 68 |
| Cadmus | 151–52 | Ittobaal I | 23, 35, 77, 81–82, 86, 105, 114, 128–29, 138, 263 |
| Cambyses | 136 | | |
| Chelbes | 134, 138 | Ittobaal II | 129–30, 138 |
| Cyrus | 134, 136 | Ittobaal III | 130, 134, 138 |
| David | 28, 36, 127, 263 | Jehu | 129 |
| Diodorus Siculus | 103 | Jezebel | 128, 263 |
| Ednibalos | 134 | Joash | 129 |
| Eiromos | 134 | Josephus | 28, 115, 125–26 |
| Eknibal | 138 | Justin | 125, 137 |
| Elibaal | 35, 81–82, 86, 212 | Khnumhotep III | 80 |
| Elissa | 129, 309 | Kilamuwa | 261, 262 |
| Elpaal | 85–86 | Lulî | 92, 100, 101, 105, 130, 138, 161, 189, 267, 309 |
| Esarhaddon | 57, 67–69, 76–77, 83, 87, 91, 93–94, 101–2, 121, 131–32, 142, 144–45, 183, 185, 212, 253–54, 267 | | |
| | | Maharbaal | 72, 138 |
| | | Manasseh | 132 |
| Eshmunazar I | 104, 106–7, 114, 143 | Matar | 213 |
| Eshmunazar II | 6, 58, 87, 91, 96, 105–7, 114, 143–44, 220, 236 | Matinu-baʻal (= Mattan-Baal I) | 57 |
| | | Mattan I | 129, 138 |
| Ethbaal I | 100 | Mattan II | 129–30, 138 |
| Eusebius of Caesarea | 182 | Mattan III | 136, 138 |
| Evagoras I | 136 | Mattan-Baal I | 65, 67 |
| Evagoras II | 114 | Matten | 70 |
| Gerʻaštart | 58, 70, 71, 72, 134, 138 | Mazday | 112 |
| Gerastartos. *See* Gerʻaštart | | Mekmer | 138 |
| Gerostratus. *See* Gerʻaštart | | Menahem | 130 |
| Hakoris | 103, 109 | Menander of Ephesus | 27, 77, 126, 262 |
| Hazael | 66, 82, 120, 129 | Menon | 58 |
| Herodotus | 4, 65, 152, 155, 187, 203 | Merbalos | 70, 134 |
| Hiram I | 13, 28, 36, 115, 119, 121, 126–28, 138, 142, 144, 203, 253, 256, 262, 263, 270, 277, 306 | Merbalus. *See* Merbalos | |
| | | Merenptah | 33 |
| | | Metenna. *See* Mattan II | |
| Hiram II | 3, 100, 104, 128, 130, 138, 267 | Methusastartus | 128, 138 |
| Hiram III | 23, 136, 138 | Milki-ašapa | 83, 86, 132 |
| Hiram IV | 138 | Milkiram | 130, 138 |
| Hirom | 23 | Mitinti | 132 |
| Homer | 3, 104, 251, 269, 306 | Mugallu | 55, 67 |
| Hophra. *See* Apries | | Muṣurī | 132 |

# PERSONAL NAMES INDEX

| | |
|---|---|
| Mutallu | 261 |
| Muwaharna | 261 |
| Myttynos | 134 |
| Na'areshmun | 72 |
| Nabû-šarru-uṣur | 68 |
| Nebuchadnezzar II | 13–14, 84, 103, 133–35, 144, 259 |
| Neco | 84, 103, 272 |
| Nergal-šar-uṣur. *See* Neriglissar | |
| Neriglissar | 135 |
| Nikokles | 112 |
| Omri | 129 |
| Osorkon I | 36, 81, 212, 272 |
| Osorkon II | 272 |
| 'Ozbaal | 34, 85–86 |
| 'Ozzimilk | 121, 137–38 |
| Palṭibaal | 85 |
| Phelles | 128, 138 |
| Philip I | 152 |
| Philo | 3, 106, 182–83, 213 |
| Pliny the Elder | 4, 180, 297–98, 300 |
| Psammetic I | 84, 103, 272 |
| Psammetic II | 103 |
| Pseudo-Scylax | 5, 7, 58, 65, 94, 121, 265 |
| Pumiyaton. *See* Pygmalion | |
| Pygmalion | 129–30, 138 |
| Qa'uš-gabri | 132 |
| Qurdi-Aššur-lamur | 126 |
| Ramesses III | 33 |
| Ramesses IV | 47 |
| Rezin | 130 |
| Rib-Adda | 75, 76, 80, 123, 124, 277 |
| Sadok-Re | 91 |
| Salamis | 58, 69, 84, 108, 136, 267 |
| Šalmaneser III | 56, 65–67, 82, 99, 126, 128–29 |
| Šalmaneser V | 92, 100 |
| Šamši-Adad V | 99 |
| Sanchuniaton | 182, 213 |
| Sanda-šarme | 55, 67 |
| Sanda-uarri | 101–2 |
| Sanduarri. *See* Sanda-uarri | |
| Sargon II | 13, 100, 259, 264, 309 |
| Sarmakaddmis | 261 |
| Sennacherib | 67, 83–84, 91–92, 94, 100–101, 121, 130–31, 161, 189, 309–10 |
| Sen-nefer | 74 |
| Seti I | 41, 123–25 |
| Shalmaneser III | 115, 120 |
| Sheshonq I | 35, 81, 212, 272 |
| Shipitbaal I | 81, 86 |
| Shipitbaal II | 83, 86, 130 |
| Shipitbaal III | 84–86 |
| Ṣil-Bēl | 132 |
| Siromus | 70 |
| Solomon | 6, 28, 36, 119, 121, 12–28, 144, 253, 256, 262–64, 277, 306 |
| Strabo | 4, 59, 65, 308 |
| Straton of Arwad ('Abd'ashtart) | 70–71 |
| Straton I (= 'Abd'aštart I) | 58, 70–71, 109–12, 213 |
| Straton II (= 'Abd'aštart II) | 111 |
| Straton Philhellene. *See* Straton I | |
| Tabnit | 104, 106, 114, 143, 176, 226–27, 229 |
| Taharqa | 102, 131, 212, 216 |
| Tawosret | 40, 99 |
| Tennes | 112–14, 145 |
| Tetramnestus | 70, 108–9, 114 |
| Thucydides | 108 |
| Thutmosis III | 64, 74, 90 |
| Thutmosis IV | 90 |
| Tiglath-pileser I | 34, 65, 80, 99, 126 |
| Tiglath-pileser III | 57, 67, 79, 83, 100, 129–30 |
| Tuba'il. *See* Ittobaal II | |
| Tu-Ba'lu (= Ittobaal III) | 67, 100, 130, 131 |
| Tushratta | 297 |
| Urikki | 261 |
| Urimilk I | 86 |
| Urimilk II | 84–86 |
| Urimilk III | 85–86 |
| Urkatel | 253 |
| Urumilki | 83 |
| Warpala | 261 |
| Wenamun | 13, 27, 34–36, 39, 77, 81, 99, 126, 144–45, 252, 272, 275 |
| Weret | 138 |

| | |
|---|---|
| Xenophon | 108 |
| Xerxes | 84, 108, 136 |
| Yakīn-Lû | 55, 67, 69, 132 |
| Yapaʿ-Adad | 98 |
| Yariris | 261 |
| Yatonmilk | 114, 197 |
| Yeḥarbaal | 85–86 |
| Yeḥawmilk | 85–86 |
| Yeḥimilk | 35, 81–82, 86, 185 |
| Yeḥumilk | 84, 144, 184, 213 |
| Yḫrbʿl | 84 |
| Zakarbaal | 27, 35–36, 77, 81, 86, 145 |
| Zimridda | 98, 119, 124 |
| Ptah Sokar | 207 |
| Rephaim | 216 |
| Reshef | 191 |
| Reshef-Mukol | 247 |
| Shadrapa | 72, 185, 186, 207, 212 |
| Shéd | 185 |
| Ṣid | 212 |
| Tanit | 187, 209, 309 |
| Tanit-Astarte | 187, 209 |
| Tiamat | 183 |
| Yahweh | 208, 306 |
| Yam | 183 |
| Zeus | 5, 187 |

## Deities

| | |
|---|---|
| Adonis | 77, 184 |
| Amon | 212 |
| Apollo | 191, 214, 220 |
| Asclepius | 214 |
| Astarte | 75, 106–7, 120–21, 128, 143–44, 181, 184–85, 204–6, 208, 213–14, 228, 244, 247, 267 |
| Astarte-Isis | 213 |
| Baal | 70, 81, 128, 184, 244, 263 |
| Baalat Gebal | 184 |
| Baal Hammon | 262 |
| Baal Malagê | 185 |
| Baalšamen | 181, 185, 187 |
| Baal Ṣaphon | 185 |
| Bastet | 207 |
| Bes | 207–8, 212, 245 |
| Eshmun | 72, 96, 103, 106–7, 109, 111, 113, 144, 184–85, 197, 207–9, 214, 247 |
| Gula | 247 |
| Hathor | 212, 213 |
| Helios | 191 |
| Heracles | 72, 122, 137, 189, 207, 214 |
| Horus | 75, 207–8, 212–13, 233, 245 |
| Isis | 72, 212, 213 |
| Melqart | 72, 100, 137, 140, 181, 185–86, 189, 203, 207, 214, 262, 297 |
| Mot | 183 |
| Osiris | 212 |
| Ptah | 207, 212 |

# Place Names Index

Abrach, Nahr el-   56, 59, 62
Abu Hawam   31, 34, 38, 42, 44, 46, 48, 120–21, 158, 160, 166, 168, 189, 284, 287, 299
Abydos   97, 274
Adana, Plain of   261
Addaru   102
Adlūn   9, 94
Aegean   4, 16, 34, 42, 99, 251, 297
Afghanistan   257
Afqa   77
Akhziv   31, 93, 121, 218–23, 230–31, 233, 236, 238, 242–45, 290, 292–93. See also Akzibu
'Akka. See Akko
Akkār   9, 11, 31, 56, 76, 91, 238
Akko   4–5, 8–11, 31, 38, 41–42, 77, 90, 92–93, 101, 119, 121, 128, 141, 148, 156, 176, 180, 246, 256–57, 270, 284, 288, 299, 300, 302, 304–8
Akshaph. See Keisan, Tell
Akzibu   92–93, 121. See also Akhziv
Alalakh   64
al-Anṣariyye Mountains   55–56, 59
Alanya   261
Aleppo   186, 236, 260, 262
al-Mina   261
Amarna, Tell el-   51, 80, 119, 123
Amathus   267
Ampa   30, 77, 93. See also Anfe
Ampi   75
'Amrit   6, 8–9, 17, 31, 54, 57, 60–62, 71–72, 140–41, 148, 150, 185–86, 188–89, 193–94, 203–4, 207, 217–19, 221–22, 224, 227, 229–32

Amuq Plain   236
Amurru   34–35, 55–57, 64–65, 67, 75–77, 81
Anatolia   12, 98, 237, 249, 255–56, 260–61
Anfe   30, 75–77, 93–94, 121, 139. See also Ampa
Anṣariyah   11
'Aqtanit   187
Arabia   249, 271, 315
Arados   5, 58, 71, 140
Aradus   58–59, 70, 280
Aram   66
Ardata   64
Arde, Tell. See Ardata
Argos   251
Arqā   260
'Arqa, Nahr   238
Arqa, Tell   19, 38, 56, 76, 139, 148, 164, 189, 195, 196, 205, 217–18, 236, 238–39, 280. See also Irqata; Irqanata
Arslan-Tash   177
Arvad. See Arwad
Arwad   2, 6, 10–11, 16–17, 23, 28, 31, 34, 36–37, 51, 54–72, 76, 82, 84, 94, 108, 132, 139–41, 148, 150, 185, 222, 229–30, 259–60, 313–14
Ashdod   34, 258, 290, 300
Ashkelon   5–6, 34, 122, 132, 150, 246–47, 255, 258, 265, 273–74, 285, 290, 293, 304, 309–11
Asia Minor   34, 103, 149, 210, 228, 236–37
Assyria   13, 66–69, 77, 83, 92, 101–2, 126, 130–33, 176, 183, 212, 216, 249–51, 258–59

Athens 109-11, 270-71
'Athlit 10, 31, 236, 272
Awwali River 96, 107-8, 188
Ayaa 114, 214, 220, 226-27
'Ayn Dara 189
'Ayn el-Ḥayyāt 9, 193
Ayn el-Helwe 220, 226
'Aytanit 187
Azor 266
Ba'asa 57
Babylon 13, 100, 112, 134-36, 183, 247, 259
Babylonia 13, 126, 250, 259, 260
Baitokaike. See Ḥuṣn Suleiman
Balanea 59
Balawat 115, 126-27, 161, 309
Balearic Islands 179
Bano 60
Bared, Nahr el- 57, 76
Barǧa. See Birgi'
Batrun. See Bitirume
Batruna 75
Beersheba 264
Beirut 5, 8-11, 15, 22, 24, 29-31, 38, 47, 73, 76, 78, 87, 90-91, 93-94, 114, 120, 139, 141, 156, 158, 160-64, 166-68, 173, 177, 180, 182, 189, 195-96, 205-6, 217-19, 222-23, 246, 253, 270, 277, 280, 298, 311, 313
Beten 121
Biqā' 2, 9, 11-12, 14, 91, 187, 212
Birgi' 93, 94
Bi'rû 93
Bit-Arḫa 75
Bīt-Gisimeya 93-94
Bitirume 30, 75-77, 82, 93
Bīt-Ṣupūri 93
Bīt Sūrāya 260
Bīt-Zitti 92-94, 121
Biyyāda. See Rās el-Abiad
Bramiyeh 220
Breij 186, 260, 262
Bṣfaray. See Bi'rû
Burak, Tell el- 9, 30-31, 90, 117, 139, 141, 148, 156-60, 163-64, 166-68, 173- 74, 201-4, 206-9, 212-13, 243, 246, 255, 258, 268, 270-71, 280-82, 284-85, 288-94, 303, 305, 311
Burj aš-šamali 203-4
Bustan esh-Sheikh 96, 10-8, 189, 197, 204, 207-9, 214
Byblos 2-3, 10-11, 23, 27-31, 34-38, 51, 56-57, 65, 73-87, 90-91, 93-94, 97, 104, 106, 120, 123, 126, 130, 132, 139-44, 146, 148-49, 152-54, 161, 165, 176, 179, 182, 184-85, 204, 208, 212, 213, 215-17, 219, 236, 252, 259-60, 270, 272, 277, 279, 289-90, 311, 313-14
Cadiz 222, 275
Canaan 2-3, 49, 72, 124, 127
Carchemish 33, 260-61
Carmel, Mount 10-11, 120-21
Carmel coast 6, 8, 10, 49, 268, 304
Carmel range 11
Carne 59, 62
Carthage 100, 128-29, 135-36, 145, 228, 241, 275, 279, 308
Cebel Ires Daği 261
Chanaan 3
Chanani 2
Chhim 30-31, 289, 295
Chna 3
Cilicia 33, 55, 67, 77, 237, 250, 260-63
Cineköy 261
Cnidos 109
Cos 106, 270
Crete 98, 250, 270-71, 297, 304, 315
Cyprus 3-4, 16-17, 20, 23, 33, 34, 37, 42, 48-49, 67, 69, 83, 98-100, 103-4, 128, 130, 149, 173-74, 176, 178, 198, 210, 237, 241, 249-50, 255-56, 266-68, 271, 275-76, 304-5
Dabaa, Tell ed- 120
Dahr el Aouq 220, 229
Dahshur 80
Dakerman 87, 97, 172, 218-20, 228, 230, 298
Dalaimme 93-94
Damascus 11-12, 66-67, 82, 91, 99, 120, 129-30, 249, 260

# PLACE NAMES INDEX

Damūr, River 91
Dan, Tel 127, 264
Daruk, Tell 56
Delhum. *See* Dalaimme
Delos 71
Delphi 256
Dor 4–6, 8, 10, 17, 20–21, 24, 26, 31, 34, 38, 42–44, 46, 48, 58, 77, 96, 106, 120–22, 155–56, 158, 161, 163, 169–70, 205, 207, 246–47, 256, 262, 268, 270, 272–73, 275–76, 280, 284–99, 304–7. *See also* Dor, Tel
Dor, Tel 21, 42–43, 46, 48, 156, 246, 276, 280, 284–87, 299. *See also* Dor
Drehem 78
Ebla 63, 79, 189
Edom 132, 249, 256
Egypt 12–13, 35–36, 40, 48, 57, 63, 80–81, 86, 90–91, 97–99, 102–4, 106, 108–9, 112, 116, 123–26, 130–32, 136, 142, 152–54, 198, 210, 212–16, 249–53, 255, 257, 264, 271–76, 286–87, 289–90, 315
Ein Hofez 256
Elam 178
Elephantine 273–74, 290, 293
Eleutherus River 9
Eleutherus Valley 103, 313
el-Mrah 220
'Elyākīn 189–90
Enfe 31
Enkomi 307, 308
Enydra 58, 59
Ethiopia 263
Etruria 178
Euboa 269
ez-Zib 121
Fadous-Kfarabida, Tell 279
Far'ah, Tell el- (South) 266
Fort Shalmaneser 177
Fukkhar, Tell el-. *See* Akko
Ğabal al-Anṣariyye 55
Ğabal al-Arba'in 189, 190
Ğabal 'Āmel 11
Ğabal Ğarmak 11
Gabala. *See* Ğabla
Ğabla 9–10, 44, 57, 59, 61–62. *See also* Tweini, Tell
Ğabla, Plain of 31, 59–62, 192, 203
Galilee 10–11, 119–22, 128, 142, 277, 296
Gambūlu 93
Ğawz, Nahr el- 75
Gaza 34, 132, 303
Ğbayl. *See* Byblos
Ghamqe, Tell 59–60, 62, 231
Gi' 93
Gibeon 290
Greece 37, 111, 151, 210, 213–15, 268, 270
Gubal. *See* Byblos
Gubla. *See* Byblos
Hadad-Ezer 56
Hama 236, 262
Ḥamat 141
Hamath 11, 57, 66, 260, 313
Hamme East, Tell 257
Hassan Beyli 261
Ḥatti 33, 92–93, 100, 131, 133, 143
Hazor 258, 264
Herodian 3
Ḥilakku. *See* Cilicia
Ḥildua 93
Hizzin, Tell 179, 212
Hlaliye 220
Homs Gap 11–12, 55, 63, 76, 141
Horbat Rosh Zayit 120, 156, 158, 163, 168, 280, 283–84, 287–90, 293, 295–96
Huelva 275
Ḥuṣn Suleiman 185
Ibirta 75
India 257, 263
Inimme 93
Ionia. *See* Yawan
Iran 129, 257
Iris, Tell 60, 61
Irmid/Ermes, Tell 120
Irqanata 56. *See also* Arqa, Tell; Irqata
Irqata 57, 76. *See also* Arqa, Tell; Irqanata

Isiḫimme 93, 94
Israel 6, 8, 21, 42–43, 126–29, 250, 262–64, 288
Italy 176, 255
Jaffa 5–6, 8, 58, 106, 293, 313
Jezreel Valley 10–12
Jezzine 91
Jiyye 30–31, 93, 148, 158, 289
Joppa 96
Jordan 3, 154, 178, 257, 307, 315
Jordan River 3
Judah 126, 132, 135, 262, 264, 296
Kabri, Tell 288
Kaizu 56
Kalb, Nahr el- 8, 9, 13, 76, 77, 84, 134, 259, 313
Kalmin 93. *See also* Ampa
Kāmid el-Lōz 91, 212
Karatepe 185, 260–61, 309, 311
Kar-Esarhaddon 93, 101–2, 131
Karnos 58
Kastina, Tell. *See* Ullaza
Kazel, Tell 15–17, 19, 31, 36–37, 44–45, 48, 55, 72, 156, 166, 189, 191, 194–95, 203, 207, 209, 270, 284
Keisan. *See* Keisan, Tell
Keisan, Tell 17, 21, 24, 26, 31, 38, 41–46, 48, 120–21, 158, 160, 166, 168–69, 256, 277, 280, 283, 288–99
Kfarshima 93
Khaldeh 47, 91, 93, 174, 217–18, 222–25, 233–34, 236, 246, 268, 270, 289
Kharayeb 31, 148, 199–200, 209
Khorsabad 13, 309
Kilmê 93
Kinet Hüyük 261
Kinneret 264
Kition 128, 247, 266–67
Knossos 269
Kommos 269
Koubba, Tell 31
Kumidi. *See* Kāmid el-Lōz
Kundi 101–2
Kusba. *See* Kašpuna
Larnaca. *See* Kition

Laruba 120–21
Lattakia 61
Lay 91
Lebanon 2, 8–9, 11–15, 29–31, 34, 56–57, 64, 73, 77, 83, 121, 134, 148, 153, 170, 172, 199, 219, 222, 228, 258–59, 263–64, 272, 290, 309, 313, 316
Lebanon, Mount 253
Lebanon Mountains 2, 11, 13, 259, 309
Limassol 267
Litani River 91, 93–94, 101, 119, 121, 131
Lixus 275
Lycus River 8, 76
Magharet al-Wardeh 307
Mahalab 130
Maḫallatu 56
Maḫalliba 92–93, 121
Main 271
Maizu 56
Marathos 58
Marathus 58–59, 70, 86
Mariamme 58, 62, 70
Ma'rubbu 94, 101, 121, 131
Mašġara 91
Medinet Habu 33
Mediterranean 8, 10, 12, 14, 29–, 40, 42, 48, 55, 91, 99, 135–36, 155, 175–76, 179–80, 210, 228, 238, 245, 249–51, 255–56, 258, 269, 274–77, 280, 287–88, 298, 303–5, 308, 315
Mediterranean Sea 10, 14
Megiddo 120, 264, 300
Memphis 103, 136, 272
Mesopotamia 12, 134, 176, 179, 210, 241, 247, 257, 316
Mgharet Tablun 177, 209, 220, 228, 236, 308
Michal, Tell 290, 293, 300
Minet el-Beida 297
Minuḫimmu 67
Miqne, Tell 255, 289
Mirhan, Tell 30, 77, 273. *See alsos* Shekka
Mišpē Yammīm. *See* Ġabal al-Arba'in
Miye-w-Miye 220

# PLACE NAMES INDEX

Mor, Tel 299
Mugharet el-Wardeh 257
Myriandros 5–6, 173, 260
Nā'me 93
Nasbeh, Tell en- 264
Nile 273
Nile River 287
Nile Valley 179
Nimrud 126, 177
Nineveh 68, 84, 102–3, 131, 133, 145, 161, 189
Nippur 260
North Africa 2, 179
Nuṣayriyye Mountains. See Anṣariyah
Olympia 256
Ophir 128, 250, 263
Orontes Valley 11–12, 55
Palaepaphos-*Skales* 266, 297
Palaetyrus. See Ušû
Palastin 16, 236, 237
Palestine 5, 10–12, 29, 34, 39, 42, 83–84, 93, 103, 121, 148–49, 151, 153–54, 170, 178–79, 201–2, 204, 210, 249, 258, 293, 296, 298, 305, 316
Paltos 59
Persian Gulf 4, 257
Philistia 266
Pithecussai 269
Plain of Sharon. See Sharon, Plain of
Qadesh 91
Qarnum, Tell 54, 59, 60, 62
Qarqar 56, 65, 82, 86, 129, 260
Qartimme 93
Qasile, Tell 266, 290
Qasimiyye 91, 94, 119, 121
Qrtḥdšt 3, 130
Que 261
Ramat Raḥel 264
Raphanée 62
Rās el-Abiad 8, 119–20
Rās el-'ayn 9, 121–23, 140
Rās en-Nāqūra 8–10, 119–20
Rās esh-Shaq'a 8–9
Ras Ibn Hani 15, 37
Rās Nahr el-Kalb 8v9

Rašidiyye, Tell el- 90, 93, 119, 121–23, 140, 218–19, 233, 236. See also Ušu
Red Sea 4, 178, 250, 257, 263, 287
Rehov, Tell 264
Rhodes 250, 270
Riblah 103
Ri'siṣurri 57
Rmayle 93
Ruād. See Arwad
Rumat az-Zahab 60
Ruqeish, Tell 266
Ruwayse 47
Sagû (modern Shekka) 76, 93
Sakka, Tell 91
Sam'al 260, 261
Samaria 130, 171, 177–78, 264
Samos 270
Samsumuruna 67
Sanam 274
Saqqara 97
Sarafand 29, 93, 173, 198, 219. See also Sarepta
Sarapta 5
Sardinia 228, 256, 264, 275, 308
Sarepta 4, 17, 20–22, 24–25, 29–30, 38–40, 43–45, 48–49, 92–94, 101, 121, 125, 131, 139, 141, 148, 151, 156, 158, 169–74, 177, 185, 187, 189, 198–99, 205–6, 208–9, 213, 218–19, 268, 270, 282, 284, 289, 298, 300–302, 304–5, 307–8
Ṣaydā. See Sidon
Sendjirli 102, 261
Serabit el-Khadim 152
Sharon Plain 10–11, 58, 96, 121, 313
Sheikh Abaroh. See Sidon-Dakerman
Sheikh Zenad 217, 219, 222
Shekka 8, 30, 31, 75–77, 93. See also Sagû; Šigata
Šḥīm. See Isiḥimme
Shiqmona 145, 270, 272, 294–95, 299
Shwayfat 9
Sianu, Tell 17, 56, 60–61, 189, 191–92, 260
Sidon 2–6, 8–12, 23, 28, 30–31, 34–36, 38–40, 43, 48, 49, 51, 56, 58, 64–65,

Sidon (cont.)
67, 69–70, 72, 76–79, 82, 84, 86–116, 118–21, 123–26, 129–31, 137, 139–43, 145, 148–50, 161, 172, 174, 176, 180, 184–85, 187–89, 197–98, 203, 208–10, 212, 214–15, 219–22, 224–30, 236, 245, 253, 256, 268–73, 276, 279–80, 282, 284, 288, 290, 293, 295, 298, 304, 306, 308–9, 313–14

Sidon-Dakerman 218
Ṣiduna 90. *See also* Sidon
Ṣiduni 90. *See also* Sidon
Šigata (modern Shekka) 30, 75, 77
Sigon 58, 70
Sikkû 93
Ṣimirra 55–57, 62–64, 313. *See also* Kazel, Tell
Sinn, Nahr es- 56, 62
Sissû 101–2
Spain 176, 228, 249, 255–56, 263, 275, 308, 310
Sudan 263, 274
Sukas, Tell 15, 31, 36, 37, 44, 47, 49, 57, 59–60, 62, 158, 166, 189–90, 192, 203, 217–18, 236–37, 262, 270, 313–14
Ṣurru 101, 114, 116, 119, 123–24, 128, 133, 140
Susa 112
Syria 4–5, 9, 12, 16, 23, 31, 33, 39, 46, 49, 54, 58–59, 63, 67, 70, 77, 83–84, 93, 124, 141–43, 149, 153–54, 172, 174, 176, 179, 210, 236–37, 241, 250, 254, 257, 260–62, 276, 313, 316
Tabal 55, 67
Tabbat el-Hammam 10, 54, 62
Tamassos 267
Tambourit 219, 236
Tarshish 249–50, 256, 263–64, 310
Tarsus 260–61, 263
Tartessos 263
Ṭarṭūs 10, 51, 56–57, 59–60, 62, 71, 140, 193, 194, 221, 227
Tašrītu 102
Ṭaybe 120, 148
Tayinat, Tell 189
Tekke 269
Thebes 269, 309
Theouprosopon 8
Til Barsip 102
Tripoli 9–11, 57, 75–76, 94
Turkey 33, 149, 237, 249, 255, 260–61
Tweini, Tell 15–18, 36, 37, 44, 60–61, 189, 191–92, 205–6, 208, 210–11, 254, 257, 279–80, 284, 288–90, 293–94, 305. *See also* Ǧabla
Tyre 2, 4–6, 8–13, 17, 20–26, 28–31, 34–36, 38–41, 43, 45, 47–49, 51, 56, 64–65, 69–70, 72, 77–79, 82–84, 90–92, 94–96, 98–105, 108, 114–26, 128–42, 144–46, 148–49, 152, 158, 161, 169, 173–74, 176, 183, 185, 187, 189, 199–200, 203–5, 208, 210, 213, 216–19, 223–24, 233, 236–37, 239–40, 242, 244–45, 249–50, 252–54, 256, 259–60, 262–63, 265, 267–72, 275–78, 280, 282, 284–85, 288–89, 297–98, 302, 304, 306, 309, 313–14
Tyre al-Baṣṣ 17, 21–22, 25, 30, 41, 47, 116, 126, 218, 223–24, 233, 236, 239–40, 244–45, 267–68, 280, 282, 284–85
Ugarit 15, 37, 56–57, 61, 80, 98, 106, 123, 125, 147, 151, 154, 182–83, 285, 297, 303, 307, 311
Ullaza 76, 80, 91
Umm el-Amed 148, 187, 208, 289
Unqi (Patina) 66
Upe 212
Usanata/Usnu 56
Usanātu 57
Usnu 56–57, 260
Ušu 90–93, 119, 121–24, 133, 136–37, 140. *See also* Rašidiyye, Tell el-
Utica 275
Wadi Araba 315
Wadi Brisa 13–14, 84, 134, 259
Wadi el-Ḥôl 152, 153
Walistin. *See* Palastin
Yanūḥ 30, 77, 142
Yarimuta 277
Yawan 250

| | |
|---|---|
| Yemen | 249 |
| Yoqneam | 264 |
| Zarqa, River | 257 |
| Zayta | 121 |
| Zeita. *See* Bīt-Zitti | |
| Zib, ez-. *See* Akhziv | |
| Zimarra | 57 |

# Modern Authors Index

Abou Abdallah, Marc 80
Abou-Assaf, Ali 189
Abou Samra, Gaby 23, 34, 148, 213, 217
Acquaro, Enrico 79, 275
Aharoni, Yohanan 12
Ahlström, G. W. 290
Al-Amri, Yosha Abdel Salam 257
Alexandre, Yardenna 156, 158, 163, 168, 176, 295, 296
Alfen, Peter Gerritt van 12, 251, 252, 258, 271
Aliquot, Julien 208
Allen, James P. 80
Al-Maqdissi, Michel 15–17, 37, 54, 59, 61–62, 71, 190–94, 232, 294–95
Amadasi-Guzzo, Maria Giulia 105–6, 149, 241, 260, 266–67
Anderson, William P. 17, 20, 22, 24–25, 39, 45, 139, 156, 169–73, 300–301, 307–8
Archi, Alfonso 64
Arnaud, Daniel 90, 92, 98
Artin, Gassia 179
Artzy, Michael 10–11, 42, 46, 120
Aruz, Joan 177
Aston, David 273
Aston, Barbara 273
Astour, Michael C. 54
Attridge, Harold W. 183
Aubet, María Eugènia 41, 47–48, 126, 173, 224, 236, 239–42, 249–51, 254–55, 260, 262, 265–68, 270, 274–75, 278
Avigad, Nahman 23
Aznar, Carolina Ana 258, 266, 304

Badawi, Massoud 61–62, 191, 205–6, 208, 294
Bader, Bettina 90, 98, 212
Badre, Leila xi, 15, 22, 24, 37–38, 45, 55, 156, 158, 161, 164–65, 194–95, 200, 209
Badreshany, Kamel 164
Bagg, Ariel M. 54, 56–57, 69, 76, 79, 92–94, 119–21
Bahn, Paul 303
Balensi, Jacqueline 42, 46, 120
Ballard, Robert D. 258, 274, 303, 309, 312
Baramki, Dimitri 4
Barnett, Richard 177
Barnett, Richard David 126
Barreca, Ferrucio 275
Baruch, Inbar 287, 299
Baruch, Uri 283
Bass, George F. 310
Baumgarten, Albert I. 182
Baurain, Claude xi, 143, 269, 270
Belmonte-Marín, Juan Antonio 51, 54–55, 58, 64, 75–76, 79, 90–93, 100, 116, 119, 121–24, 277
Bennett, W. J. 173
Ben-Shlomo, David 266
Ben-Yosef, Erez 256
Benz, Frank L. 70–71, 148, 212
Bertsch, Julia 90
Bettles, Elizabeth 173, 252–54, 258, 273, 303–4, 306
Bienkowski, Piotr 236–38
Bierling, Marilyn 275

Bikai, Patricia Maynor 17, 22, 25–26, 30, 39–41, 45, 116, 122–23, 125, 171, 173, 265–68, 276, 302
Biran, Avraham 127
Blakely, Jeffrey A. 173
Bloch-Smith, Elizabeth 6
Blomquist, Tina Haettner 202
Boaretto, Elisabetta 42, 266, 268, 275
Bode, Michael 256
Bondì, Sandro Filippo 275
Bonechi, Marco 63, 78
Bonnet, Corinne xi, 1, 143, 181–85, 216, 241, 262, 269–70
Bordreuil, Pierre 23, 34, 72, 119, 148, 151, 238
Borger, Rykle 69, 131, 253
Boschloos, Vanessa 213
Bounni, Adnan 37
Boyes, Philip J. 105
Braemer, Frank 46, 158, 168
Braidwood, Robert John 54
Bretschneider, Joachim 15–16, 18, 44, 61, 254–55, 280, 294
Briend, Jacques 26, 41, 45–46, 120, 158, 160, 277
Briquel-Chatonnet, Françoise 55, 63–67, 126, 128, 150, 262–63, 265
Brody, Aaron Jed 264
Bron, François 261
Brossé, C.-L. 222
Brun, Jean-Pierre 290
Buccianti-Barakat, Liliane 9, 11, 15
Buhl, Marie-Louise 227, 262
Bunnens, Guy 274
Çakırlar, Canan 246, 284–85
Çambel, Halet 261
Capet, Emmanuelle 16, 19, 37, 45, 166
Carayon, Nicolas 89, 115, 118
Carmona, Pilar 115–16
Casson, Lionel 311
Caubet, Annie 60, 177, 179, 257
Chahoud, Jwana 284
Chamussy, Henri 9, 11, 15
Chéhab, Maurice 28, 106, 107, 122, 148, 213, 219, 236, 298

Chirpanlieva, Iva 174
Clawson, M. Don 226
Coffey, Helena 177
Coldstream, Nicholas 174, 270
Conrad, Diethelm 302
Counts, Derek B. 17, 21
Cowley, Arthur E. 290
Cross, Frank Moore 148, 234, 307
Crowfoot, Grace M. 177, 264
Crowfoot, John Winter 177, 264
Culican, William 205, 219, 230, 267
Curtis, John 126
Curvers, Hans H. 38, 139, 161, 163–65
Da Riva, Rocío 84, 134
Darnell, John Coleman 152
Davie, Michael F. 9
Dayagi-Mendels, Mikhal 220, 231, 233–34
De Bertou, Jules 115
Deckers, Katleen 278–82, 294
Delavault, Bernard 148
Demesticha, Stella 258
Deutsch, Robert 23
Diakonoff, Igor M. 249
Dils, Peter 2
Dinçol, Belkis 261
Dixon, Helen 223–24, 229, 237, 247
Doak, Brian 203
Dongen, Erik van xiv, 175
Donner, Herbert 81
Dossin, Augustin-Georges Barrois 177
Dothan, Moshe 41, 148, 302, 306–7
Doumet, Claude. *See* Doumet-Serhal, Claude
Doumet-Serhal, Claude 30, 40, 89–91, 97–99, 122, 148, 174, 180, 198, 209, 212, 218–19, 225, 236, 268, 270, 284
Dunand, Maurice 28, 38, 60, 71–72, 74, 79, 96, 97, 102, 148, 165, 172, 177, 193, 207, 213, 228
Durand, Jean Marie 2
Duru, Raymond 148, 213
Dussaud, M. René 11–12, 121, 212
Duyrat, Frédérique 63
Edrey, Meir 246–47

Elayi, Alain G.   54, 122, 136, 148, 306
Elayi, Josette   xi, xv, 1, 4, 12, 22, 23–24, 54, 58–60, 63–64, 66, 70–72, 76–77, 79, 82–83, 85–86, 90–91, 94, 96, 101, 103–7, 109, 111–12, 114, 122, 135–39, 145, 148, 156, 158, 166, 195, 206, 213, 221–22, 227–31, 254, 306
Elgavish, Joseph   295
El-Hélou, Michel   118
Eschel, Tzilla   256
Faber, Alice   150–51
Fales, Frederick Mario   250, 259, 261
Fantalkin, Alexander   293
Feldman, Marian   251
Finkbeiner, Uwe   38, 139, 161, 165, 246
Finkelstein, Israel   21–22, 29, 127
Fischer-Elfert, Hans-Werner   119
Fleming, Stuart   290
Fleming, Wallace Bruce   122
Flinders, Matthew   152
Fontan, Elisabeth   177
Forstner-Müller, Irene   90, 98, 212
Francis-Allouche, Martine   78
Frankel, Rafael   289, 295–96
Frede, Simone   220, 222, 225, 227
Friedrich, Johannes   149
Frost, Honor   30, 54, 78, 89, 116–17
Fuchs, Andreas   259
Gal, Zvi   120, 156, 158, 163, 168, 289, 295–96
Garbini, Giuseppe   149–51
Gardiner, Alan H.   152
Gasull, Pepa   236, 238
Genz, Hermann   33, 212, 273
Geva, Shulamit   265
Ghadban, Ch.   176, 210, 220, 228–29
Ghantus, M.   223
Gibson, John Clark Love   96, 108, 148, 260
Gilboa, Ayelet   4, 6, 20–21, 26, 41–44, 46–49, 169–70, 253, 264, 266, 268–73, 275, 286, 303–4, 306
Gitin, Seymour   275
Giulia, Maria   105
Goedicke, Hans   27, 35, 77

Goldman, Hans   261
Goldwasser, Orly   152, 154
Goren, Yuval   264, 268, 272, 303–4
Graesser, Carl F.   202
Graeve, Marie-Christine de   309, 311
Gras, Michel   xi, 179, 237–38, 269
Grayson, Albert Kirk   34, 56, 57, 65–67, 76, 82–83, 99, 100–101, 120, 126, 129, 260
Grimal, Nicolas   78
Gubel, Eric   xi, 45, 57, 156, 177, 194–95, 209
Guigues, Paul-Émile   47
Hachmann, Rolf   12, 212
Hadas, Daniel   2
Haggi, Arad   10–11
Haidar, M.   111
Haines, Richard C.   189
Halpern, Baruch   33, 247
Hamdy Bey, Osman   214, 220, 226, 229
Hamilton, Robert   158
Harden, Donald   74
Hawkins, John David   16, 33, 260
Haykal, Mohammed R.   54, 60, 71, 221–22, 227, 229–31
Helck, Wolfgang   2, 35, 74, 78, 80, 123–24, 272
Helzer, Michael   246
Herrera, Maria D.   42, 46, 120
Herrmann, Georgina   177
Herzog, Ze'ev   293
Higginbotham, Carolyn R.   215
Hill, George Francis   115, 297
Hodder, Ian   169
Hodos, Tamar   191, 261, 270
Hoftijzer, Jacob   79, 96
Hölbl, Günther   215
Hoover, Oliver D.   125
Horn, Siegfried H.   78
Horwitz, Liora K.   78, 284, 287–88
Houghton, Arthur   125
Huehnergard, John   150
Humbert, Jean-Baptiste   21, 26, 41–42, 45–46, 120, 158, 160, 277
Hvidberg-Hansen, F. O.   187

Iacovou, Maria 17, 21
Ishaq, Eva 17, 61–62, 71, 191, 193–94, 205–6, 208, 211, 217–19, 221, 230–32
Jabak, S. 173
Jablonka, P. 161
Jans, Greta 15–16, 18, 44, 294
Jean, Charles-François 79
Jericke, Detlef 202, 268
Jessup, Henry Harris 229
Jidejian, Nina 79, 144, 212, 272
Johns, C. N. 236
Jones, Richard 59, 269
Jongeling, Karen 96
Kahrstedt, Ulrich 7
Kamlah, Jens 90, 139, 141, 156, 163, 173, 189–90, 201, 206, 212, 246, 270, 280–81
Kaniewski, David 15, 277
Kaoukabani, Ibrahim 148, 199, 209
Karageorghis, Vassos xi, 174, 218, 266–68, 270
Karmon, Nira 298–99
Katz, Solomon 290
Katzenstein, H. Jacob 2–3, 82, 92, 100, 104, 115–16, 119–22, 124–25, 128–32, 135–36, 150, 249, 253, 260, 261, 272
Kaufmann, Asher xv
Keel, Othmar 215, 245
Kerr, Robert M. 2
Kessler, Karlheinz 57
Kestemont, Guy 129, 260, 262
Khalifeh, Issam 17, 24, 39, 45, 172–73, 300
Killebrew, Ann E. 34, 307
Kinderlen, Moritz 256
Kislev, M. E. 283
Kitchen, Kenneth A. 12
Klengel, Horst 12
Kletter, Raz 148
Knapp, A. Bernard 258
Koehl, Robert B. 173–74, 268, 270
Kopetsky, Karin 90, 98, 212, 273
Kourou, Nota 269
Krings, Véronique xi
Kukahn, E. 227

Kuschke, A. 12, 91
Lagarce, E. 37
Lagarce, Jacques 37
Laidlaw, Stuart 177
Lancel, Serge 275
Lange, Matthias 242
Lapérouse, Jean-François de 177
Lauffray, Jean 87–89
Lebrun, René 260–61
Leclant, Jean 272
Lehmann, Gunnar 34, 41, 172–74, 270
Lehmann, Reinhard G. 82
Lehmann-Jericke, K. 268
Leichty, Erle 67, 76, 83, 87, 92–94, 100–102, 121, 131, 145, 212
Le Lasseur, Denyse 120
Lemaire, André 23, 27, 34–35, 66, 81, 85, 96, 120–22, 128, 130, 145, 148, 155, 208, 213, 241, 261, 263, 265
Lembke, Katja 104, 111, 220, 225–29
Le Meaux, Hélène 269
Lerberghe, Karel van 61, 254–55, 294
Lernau, Omri 287–89
Levy, Thomas Evan 179, 256
Lidzbarski, Mark 274
Linseele, Veerle 257, 284
Lipiński, Édouard 1, 64, 142, 148, 172, 181, 184–85, 187, 212, 260–61, 307
Lipschitz, N. 283
Liverani, Mario 249, 256
Loffet, Henri Charles 174, 218, 268, 270
Lohwasser, Angelika 274
Lopriano, Antonio 103
Lorber, Catharine C. 125
Lund, John 45, 158, 166
Macridy Bey, Theodor 122, 219–20, 229, 233, 236
Maeir, Aren M. 273
Maïla-Afeiche, Anne-Marie 9
Mainberger, Martin 117
Malbrant-Labat, Florence 119
Marcus, Ezra 80, 153
Margueron, Jean-Claude 73, 74
Mark, Samuel 310–11
Markoe, Glenn E. xi, 161, 175–76, 204

Marriner, Nick 89, 118
Marti, Lionel 102
Martin, Robert xii, 103, 111, 114, 148, 175, 179, 214, 251, 297, 299
Martin, S. Rebecca 174
Marzoli, Dirce 275
Masson, Olivier 266–67
Master, Daniel M. 293
Mathys, H.-P. 96, 103, 106–7, 148, 207
Matoïan, Valérie xi, 214
Matthiae, Paolo 189
Mazar, Amihai 264
Mazar, Eliat 213, 219–21, 231, 233–34, 236, 238, 242–45, 266, 292, 293
McGovern, Patrick 290
McLynn, Neil 2
Melamed, Y. 283
Mettinger, Tryggve N. D. 202–3
Metzger, Martin 233
Miller, Robert 257
Monchambert, Jean-Yves 30, 77, 142
Montero, Mabel 284–85
Moran, William L. 2, 75–76, 79, 90, 98, 119, 123, 124, 277, 297
Morhange, Christophe 78, 87, 89–90, 117–18
Morstadt, Bärbel xi, 176, 210
Mosca, Paul G. 261
Moscati, Sabatino xi, 179, 213
Moulins, Dominque de 280
Mouterde, René 9
Mura, Barbara 174, 222–24
Najjar, Mohammad 256
Nashef, Khaked 54
Naveh, Joseph 127, 269
Negueruela, Iván 310
Nibbi, Alessandra 2
Niehr, Herbert 181–85, 187, 216, 241, 262
Nitschke, Jessica 297, 299
Noureddine, Ibrahim 118
Novotny, Jamie R. 55, 67–69, 83, 100–101, 132–33
Nuñez, Francisco J. 17, 20–22, 25, 41, 172–73, 224, 239–42, 267–68

Nunn, Astrid 174
Oden, Robert A., Jr. 183
Oggiano, Ida 199–200
Opificius, Ruth 79
Orendi, Andrea 278, 280–82, 294
Orsingher, Adriano 234
Pardee, Dennis 235
Parpola, Simo 77, 131, 142, 253
Parrot, André 213
Peckham, Brian xi
Petrie, William 152
Pettinato, Giovanni 63, 78
Pfeiffer, Robert H. 68
Poidebard, Antoine 54, 87–89, 116–17
Porada, Edith 34
Prausnitz, Moshe W. 231, 242
Pritchard, James B. 29–30, 115, 141, 148, 156, 158, 161, 172, 177, 198–99, 205–9, 213, 259, 290, 300–301, 307–8
Puech, Émile 236
Pulak, Cemal 310
Quinn, Josephine xi–xiii, xv, 1–3, 105, 175, 182
Raban-Gerstel, Noa 284, 286
Reese, David 284, 297–99
Rehm, Ellen 82
Rehren, Th. 257
Reinach, Théodore 214, 220, 226
Renan, Ernest 9, 28, 54, 60–61, 193, 204, 220, 222, 225–26, 230, 236
Renfrew, Colin 303
Rey-Coquais, Jean-Paul 54, 62–63, 71, 187
Reyes, A. T. 266
Ribichini, Sergio 216
Riehl, Simone 279
Riis, P. J. 37, 47, 189–90, 217, 236
Robin, Christian 271
Röllig, Wolfgang 1, 29, 81, 148–49, 261, 274
Rouillard, Pierre xi, 179, 237–38, 270
Rovira, N. 282
Ruiz, Jose Miguel 115–16
Russel, James 261

Sader, Hélène        xiii, xv, 12, 23, 34, 51, 55, 76, 90–91, 93–94, 96, 139, 141, 148, 156, 163, 173, 187, 201, 203, 206, 209, 211–12, 219, 231, 239, 246, 270, 281
Saggs, Henry W. F.        126, 253
Saidah, Roger    47, 97, 172, 174, 218–20, 222–25, 230, 236, 246, 270
Salamé-Sarkis, Hassan        9
Saliby, Nassib    60, 71, 72, 148, 193, 207
Salles, Jean-François    38, 74, 217, 219, 236
Salskov Roberts, Helle        174
Sapin, J.        57
Sapir-Hen, Lidar        246, 284, 286
Sartre, Maurice        58, 114
Sass, Benjamin        13, 21–23, 34, 35
Satzinger, Helut        153–54
Sayegh, Hala    22, 24, 139, 156, 158, 166, 195, 206, 254
Scandone, Matthiae Gabriella        212
Schloen, J. David        293
Schmitt, Aaron    139, 141, 156, 163–64, 173–75, 201, 206, 258, 270, 281–82, 296, 302, 305
Schmitz, Philip C.        23, 148
Schreiber, Nicola        173
Seeden, Helga        30, 239
Seif, A.        228
Shalev, Yiftah        297, 299
Shanklin, W.        223
Sharon, Ilan    4, 6, 20–21, 26, 28, 41–44, 47–48, 156, 158, 163, 169–70, 266, 268, 275, 286, 306
Shipley, Graham        5, 58
Silberman, Neil Asher        29, 127
Singer-Avitz, Lily        264
Skaggs, Sheldon        256, 264
Sollberger, Edmond        78
Sommer, Michael        xi
Spanier, Ehud        298–99
Spanò Giammellaro, Antonella        279
Stager, Lawrence    246–47, 258, 265, 274, 290, 293, 303, 309, 312
Stampolidis, Nikolaos C.        xi

Starcky, Jean        35, 216
Starr, Ivan        68
Steen, Eveline van der        257, 307
Stefaniuk, Lise        78
Stern, Ephraim    6, 20, 42, 170, 206, 208
Stewart, Andrew        174
Stuart, Barbara    47, 139, 218–19, 222
Stucky, Rolf A.    96, 178–79, 197–98, 204, 207, 214
Sukenik, E. L.        177, 264
Suleiman, Antoine        61, 185
Suriano, Matthew J.        11
Sznycer, Maurice        153, 266–67
Tadmor, Hayim    57, 67, 83, 129–30
Tallis, Nigel        126
Taraqji, Ahmed Ferzat        91
Teixidor, Javier    xi, 23, 134–35, 148, 172, 179, 187, 230, 237–38, 270
Tekoğlu, Recai        261
Thalmann, Jean-Paul    xi, 19, 38, 74, 164, 195, 217, 236, 238–39
Thompson, Christine        256, 264
Thureau-Dangin, François        102, 177
Trellisó, Laura        267
Tropper, Josef        152
Tusa, Vincenzo        275
Unger, Eckhard        134–35, 260
Vaelske, Veit        256
Vanel, Antoine        148
Van Neer, Wim        288
Van Vyve, Anne-Sophie    16, 18, 44, 294
Veldhuijzen, Xander        257, 307
Venturi, Fabrizio        33, 46, 170
Vidal, Jordi        64
Vila, Emmanuelle        284
Volney, Constantin-François    87, 116
Waiman-Barak, Paula    264, 269, 272, 304
Waliszewski, Tomasz    30, 94, 158
Walsh, Carey Ellen        290
Ward, William A.        239
Wartke, Ralf-Bernhard        102
Watanabe, Kazuko    77, 131, 142, 253
Waterfield, Robin    70, 122, 136
Weidner, Ernst        69, 134, 259

Wein, Erwin J. 79
Weissbach, Franz Heinrich 9, 134
Wightman, G. J. 195
Wiseman, Donald J. 64
Woolmer, Mark xi–xii, 1, 35, 109–10, 177, 310–11
Xella, Paolo 106–8, 148, 182, 213, 307
Yadin, Yigael 264
Yakubovich, Ilya 262
Yamada, Shigeo 121
Yardeni, Ada 274
Yon, Marguerite 56, 60
Younger, K. Lawson, Jr. xiii, 66
Zamora, José Á. 103, 106–8, 148, 241
Zernecke, Anna 184
Zorn, Jeffrey 290
Zwickel, Wolfgang 257

www.ingramcontent.com/pod-product-compliance
Lightning Source LLC
Chambersburg PA
CBHW021929290426
44108CB00012B/779